THE MAKING OF AN IMPERIAL POLITY

Bringing to life the interaction between America, its peoples, and metropolitan gentlemen in early seventeenth-century England, this book argues that colonization did not just operate on the peripheries of the political realm, and confronts the entangled histories of colonialism and domestic status and governance. The Jacobean era is reframed as a definitive moment in which the civil self-presentation of the elite increasingly became implicated in the imperial. The tastes and social lives of statesmen contributed to this shift in the English political gaze. At the same time, bringing English political civility in dialogue with Native American beliefs and practices speaks to inherent tensions in the state's civilizing project and the pursuit of refinement through empire. This significant reassessment of Jacobean political culture reveals how colonizing America transformed English civility and demonstrates how metropolitan politics and social relations were uniquely shaped by territorial expansion beyond the British Isles. This title is also available as Open Access on Cambridge Core.

LAUREN WORKING is Research Associate on the ERC-funded TIDE project (Travel, Transculturality, and Identity in England, 1550–1700) at the University of Oxford. She has held fellowships at the Jamestown archaeological site and the Royal Anthropological Institute, where she continues to develop methodologies and projects that explore indigeneity, colonial legacies, and heritage in English museums.

CAMBRIDGE STUDIES IN EARLY MODERN BRITISH HISTORY

SERIES EDITORS

MICHAEL BRADDICK
Professor of History, University of Sheffield

ETHAN SHAGAN
Professor of History, University of California, Berkeley

ALEXANDRA SHEPARD
Professor of Gender History, University of Glasgow

ALEXANDRA WALSHAM
Professor of Modern History, University of Cambridge

This is a series of monographs and studies covering many aspects of the history of the British Isles between the late fifteenth century and the early eighteenth century. It includes the work of established scholars and pioneering work by a new generation of scholars. It includes both reviews and revisions of major topics and books which open up new historical terrain or which reveal startling new perspectives on familiar subjects. All the volumes set detailed research within broader perspectives, and the books are intended for the use of students as well as of their teachers.

For a list of titles in the series go to
www.cambridge.org/earlymodernbritishhistory

THE MAKING OF AN IMPERIAL POLITY

Civility and America in the Jacobean Metropolis

LAUREN WORKING

University of Oxford

CAMBRIDGE
UNIVERSITY PRESS

CAMBRIDGE
UNIVERSITY PRESS

University Printing House, Cambridge CB2 8BS, United Kingdom

One Liberty Plaza, 20th Floor, New York, NY 10006, USA

477 Williamstown Road, Port Melbourne, VIC 3207, Australia

314–321, 3rd Floor, Plot 3, Splendor Forum, Jasola District Centre, New Delhi – 110025, India

79 Anson Road, #06–04/06, Singapore 079906

Cambridge University Press is part of the University of Cambridge.

It furthers the University's mission by disseminating knowledge in the pursuit of education, learning, and research at the highest international levels of excellence.

www.cambridge.org
Information on this title: www.cambridge.org/9781108494069
DOI: 10.1017/9781108625227

First published 2020

Printed in the United Kingdom by TJ International Ltd, Padstow Cornwall

A catalogue record for this publication is available from the British Library.

Library of Congress Cataloging-in-Publication Data
NAMES: Working, Lauren, 1985– author.
TITLE: The making of an imperial polity : civility and America in the Jacobean metropolis / Lauren Working.
OTHER TITLES: Savagery and the state
DESCRIPTION: Cambridge, United Kingdom ; New York, NY : Cambridge University Press, 2020. | Series: Cambridge studies in early modern British history | Revision of author's thesis (doctoral) – Durham University, 2015, titled Savagery and the state : incivility and America in Jacobean political discourse. | Includes bibliographical references and index.

IDENTIFIERS: LCCN 2019028608 (print) | LCCN 2019028609 (ebook) | ISBN 9781108494069 (hardback) | ISBN 9781108625227 (epub)
SUBJECTS: LCSH: Indians – History – 17th century. | Indians – Foreign public opinion, British – History – 17th century. | Public opinion – Great Britain – History – 17th century. | Imperialism – Public opinion – History – 17th century. | Etiquette – England – History – 17th century. | Great Britain – Politics and government – 1603–1625. | Great Britain – Colonies – America – Public opinion – History – 17th century. | Great Britain – Colonies – America – History – 17th century. | Great Britain – Civilization – American influences. | Great Britain Civilization – 17th century. | England – Social life and customs – 17th century.
CLASSIFICATION: LCC DA391 .W67 2020 (print) | LCC DA391 (ebook) | DDC 970.02–dc23
LC record available at https://lccn.loc.gov/2019028608
LC ebook record available at https://lccn.loc.gov/2019028609

ISBN 978-1-108-49406-9 Hardback

Riches, *and* Conquest, *and* Renowne *I sing*

Riches *with honour,* Conquest *without bloud.*[1]

Kekuttokâunta, *Let us speake together.*[2]

[1] George Chapman, 'De Guiana, Carmen Epicum', in Lawrence Kemys, *A relation of the second voyage to Guiana* (1596; STC 14947), sig. Av.

[2] Roger Williams, *A key into the language of America* (1643; Wing W2766), sig. E5r.

Contents

Figures

Acknowledgements

Knowledge, wrote Marcel Proust, is a journey of discovery that no one else can take or spare us. Luckily I have received generous assistance along the way. I am indebted to Adrian Green, my PhD supervisor at Durham University, for his unflagging support and his discerning and deeply humane insights into the past. This research would not have been possible without a Durham Arts and Humanities Doctoral Studentship, nor without smaller grants for archival visits from the Durham History Department and the Institute of Medieval and Early Modern Studies. I would also like to thank Natalie Mears, Nicole Reinhardt, and Andy Wood for their advice and feedback on my work, and Ludmilla Jordanova for encouraging my involvement with the National Portrait Gallery.

My postdoctoral associateship on the TIDE project (Travel, Transculturality, and Identity in England, 1550–1700) has enabled me to develop my PhD research into a monograph. This project received funding from the European Research Council (ERC) under the European Union's Horizon 2020 research and innovation programme (grant agreement no. 681884). My warmest thanks to the principal investigator, Nandini Das, and to all my colleagues on the project and in the School of the Arts at the University of Liverpool for widening my perspectives on global encounters (and many facets of English literature) in a stimulating atmosphere of collegiality.

Further funding and fellowships have been critical to transforming my work. This included two short-term fellowships at Jamestown, one funded by the Colonial Williamsburg Foundation in 2014, the other by the Omohundro Institute of Early American History and Culture in 2016. Spending time in Virginia gave me the opportunity to meet the Jamestown archaeological team, including Jim Horn, Merry Outlaw, William Kelso, and Dave Givens. The archaeologists, curators, and researchers at Jamestown Rediscovery and the Omohundro brought my interest in material culture beyond a fascination with transatlantic 'things' into more practical ways of achieving cross-disciplinary work. I re-wrote a substantial portion of my material on sociability during a short-term fellowship at the Huntington Library in the summer of 2016, fuelled by many iced coffees and desert garden jaunts. Finally, my time as a 2018 Royal Anthropological Institute Library fellow at the British Museum was immeasurably enrichening, starting with the confidence the committee expressed in the value and importance of bringing indigeneity into the story of English heritage. Learning to approach my material both archae-ologically and anthropologically has profoundly influenced my work, the seeds of which have been planted, I hope, in this study.

Several events, and conversations with all their participants, have also been invaluable to developing this book. This includes the 'Jamestown at 1619' conference at Dartmouth College in 2017 organized by Jim Horn, Peter Mancall, and Paul Musselwhite, and the 'Intoxicants, Space, and Material Culture' workshops at the Victoria & Albert Museum in London in 2017 and the Beinecke Library at Yale University in 2018 with Phil Withington, Kathryn James, and Angela McShane. At Dartmouth, Nicholas Canny asked me about female interest in colonization. While that is not the subject of this book, I have thought a great deal about his question since. The topic deserves equal attention to that of masculine interest, and I hope to give a fuller reply in my next project.

Since the American Indian Workshop at Goldsmith's in London in 2017, conversations with Native Americans have become essential. These have begun to unlock a long history of interaction with indigenous Americans and their cultures that I did not always fully appreciate growing up in America, from the salmon iconographies by Coast Salish artists committed to protecting waterways around Seattle, to visiting Chumash nature reserves in Santa Barbara County. I am deeply appreciative to all those who have shared their histories and songs with me at conferences, museums, and powwows. A special thank you to Stephanie Pratt for our many conversations and for a memorable afternoon at the British Museum, viewing John White's Roanoke watercolours with the prints and drawings curator, Kim Sloan.

The editorial team at Cambridge University Press, led by Liz Friend-Smith and with the assistance of Atifa Jiwa, have been a pleasure to work with. I am deeply obliged to Michael Braddick, Ethan Shagan, Alexandra Shepard, and Alexandra Walsham for providing the insightful feedback that transformed my draft into a more complete book, asking questions of my material that provoked a richer consideration of it. A portion of Chapter 2 draws on "'The Savages of Virginia Our Project': The

Powhatans in Jacobean Political Thought', my contribution to *Virginia 1619: Slavery and Freedom in the Making of English America*, ed. Paul Musselwhite, Peter Mancall, and James Horn (Chapel Hill: University of North Carolina Press, 2019), 42–59. Chapter 5 engages with some material from my article 'Locating Colonization at the Jacobean Inns of Court', *The Historical Journal*, 61 (2018), 29–51, published by Cambridge University Press. Both are reproduced here with permission.

My family, though closer to the place of Francis Drake's landing in California than to London, offered wholehearted support from 5,000 miles away, and have always nurtured my rather fanciful love of history. And a book that ends with a discussion of friendship is keenly aware of the importance of friends. I am grateful to those kindred spirits I have found within academia, particularly Finola Finn, and to all those outside of it, who indulged my talk about humanists and featherwork while knowing when to lure me to distraction, and who reminded me that writing a book about Protestant politics could leave room for sweet disorder and a little baroque. While Ciceronian evocations of twinned hearts and blazing souls may seem somewhat extravagant today, the gratitude remains.

Note on Conventions

Original spellings and punctuations have not been altered, except to distinguish between vowels and consonants at a time when *u* and *v*, and *i* and *j*, were often used interchangeably. Scribal abbreviations in manuscripts have been expanded for clarity, designated in the text with brackets. Dates are given in the Old Style (the Julian calendar), with the year adjusted to begin on 1 January. Unless otherwise stated, early modern books were printed in London.

Introduction

In 1614, the lawyer and wit Richard Martin approached the bar in Parliament to deliver a humbling apology. Martin had given members of the House of Commons something of a history lesson, speaking at length of recent geographical discoveries, notions of conquest, previous European colonial efforts, the failed English settlement on Roanoke, and the means through which Virginia might strengthen the English foothold in the Atlantic.[1] What most displeased the Members of Parliament (MPs), however, was not his detailed account of colonization but the ease with which he had slipped into discussing other matters of state. Martin's speech fluctuated away from and then 'fell in again, as it were [to] the Council of Virginia', speaking 'as a School-master, to teach his Scholars'.[2] Colonial supporters from the House of Lords who had accompanied Martin to the Commons were livid. Among clamours for Martin to kneel to deliver his apology, the barrister Francis Ashley maintained that although at fault, Martin 'had his Heart sound and intire', and his 'Love of the State [was] great'.[3]

Martin's defence of Virginia and subsequent digression offer a glimpse into the entangled nature of early colonial interests in Jacobean London, and into the intensely interpersonal environment in which these projects occurred. Martin's behaviour risked damaging the Virginia Company's efforts – and, by extension, the honour and standing of its elite share-holders who were deeply committed to the enterprise. When members of the Virginia Company were asked to leave the chamber while the Commons deliberated Martin's punishment, the lawyer Christopher Brooke refused, 'this being a mixed action' that could not be neatly divided between the integrity of the Lower House and Virginian affairs.[4] The

---

[1] 'Virginia Company', 17 May 1614, in *Journal of the House of Commons, Vol. 1, 1547–1629* (London: His Majesty's Stationary Office, 1802), 487–8.

[2] Ibid.; *Proceedings in Parliament, 1614*, ed. Maija Jansson (Philadelphia, PA: American Philosophical Society, 1988), 276.

[3] 'Virginia Company', 18 May 1614, in *Journal of the House of Commons*, 488.   [4] Ibid.

outcome of the incident is also revealing. Contrary to fears, Martin's transgression seems not to have damaged colonial support. The speaker of the House of Commons reiterated that Martin had 'done himself much Right in the Beginning', and that the 'Remembrances of the Plantation [were] well accepted, and looked upon with the Eyes of our Love'.[5]

Increasingly, the colonial endorsement of gentlemen and their 'love of the state' became difficult to pick apart. In the space of some forty years, from unsuccessful efforts to colonize Roanoke in the mid-1580s to the creation of a royal Virginia in 1624, America, to the English, went from a terra incognita to an integrated component of early seventeenth-century political culture. This book examines how and why this happened, integrating America into the politics and social lives of Jacobean gentlemen and arguing that demonstrations of their civility were increasingly contingent on participating in the colonial. This challenges long-standing assumptions that gentlemen had little interest in the Atlantic prior to larger-scale migration during the reign of Charles I and the civil wars, and establishes a fundamental connection between the proclaimed desire to 'civilize' other peoples and changing notions of civility and refinement in London itself. The civilizing project that the English extended to America did more than stimulate colonization in the Atlantic: it created the foundations of an imperial polity at home.

Scholars of the eighteenth to the twentieth centuries have long considered the impact of empire on London, acknowledging that questions over the burdens, responsibilities, and economic potential of empire informed how the English understood themselves as a nation and how they conceived of their place in the wider world. Historians, writes Catherine Hall, 'need to open up national history and imperial history, challenging that binary and critically scrutinizing the ways in which it has functioned as a way of normalizing power relations and erasing dependence on and exploitation of others'.[6] In *Evaluating Empire and Confronting Colonialism*, the American historian Jack P. Greene admits that although he sought to shed light on developments in the Atlantic outside the imperial centre, de-centred approaches could at times distract from the fact that metropolitan policy-makers were not just implicated in imperial intervention but often 'the principal agents of it'.[7]

---

[5] Ibid.
[6] Catherine Hall and Sonya O. Rose, 'Introduction', in *At Home with the Empire: Metropolitan Culture and the Imperial World*, ed. Catherine Hall and Sonya O. Rose (Cambridge: Cambridge University Press, 2007), 5.
[7] Jack P. Greene, *Evaluating Empire and Confronting Colonialism in Eighteenth-Century Britain* (Cambridge: Cambridge University Press, 2013), xix.

Many studies of early seventeenth-century English politics have none-theless kept national and imperial histories separate. Statesmen in Jacobean London are often seen as thinking about and acting on others while remaining untouched by those they sought to colonize. The Jamestown colony under James I is seen as having little or no significance at the time, dwarfed by English travels to a multitude of territories around the world.[8] Until Oliver Cromwell's Western Design and the rapid economic growth of English plantations in the Caribbean, English colonization is often considered peripheral to political practice, lacking a unified vision or coherent ideology.[9] The result has been that fundamental issues about the cost and consequences of creating an imperial polity have remained muted in studies of English socio-political history. American and colonial scholars have examined the complex relationships between peoples, groups, and institutions on the ground, while global history has opened up remarkable studies on the cross-cultural encounters of merchants, chaplains, sailors, and other transoceanic go-betweens and joint-stock company agents with diverse peoples across the globe. Yet the sense remains that colonization happened 'over there' somewhere, meaning the English impetus to expand their territories through colonization seems to bear little on shifts in domestic thought and behaviour. A focus on James' English reign (1603–25) offers a corrective to assumptions that the Jacobean contribution to colonization was haphazard and minimal, and revises the notion that English experiences in America existed outside Jacobean political culture.

This research began with an investigation into why America appeared so frequently in a range of English discourses beyond the expected cosmographies and travel reports. Why did churchmen evoke the practices of indigenous South Americans in sermons about moral corruption, or pamphleteers deem the Gunpowder Treason conspirators 'tobacconists'? What induced a soldier, in a court deposition, to verbally defend his Protestantism by professing he was no more an atheist than he was a cannibal? Representations of Native Americans featured in unexpected

---

[8] Peter C. Mancall, 'Introduction', in *The Atlantic World and Virginia, 1550–1624*, ed. Peter C. Mancall (Chapel Hill: University of North Carolina Press, 2007), 1–28, at 2.

[9] L. H. Roper, *Advancing Empire: English Interests and Overseas Expansion, 1613–1688* (Cambridge: Cambridge University Press, 2017); Ernest B. Gilman, 'Madagascar on the Mind: The Earl of Arundel and the Arts of Colonization', in *Early Modern Visual Culture: Representation, Race, and Empire in Renaissance England*, ed. Peter Erickson and Clark Hulse (Philadelphia: University of Pennsylvania Press), 284–314, at 311–12; David L. Smith, *A History of the Modern British Isles, 1603–1707: The Double Crown* (Oxford: Blackwell, 1998), 188; David Armitage, *The Ideological Origins of the British Empire* (Cambridge: Cambridge University Press, 2000).

places, appearing on architectural sketches for ceilings and in paintings hanging on walls in royal palaces.[10] Walking through banqueting halls and chapels, a visitor to Hampton Court in 1599 noticed 'the lively and lifelike portrait of the wild man and woman captured by Martin Frobisher ... and brought back to England' in the corridors on the way to the inner apartments.[11] These were the Inuit Arnaq and Kalicho, captured by the English in 1577 along with an infant, Nutaaq. Though the visitor deemed them 'savages', clad in skins and 'Indian dress', images of these Native Americans were widely replicated, from the colonist John White's water-colours to their appearance in the 'America' engraving by the artist Marcus Gheeraerts the elder, who spent time in London.[12] Amidst tapestries and tiled floors, tainted glass and ornate tableaux, representations of the people, flora, and fauna of North and South America – including 'captured' individuals – inhabited the world of the political elite.

By this time, several Native Americans also lived in England as servants, guests, and intelligencers, including in the households of Walter Ralegh and James' secretary of state, Robert Cecil.[13] References to the Chesapeake, tobacco, and cannibals, and slurs about 'savage' or 'Indian-like' behaviour, could be found in commonplace books, Parliament speeches, wit poetry, sermons, popular print, cabinets of curiosities, and court masques. Over the course of this research, it became apparent that these references, while intriguing in and of themselves, were the result of a much larger process of domestic change. On one level, they catalogue the far-reaching effect that English colonization, and the first sustained encounters with Native American peoples, had on English discourse, politics, and sociability in the earliest decades of contact. However, these were not just manifestations of curiosity about other peoples and places, but reflect imperial intent. By extending the civilizing project, so integral to post-Reformation humanistic reform and political stability, to America, English gentlemen began to view their own civil integrity in relation to the project of empire, and they began to fashion themselves accordingly.

---

[10] Design for a ceiling [plan 1/12], *c.* early seventeenth century, Hatfield House, CPM I 12; *Thomas Platter's Travels in England 1599: Rendered into English from the German*, tr. and ed. Clare Williams (London: Jonathan Cape, 1937), 201.

[11] Ibid., 201.

[12] Ibid.; Marcus Gheeraerts the elder, 'America', *c.* late sixteenth century, Victoria & Albert Museum, E. 371–1926.

[13] Coll Thrush, *Indigenous London: Native Travelers at the Heart of Empire* (New Haven, CT: Yale University Press, 2016), 47, 58.

Expansion and the Civilizing Project

To interrogate civility and America in the Jacobean metropolis is to delve into the heart of the troubled relationship between nascent imperialism and English concepts of honour and political identity. Like studies that focus on the abolition of slavery without placing due emphasis on the intentionality behind its beginnings, so an understanding of civility and its implications for participation in civil life is incomplete without acknowledging the fraught, often conflicting ideas that operated within this term.[14] The enduring myths of a trade-based empire undergirded by common law rather than exclusion, liberty rather than conquest, do not match up to the knowing endorsement of subjugation that emerges from civility's political meanings. Neither do such narratives fully explain the elite's commitment to empire for centuries after. By the eighteenth century, the English view of themselves as 'a Race of Men, who prefer the publicke Good before any narrow or selfish Views – who choose Dangers in the defence of Their Country [and] an honourable Death before the unmanly pleasures of a useless and effeminate life' was an entrenched prototype of the ideal gentleman.[15] This 'Race of Men' equated 'Birthright' to bringing 'Good Manners' and Protestantism to distant parts of the world, refracting the language of colonial treatises and pro-imperial poems constructed in the sixteenth and seventeenth centuries.

The discussion of the civilizing project in this book is a means of exploring the dual sense of English identity that emerged as a result of expansion and reform. The Reformation fractured ideas of a unified Christian Europe. Henry VIII's break from Rome imbued the English monarch with claims to religious and political sovereignty while leaving many practical questions over what such sovereignty entailed. Humanists turned to history and queried the language, literature, and institutions of their own past in the hopes of understanding what it meant to be English.[16] The Reformation also shifted the relationship between the English and the rest of the British Isles, where Ireland and parts of Scotland remained resistant to the religious and political reforms of the late Tudor state. Colonization was in many ways the large-scale consequence of changing

---

[14] William A. Pettigrew, *Freedom's Debt: The Royal African Company and the Politics of the Atlantic Slave Trade, 1672–1752* (Chapel Hill: University of North Carolina Press, 2013), 3–4.

[15] Kathleen Wilson, 'The Good, the Bad, and the Impotent: Imperialism and the Politics of Identity in Georgian England', in *The Consumption of Culture, 1600–1800: Image, Object, Text*, ed. Ann Bermingham and John Brewer (New York: Routledge, 1995), 237–62, at 237.

[16] Cathy Shrank, *Writing the Nation in Reformation England, 1530–1580* (Oxford: Oxford University Press, 2004).

strategies for domestic governance, where the Tudor governing regime drew on the concept of civility to subject individuals to the authority of the state.

Even as the English looked to their past and their borders to form their identity, increased trade routes and travel impelled them to profess their legitimacy on a global stage. Proud of their status as an island nation while acutely aware of their inferior reputation in the eyes of many Europeans, the English began to assert a sense of national feeling influenced by Protestantism and inflected by a larger international cosmopolitanism.[17] A desire to contend with the status of other European nations, and what J. H. Elliott calls the imperial envy of the English, propelled their outward-looking ambitions in the Atlantic.[18] The frontispiece to the 1625 edition of the geographer and clergyman Samuel Purchas' *Purchas his pilgrimes* depicted James wearing an imperial crown and his son Charles stepping forward to accept the call to further effect the plantation projects begun by his father. Psalms 147:20 appeared below him, reinforcing the English belief of themselves as providentially elect: 'He shewed his word unto Jacob, and he hath not dealt so with any nation'.[19] Purchas' frontispiece depicted Scotland and England as united realms, but he also mapped English spaces in Newfoundland, Virginia, Guiana, Brazil, and Peru, challenging the territories claimed by the French in Florida and by the Spanish in New Spain. The works of Richard Hakluyt and Samuel Purchas embodied what J. G. A. Pocock describes as the English belief that they were 'occupying a moment and possessing a dimension in sacred history', one in which each individual was called to act.[20] To many Jacobean Englishmen, colonization was a national imperative.

The humanist 're-discovery' of England played an important role in how imperial-minded gentlemen conceived of colonization. As Colin Kidd argues, the outward-looking ideological imperatives of the English were shaped by conceptions of their own history, marked by repeated conquests and new settlements by the Romans, Saxons, and Normans.[21] Humanists drew on classical models and histories to mould their national

---

[17] Adrian Green, *Building for England: John Cosin's Architecture in Renaissance Durham and Cambridge* (Durham: Institute of Medieval and Early Modern Studies, 2016), 14.

[18] J. H. Elliott, *Spain, Europe, and the Wider World, 1500–1800* (New Haven, CT: Yale University Press, 2009), 33.

[19] Samuel Purchas, *Purchas his pilgrimes* (1625; STC 20509), frontispiece.

[20] J. G. A. Pocock, *The Machiavellian Moment: Florentine Political Thought and the Atlantic Republican Tradition* (Princeton, NJ: Princeton University Press, 1975), 344–5.

[21] Colin Kidd, *British Identities before Nationalism: Ethnicity and Nationhood in the Atlantic World, 1600–1800* (Cambridge: Cambridge University Press, 1999), 75.

image. The imperial language of ancient Rome heavily influenced political thinkers in Elizabethan England, where *imperium* related both to territorial expansion and to the power of the monarch at home.[22] Coins and portraits, courtly performances and the frontispieces of books likened Elizabeth and James to classical emperors, often crowned with the closed imperial crown of Roman rulers. Elizabeth and James were compared to the emperor Constantine, not only for his ability to rule but also for his desire to create a Christian empire that involved a concerted attack on the pagan world.[23]

Elizabethan and Jacobean antiquarians including William Camden, John Selden, and Robert Cotton were also lawyers and politicians, and did not see history as distinct from, but integral to explaining the legitimacy of English customs.[24] English statesmen and colonists claimed they were well placed to 'civilize' Native Americans since they themselves had benefitted, and continued to benefit, from having been civilized by Roman occupation.[25] '[F]or his Majesty to reach his long royall armes to another World' in the present moment was to do as the Romans had done, since the '*Roman* Empire sowed *Roman* Colonies thorow the World, as the most naturall and artificiall way to win and hold the World *Romaine*'.[26] The antiquarian Henry Spelman, an active officeholder and treasurer of the Guiana Company in 1627, sent his own nephew Henry to Virginia in 1609, where Henry learned Algonquian languages and became an important mediator in Anglo–Algonquian relations. Even more so than the Greek polis, the Roman pursuit of the civil life involved a demonstrable interest in empire and the exportation of their customs abroad, in models that Jacobeans demonstrably sought to emulate.[27]

Colonization implicated the political elite in a significant way, requiring sustained regulation and oversight. This began with Ireland. Henry VIII's self-conscious declaration of political legitimacy and his rejection of papal authority necessitated more vigorous campaigns to instil conformity as the state began to look beyond its borders.[28] The influential Elizabethan statesmen Francis Walsingham and William Cecil, Lord Burghley, as well as Elizabeth's keeper of the privy seal, Thomas Smith, and Cecil's

---

[22] Anthony Pagden, *Lords of All the World: Ideologies of Empire in Spain, Britain, and France, 1500–1800* (New Haven, CT: Yale University Press, 1995), 11.

[23] Ibid., 18.

[24] See Graham Parry, *The Trophies of Time: English Antiquarians of the Seventeenth Century* (Oxford: Oxford University Press, 1995).

[25] Kidd, *British Identities before Nationalism*, 35.

[26] Purchas, *Purchas his pilgrimes*, sig. Mmmmmmm3v.   [27] Pagden, *Lords of all the World*, 22.

[28] Michael Hechter, *Internal Colonialism: The Celtic Fringe in British National Development*, 2nd ed. (London: Transaction Publishers, 1999), 66.

son, Robert, oversaw the colonization of Ireland in the second half of the sixteenth century. Irish scholars have established how humanism and the Reformation shaped English colonial intervention and provoked varying levels of resistance and accommodation on the part of local peoples. This involved attempts to subject the Gaelic Irish, but also the Catholic 'Old English' descendants of the twelfth-century Norman conquest of Ireland, to Protestant visions of reform. The humanist statesman Francis Bacon, like the colonist Edmund Spenser, portrayed the colonization of Ireland as a civilizing project modelled on Greco-Roman political histories and the imperial ambitions of Rome.[29] The language of savagery set against the civilizing initiatives of the English state provided consistent rhetoric in favour of colonization among policy-makers and their agents.[30]

Events in Ireland during the Nine Years' War (1594–1603) led to more stringent policies against the Irish, and influential treatises by Richard Becon and John Davies argued that the English colonization of Ireland had hitherto failed precisely because colonists were accepting and even imitating the mores of local inhabitants.[31] Interactions between the New English, Gaelic nobility, Irish tenants, town dwellers, and Old English were characterized by negotiation as well as brutality, depending on the policies of individual governors and their rapport with local populations.[32] Nonetheless, English colonization altered the Irish landscape. Even during the atrocities of the Cromwellian regime in the 1640s, poetry explicitly attributed the destruction of Gaelic ways of life to James' reign and to the violent redistribution of land: '[James] ordered their lands to be measured with ropes, he replaced the pure Irish with Saxons, and transplanted them all'.[33] As attorney general in

---

[29] Nicholas Canny, *Making Ireland British, 1580–1650* (Oxford: Oxford University Press, 2001), 197–8.

[30] Nicholas Canny, 'The Ideology of English Colonization: From Ireland to America', *The William and Mary Quarterly*, 30 (1973), 575–98; Paul Slack, *The Invention of Improvement: Information and Material Progress in Seventeenth-Century England* (Oxford: Oxford University Press, 2014), 68; Nicholas Canny, *Kingdom and Colony: Ireland in the Atlantic World, 1560–1800* (Baltimore, MD: Johns Hopkins University Press, 1988); Audrey Horning, *Ireland in the Virginian Sea: Colonialism in the British Atlantic* (Chapel Hill: University of North Carolina Press, 2013).

[31] John Davies, *A discourse of the true causes why Ireland was never entirely subdued* (1612; STC 6348); Edmund Spenser, *A View of the State of Ireland*, ed. Andrew Hadfield and Willy Maley (Oxford: Blackwell, 1997); Richard Becon, *Solon his follie, or a politique discourse* (Oxford, 1594; STC 1653); Hans Pawlisch, *Sir John Davies and the Conquest of Ireland: A Study in Legal Imperialism* (Cambridge: Cambridge University Press, 1985); Nicholas Canny, *The Elizabethan Conquest of Ireland: A Pattern Established, 1565–1576* (Hassocks: Harvester Press, 1976).

[32] Steven G. Ellis, *Ireland in the Age of the Tudors, 1447–1603: English Expansion and the End of Gaelic Rule* (London: Longman, 1998); *British Interventions in Early Modern Ireland*, ed. Ciaran Brady and Jane Ohlmeyer (Cambridge: Cambridge University Press, 2005). For examples of how the English might benefit from lenience towards local populations, see Canny, *Making Ireland British*, 79.

[33] Canny, *Making Ireland British*, 214, 575.

Ireland, Davies emphasized the reforming power of the law and the responsibilities of authorities to inaugurate English institutions and values to ensure the success of colonization. At the same time, the initiatives on the part of the English were frequently imperiled and only partially successful. The contracted military campaigns and failures to assimilate Gaelic cultures only deepened the English belief in the importance of conformity in upholding an ordered civil society.

This book picks up policy-makers' civilizing impetus as they began to apply it further west. The English believed Irish landscapes and industries could be financially beneficial to the state, but the 'newness' of America and the competition among European states to claim its sizeable territories added to its appeal. The 'fourth part of the world', unknown to the very Greeks and Romans whose authority and civil refinement captivated early modern individuals, seemingly lay ready for possession, infusing Elizabethan and early Jacobean discourse with a sense of opportunity and optimism. Colonial promoters expressed an awareness that their era offered a distinct moment of opportunity. 'No nation in Christendom is so fit for this action [of colonization] as England', pressed Edward Hayes in 1602, 'by reason of . . . our long domesticall peace'.[34] While later Elizabethan colonial projects were hampered by war with Spain, the Anglo–Spanish peace treaty of 1604 allowed the English to devote unprecedented energy to American colonization. New investment opportunities from 1600 reflected this intent. The Virginia Company (1606), the Newfoundland Company (1610), the Somers Islands/Bermuda Company (1615), and the Amazon Company (1619) were Jacobean innovations, contributing to a pitch of interest in America at the time. 'I knowe of some and heare of more of our nation who endevoure the finding out of Virgenia, Guiana and other remote and unknowen Countries', complained the king's lord deputy in Ireland, Arthur Chichester, in 1605, while neglecting the 'makinge Cyvell of Ireland'.[35]

A focus on the Atlantic is not intended to diminish the many relations that the English had with the rest of the world. The global turn in early twenty-first-century historiography has emphasized broad patterns of movement and global connectivity, focussing on diasporas and migration patterns, company agents and other go-betweens.[36] As Hakluyt and Purchas' vast travel

---

[34] Edward Hayes in John Brereton, *A briefe and true relation of the discoverie of the north part of Virginia* (1602; STC 3611), sig. C2r.

[35] Arthur Chichester to the Earl of Salisbury, 2 October 1605, The National Archives, SP 63/217, f. 165v.

[36] Miles Ogborn, *Global Lives: Britain and the World, 1550–1800* (Cambridge: Cambridge University Press, 2008); *The Atlantic in Global History, 1500–2000*, ed. Jorge Cañizares-Esguerra and Erik

compendia indicated, English aspirations in North and South America were part of a much larger project of trafficking and exchange. Europeans first turned to America in their search for India. The interest in spices and silks is apparent in many surviving maps of the time, where the label 'Oriens' reinforced the European desire to orient themselves, quite literally, towards the East. Prior to the establishment of sugar plantations in the Caribbean from the 1630s, pursuing trade with the Ottoman and Mughal empires far outweighed the economic potential of the English Atlantic.

The westward enterprises can be placed within multiple processes of global exchange that were relational, but distinct. Rather than pitting the Atlantic as an alternative approach to English post-Reformation history, America becomes a vital component of the Protestant vision of reform that emerged from the upheavals and traumas of religious and political controversies in Europe and beyond. When gentlemen copied excerpts from geographies in their commonplace books ('Africa is greater than Europe. Asia then Africa. and America bigger then all'), or purchased engravings that personified America as a woman awaiting possession, they perpetuated widely accepted geopolitical assumptions about a civil Europe engaged with other parts of the globe in a series of interconnected but specific relationships.[37] The English celebrated American plantation as a vital means of sourcing the commodities that characterized Eastern wealth while opposing Catholic ascendancy in the Atlantic. Virginia's soil and climate rivaled that of Persia, wrote James' silkworm expert John Bonoeil, and was not silk the staple commodity of 'that great Empire', forming the 'sinewes of the *Persian* state'?[38] The vast American continents, not Ireland, would allow the English to become global contenders, turning 'the Easterne world . . . Spectators of the Western Worth'.[39]

R. Seeman (Upper Saddle River, NJ: Pearson Prentice Hall, 2007); *Bringing the World to Early Modern Europe: Travel Accounts and Their Audiences*, ed. Peter C. Mancall (Leiden: Brill, 2007); *Collecting across Cultures: Material Exchanges in the Early Atlantic World*, ed. Daniel Bleichmar and Peter C. Mancall (Philadelphia: University of Pennsylvania Press, 2011); *Travel and Travail: Early Modern Women, English Drama, and the Wider World*, ed. Patricia Akhimie and Bernadette Andrea (Lincoln: University of Nebraska Press, 2019).

[37] Cosmographical commonplace book, *c.* early to mid-seventeenth century, Beinecke Library, Osborn b337; 'The Four Continents' engravings, *c.*1625–35, The British Museum, 1870,0514.1176–79; Robert Stafford, *A geographicall and anthologicall description of all the empires and kingdomes* (1618; STC 23136), sig. I2v; Edmond Smith, 'De-personifying Collaert's *Four Continents*: European Descriptions of Continental Diversity, 1585–1625', *European Review of History*, 21 (2014), 817–35.

[38] John Bonoeil, *His Majesties gracious letter to the Earle of South-Hampton* (1622; STC 14378), sig. I4r. See also Thomas Hariot, *A briefe and true report of the new found land of Virginia* (1590; STC 12786); Robert Johnson, *Nova Britannia* (1609; STC 14699.5).

[39] Quoted in Jonathan Eacott, *Selling Empire: India in the Making of Britain and America, 1600–1830* (Chapel Hill: University of North Carolina Press, 2016), 30.

As the first permanent English colony in America, Virginia held particular importance to statesmen and emerges as a major influence on Jacobean articulations of their emergent transatlantic polity. Travelling from Cape Cod to the Chesapeake, one gentleman called Jamestown 'the London colonie', highlighting its strong associations with the metropolis.[40] The Virginia Company years (1606–24) align closely with James' English reign (1603–25), rendering it a distinct feature of the era. Not only did the colony provide the first large-scale American export for England – tobacco – but it was to be a point of entry for the creation of an English Atlantic, a land base where the English could begin the industries, trades, and settlements that would enable them to transplant their civil society. The English were 'growing and multiplying into kingdomes', with Virginia the portal to '*New England, New found land* ... and other Ilands [that] may be adopted and legall Daughters of England'.[41]

Virginia informed many of the approaches to colonization that followed. The puritan George Mourt wrote in 1622 that the colonists' hopes for Massachusetts would be effected through 'the example of the hon[ourable] *Virginia* and *Bermudas* Companies' whose ability to overcome a litany of failures 'may prevaile as a spurre of preparation'.[42] English Separatists, sailing from the Netherlands, received permission to settle south of Cape Cod in 1619, arriving in Plymouth in 1620. The official charter for the Massachusetts Bay colony did not appear under James, but under Charles. Given this book's focus on state politics, the communities that began to prosper in New England in the last few years of James' reign – many of them created to escape Jacobean politics and what they saw as the corruptions of the Anglican Church – had a less demonstrable impact on metropolitan political thought and practice in this period, though this changed after the establishment of the Commonwealth in 1649. In the poet Thomas Carew's court masque of 1634, 'the plantation in *New-England*' served as a place to send dissenters, not aspiring statesmen. As the character Momus quipped, the colony had 'purg'd more virulent humours from the politique body' than West Indian drugs had purged physical bodies at home.[43]

As this book argues, something is lost when colonization is viewed solely as another form of global exchange. The stated method of 'civilizing' others

---

[40] Thomas Holland to the Earl of Salisbury, 30 October 1609, Hatfield House, CP 128/24r.

[41] Purchas, 'Virginias Verger', in *Purchas his pilgrimes*, sig. Mmmmmmm3v.

[42] George Mourt, 'To the Reader', in William Bradford [and Edward Winslow], *A relation or journall of the beginning and proceedings of the English plantation settled at Plimoth* (1622; STC 20074), sig. Bv.

[43] Thomas Carew, *Coelum Britanicum. A masque at White-hall* (1634; STC 4618), sig. C2v.

as a means of extending territorial authority politicized the enforcement
of manners and social habits. Different dynamics of power were inher-
ently at play, leaving deep wounds and legacies. Native American scholarship refers to indigenous peoples' persistent refusal to be subsumed by
settler colonialism as 'survivance'.[44] This term refers to the ability of
Native groups to not only endure trauma but to thrive in spite of it, while
also making clear that the flourishing of indigeneity into the present day
happened *despite* Europeans' persistent attempts to eradicate their ways
of life. While the political elite's conceptions of civility were repeatedly
challenged by those they sought to colonize, ignoring the intent behind
colonization presents a skewed understanding of how English civility
developed in the seventeenth century. Rather than viewing the enforcement of civility as a process – which implies its fulfilment – the 'civilizing
project' explored in this book is a means of focussing on the beliefs and
ambitions of statesmen and the effect of colonization on their understanding of themselves. When the Virginia Company councillor
Nicholas Ferrar made a list in the 1620s of all the languages spoken in
the king's dominions, he included '[t]he language spoken by the savages
in the Virginia plantation' and '[t]hat other kind also spoken in New
England'.[45] To Ferrar, English colonies in eastern North America were
a part of the English nation.

Civility and the Jacobean Polity

The popularity of Atlantic and global history has in some ways discouraged
joined-up studies of colonization and the practice of politics in England.
Whereas American scholars tend to view the early colonies as the prelude to
the foundation of a new republic, English political historians often assume
that American schemes were the fancies of merchants and poets, largely
outside the domain of concerted political interest before the mid-
seventeenth century. The global activities of merchant corporations were
profoundly important in developing overseas governance, but it is equally
important to recognize the active and willing role that policy-makers
played in bringing imperial interests into state institutions. Gentlemen
sought to contend with expansion, not only in the formal structures of
metropolitan government but also in grappling with wider questions about

---

[44] *Survivance: Narratives of Native Presence*, ed. Gerald Vizenor (Lincoln: University of Nebraska
Press, 2008).
[45] John Ferrar, 'Life of Nicholas Ferrar', in *Nicholas Ferrar: Two Lives*, ed. J. E. B. Mayor (Cambridge:
Macmillan, 1855), 157.

their responsibilities in asserting their authority abroad. While scholars, therefore, have raised attention to the lack of a coherent vision of empire in Elizabethan England and pointed to policy-makers' frequent invocation of classical writers like Tacitus, who expressed concern at the moral corruption that empire engendered, these ambiguities should not obscure policy-makers' clear desire to participate in the political project of empire.[46] Though Pocock and others established the insufficiency of the 'one-way imperial success story' in understanding English identity in this period, a sense remains that the English acted on others but that the colonial experience bore little on elite self-perception.[47]

Coming from a long line of Scottish kings who expressed their authority in imperial terms, James actively promoted civility as a means of transforming individuals into obedient subjects.[48] He fashioned himself as a learned and civilizing king, though centuries of historiography have turned his earnestness into something of a joke. James has never been considered the embodiment of the classical Renaissance prince. He hates dancing and music, wrote one ambassador of the eighteen-year-old Scottish king in 1584, his manners 'very ... uncivil'.[49] A controversial Latin text published anonymously on the Continent in 1615 viciously attacked the correlation between James' bodily carriage and his inner morality. The authors described James' physicality in scathing detail, lingering on the king's disproportionate features. 'You appear to have been made more by design than by chance, more for the needs of a scholar than a king', the discourse went. 'Your body does depart from the basic principles of nature ... [Those who fault it] are surely too delicate and certainly unable to comprehend that this is the beauty of a man ... even if it seems an ugly or very near ugly thing'.[50] Contemporaries

---

[46] David Armitage, 'The Elizabethan Idea of Empire', *Transactions of the Royal Historical Society*, 14 (2004), 269–77, at 276; Andrew Fitzmaurice, *Humanism and America: An Intellectual History of English Colonization, 1500–1625* (Cambridge: Cambridge University Press, 2003).

[47] J. G. A. Pocock, 'The New British History in Atlantic Perspective: An Antipodean Commentary', *The American Historical Review*, 104 (1999), 490–500; Jane Ohlmeyer, 'Seventeenth-Century Ireland and the New British and Atlantic Histories', *The American Historical Review*, 104 (1999), 446–62; *The Stuart Kingdoms in the Seventeenth Century: Awkward Neighbours*, ed. Allan I. Macinnes and Jane Ohlmeyer (Portland, OR: Four Courts Press, 2002); Nicholas Canny, 'Writing Early Modern History: Ireland, Britain, and the Wider World', *The Historical Journal*, 46 (2003), 723–47; John Kerrigan, *Archipelagic English: Literature, History, and Politics, 1603–1707* (Oxford: Oxford University Press, 2008).

[48] Roger A. Mason, 'Scotland, Elizabethan England and the Idea of Britain', *Transactions of the Royal Historical Society*, 14 (2004), 279–93.

[49] Monsieur Fontenay to Mary [Queen of Scots], 15 August 1584, The National Archives, SP 53/13, f. 159r.

[50] *Corona Regia*, ed. Winfried Schleiner and Tyler Fyotek (Geneva: Librarie Droz, 2010), 87–9.

portrayed James as playing at civility while unaware, in his indulgent lasciviousness, of his own appalling deformities.

Although James was criticized for failing to embody courtly grace, his conception of civility went beyond manners to fundamental ideas of civil, godly order, and he championed the monarchy as a civilizing force in ways that encouraged empire. James' reputation has benefitted from more favourable assessments of his reign over the past few decades.[51] At the same time, the enduring attention to issues around authorship, frictions with Parliament, and Anglo–Scottish Church disputes have continued to sideline the place of overseas involvement in the king's conception of sovereignty. In 1598, James urged his son and heir, Henry, to 'follow forth the course that I have intended . . . planting civilitie' in the lives of the 'barbarous and stubborne sort'.[52] As Jane Ohlmeyer argues, James' civilizing initiatives were based on strong personal conviction. He retained an interest in affairs in Scotland and Ireland and frequently invoked the duties of his nobility to promote civility as a method of rule.[53] Before becoming king of England, James sent his royal favourites in Scotland to carry out missions into the Highlands and the Hebrides, using a coterie of 'Gentlemen Adventurers of Fife' in attempts to quell the Isle of Lewis in the 1590s. This reflected a nascent pattern of expansion in which the king used high-ranking members of the court in campaigns to restore order to the territories claimed by the Crown.[54] The intervention of the English in Shetland, Orkney, the Isle of Man, and the Anglo–Scottish borders, as in Munster and Ulster and then America, indicated aggressive attempts to push 'the political frontier gradually westward'.[55]

Although vehemently contested by lawyers and MPs in England, James' commitment to the notion of a unified 'Britain' created a language of imperial sovereignty that writers and policy-makers frequently drew upon.

---

[51] *James VI and I: Ideas, Authority, and Government*, ed. Ralph Houlbrooke (Aldershot: Ashgate, 2006); Pauline Croft, *King James* (New York: Palgrave, 2003); *Scots and Britons: Scottish Political Thought and the Union of 1603*, ed. Roger A. Mason (Cambridge: Cambridge University Press, 1994); Maurice Lee, *Great Britain's Solomon: James VI and I in His Three Kingdoms* (Urbana: University of Illinois Press, 1990); *Royal Subjects: Essays on the Writings of James VI and I*, ed. Daniel Fischlin and Mark Fortier (Detroit, MI: Wayne State University Press, 2002); John Cramsie, *Kingship and Crown Finance under James VI and I, 1603–1625* (Woodbridge: Boydell Press, 2002).

[52] James I, 'Basilikon Doron', re-printed in *The workes of the most high and mightie prince, James* (1616; STC 14344), sig. O2r.

[53] Jane Ohlmeyer, '"Civilizinge of Those Rude Partes": Colonization within Britain and Ireland, 1580s–1640s', in *The Oxford History of the British Empire: Vol. 1*, ed. Nicholas Canny (Oxford: Oxford University Press, 1998), 124–47, at 144.

[54] Jenny Wormald, 'A Very British Problem: The Stuart Crown and the Plantation of Ulster', *History Ireland*, 17 (2009), 20–3, at 21.

[55] Ohlmeyer, 'Civilizinge of those Rude Partes', 125–6.

The cartographer John Speed praised 'the royall Person of our now-*Soveraigne*' for unifying 'Britannia', where '[t]he Cordes of whose *Royall Tents*, we pray, may be further extended, that those naked *Virginians* may be covered under the Curtaines of his most Christian Government'.[56] Merchants too fostered this conceit. The motto on the arms of the Merchants of Virginia, *en dat Virginia quintam*, or, 'behold, Virginia gives us a fifth dominion', referred to English claims to territories beyond England, Ireland, Scotland, and France.[57] This made explicit Virginia's prime role in the English imaginary as a cornerstone of the transatlantic polity.

Historians' conception of political change in this period owes much to the sociologist Norbert Elias' work on civility and state formation, a connection he believes was fundamental to the creation of modern European society.[58] To Elias, the 'civilizing process' brought manners and the individual body into discourses about the body politic. Mastering strict codes of conduct allowed individuals to access spheres of political power and to assert authority in governing others. Elias attributes this shift to the sixteenth century, when aristocratic values moved from a martial, knightly ethos of courtliness to new codes of manners and principles of shame. Elias attributes particular importance to the humanist Desiderius Erasmus' *On civility in children* (1530), which established manners as essential to priming members of the nobility for politics.[59]

It has become commonplace to criticize Elias' confidence in the progression of civilization, but historicizing his claims do not make them a less useful departing point. While few scholars today draw a linear correlation between a 'civilizing process' and the concept of civilization, historians have established the prominence of civility as a tool in the formation of the early modern state.[60] As Anna Bryson finds, 'civility' in late sixteenth-century England began to supplant other terms in the vocabulary of manners while retaining politically charged meanings.[61] This internal

---

[56] John Speed, *The theatre of the empire of Great Britaine* (1612; STC 23041), sig. Ppppp3r.

[57] John Stow, *The survey of London* (1633; 23345.5), sig. Ggg4v.

[58] Norbert Elias, *The Civilizing Process*, tr. Edmund Jephcott (Oxford: Blackwell, 1978), xvi; Stephen Mennell, *Norbert Elias: An Introduction* (Oxford: Blackwell, 1992), 31.

[59] Elias, *The Civilizing Process*, 54.

[60] Mennell, *Norbert Elias*, 30; Michael Braddick, *State Formation in Early Modern England, 1550–1700* (Cambridge: Cambridge University Press, 2000); Steve Hindle, *The State and Social Change in Early Modern England, 1550–1640* (Basingstoke: Palgrave, 2000); Michael Braddick, 'Introduction: The Politics of Gesture', *Past & Present*, 203 (2009), 9–35.

[61] Anna Bryson, *From Courtesy to Civility: Changing Codes of Conduct in Early Modern England* (Cambridge: Cambridge University Press, 1998), 48.

shift occurred precisely at the time that the English also looked to ancient Rome for their articulations of empire. Rooted in classical political philosophy, gentlemanly civility evoked the necessity of social order and celebrated participation in the common good. This did not just involve the monarchy and the court. Urban, town-dwelling individuals were deemed more civil than those beyond the city, while 'savages' were frequently characterized as living beyond the pale of human society and outside the bounds of citizenship. Far from being a term used among the elite alone, litigations and parish court records suggest that early Stuart subjects regarded civility an important form of social currency. Appealing to the civility (or the incivility) of others became a means of articulating honour and good standing across communities, as when women defended their reputations by professing their chastity and by using modest speech.[62]

The political weight behind civility and savagery differed from other terms the English used to describe incivility, such as 'heathen' or 'pagan'. These were largely biblical terms that denoted non-Christians, particularly polytheists. While 'pagan' resonated with the classical past, 'heathen' played a particularly central role in post-Reformation theological debate, closely associated with Old Testament language and widely employed by puritans to discuss providentialism and salvation.[63] For this reason, 'heathen' frequently appeared in the writings of colonists in New England, especially during conflict with the Pequots in the 1630s. Both terms also evoked classical discourses about the East and its luxuries to denounce the hazards of indulging in sensual pleasures that distracted from contemplating the spiritual. Frequent encounters with non-Christians through trade and expansion added potency to long-standing English associations between heathenism and religious error, but also with dangerous extravagance.

While 'heathen' or 'pagan' were sometimes used interchangeably with 'savage', the political language of the English civilizing project overwhelmingly drew on ideas of savagery. This is evident in the recurrent manner in which Native Americans were labelled 'savages'. Since English civility

---

[62] *Civil Histories*, ed. Peter Burke, Brian Harrison, and Paul Slack (Oxford: Oxford University Press, 2000), v; Anthony Pagden, *European Encounters with the New World: From Renaissance to Romanticism* (New Haven, CT: Yale University Press, 1993); Sara Mendelson, 'The Civility of Women in Seventeenth-Century England', in *Civil Histories*, 112–25.

[63] Alexandra Walsham, *The Reformation of the Landscape: Religion, Identity, and Memory in Early Modern Britain and Ireland* (Oxford: Oxford University Press, 2011); Alexandra Walsham, *Providence in Early Modern England*, 2nd ed. (Oxford: Oxford University Press, 2001); John Marenbon, *Pagans and Philosophers: The Problem of Paganism from Augustine to Leibniz* (Princeton, NJ: Princeton University Press, 2015).

involved a concept of historical development, of 'a civil state of polity and society [emerging] out of an original condition of savagery', grouping the complexities of Native American societies under a single word served to dismiss their cultures while expressing colonial intervention as a positive act.[64] Colonial literature informing readers 'How the Salvages became subject to the English' perpetuated myths of passive Native Americans while propagating fundamental beliefs about the necessity and seeming success of the civilizing project abroad.[65] While Catholics often viewed conversion as an immediate aim achieving colonial ascendancy, English Protestants voiced that they themselves had been 'first Civilized by the Romane Conquests, and mixture of their Colonies with us [brought] Religion afterwards'.[66] Protestant evangelism was an entrenched obligation in joint-stock company charters, providing a moral framework through which civil society would be upheld and successfully governed. At the same time, conversion involved time, education, and rigorous self-searching through theological query, something that could only come after Native Americans were better integrated within English society. It was communication – civil conversation – that the New England colonist Roger Williams saw as laying the groundwork for conversion, for 'by such converse it may please the *Father* . . . to spread *civilitie* (and in his owne most holy Season), *Christianitie*'.[67]

In her study of early modern masculinity, Alexandra Shepard illustrates how men in early Stuart England increasingly defined themselves through social distinction and civility.[68] Self-control became a manifestation of the ability to manage and govern one's household and, by extension, the state.[69] Colonization inflected these expressions of authority. Plantation, preached William Crashaw in 1609, would bring Algonquians '1. Civilitie for their bodies, 2. Christianity for their soules. The first to make them men: the second happy men'.[70] In its role in 'making men' and displaying the right to rule, the civil body became equated with virtuous manhood,

---

[64] Bryson, *From Courtesy to Civility*, 277.

[65] John Smith [ed. William Symonds], *A map of Virginia* (1612; STC 22791), sig. Lv.

[66] John White, *The planters plea: Or the grounds of plantations examined* (1630; STC 25399), sig. C2r.

[67] Roger Williams, *A key into the language of America* (1643; Wing W2766), sig. A3r. On English Protestantism and expansion, see Carla Gardina Pestana, *Protestant Empire: Religion and the Making of the Atlantic World* (Philadelphia: University of Pennsylvania Press, 2009).

[68] Alexandra Shepard, *Meanings of Manhood in Early Modern England* (Oxford: Oxford University Press, 2003), 252–3.

[69] Hindle, *The State and Social Change*; Braddick, *State Formation in Early Modern England*, part 2.

[70] William Crashaw, *A sermon preached in London before the right honorable the Lord Lawarre* (1610; STC 6029), sig. D4r.

one that distinguished itself from other bodies, whether those from invaded territories or social inferiors including women. Write not to me 'of your Savages', the poet Michael Drayton wrote to his friend, the colonist George Sandys, for '[a]s savage slaves be in great *Britaine* here/ As any one that you can shew me there'.[71] In 1628, the Newfoundland colonist Robert Hayman drew on decades-old tropes about uncivil women and untamed landscapes, where a 'rude' Newfoundland, when 'decked with neat husbandry', would be like a 'sluttish' woman made 'pretty pert ... with good cloathes on'.[72] By the early seventeenth century, American 'savages' and domestic social differentiation were already being melded together in ways that connected imperial success and household authority.

Before establishing sustained plantation economies, English categorizations of human difference depended more on what Colin Kidd calls 'ethnic theology' than on later concepts of race.[73] While Africans in sixteenth- and seventeenth-century England might occupy roles similar to those of servants, the label 'blackamoor', like descriptions of Native Americans' 'tanned' or 'tawny' skin, nevertheless depended on categorizing people based on skin colour.[74] John Hawkins' and Francis Drake's voyages involved trafficking humans, and English merchants, seafarers, and policymakers were well aware of the presence of enslaved Africans and Native Americans in the West Indies and Central and South America.[75] While the English found no indigenous inhabitants when they first landed in Bermuda in 1609, they quickly brought Africans and Native Americans to the island as skilled tobacco cultivators and pearl divers.[76] In London,

---

[71] Michael Drayton, 'To Master George Sandys, Treasurer for the English Colony in Virginia', in *The battaile of Agincourt ... Elegies upon sundry occasions* (1627; STC 7190), sig. Bbv.

[72] Robert Hayman, *Quodlibets ... composed and done at Harbor-Grace in Britaniola, anciently called Newfound-land* (1628; STC 12974), sig. F2r. For discussions of gender and possession, see Louis Montrose, 'The Work of Gender in the Discourse of Discovery', *Representations*, 33 (1991), 1–41.

[73] Kidd, *British Identities before Nationalism*, 12; Joyce E. Chaplin, 'Race', in *The British Atlantic World, 1500–1800*, 2nd ed., ed. David Armitage and Michael J. Braddick (Basingstoke: Palgrave, 2009), 173–92, at 173; Karen Ordahl Kupperman, 'Presentment of Civility: English Reading of American Self-Presentation in the Early Years of Colonization', *The William and Mary Quarterly*, 54 (1997), 193–228; *Race in Early Modern England: A Documentary Companion*, ed. Jonathan Burton and Ania Loomba (Basingstoke: Palgrave, 2007).

[74] Kim F. Hall, *Things of Darkness: Economies of Race and Gender in Early Modern England* (Ithaca, NY: Cornell University Press, 1995); *Black Africans in Renaissance Europe*, ed. Thomas Foster Earle and Kate J. P. Lowe (Cambridge: Cambridge University Press, 2005).

[75] Michael Guasco, *Slaves and Englishmen: Human Bondage in the Early Modern Atlantic World* (Philadelphia: University of Pennsylvania Press, 2011).

[76] Virginia Bernhard, 'Bermuda and Virginia in the Seventeenth Century: A Comparative View', *Journal of Social History*, 19 (1985), 57–70; Virginia Bernhard, 'Beyond the Chesapeake: The

the appearance of Native American iconographies on tobacco advertisements and shop signs, and the depiction of 'blackamoors' smoking pudding roll tobacco (the cigar-like methods of packaging and imbibing tobacco in Spanish colonies) created visual primers that normalized conceptions of human difference and the knowing exploitation of human labour in the Atlantic. Writing from Barbados in 1631, the Essex gentlemen Henry Colt noted that the sun never 'tannes the skin ... I never ware gloves, & yett my hands were never whiter'.[77] Even before institutionalized slavery in English America, civil gentlemen sought to demonstrate the value of remaining white.

Politics, Sociability, and Taste

Early modern political practice was imbedded in the social.[78] The state relied on networks of affiliations to sustain and extend its authority, where a large administrative apparatus linked Parliament and the Privy Council to officeholders in towns and parishes.[79] The social life of politics involved increasing dialogue about political affairs through a range of media, where the circulation of print, manuscript, and news increased political awareness among subjects in the metropolis and the localities.[80] As Felicity Stout argues, using Russia as a case study, travel literature began to inform the practice of politics in new ways during this time.[81] Humanist statesmen understood history and travel writing to serve practical functions in the *vita activa*. Merchants, travellers, diplomats, and sailors carried and circulated news that generated discussion and participation in state affairs. Fantastical imaginings of faraway nations gave way to valuing observation-based

Contrasting Status of Blacks in Bermuda, 1616–1663', *The Journal of Southern History*, 54 (1988), 554–64.

[77] 'The Voyage of S[i]r Henrye Colt Knight', 1631, in *Colonizing Expeditions to the West Indies and Guiana, 1623–1667*, ed. V. T. Harlow (Surrey: Ashgate, 2010), 73.

[78] Philip J. Stern, *The Company-State: Corporate Sovereignty and the Early Modern Foundations of the British Empire in India* (Oxford: Oxford University Press, 2011); Braddick, *State Formation in Early Modern England*; Phil Withington, *Society in Early Modern England: The Vernacular Origins of Some Powerful Ideas* (Cambridge: Polity, 2010).

[79] Noah Millstone, *Manuscript Circulation and the Invention of Politics in Early Stuart England* (Cambridge: Cambridge University Press, 2016), 324; Braddick, *State Formation in Early Modern England*.

[80] Millstone, *Manuscript Circulation and the Invention of Politics*, 6–7.

[81] Felicity Jane Stout, *Exploring Russia in the Elizabethan Commonwealth: The Muscovy Company and Giles Fletcher, the Elder (1546–1611)* (Manchester: Manchester University Press, 2015); Ken Macmillan, *The Atlantic Imperial Constitution: Centre and Periphery in the English Atlantic World* (New York: Palgrave, 2011); Robert Brenner, *Merchants and Revolution: Commercial Change, Political Conflict, and London's Overseas Traders, 1550–1653* (London: Verso, 2003).

knowledge, where diplomacy and trade stimulated a proliferation of treatises and reports about global politics.[82] Ideas of civility and legitimacy of rule were constructed against and through an awareness of other territories and political systems, so that writing about other states and nations became a way of mediating events and encouraging strategic decision-making.[83]

Reconstructing the world of Jacobean political actors therefore necessitates a wide range of material, including print and manuscript sources that served different though often complementary functions in the practice of statecraft. Jacobean statesmen relied on intelligence-gathering from a range of informants and sources to provide reliable news. Diaries, correspondences, and other forms of the 'political gaze' through observation gained ascendancy over traditional modes of counsel such as political philosophy and advice literature.[84] The privy councillor and bencher Julius Caesar collected letters from his brother-in-law Captain John Martin in Jamestown alongside copies of the Virginia Company's printed propaganda. To study one mode of discourse in isolation risks presenting a skewed picture of political participation and colonial promotion. An approach focussing purely on Virginia Company print, for example, downplays the role of elite networks and manuscript circulation at a time when gentlemen still disdained print as the recourse of lesser political actors. 'In publishing this Essay of my Poem', Drayton wrote in *Poly-Olbion* (1612), 'there is this great disadvantage against me; that it commeth out at this time, when Verses are wholly deduc't to Chambers, and nothing esteem'd in this lunatique Age, but what is kept in Cabinets, and must only passe by Transcription'.[85] Among the many concurrent modes of communication, popular politics and the 'public sphere' operated alongside state-level decision-making that continued to occur in 'chambers' and 'cabinets'.[86]

---

[82] Stout, *Exploring Russia in the Elizabethan Commonwealth*, 228; Susan E. Whyman, *Sociability and Power in Late Stuart England: The Cultural World of the Verneys, 1660–1720* (Oxford: Oxford University Press, 2002).

[83] Stout, *Exploring Russia in the Elizabethan Commonwealth*, 7.

[84] Pocock, *The Machiavellian Moment*, 353; Noah Millstone, 'Seeing Like a Statesman in Early Stuart England', *Past & Present*, 223 (2014), 77–127.

[85] Michael Drayton, *Poly-Olbion* (1612; STC 7226), sig. Ar.

[86] *The Politics of the Public Sphere in Early Modern England*, ed. Peter Lake and Steve Pincus (Manchester: Manchester University Press, 2007); Alastair Bellany and Thomas Cogswell, *The Murder of King James* (New Haven, CT: Yale University Press, 2015); Peter Lake and Steve Pincus, 'Rethinking the Public Sphere in Early Modern England', *Journal of British Studies*, 45 (2006), 270–92; Alexandra Halasz, *The Marketplace of Print: Pamphlets and the Public Sphere in Early Modern England* (Cambridge: Cambridge University Press, 1997).

This is not to obscure the social depth of political participation at this time. Attitudes to empire emerged from a multiplicity of agendas, voices, and places. Non-elite men and women successfully participated in the political life of the realm through patronage, petitioning, and trade.[87] Anne of Denmark cultivated colonial interests at her court, and several women invested in the Virginia Company and offered financial support for ships or Algonquian schools. As policies towards plantation began to favour sustained settlement in the late 1610s and early 1620s, women began migrating to the colonies in greater numbers. Whether travelling to America, consuming tobacco, overseeing projects, or investing in joint-stock companies, English subjects quickly became participants in a budding imperial system. The social and political worlds of metropolitan gentlemen contributed one part of this complex process through which the English envisaged and enacted empire.

The body politic comprised overlapping corporate bodies, in formal and informal networks held together by sociability and civil conversation.[88] The term 'political culture' as it is used in this book probes the relationship between state and society, between political ideas and how they operated in practice. Political scientists have employed this concept to interrogate 'a combination of practice and discursive dimensions' including writing, thought, and behaviour.[89] Investigating Jacobean political culture does not imply a uniform or single vision of politics in England, but incorporates a range of values, pressures, and experiences that shaped political environments in the metropolis. Moving beyond the dichotomies of 'us' and 'other' often apparent in print polemic, the relational aspect of political culture encourages a deeper consideration of how gentlemen confronted, both imaginatively and actually, the non-English peoples they proposed to govern.

A central claim of this book is that colonization in America infused expansionist discourses with the language of political duty but also encouraged gentlemen to lavishly imagine how plantation might improve the civil life. Rich studies have emerged on the administrative or

---

[87] Andy Wood, *Riot, Rebellion, and Popular Politics in Early Modern England* (Basingstoke: Palgrave, 2002); *Negotiating Power in Early Modern Society: Order, Hierarchy, and Subordination in Britain and Ireland*, ed. Michael J. Braddick and John Walter (Cambridge: Cambridge University Press, 2001).

[88] Stern, *The Company-State*, 323; Stefano Guazzo [tr. George Pettie], *The civile conversation* (1581; STC 12422); Markku Peltonen, *The Duel in Early Modern England: Civility, Politeness and Honour* (Cambridge: Cambridge University Press, 2003).

[89] Stephen Welch, *The Theory of Political Culture* (Oxford: Oxford University Press, 2013); Candida Yates, *The Play of Political Culture, Emotion and Identity* (Basingstoke: Palgrave, 2015).

mercantilist side of imperial policy and its intellectual origins.[90] The charters and laws made in the council chamber were in many ways the product of other kinds of less formal interactions between individuals and their social networks, where sociability and consumption helped to drive the appeal of expansion. Gentlemen celebrated the bonds of friendship and trust that made civil society not only necessary but satisfying, and they related this to their conception of politics, equating '[p]oliticke government' to 'Civilitie [or] Civile societie'.[91] While relying on aspirations to good, civil society also encompassed what was 'profitable' and 'pleasant' as well as what was 'honest'.[92] The politics of manners was not just about constraint, therefore, but also about pleasure, involving those 'passions' or senses that gentlemen celebrated when they met together to drink, socialize, share poetry, and smoke. When Crashaw preached his sermon to colonial promoters in London, he declared that 'he that hath 1000. acres, and being a *civill* and *sociable* man knowes how to use it, is richer then he that hath 2000. and being a savage, cannot plow, till, plant nor set'.[93] This not only defended English intervention in Virginia on the grounds of improvement – 'when they are *civilized* [they will] see what they have received from us' – but it drew a connection between plantation, civil order, and 'the social man'.[94]

The 'social man' performed civility in the things he wore, carried, and possessed. The economic reality of consumption and the demand for 'things' saturated discourses about civility and must be seen as having a profound effect on developments in political culture. Attitudes towards civil refinement in London arose not through the separation, but the overlap, of Whitehall and the commercial sphere of City merchants.[95] The Greco-Roman model of civility centred on urban centres partly because of their proximity and access to goods, and gentlemen expressed a taste for material consumption while praising the effects of trade in achieving political stability abroad.[96]

---

[90] Fitzmaurice, *Humanism and America*; Macmillan, *The Atlantic Imperial Constitution*; Brenner, *Merchants and Revolution*; Roper, *Advancing Empire*; Edmond Smith, 'The Global Interests of London's Commercial Community, 1599–1625: Investment in the East India Company', *Economic History Review*, 71 (2018), 1118–46.

[91] Guillaume de la Perrière, *The mirrour of policie* (1598; STC 15228.5), sig. Ar.

[92] Crashaw, *A sermon preached in London*, sig. D4r.   [93] Ibid.   [94] Ibid., sig. D4v.

[95] Peltonen, *The Duel in Early Modern England*, 300.

[96] Keith Thomas, *In Pursuit of Civility: Manners and Civilization in Early Modern England* (Waltham, MA: Brandeis University Press, 2018), 139; Braddick, 'Civility and Authority', 124; Phil Withington, *The Politics of Commonwealth: Citizens and Freemen in Early Modern England* (Cambridge: Cambridge University Press, 2005).

Situating 'the desire, appropriation, and use of things' within the social lives of statesmen is crucial to explaining the imperial-mindedness of gentlemen at this time.[97] Self-presentation depended on an array of textiles, dyes, drugs, spices, pigments, skins, and foods, linking civility to the ability to access markets and sustain manufacture. Archaeologists at Jamestown have uncovered an overwhelming number of European-made objects at the fort, including signet rings, silver grooming tools, armour, books, silk fragments, locks, keys, and even a Roman lamp, thought to have belonged to a gentleman's cabinet of curiosities, all evidence of the immense effort gentlemen took to replicate their lives in England.[98]

As Noah Millstone maintains, political culture should include an assessment of material culture embedded in practice, taking into account imbalances of power and developments in political thought.[99] Comparative anthropology and material culture complicates the rhetoric of free trade, liberty, and other ostensible benefits championed by endorsers of the civilizing project.[100] What gentlemen did with objects, and which they valued, mattered to their expressions of civility. Absence can be as indicative as what does appear in inventories, portraits, and archaeological sites. While they valued Eastern goods like Chinese porcelain or Indian textiles, Londoners and colonists alike showed less appreciation for indigenous-made artefacts. Descriptions of Tupi or Algonquian peoples as 'naked' distracted from the jewellery, shells, and dyed and embellished animal skins that circulated in Anglo–Native American exchanges and played an important part in indigenous self-expression and social cohesion. Tobacco, a sacred indigenous intoxicant, became equated with sociability only after gentlemen re-contextualized and re-packaged the commodity in specific ways, as Chapter 4 demonstrates. The civility that emerged from expansion involved inherent tensions and the possibilities of ruthless exploitation.

---

[97] Frank Trentmann, *Empire of Things: How We Became a World of Consumers, from the Fifteenth Century to the Twenty-First* (London: Penguin, 2016), 119.

[98] Objects discussed in this book were examined during two short-term fellowships at Jamestown Rediscovery. For a discussion of some of the objects taken to Virginia by one of its early colonists, see 'George Percy's "Trewe Relacyon": A Primary Source for the Jamestown Settlement', ed. Mark Nicholls, *The Virginia Magazine of History and Biography*, 113 (2005), 212–75, and the 'Jamestown, 1607–2007' special issue of *Post-medieval Archaeology*, 40 (2006).

[99] Millstone, *Manuscript Circulation and the Invention of Politics*, 13, 16.

[100] Thomas, *In Pursuit of Civility*, 255.

'Betweene the olde world and the newe'

By 1600, the two entities of Westminster and the City of London were the 'emergent centre of industry and empire'.[101] As a major port city, London brought together the local, national, and international, where frequent waves of migration shaped the character of the city and its parishes.[102] Within the ancient Roman city walls, merchants and guilds contributed substantial funds to colonizing expeditions. For news, individuals gathered at Paul's Walk and its nearby printers' shops to procure recent accounts of Bermuda shipwrecks or raids on Spanish settlements in the Caribbean. In November 1622, colonial councillors were charged with finding rooms for their meetings in the commercial environment of the New Exchange, built earlier in James' reign, where they discussed trade and Anglo–Algonquian relations with colonial governors, captains, and investors.[103] At Paul's Cross, sermons about the Virginia enterprises exposed large and diverse audiences to the Virginia Company's expansionist aims. Political interest in colonization stretched far beyond London, from the family ties of West Country explorers to the port cities of Bristol and Plymouth. Centralized decision-making, however, happened at the royal court and Parliament, and the London 'season' brought the nobility and the gentry to the metropolis, dictating changing tastes and fashions. Unlike Elizabeth, James did not travel on progress, further influencing the nobility's desire to acquire permanent residences in London.[104]

Here, gentlemanly aspirations to state-level careers converged with the pleasures that the city afforded. London provided many of the spaces – council chambers, private residences, taverns, playhouses, tobacco shops, printers, libraries, gardens, churches – where subjects encountered, debated, and performed America. Young, moneyed gentlemen came to the metropolis to debate the politics of the realm and to seek preferment in the context of refined urbanity, and these social milieus are key to understanding the rising imperial-mindedness of the elite. The building projects of courtiers who benefitted from the redistribution of medieval Church lands also created spaces for colonial promotion. Walter Ralegh, Robert

---

[101] J. F. Merritt, *The Social World of Early Modern Westminster: Abbey, Court, and Community, 1525–1640* (Manchester: Manchester University Press, 2005), 2; *Material London, ca. 1600*, ed. Lena Cowen Orlin (Philadelphia: University of Pennsylvania Press, 2000), 3; Deborah Harkness and Jean E. Howard, 'Introduction: The Great World of Early Modern London', *Huntington Library Quarterly*, 71 (2008), 1–9.

[102] Jacob Selwood, *Diversity and Difference in Early Modern London* (Farnham: Ashgate, 2010), 13.

[103] Minutes of the Council of New England, 16 November 1622, in *Calendar of State Papers: Colonial: America and West Indies, Vol. 1, 1574–1640*, ed. W. Noel Sainsbury (London: Longman, 1860), 34.

[104] Linda Levy Peck, *Consuming Splendour: Society and Culture in Seventeenth-Century England* (Cambridge: Cambridge University Press, 2005), 201.

Figure 1 Thomas Hariot, *A briefe and true report of the new found land of Virginia* (1590). Although this is a highly stylized image, important elements of Algonquian lifeways are evoked in the deerskin clothing, tobacco pouches, feathers, and corn. Courtesy of the Huntington Library.

Cecil, George Villiers, Thomas Howard, and Henry Wriothesley all had households on the Strand, where they offered patronage to colonial supporters, oversaw extravagant entertainments that celebrated conquest, furnished their cabinets of curiosities, and provided meeting places for company meetings. Cecil employed Richard Hakluyt as his personal chaplain. Ralegh encouraged Thomas Hariot to compile his Algonquian dictionary in London with the help of resident indigenous interpreters, and supported the French Huguenot artist Jacques le Moyne de Morgues, who had been to Florida and produced vivid drawings of its peoples.

Living, breathing cross-cultural exchange existed alongside stylized depictions of indigeneity in woodcuts, watercolours, and engravings. The

images in the 1590 edition of Hariot's *A briefe and true report*, a text that
gentlemen in the metropolis frequently cited and discussed, trapped
Algonquians within stylized mannerist forms, conveying a sense of civility
and abundance that drew on the values of classical antiquity (Figure 1). At
the same time, these engravings, like the Algonquian depicted at St James'
Park in a traveller's *album amicorum* from the mid-1610s, were enlivened by
the presence of Native Americans and their objects in households like
Ralegh's.[105] As Coll Thrush points out, colonization was 'an urban process', and it is a pervasive myth of colonial discourse that Native Americans
operated purely outside these metropolitan spaces.[106]

In addition to the better-known examples of two abducted eastern
Native Americans, the young Powhatan/Pamunkey woman Pocahontas
(also known as Matoaka and Amonute), and the Pawtuxet man
Tisquantum (Squanto), scholars have uncovered dozens of North and
South Americans who walked the streets of Elizabethan and Jacobean
London. In the 1580s, a man named Towaye was in London, along with
the Croatan Manteo and Wanchese of Roanoke.[107] An Abenaki *sagamore*,
or Algonquian leader, arrived in London in 1605 and lived in the household
of the jurist John Popham.[108] Captain Christopher Newport exchanged
the boys Totakins and Namontack for several English youths who lived
among the Algonquians to learn their language for diplomatic purposes.[109]
Totakins lived in the household of the Virginia Company merchant
Thomas Smythe, while the puritan minister William Gouge kept an
Algonquian woman christened Mary.[110] In 1622, the minutes for the
council of New England included an order 'to Leonard Peddock to take
over with him a boy, native of New England, called Papa Whinett,
belonging to Abbadakest, Sachem of Massachusetts'.[111] In 1610, the puritan
MP Edwin Sandys lamented that the young Algonquian boy Nanawack

---

[105] The *album amicorum* ('friendship book') of Michael van Meer, *c*.1615–16, Edinburgh University
Library, Laing MS III 283, f. 264v. This Algonquian was likely Eiakintomino, the watercolour
based on the Virginia Company lottery broadside, *A declaration for the certain time of drawing the
great standing lottery* (1616; STC 24833.8). Though a stock image, the watercolour suggests a market
for images of Native Americans produced in workshops in London.

[106] Thrush, Indigenous London, 38; Thomas King, *The Inconvenient Indian: A Curious Account of
Native People in North America* (Toronto: Anchor, 2013). See also Alden T. Vaughan, *Transatlantic
Encounters: American Indians in Britain, 1500–1776* (Cambridge: Cambridge University Press,
2006).

[107] Thrush, *Indigenous London*, 44. For an imagining of Algonquians' possible reactions to London,
see 50–5.

[108] Ibid., 47.   [109] Ibid.   [110] Ibid., 47–8.

[111] Minutes of the Council of New England, 19 November 1622, in *Calendar of State Papers: Colonial,
Vol. 1*, 34.

had been living in London for several years, where he 'heard not much of Religion, but saw and heard many times examples of drinking, swearing, and like evills, [and] remained as he was a meere Pagan'.[112] Attempts at 'civilizing' and converting Algonquians operated beyond the abstract, and indicate much about the attitudes and aspirations of the English who housed them.

The indigenous presence in London reflected the increased contact that the English had with large numbers of diverse Native American groups in the Atlantic. In Virginia, this included the thousands of Algonquians within and beyond the dominant Powhatan confederacy.[113] South America and the Caribbean also remained important spaces for Anglo–indigenous encounters. Carib and Tupi groups featured in Jacobean anti-Spanish propaganda, discourses about commodities and production, and articulations of violence and cultural difference. As Chapter 3 argues, discussions of the practice of cannibalism in Jacobean discourse were often the result of the English directly entering Native American spaces. Drawing on historical anthropology helps to redress the older historiographical usage of 'the natives', a blanketing term that obscured the complexities of indigenous societies and risked effacing Native American agency. This book cannot, nor should it, offer an indigenous perspective on the history of colonization, but it does raise attention to Native American peoples, practices, and terms that Jacobean writers regularly engaged with when they debated civility and state policies.

Rather than offer a complete or chronological study of the colonies, this study traces the concepts, motifs, and objects that animated and spurred domestic debates over conformity and social order, rituals of violence, and political participation. Though they developed distinct identities, New England, Bermuda, Newfoundland, the Chesapeake, and failed colonies like Roanoke and Guiana remained overseen by many of the same councillors in London, contributing to the elite's sense of governance and political participation through colonial oversight. Even as godly ministers petitioned to build their 'new Jerusalem' in America, colonial projects in Massachusetts continued to be influenced by courtiers including George Villiers, the Duke of Buckingham, Ferdinando Gorges, and Thomas Howard, fourteenth Earl of Arundel, many of whom drew on the language of civility and hierarchical order to advocate their authority over both

---

[112] Quoted in Thrush, *Indigenous London*, 57–8.
[113] For the political complexities of the Algonquian Chesapeake, see James Rice, 'Escape from Tsenacommacah: Chesapeake Algonquians and the Powhatan Menace, 1300–1624', in *The Atlantic World and Virginia, 1550–1624*, 97–140.

unruly colonists and Native Americans.[114] Certain commonalities in elite attitudes to governance raise attention to the interconnectedness of the civilizing project, one that created enduring structures and expectations even after the English sought to colonize other parts of the globe.

Taken together, these chapters probe how policy-makers increasingly committed their civil designs to those of empire, setting structures and expectations in place that endured well beyond these initial Western projects. The first chapter presents an overview of the expansionist projects endorsed by gentlemen in Whitehall, Parliament, and the localities, and relates the enthusiasm for overseas plantation to the rise in domestic surveying and estate management. Chapter 2 examines the influence of Virginia on political debate in London. The Jamestown–London connection was vital to substantiating English claims to an imperial polity, and its setbacks and failures shaped the articulations of empire that emerged as a result. Chapter 3 approaches Norbert Elias' claims about violence and state authority through the remarkable proliferation of accounts of cannibalism in Jacobean discourse. Drawing on Elias' discussion about civility and the monopolization of force, this chapter establishes how writers drew on Carib and Tupi ethnography to articulate the necessity of the law in the fraught confessional climate of the 1610s and 1620s.

Chapters 4 and 5 turn to how gentlemen incorporated America into their expressions of masculine sociability. Chapter 4 charts the changing policies towards tobacco that emerged in parliamentary debates about moral regulation and consumption. Despite tobacco's association with political subversion, pro-imperial MPs increasingly understood it as essential to their colonial designs. Tobacco consumption became a manifestation of imperial intent, integrated into the broader political culture of parliamentary debate and its related sociability. The final chapter turns to the coteries and friendships in and around the Inns of Court, where urbane young gentlemen brought colonial interests and commodities within provocative re-definitions of civility. The sense of moral responsibility that developed alongside a celebration of fraternal sociability and literary composition created a distinct vision of civil manhood that did not eschew but subordinated the allure of America to English political life.

In 1597, seventeen years before his disastrous performance in Parliament, Martin had played the coveted role of the Prince d'Amour in the raucous

---

[114] 'Minutes of the Council of New England', 17 December 1622, in *Calendar of State Papers: Colonial, Vol. 1*, 35; Gorges complained that merchants in New England, including 'a worthlesse fellow of our Nation' who 'set out by certaine Merchants for love of gaine' were enslaving Native Americans, *A briefe relation of the discovery and plantation of New England* (1622; STC 18483), sig. B3r.

Christmas revels at the Middle Temple. Epitomizing graceful civility – '*[w]it, and Beauty* in their exact perfection' – the 'prince' paraded through the hall in command of the forces of Venus, but the classical and chivalric resonances in the performance existed alongside the geographical realities of invaded and explored territories from Florida to the Amazon.[115] Like an earlier performance from the 1590s, where Robert Devereux, second Earl of Essex, hosted an entertainment for Elizabeth that centred on the arrival of an 'Indian Prince' from Greater Amazonia, orators praised the queen for 'civilizing her subjects' and demonstrating 'infinite moderation in counterpoising the uneven parts of the world'.[116] England was an island '[s]eated betweene the olde world and the newe/A land . . . no other land may touche'.[117] The establishment of colonies in America in subsequent decades quickly revealed the impossibility of such fantasies of bloodless conquests and willing submission to 'wit refined'. Nor were the English inclined to remain inhabitants of an isolated island. Instead, they imagined new boundaries and balances of power. '*Virginia* and *Summer Ilands* seeme to this *English* bodie as two *American* hands', Purchas wrote in 1625, 'two Armes to get, encompasse, embrace'.[118] This image of America and England as one body, hands outstretched to embrace and encompass the world, invites a re-consideration of the Jacobean body politic, in terms of its ambitions and in the ardent ways in which such aspirations were expressed. The personal bonds between gentlemen that drove politics and expansion at this time laid the foundations for a vision of civil society that bonded England and America together.

---

[115] 'The Prince of Love', 1597, later printed based on a transcription by Benjamin Rudyerd, who attended the events, as *Le prince d'amour; or the prince of love* (1660; Wing R2189), sigs. A2v–A3r, B7r.

[116] Ibid., sig. B7r.

[117] 'A device by the Earl of Essex for the Queen's entertainment' [written by Francis Bacon?], 17 November 1595, The National Archives, SP 12/254, f. 139r.

[118] 'Virginias Verger', in Purchas, *Purchas his pilgrimes*, sig. Nnnnnnnv.

CHAPTER I

Cultivation and the American Project

The networks and spaces of information exchange that fostered expansion come to life in Robert Cecil's testimony at Walter Ralegh's trial for treason in 1603. The jury accused Ralegh of possessing a seditious book written against the sovereignty of kings, one that had been kept from public view in the private study of the late lord treasurer William Cecil, Lord Burghley. Burghley's son Robert, James' secretary of state, suggested Ralegh may have stolen the book when visiting Burghley's study to consult his cosmographical works. Ralegh often visited their residence on the Strand, Cecil acknowledged. 'Sir *Walter* desired to search for some Cosmographycall descriptions of the West-Indies which he thought were in his study, and were not to be had in print, which he [Cecil] granted'.[1] Before 'the bonds of his affection had been crackt', Cecil admitted, he had admired Ralegh and had supported Ralegh's ventures to North America and Guiana.[2]

The first part of this chapter investigates the breadth of colonial interest among members of the elite within this interpersonal world of patronage and political alliance, tracing colonial endorsement in converging, at times competing, metropolitan circles. The chapter then turns to what colonizing projects actually meant to the elite who became involved with them. While the colonist John Smith remained on the margins of Jacobean politics, gentlemen commended his role in clearing landscapes for intervention. Prefatory verses in *The generall historie of Virginia, New-England, and the Summer Iles* (1624) lauded Smith for forcing Native Americans to 'bow unto subjection', so that 'brave projects' would 'forge a true Plantation'.[3] Governors

---

[1] *The arraignment and conviction of S[i]r Walter Rawleigh* (1648; Wing A3744), sigs. Bv–B2r.

[2] Ibid., sig. Bv; Walter Ralegh to Robert Cecil, 13 November 1595, in *Calendar of the Manuscripts of the Most Honourable the Marquis of Salisbury, Vol. 5, 1591–1595*, ed. R. A. Roberts (London: Her Majesty's Stationary Office, 1894), 475; Lady Ralegh to Cecil, September 1595, in ibid., 396.

[3] S. M., 'A Gentleman desirous to be unknowne, yet a great Benefactor to *Virginia*', in John Smith, *The generall historie of Virginia, New-England, and the Summer Iles* (1624; STC 22790), prefatory verses.

and colonists, but also domestic benefactors, were called to 'Spend money, [and] Bloud' to receive God's blessing and to facilitate territorial possession.[4] The ability to subordinate both human nature and the natural world was inherent in cultivation, suggesting that planting colonies was not a benign alternative to conquest. The transformation and restraint of nature was a painful, often destructive process, frequently deemed necessary for achieving political control.

The final section connects changing attitudes to landscapes in post-Reformation England to gentlemanly aspirations in America. For the Jacobean elite, the pursuit of a fulfilling and pleasurable civil life was deeply rooted in property and governance. Fundamental attitudes towards land underpinned the impetus to civilize. This became especially apparent from the later 1610s, as the gentry began to show a greater interest in surveying and managing plantations as the most efficient method of colonizing Bermuda and Virginia. 'Christ hath given us', Samuel Purchas proclaimed, 'the Universe in an Universall tenure'.[5] In contrast to hopes for quick profit through joint-stock investment, land became critical to the elite vision of how a transatlantic polity might be sustained. Land committed gentlemen to overseeing an empire held together not only by trade, but also by the hierarchical structures of governance that accompanied traditional estate-holding.

Planting in the Age of Projection

From the 1570s to the 1630s, a distinct language of planting emerged, surpassing other tactics and models for colonization.[6] Elizabethan statesmen drew on a humanist vision of expansion that united the possibilities of exploitation with a strong strain of civic responsibility, encouraging the pursuit of Atlantic projects in Ireland and further west.[7] Seeking to advance a model of Protestant society that differentiated English colonization, at least in theory, from Spanish methods of conquest, Richard Hakluyt the younger composed his 'Discourse of Western Planting' for Elizabeth at the behest of Ralegh in 1584.[8] Though Elizabeth may never have read the document, the text indelibly influenced the language and rhetoric of future projects, where the English right to plant in North America was related to global competition with Spain and legitimized

---

[4] Ibid.   [5] Purchas, *Purchas his pilgrimes*, sig. Llllll6v.
[6] David B. Quinn, 'Renaissance Influences in English Colonization: The Prothero Lecture', *Transactions of the Royal Historical Society*, 26 (1976), 73–93.
[7] Ibid., 73.   [8] Ibid., 82.

partly by promising to 'civilize' and convert its local inhabitants.[9] At the same time, the early seventeenth century saw developments in the concept of 'improvement', which began to apply not just to land and property, but 'to every aspect of human and social behaviour'.[10]

Proposals to convert indigenous Americans while ridding the realm of overpopulation by sending labourers to the colonies appeared repeatedly in charters, parliamentary debates, and royal proclamations, but the overall appeal and success of investment hinged on hopes of financial benefit. Schemes to find precious metals and to cultivate tobacco, iron, timber, silk, and other commodities were integral to the writings of colonial promoters from Hakluyt and Ralegh in the 1580s to gentry MPs in the 1620s. The projects by merchants including William Cockayne and Thomas Smythe that looked eastwards to Europe and Asia were matched by others centring on Virginian tobacco and Newfoundland cod by Robert Johnson, Richard Whitbourne, and Roger North. That the 'fourth part of the world, and the greatest and wealthiest part of all the rest, should remaine a wilderness, subject ... but to wilde beasts ... and to savage people, which have no Christian, nor civill use of any thing' forged a relationship between the possibilities of wealth and the need to civilize other peoples.[11]

Commerce and trade heavily informed policy-makers' reformist politics, where 'radical transformations and controversies in ways of thinking about the universe, the natural world, and the body politic' shaped attitudes towards private gain and common good.[12] Insofar as the voyages fit within his vision of a unified 'Great Britain' strengthened by industry and inhabited by faithful, conforming subjects, James was happy to affix the royal seal to Atlantic enterprises. James' personal style of kingship made policy-making a matter of 'patronage politics', where the Crown and the court placed financial stakes in projects on an unprecedented level.[13] The possibilities of enriching the Crown through trade and industry attracted a king who experienced notorious difficulty convincing Parliament to subsidize Crown expenses. Though the Crown, under Elizabeth, had attempted to restrict expenditure, James inherited substantial debts even before he

---

[9] Ibid., 83.   [10] Slack, *The Invention of Improvement*, 5.   [11] Johnson, *Nova Britannia*, sig. A4r.
[12] Philip Stern and Carl Wennerlind, 'Introduction', in *Mercantilism Reimagined: Political Economy in Early Modern Britain and Its Empire*, ed. Philip Stern and Carl Wennerlind (Oxford: Oxford University Press, 2014), 3–24, at 4.
[13] John Cramsie, 'Commercial Projects and the Fiscal Policy of James VI and I', *The Historical Journal*, 43 (2000), 345–64, at 346–7. See also Joan Thirsk, *Economic Policy and Projects: The Development of a Consumer Society in Early Modern England* (Oxford: Clarendon, 1978).

increased the deficit with his lavish spending.[14] Members of the Privy Council were unable to mitigate the long-term consequences that accompanied the Crown's need to sell its lands to meet expenses. Monopolies on colonial commodities remained a consistent point of contention and opportunity in the Crown's desperate search for sources of revenue, while Members of Parliament used the more lucrative aspects of Atlantic trade to promote industry and bargain for certain rights and privileges.

When the merchants and economic writers Gerard Malynes and Thomas Mun offered financial counsel to the Crown, and James' treasurers sought to revise the king's means of securing revenue, they did so with the recognition that the need to find and circulate wealth would not only benefit their and the king's interests, but also contained consequences for the realm as a whole.[15] Speaking to the Commons on the dire state of economic affairs in 1621, Sandys showed concern that 'if we bring [the English] so slender comfort as these poor bills, we make their discontents and dislike of their miserable fortunes reflect upon the higher powers'.[16] Members of Parliament expressed a sense of responsibility towards social welfare, and many of the men who displayed the most zeal in addressing the realm's social ills were also those, like Sandys, who promoted colonization as a natural solution to a range of problems the English faced under James, including finding employment for the poor and pursuing manufactures. 'O[u]r cuntrie is strangely anoyed w[i]th ydell, loose and vagrant people', wrote the brothers Edward and Thomas Hayes in their efforts to promote colonization, but 'the State hath wisely in p[ar]liam[en]t sought redress'.[17]

Vivid accounts of colonial horrors in the early decades of English expansion can distract from the levels of enthusiasm evident in the metropolis. Jamestown offered a chronicle of miseries, from rumours of colonists eating each other during the Starving Time of 1609/10 to the ensuing martial law that imparted governors with the power to execute colonists for stealing food or fleeing to Powhatan villages. By 1624, a report from Virginia recorded 1,275 people in the colony, despite the thousands of English men and women who had migrated from England over the

[14] Mark Kishlansky, *A Monarchy Transformed: Britain 1603–1714* (London: Penguin, 1996), 83–5; Linda Levy Peck, '"For a King not to be bountiful were a fault": Perspectives on Court Patronage in Early Stuart England', *Journal of British Studies*, 25 (1986), 31–61; Daniel W. Hollis, 'The Crown Lands and the Financial Dilemma in Stuart England', *Albion*, 26 (1994), 419–42.

[15] Stern and Wennerlind, 'Introduction', 9.

[16] Quoted in Theodore K. Rabb, *Jacobean Gentleman: Sir Edwin Sandys, 1561–1629* (Princeton, NJ: Princeton University Press, 1998), 256.

[17] Edward and Thomas Hayes to the Earl of Salisbury, 4 September 1605, Hatfield House, CP 112/53r.

previous seventeen years.[18] Though 4,000 people migrated between the late 1610s and the early 1620s, the population remained reduced to a quarter of that number, with death rates in the earliest years estimated at more than 80 per cent.[19] The Virginia Company, for all its propaganda campaigns celebrating fruitful landscapes, raised a total stock of 37,000l., a 'trifling' sum when compared to the corporations establishing trade with India or the Levant.[20] When the state secretary George Calvert finally went to his Ferryland colony in Newfoundland in 1629 after years of painstaking preparation, he found himself unable to conform to the rhetoric of abundance that had lavished his previous letters. 'In this part of the world, crosses and miseryes is my portion', Calvert wrote. 'I am so over-whelmed with troubles . . . I am forced to write but short and confusedly'.[21]

A different perspective emerges when examining colonization from within the metropolis, rather than its initial settlements. The court admin-istrator Walter Cope, who regularly entertained the king and queen in London, wrote a letter to Cecil in 1607 that brimmed with news from Virginia, including details about pearls and Wahunsenacah/Powhatan (Figure 2). 'When the busines [sic] of Virginia was at the highest, in that heat', the letter writer John Chamberlain reported in 1613, 'many gentle-men and others were drawn by perswasion and importunity of frends to under-write theyre names for adventurers'.[22] Chamberlain acknowledged that gentlemen were less willing to part with their money than they were to write their names to paper, but the 'perswasion' of 'frends' evokes a rising metropolitan fashion for subscribing to colonial projects. '[T]here was much suing for Patents for Plantations', John Smith recalled of the early 1620s, and 'much disputing concerning those divisions, as though the whole land had been to [sic] little for them'.[23] Englishmen far beyond London, complained the Somerset vicar Richard Eburne, had been so enamoured with the idea of supporting the Virginia Company, despite the risks, that they had lacked 'the wit, not to run out by it, to their undoing'.[24]

[18] 'List of the Names of the Living in Virginia', 16 February 1624, in *Calendar of State Papers: Colonial, Vol. I*, 57.

[19] Karen Ordahl Kupperman, *The Jamestown Project* (Cambridge, MA: Harvard University Press, 2007), 293; Horning, *Ireland in the Virginian Sea*, 276.

[20] Slack, *The Invention of Improvement*, 70.

[21] George Calvert to [Sir Francis Cottington], 18 August 1629, in *Newfoundland Discovered: English Attempts at Colonization, 1610–1630*, ed. Gillian T. Cell (London: Hakluyt Society, 1982), 292.

[22] John Chamberlain to Dudley Carleton, 1 August 1613, The National Archives, SP 14/74, f. 101r.

[23] Smith, *The generall historie*, sig. T3r.

[24] Richard Eburne, *A plaine path-way to plantations* (1624; STC 7471), sig. Ir.

Figure 2 Letter from Sir Walter Cope to the Earl of Salisbury, August 1607.
Reproduced with the permission of the Marquess of Salisbury, Hatfield House.

The precariousness of English settlements in the Chesapeake, Bermuda, and New England ensured these places retained a place in political debates in London. In 1620, the contentious governor of Bermuda, Nathaniel Butler, complained to his patron, Nathaniel Rich, that being governor of Bermuda had proved 'an extreame discouragement' because 'every petty Companion and member of your Court and Company . . . upon the least false and base Intelligence fastened upon their precipitate credulitie . . . snarle and braule his fill at him'.[25] This invokes Chamberlain's remark that

---

[25] Nathaniel Butler to Sir Nathaniel Rich, 23 October 1620, *The Rich Papers: Letters from Bermuda, 1615–1646*, ed. Vernon A. Ives (Toronto: University of Toronto Press, 1984), 195.

debates about Virginia and Bermuda at Whitehall had led to public outbursts and even brawls.[26] These reports heavily suggest that the 'snarls and
brawls', the political contests over colonization schemes, were a formative
part of London policy-making, though it would be the inhabitants of the
colonies who suffered most from the consequences of inconsistent policies.
While colonists in Bermuda complained that 'ther is not scarce
a thought ... amongst the Company [in London] of sending us any
shippynge from England above once a yeare, and then [only] for our
Tobacco', policy-makers in England saw their involvement as a means of
advancing the interests of the realm by actively engaging in contemporary
politics and associated debates about the welfare of their civil society.[27]

While James' son, Henry, vigorously cultivated the image of a Protestant
military prince, the king's interest in colonization can admittedly appear
scant. In 1609, Henry Wriothesley, third Earl of Southampton, wrote to
Cecil informing him of James' interest in acquiring a flying squirrel.
'Talkinge w[i]th the K[ing]', Southampton wrote, 'by chance I tould him
of the Virginia squirrels w[hi]ch they say will fly ... & hee, presently & very
earnestly asked mee if none of them was provided for him'.[28] Southampton's
record of his discussion with James about Virginia and its fauna seemed to be
an afterthought, added at the close of his letter. It was 'by chance' that
Southampton had raised the matter, and he added that 'I would not have
trobled you w[i]th this but that you know so well how [the King] is affected
to these toyes.'[29] James' delight at the prospect of a winged rodent gives little
sense that he had spoken seriously with Southampton about what else had
been happening in 1609, including a campaign by members of the Virginia
Company in London to stimulate colonial support through a series of print
publications and sermons following the signing of the second company
charter.[30]

Until Cecil's death in 1612, most letters by investors or colonial promoters were sent to Cecil rather than to James. Yet assumptions of James'
disinterest are misleading in several ways. Firstly, this indifference should
not be seen as indicative of James' reign as a whole. From 1619 in particular,
the king began to take active interest in the affairs and government of the

---

[26] John Chamberlain to Dudley Carleton, 19 April 1623, SP 14/143, f. 30v; Attorney General [Thomas] Coventry to the Council, 8 January 1624, The National Archives, SP 14/158.

[27] Nathaniel Butler to Sir Nathaniel Rich, 15 March 1620, in *The Rich Papers*, 178.

[28] The Earl of Southampton to the Earl of Salisbury, 15 December 1609, The National Archives, SP 14/50, f. 130v.

[29] Ibid.

[30] For a discussion of the 1609–10 campaign, see Fitzmaurice, *Humanism and America*, 70–7.

Virginia Company, as Chapter 2 demonstrates. Secondly, correspondences between Spanish ambassadors hint at James' shrewdness. When asked by Pedro de Zúñiga about English plans at Jamestown in 1607, the king 'answered that he was not informed as to the details of what was going on ... and that he had never known that Your Majesty [Philip II] had a right to it ... it was not stated in the peace treaties with him and with France that his subjects could not go [where they pleased] except the Indies'.[31] This seems less the rejoinder of a hapless monarch, and more like the response of one who knows when to feign ignorance. 'The King said to me', Zúñiga continued, 'that those who went, went at their own risk, and if they were caught there, there could be no complaint if it were punished' – a remark that may have held true for the Indies, but not for Virginia, since the king had signed dispensations for Richard Hakluyt, Robert Hunt, and numerous others to venture there in late 1606 and early 1607.[32]

Ambiguous Crown interest in North and South America might be indicative of James' reluctance to upset the shaky nature of Anglo–Spanish peace rather than actual disinterest.[33] Negotiations over territorial acquisition in the West Indies were so contentious in the 1604 Anglo–Spanish peace negotiations that the treaty ignored the issue altogether when no concession could be reached. Cecil's refusal to concede to Spanish territorial claims in the Atlantic became vital to allowing the English to settle parts of North and South America in subsequent decades.[34] It was with immense pressure from the Spanish Crown that James sanctioned ventures led by Thomas Roe, Walter Ralegh, Roger North, William White, Charles Leigh, and Robert Harcourt, even as Spanish agents beseeched James to 'looke carefully to the busines of not p[er]mitting such a voyage to be made'.[35] However much he valued the Anglo–Spanish peace, James did not allow English exploration in the West Indies to stop altogether.

[31] Pedro de Zúñiga to Philip III, 8 October 1607, in *The Jamestown Voyages under the First Charter, 1607–1609, Vol. 1*, ed. Philip L. Barbour (Cambridge: Cambridge University Press, 1969), 118.

[32] Dispensation for Richard Hakluyt and Robert Hunt, 24 November 1606, in ibid., 62; Orders for the Council of Virginia, 10 December 1606, in ibid., 45. Hakluyt did not end up travelling to Virginia.

[33] For the Elizabethan voyages to South America, see K. R. Andrews, 'Beyond the Equinoctial: England and South America in the Sixteenth Century', *The Journal of Imperial and Commonwealth History*, 10 (1981), 4–24.

[34] Joyce Lorimer, 'The Failure of the English Guiana Ventures 1595–1667 and James I's Foreign Policy', *The Journal of Imperial and Commonwealth History*, 21 (1993), 1–30, at 12.

[35] Julian Sanchez de Ulloa to James, 29 February 1620, in *English and Irish Settlement on the River Amazon, 1550–1646*, ed. Joyce Lorimer (London: Hakluyt Society, 1989), 198.

From 1612 to 1618, while the Virginia colony struggled to find stability, many members of the gentry turned to Bermuda. Of the 117 founding investors, 5 were noblemen, 18 were knights, and 21 were MPs.[36] All but ten held shares in the Virginia Company, many of them also involved with the East India Company and voyages in search of the Northwest Passage.[37] The second Earl of Warwick and other members of the Rich family dispatched ships to send 'negroes to dive for pearls' and to bring back tropical plants, plantains, figs, and other 'West Indy' goods.[38] Merchants returned from the island with pearls, coral, ambergris, pineapples, and tobacco.[39] A chance finding of a lump of ambergris – whale secretion used for perfume – gained as much as 12,000l. for the ailing Virginia Company at a time when the same London councillors had joint oversight of Virginia and Bermuda.[40] Even before its successful planting, Silvester Jourdain wrote in 1610 that Bermuda contained 'plenty of Haukes, and very good Tobacco', appealing to the civil pursuits of landed gentlemen while promoting the colonization of this 'richest, healthfullest, and pleasing land'.[41] Although the island seemed remote, Jourdain wrote, it held all the promise that the best colonies contained. By the mid-1610s, the surveyor Richard Norwood had mapped out the land divisions on the entire island. Norwood's surveying of the landscape served to delineate property lines, but it also established relationships and obligations between the English land-holding elite and their colonial tenants.[42] Company meetings in London remained essential to the development of the island, and the strong correlation between metropolitan interest and the survival of the colony is evident in the letters colonists sent back to London in this period.[43]

Countless individuals took it upon themselves to pursue various schemes at their own personal cost. William Alexander received substantial support from James and then Charles to conduct voyages to New Scotland (Nova Scotia). After his patron, Prince Henry, died, Alexander became gentleman usher to Henry's brother Charles. He spent a prodigious 6,000l. of his own money to prepare a voyage in 1622, contributing further funds for two other attempts until Charles I conceded Nova Scotia to the French

---

[36] Michael Jarvis, *In the Eye of All Trade: Bermuda, Bermudians, and the Maritime Atlantic World, 1680–1783* (Chapel Hill: University of North Carolina Press, 2010), 19–20.

[37] Ibid.   [38] Ibid., 26.

[39] Lorena S. Walsh, *Motives of Honor, Pleasure, & Profit: Plantation Management in the Colonial Chesapeake, 1607–1763* (Chapel Hill: University of North Carolina Press, 2010), 32.

[40] Jarvis, *In the Eye of All Trade*, 18.

[41] Silvester Jourdain, *A discovery of the Barmudas* (1610; STC 14816), sigs. C3v, B3v.

[42] Jarvis, *In the Eye of All Trade*, 35.   [43] Ibid., 40–1.

in the early 1630s. Alexander advocated intermarriage with Native Americans, believing that 'lawfull allyances ... by admitting equalitie remove contempt'.[44] His support of intermarriage was rare, though many of his other attitudes to colonial policy were representative of those shared by the English and Scottish elite. Plantations were to establish civil life for its inhabitants, 'not to subdue but to civillize the Savages' so that they 'by their Posteritie may serve to many good uses', while Europeans must not succumb to 'naturalizing themselves where they are, [lest] they must disclaime their King and Countrey' with their 'affections altered'.[45] Alexander's tract showed a clear vision of the colonies in Virginia, New England, Newfoundland, Ireland, and Bermuda as encompassing a wider, more singular project.

Failed projects also offer insight into the interworking of Jacobean political networks. Ralegh's hopes for extracting precious metals and stones in Guiana were supported by Thomas Roe, later made a gentlemen of James' privy council, who travelled to South America in 1611. Roe was a product of the early Jacobean Middle Temple milieu, a particularly strong site for imperial projects due to its ties to the West Country. Benchers at the Middle Temple made Francis Drake an honorary member of its society after he circumnavigated the globe in 1580. There was a 'fervour' in 'this business ... this most christian and Noble enterprise of plantation', Roe wrote to his patron, Cecil, in 1607.[46] '[D]ivers Noblemen and Gentlemen have sent in theyr mony', but also 'divers attend in person, enough to performe this project'.[47] Schemes in South America, Roe believed, would bring profit to the nation and combat the dishonour of allowing Spanish ascendancy in the Atlantic, while making 'provinciall to us a land ready to supply us with all necessary commodytyes'.[48]

The creation of the short-lived Amazon Company led James to irritably profess that he 'had never seen an enterprise so supported' as Roger North's plans for Guiana in the early 1620s.[49] The list of investors for the voyage exhibits a high level of engagement with the project. The Spanish ambassador at James' court, Diego Sarmiento de Acuña, Count Gondomar, cited seven of the thirty-four privy councillors of 1620 as

---

[44] William Alexander, *An encouragement to colonies* (1624; STC 341), sig. E3r. [45] Ibid., sig. F4r.
[46] Sir Thomas Roe to the Earl of Salisbury, 1607, Hatfield House, CP 124/125r. [47] Ibid.
[48] Ibid.
[49] Count Gondomar to Philip III, 30 May 1620, in *English and Irish Settlement on the River Amazon*, 208. For Lorimer's challenge of the 'traditionalist assumption' that North America was the most logical arena for English colonization in this period, see Lorimer, 'The Failure of the English Guiana Ventures', 1.

members of the Amazon Company, meaning 20 per cent of James' coun-
cillors regarded the company as a useful potential arena to advance their
interests and to pursue an anti-Spanish agenda.[50] George Villiers, Duke of
Buckingham, Ludovick Stuart, Duke of Lennox, Henry Herbert, Earl of
Pembroke, George Abbot, Archbishop of Canterbury, Robert
Rich, second Earl of Warwick, and Henry Wriothesley, third Earl of
Southampton, were cited as prominent supporters of this inference against
Spanish colonial designs. Gondomar recognized them as 'the foremost
personages of this kingdom'.[51] The Duke of Lennox had conducted cam-
paigns on James' behalf in parts of Gaelic Scotland in the 1590s.
Southampton was treasurer of the Virginia Company at the time. The
Earl of Warwick, aggressively exploiting the opportunities colonization
offered, made his kinsman Nathaniel a Somers Islands Company agent and
worked closely with him in overseeing plantations.

James' ruling elite actively pursued colonization despite, or perhaps because
of, the king's own hesitation to directly embroil the Crown in territorial
disputes involving lands already claimed by the Spanish. Imprisoned on
charges of treason since 1603, Ralegh pursued his advancement of English
territories from the Tower. Seeking royal sanction for another voyage to
Guiana, he complained to Queen Anne in 1611 that, if anything, James did
not show enough desire for wealth. He had only sought, Ralegh lamented, 'to
have done him such a service as hath seildome bine p[er]formed for any king',
but James continually rejected those 'riches wich God hath offred him, therby
to take all presumption from his enemies, arising from the want of tresor, by
which (after God) all states are defended'.[52] Ralegh's letter demonstrates the
way that colonial projects informed the 'more flexible notions of public
interest and the public good' emerging from early seventeenth-century economic understandings of commonwealth, where God-given riches enabled
states to declare and extend their sovereignty.[53]

For the more militant supporters of colonization in the first decade of
the seventeenth century, the solution to James' desire for reconciliation
with Spain was to seek patronage in the courts of Anne of Denmark at
Greenwich and Somerset House, and Prince Henry at St James' Palace.
Henry promoted an interest in navigation, cosmography, and art that
reflected his pro-expansionist foreign policy, adopting militant sensibilities
that stood in stark contrast to his father's iconography of divine right and

---

[50] Count Gondomar to Philip III, 30 May 1620, in *English and Irish Settlement on the River Amazon*, 204.
[51] Ibid.   [52] Walter Ralegh to the Queen, 1611, The National Archives, SP 14/67, f. 196r.
[53] Slack, *The Invention of Improvement*, 54.

compromise.[54] 'We suffer the Spanish reputation and powre', wrote a frustrated Roe in 1607, 'to swell over us'.[55] Henry explicitly chose to surround himself with tutors, artists, and counsellors who shared more combative pro-Protestant policies, filling the roles of Gentlemen of the Bedchamber and Privy Chamber with men who had participated in colonial projects in various capacities. Letters from Virginia specifically addressed to the prince reported the safe arrival of the English almost immediately after the establishment of James Fort.[56]

When the Jamestown governor Thomas Dale heard of Henry's death in 1612, he lamented that the demise of his principal patron would be both his undoing and the unravelling of the entire colony.[57] It was in Henry's court that plans for a Guiana Company and Northwest Passage expeditions took shape, and where playwrights like George Chapman wrote *The memorable masque* for Elizabeth and Frederick's nuptials, a performance that featured masquers apparelled as indigenous Americans. Henry had judiciously overseen 'the North West Passage, Virginia, Guiana, the Newfoundland, etc., to all which he gave his money as well as his goodly word'.[58] The interest Henry fostered in pursuing colonization, coupled with his contempt for Catholicism, created an environment where Protestant courtiers, gentlemen, poets, and playwrights might advance their political agendas, especially during the years of the Catholic Howard family's ascendancy in James' court. The prince's widely mourned death cut short the more active, militant role that royalty held in promoting colonization, but gentlemen in Parliament and the Inns of Court stepped up to the task.

The failure to enlist James' more overt interest in colonization motivated an anonymous petition to the queen in 1610, beseeching Anne to follow Queen Isabella of Castile's lead by patronizing voyages to America. The petitioners asked that Anne be 'the meanes for the furthering' of plantation, not only to 'augment the number of gods church, but also procure great benifitt by plenty of trade' so that 'his Ma[jes]t[ie]s kingdomes might be made the storehouse of all Europa'.[59] The letter

---

[54] Roy Strong, *Henry, Prince of Wales and England's Lost Renaissance* (London: Thames, 1986), 103.

[55] Roe to Salisbury, 1607, CP 124/125v.

[56] Robert Tindall to Prince Henry, 22 June 1607, in *The Jamestown Voyages under the First Charter, Vol. I*, 104.

[57] Thomas Dale to [Nicholas Ferrar?], 10 June 1613, in *Jamestown Narratives: Eyewitness Accounts of the Virginia Colony: The First Decade: 1607–1617*, ed. Edward Wright Haile (Champlain, VA: Roundhouse, 1998), 761.

[58] From a letter by Sir John Holles to Lord Gray, written to the year after Henry's death, quoted in Strong, *Henry Prince of Wales*, 2.

[59] [Unknown] to the Queen, [1610?], Hatfield House, CP 196/142r.

emphasized the zeal of the realm's subjects, suggesting that the king might 'erect an order of knighthood ... to the w[hi]ch our Lo[rd]: the prince of wales his Excellencie to be cheife Lo[rd] Paramount', where 'divers knights and esquiers of the best sort of noble descent' would provide for 'the planting' of North America.[60] An American knighthood, led by Henry, would likely have appealed to the prince's militant sensibilities, but the letter also viewed Anne as the 'meanes' through which colonization would occur.

The letter to Anne offers a small window into female interest in colonization. In 1617, Lady Ralegh sold her house and lands in Mitcham, Surrey, valued at 2,500l., to provide funds for her husband's Guiana venture.[61] In 1620, the Virginia Company recorded a handful of female investors.[62] These included Elizabeth Carew, Viscountess Falkland (one share), Elizabeth Gray, Countess of Kent and Katherine West, Lady Conway (two shares each), Mary Talbot, Countess of Shrewsbury (four shares), and Sarah Draper (one share).[63] Female investment in the Virginia Company suggests a tantalizing possibility that women from both middling and elite backgrounds saw investment as an opportunity to participate in fiscal-political affairs in the realm. Lucy Russell, Countess of Bedford, appeared on the patent for the governing council of the Virginia and Somers Islands Company in 1612. Her name came second only to the Earl of Southampton's in the Bermuda charter of 1615, after the Somers Islands/Bermuda left the aegis of the Virginia Company.[64]

Bedford was a patron of Michael Drayton, Roe, John Donne, and other colonial enthusiasts who navigated the orbit of Prince Henry's court. In this light, Donne's references to Virginia in a poem dedicated to the countess may actually reflect an interest of *hers* as much as his. Donne painted a charming picture of a man's body as an American microcosm: 'who e'er saw ... That pearl, or gold, or corn in man did grow?'[65] The glow of alchemized precious metals, the sensual pearl, and abundant maize intimately brought the allure of the Chesapeake into the human frame.

[60] Ibid.
[61] *The Western Antiquary, Vol. 4*, ed. W. H. K. Wright (Plymouth: W. H. Luke, 1885), 85; see also a possible reference to this transaction in John Haywarde to Nicholas Carew, 12 February 1617, Folger Shakespeare Library, MS V.b.288.
[62] Council for Virginia, *A declaration of the state of the colonie and affaires in Virginia* (1620; STC 24841.4).
[63] Ibid. On later female investment, see Amy M. Froide, *Silent Partners: Women As Public Investors during Britain's Financial Revolution, 1690–1750* (Oxford: Oxford University Press, 2017).
[64] 'The Bermudas Charter', in *Calendar of State Papers: Colonial, Vol. 1*, 17.
[65] John Donne, 'To the Countess of Bedford', in *The Complete Poems of John Donne*, ed. Robin Robbins (Harlow: Longman, 2010), 710.

'We've added to the world Virginia,' Donne wrote to a woman who may have been as enticed by effecting colonization as he was.[66]

Beyond Whitehall and the royal courts, large numbers of gentry MPs supported westward colonization.[67] More than half of the Virginia Company's 560 gentry were MPs.[68] All but three individuals on the initial Virginia charter of 1606 sat in the House of Commons, and half held some royal office, indicating policy-makers' attempts to give political weight to North American enterprises.[69] The gentry faction of the Virginia Company led by Edwin Sandys and Southampton gained sway over the merchant faction headed by Thomas Smythe and the Earl of Warwick in 1619, and their leadership steered plantation towards a traditional gentry land-holding system governed by the common law and elected representatives.[70]

Sandys, an extraordinary figure in the Jacobean Parliaments and the Virginia Company, considered overseas involvement and trade to be a key part of how the English gentry might promote the good of the realm. Sandys played on the changing nature of political roles open to gentlemen in society, particularly in peacetime. 'What else shall become of Gentlemens younger Sons', he asked in 1604, 'who cannot live by Arms, when there is no wars, and Learning preferments are common to all, and mean? Nothing remains fit for them, save only [to] Merchandize'.[71] John Oglander expressed similarly: 'It is impossible for [a] mere country gentlem[a]n ever to grow rich or raise his house. He must have some other vocation with his inheritance … If he hath no other vocation, let him get a ship and judiciously manage her'.[72] Younger sons of country gentlemen served as MPs and in minor offices of state while helping with the colonial interests of their patrons, serving as secretaries, or employing agents to trade in New England beaver furs. Concerns to prevent 'our warlike discipline [to] decay not, and so sincke … the honor of our state and Countrey', in the words of another MP, made involvement in overseas expansion and war in a Protestant cause a viable option for gentlemen, as when Anthony Knivet, an illegitimate son of a country knight, travelled to Brazil in the service of the explorer Thomas Cavendish.[73] The frontispiece

---

[66] Ibid.   [67] Fitzmaurice, *Humanism and America*, 61.   [68] Ibid.

[69] Rabb, *Jacobean Gentleman*, 320–1.   [70] Ibid.; also see Slack, *The Invention of Improvement*, 70.

[71] Edwin Sandys, 'Report of the Travel and Proceeding of the Committee in the Two Bills for Free Trade', 19 May 1604, in *Journal of the House of Commons*, 214–15.

[72] Quoted in Gillian T. Cell, 'The Newfoundland Company: A Study of Subscribers to a Colonizing Venture', *The William and Mary Quarterly*, 22 (1965), 611–25, at 618.

[73] Thomas Digges, *Foure paradoxes, or politique discourses concerning militarie discipline* (1604; STC 6872), sig. O2v; 'The admirable adventures and strange fortunes of Master Antonie Knivet', in Purchas, *Purchas his pilgrimes*, sig. Ggggg3r.

to Richard Brathwaite's *The English gentleman* (1633) aptly conveyed the role of travelling across the seas in gentlemanly participation in civil life. Brathwaite portrayed the ideal gentleman, clad in fashionable but sober dress, as well educated, moderate, and godly, standing above 'Vocation', who 'fixeth his eye on a Globe, or Marine Map'.[74]

Gentry interests were linked to a wider network of colonial support bolstered by the efforts of captains and churchmen. A Captain Baily frequently presented plantation schemes to the Privy Council, which he believed would empty overcrowded English prisons and allow people in the localities to partake in the evangelizing mission. He proposed that every man in England and Wales who gave a penny annually for ten years should receive the same stock-holding privileges as those who ventured 1,000l. The Privy Council noted that Baily claimed to have made his project known 'to many thousands', some of whom had already subscribed up to 10l. per annum, and none less than 2s 6d.[75] Four months later, the council reported to have conferred with Baily about his proposals, but ultimately decided that the sums he promised could not be realistically levied. Baily continued with his petitions, adapting his plans and confident that interest in the localities would eventually convince the king and his council of their commitment.[76] The Virginia Company lotteries also brought colonial promotion to the localities and shed light on non-elite investment in colonial schemes.[77] In 1610, 'the Mayor and Commonality of Dover' invested in the company, hoping to gain 'full part of all suche landes' or whatever might be found on them, including precious metals and pearls.[78] Stamped with the royal seal, these lottery certificates demonstrate an intersection between plantation and the parishes, between the endorsement of the Crown and the initiatives of individuals outside the aristocracy to subordinate America to English interests.

While the impressions of individuals who supported the imperial project are not always recoverable, the diary of Stephen Powle offers a glimpse into how gentlemen understood their endorsement of colonization on a personal level. Between financial reports and Latin verses, Powle included news from overseas voyages, situating these within a providential

---

[74] Richard Brathwaite, *The English gentleman* (1633; STC 3564), frontispiece.

[75] 'Project by Captain Baily', July 1623, in *Calendar of State Papers: Colonial, Vol. 1*, 49–51.

[76] Sir Thomas Smythe, John Wolstenholme et al. to Secretary Conway, November 1623, in ibid., 54; 'Project concerning Virginia', December 1623, in ibid., 56.

[77] E. M. Rose, 'Notes and Documents: The "Bewitching Lotteries for Virginia", 1616–1621: A List of Sites and Charitable Donations', *Huntington Library Quarterly*, 81 (2018), 107–19.

[78] 'Certificate of a payment made by the Mayor and Commonality of Dover for a share in a venture to Virginia', 23 May 2610, British Library, Egerton MS 2087, f. 3.

framework. 'I delivered to Sir Thomas Smith Treasorer of the viage to Virginia the summe of fifty powndes', Powle recorded in 1609, 'and I am to be one of the Counsell of this expedition ... The success of whitch undertakinge I referre to god allmighty'.[79] Several months later, Powle noted that the ships under Thomas Gates had departed, and he wished 'god blesse them and guide them to his glory and our goode'.[80] Nor were Powle's interests for Virginia alone. He also followed Roe's plans in 1610 to command the expedition in Guiana. Southampton had invested 800l., Powle noted, and Ralegh 600l.[81] Powle contributed 20l., but his reference to 'my sealf' suggests a sense of collective association, in which investing made him a significant contributor. News about these ventures circulated in letter-writing networks, as in the 1611 newsletter containing reports on the settlements in Ulster, Virginia, Newfoundland, and Bermuda.[82] Competing for capital from City merchants, the newsletter stressed that while the citizens of London were 'exceding wearye of theyre Ireyshe plantacion', '[t]he state and hope of the Bermodes' remained high.[83] The Newfoundland governor John Guy sent deerskins and wolf and fox furs 'for [t]estymony' of its bounty, and prepared 'for further plantacion ... wherunto all men are very forward to put in theyre moneyes, by reason this plantacion is very honest peacefull, And hopefull, And very lykely to be profytable'.[84]

Savagery and Improvement in the Language of Reform

Deep-rooted convictions about land, governance, and authority under-pinned the elite's financial and political interest in colonization. While profit remained an obvious motivation for imperial pursuits, the risks involved in joint-stock investment remained high. Most investors lost rather than gained assets when the Virginia Company went bankrupt in 1624. Investing in Eastern trade or in domestic manufactures often proved more profitable. A better understanding of the relationship between plan-tation and civility demonstrates how, and why, gentlemen viewed 'civiliz-ing' savagery as a moral imperative and a political act. The belief in their prescribed role in upholding order, and their attitudes to cultivating

---

[79] David B. Quinn, 'Notes by a Pious Colonial Investor, 1608–1610', *The William and Mary Quarterly*, 16 (1959), 551–5, at 553.
[80] Ibid., 554.   [81] Ibid.
[82] David B. Quinn, 'Advice for Investors in Virginia, Bermuda, and Newfoundland, 1611', *The William and Mary Quarterly*, 23 (1966), 135–45.
[83] Ibid., 144–5.   [84] Ibid., 145.

'savage' landscapes – territories that needed to be enclosed, tilled, and continually managed – enabled gentlemen to reconcile profit and virtue while promoting the creation of a transatlantic polity.

As Paul Slack argues, 'improvement' in seventeenth-century England 'became a fundamental part of the national culture, governing how the English saw themselves and the condition of the nation to which they belonged', more so than in other European countries.[85] Plantation was both objective and method, related to the management of land and the hopes of capitalizing on natural resources. At a time when gentlemen sought to claim and enclose the lands around their estates, a lack of tillage seemed to offer a 'reproach' to the authority of households.[86] Land management through surveying and husbandry contributed to a landholder's sense of civility. Copying out aphorisms by the Roman senator Cato, one Jacobean individual related multiple adages to the word 'husbandry' – not only maxims on labour but others on fate, caution, and spending money.[87] Far outnumbering any other words in the marginalia, associations with 'husbandry' suggested a sense of the word as related to personal virtue and moral responsibility as well as to the physicality of the natural environment.

The perceived rawness of America and its peoples invited interference and a sense of opportunism. William Bradford, recounting the Separatists' first arrival on the shores of Cape Cod in 1620, described the initial encounter with the landscape in identical terms to those expressed by Londoners. It was:

> a hideous and desolate wilderness, full of wild beasts and wild men . . . the whole country, full of woods and thickets, presented a wild and savage hue. If they looked behind them, there was the mighty ocean which they had passed and was now as a main bar and gulf to separate them from all the civil parts of the world.[88]

In 1613, Samuel Purchas expressed the commonplace belief that 'savage' peoples and landscapes were locked in a particular relationship with each other. The Algonquians 'seeme to have learned the savage nature of the wild Beasts, of whom and with whome they live'.[89] Gentlemen associated

---

[85] Ibid., 3.

[86] Keith Thomas, *Man and the Natural World: Changing Attitudes in England, 1500–1800* (London: Allen Lane, 1983), 254.

[87] 'Catoes Distinctions concerninge manners, in English', *c.*1608, Huntington Library, mssHM 78, ff. 4v, 5r, 5v, 7r, 7v.

[88] William Bradford, *Of Plymouth Plantation, 1620–1647: The Complete Text*, ed. Samuel Eliot Morison (New York: Knopf, 1952), 62.

[89] Samuel Purchas, *Purchas his pilgrimage* (1613; STC 20505), sig. Lll4v.

a perceived lack of land cultivation with the lack of human culture. James granted charters to North America 'for the inlarging of our Government, increase of Navigation and Trade, and especially for the reducing of the savage and barbarous people of those parts to the Christian faith'.[90] The Privy Council sanctioned voyages to Guiana because South America was 'inhabited with Heathen and savage people, that have no knowledg [sic] of any Christean Religion for the salvac[i]on of their Soules, and that are not under the Gover[n]ment of any Christian Prince or state'.[91] These words emphasized that, at least formally, the Crown supported colonization primarily to introduce 'savage' people to the civil life, where education would impart indigenous peoples with the capacity to comprehend Christianity and divine order. Even the vim of Richard Whitbourne's discourse on Newfoundland did not avoid the usual tropes, declaring the venture useful for industry while noting that the inhabitants, being 'rude and savage people[,] having neither knowledge of God, nor living under any kinde of civill government', were failing to usefully achieve settlement.[92]

To implement civility, the English needed to establish a permanent presence in America, as degeneration was believed to flourish anywhere that was not continuously cultivated. Purchas' 'Virginia's Verger', appearing in *Purchas his pilgrimes* (1625), is in many ways a husbandry manual for state-building. Referencing Genesis 1:29 ('Behold, I have given you every herbe bearing seede, which is upon the face of all the earth', KJV), Purchas stated at the start of his tract that 'we have *Commission from* [God] to plant'.[93] Man, created in God's image, had been given dominion over nature. God had made Adam and Eve cultivators, and had told his chosen people that 'ye shall be tilled and sown' and purified as a result (Ezekiel 26:9, KJV). Referring to the lost settlers of Roanoke, Purchas evoked the quasi-mystical language of sacrifice and fertility, in which the blood of the dead colonists proclaimed an ownership of the land: 'Their carcasses ... have taken a morall immortall possession, and being dead, speake, proclaime, and cry, *This our earth is truly English*'.[94] Unconstrained savagery, including English assumptions of indigenous paganism, would be removed by possessing the soil and fertilizing it with English blood.

---

[90] *By the King. Whereas at the humble suit and request of sundry our loving and well disposed subjects ...* (1621; STC 8660).

[91] Privy Council to Sir Thomas Coventry, 18 April 1619, The National Archives, PC 2/30, f. 159.

[92] Richard Whitbourne, *A relation of the New-found-land* (1620), in *Newfoundland Discovered*, 117.

[93] Purchas, *Purchas his pilgrimes*, sig. Lllllllv.   [94] Ibid., sig. Mmmmmmm2r.

The gentlemen who invested money and time in projects were not subscribing just to the ventures themselves, in other words, but also to the ideas about savagery and authority that underpinned them. Purchas described Native Americans as possessing 'little of Humanitie but shape, ignorant of Civilitie, of Arts, of Religion', rendering them 'more brutish then [*sic*] the beasts they hunt, more wild and unmanly then that unmanned wild Countrey, which they range rather then inhabite'.[95] Here Purchas made explicit this link between a lack of husbandry and the need for civil society, while 'unmanly' raised the connection between masculinity and the obligations of gentlemen to subdue the unruly. Francis Bacon criticized merchants for looking 'ever to the present gaine', expressing the belief that they were ill suited to establish plantations because hopes for immediate profit would always outweigh moral responsibility towards good governance.[96] The process of subjugating '[s]avagenesse to good manners and humaine polity' would create a system of transatlantic rule, inspiring '*English* hearts in loyal subjection to your Royall Soveraign'.[97]

Horticultural metaphors were widely used to express the necessity of subjection as an act of creating subjects. Algonquians seemed to possess 'unnurtured grounds of reason', wrote the colonist and minister Alexander Whitaker, that 'may serve to encourage us' to nurse promising seeds to fruition.[98] When the literary scholar Rebecca Bushnell set out to research gardening manuals of the sixteenth century, she found her sources to be as concerned with moral behaviour as with botany, where attitudes to land and education reflected wider concerns about the nature of authority and control.[99] 'Ther can not be a greater or more commendable worke of a Christian prince', wrote Arthur Chichester from Ireland in 1605, 'then to plant cyvilytie w[i]th the trewe knowledge and service of God in the hartes of his subjectes'.[100] In Latin, *cultura* signified the cultivation of land,

---

[95] Ibid., sig. Mmmmmmmm2v. For overviews of stereotypes of savagery, see Keith Pluymers, 'Taming the Wilderness in Sixteenth and Seventeenth-Century Ireland and Virginia', *Environmental History*, 16 (2011), 610–32; James E. Doan, '"An Island in the Virginian Sea": Native Americans and the Irish in English Discourse, 1585–1640', *New Hibernia Review*, 1 (1997), 79–99; Margaret T. Hodgen, *Early Anthropology in the Sixteenth and Seventeenth Centuries* (Philadelphia: University of Pennsylvania Press, 1964).

[96] Francis Bacon, 'Of Plantations', in *The essays, or councils, civil and moral, of Sir Francis Bacon* (1696; Wing B296), 94.

[97] Purchas, *Purchas his pilgrimes*, sigs. Mmmmmmmm4r, Nnnnnnnr.

[98] Alexander Whitaker, *Good newes from Virginia* (1613; STC 25354), sig. G4r.

[99] Rebecca Bushnell, *Green Desire: Imagining Early Modern English Gardens* (Ithaca, NY: Cornell University Press, 2003).

[100] Arthur Chichester to the Earl of Salisbury, 2 October 1605, The National Archives, SP 63/217, f. 165v.

and Cicero, Ovid, and Tacitus used *colere*, to cultivate or tend, to denote agricultural work but also nourishing in a metaphysical sense. 'Culture' invariably entailed the cultivation of land or industries as well as the development of the mind, faculty, and manners. This made culture a moral imperative, for, in the words of Cicero, 'just as a field however fertile cannot be fruitful without cultivation, neither can the soul without instruction'.[101] In the language of planting, pro-imperial gentlemen condemned savagery while simultaneously proposing a practical solution to eradicate it.

The idea of planting begins to reconcile what initially seems to be a contradiction between civilizing and violence. Anti-Spanish rhetoric in England continuously pitted Spanish conquest against the refining projects of English plantation. But although the English styled themselves as benevolent ushers of order, cultivation contained ingrained theories about the need to restrain or remove malign influences. Destruction was not antithetical but inherent to growth. 'As seeds and roots of noisome weeds', Robert Johnson wrote in his promotion of Virginia, unchecked English behaviour would 'soone spring up to such corruption in all degrees as can never bee weeded out'.[102] The English believed they had a responsibility to redress savagery and to 'manage [the Algonquians'] crooked nature to your forme of civlitie'.[103] America became an example of what a neglect of cultivation could lead to. It was necessary 'by cutting up all mischiefs by the rootes' to render 'the state of their common-weales' prosperous by forceful interference.[104]

Justifications for the use of force derived from Christian but also classical thought. Although historians have seen the tactics of Robert Devereux, Earl of Essex, or John Smith as exercising 'a Machiavellian critique of the prevailing Ciceronian model of colonization', Cicero had not hesitated to recommend violence as a principal instrument at the disposal of political actors.[105] Law separated 'life thus refined and humanized, and that life of savagery', Cicero wrote, but 'if the choice is between the use of violence and the destruction of the state, then the lesser of the two evils must prevail'.[106] To Cicero, violence was justified when savage behaviour imperilled the state. In such cases, violence might be legitimately used for the sake of

---

[101] Marcus Tullius Cicero, *Tusculan Disputations*, tr. A. E. Douglas (Warminster: Aris and Phillips, 1990), 23.
[102] Robert Johnson, *The new life of Virginea* (1612; STC 14700), sig. E4r.   [103] Ibid., sig. E4v.
[104] Becon, *Solon his follie*, sig. Fv.   [105] Fitzmaurice, *Humanism and America*, 168.
[106] Neal Wood, *Cicero's Social and Political Thought* (Berkeley: University of California Press, 1991), 86, 189.

common interest, an idea that became a recurrent theme in Elizabethan and Jacobean writings about the use of violence in expansion. The 'feed-fights', or burning of crops, that the English conducted in Ireland and Virginia, sometimes when in perilously short supply of food themselves, were assertions over the landscape that sought to subject local peoples to a recognition of English ascendancy. The Irish, wrote Chichester in 1605, were 'generally so ... uncyvell ... the best we can do is plant and countenance some Englyshe', but such planting required clearing the soil first.[107]

James himself employed metaphors that demonstrated his understanding of cultivation as a necessary act of force. In 1624, Nicholas Ferrar recorded heated speeches in Parliament following Prince Charles' controversial visit to the Continent to court the Spanish Infanta Maria Anna. According to Ferrar, James had proclaimed himself 'not onely a good Husband butt a good Husbandman, who doth not onely plante good Plantes butt weede upp ye weedes that would else destroy the good Plantes'.[108] James' play on 'husband' and 'husbandman' emphasized the patriarchal framework through which order was achieved. The widespread significance of the term 'husbandry' is evident from its proliferation in gardening manuals, Parliament speeches, domestic advice books, commonplace books, treatises, and sermons. 'The people wherewith you plant', wrote Francis Bacon in his essay 'Of Plantations', should include skilled labourers and 'Gardeners, Plough-men, Labourers', not vagrants or soldiers.[109] In short, ideal colonists were those best equipped to efface savagery through husbandry.

James also made clear that, like a gardener who uprooted the weeds that threatened the health of a garden, 'hee did indeed thinke fit like a good horseman not allwaies to use the Spurr butt sometimes the bridle'.[110] As Ethan Shagan argued in *The Rule of Moderation*, a 'coercive moderation' dictated relationships within the hierarchical structures of early modern English society, meaning ideas of subjection were ingrained in notions of civil order.[111] The figurative language James used articulated this belief and justified action, seen in James' rigorous campaigns against peoples in

---

[107] Chichester to Salisbury, 2 October 1605, SP 63/217, ff. 165r–v.
[108] 'Nicholas Ferrar's Diary, 12 February–8 March 1624', in *Seventeenth-Century Political and Financial Papers: Camden Miscellany XXXIII, Camden Fifth Series Vol. 7*, ed. David R. Ransome (London: Royal Historical Society, 1996), 12.
[109] Bacon, 'Of Plantations', 92.   [110] 'Ferrar's Diary', 13.
[111] Ethan Shagan, *The Rule of Moderation: Violence, Religion, and the Politics of Restraint in Early Modern England* (Cambridge: Cambridge University Press, 2011), 182, 212.

Ireland and the Scottish Highlands. Those who dwelled 'in our maine land, that are barbarous for the most part, and yet mixed with some shew of civilitie', James told his son Henry in 1598, differed from those 'that dwelleth in the Iles [and] are alluterly barbares, without any sort or shew of civilitie'.[112] It would be easy to subdue the former, James wrote, by targeting the nobility and securing their allegiance to him. For the Gaelic Scots, James believed that plantation offered the best solution, 'that within short time may reforme and civilize the best inclined among them; rooting out and transporting the barbarous and stubborne sort, and planting civilitie in their rooms'.[113] The idea of planting civility 'in their rooms' presents an evocative image of the intersection between the control of nature ('rooting', 'planting') and the flourishing of the ordered domestic environment ('rooms'). James supported the expeditions that colonizers promoted in America because they aligned well with a more general view that 'sharp conflicts' would 'civilize and reform the savage and barbarous Lives, and corrupt Manners of such peoples', enabling 'a solid and true foundation of Pietie . . . conjoined with fortitude and power'.[114]

Once an area was successfully planted, education would allow a civil polity to flourish. Schools were 'nurseries' where the fruitful soil of impressionable minds were tended and taught obedience. Protestant reformers advocated education, including literacy, as a means of equipping individuals with the tools to develop their rational faculties and to serve the realm. The schoolmaster John Brinsley dedicated his treatise on grammar school education to colonial promoters including Henry Cary, the lord deputy of Ireland, and members of the Virginia council in London. To Brinsley, bringing a humanist education to Native Americans was a natural extension of the growing access to education in the British Isles, where the conversion and salvation of 'savages', and the 'preservation of our owne countrie-men there already', might be 'rightly put in practise' through education.[115] This would create a 'sure foundation . . . for all future good learning, in their schools, without any difference at all from our courses received here at home'.[116] His view was entirely in keeping with that of many colonial promoters, from members of the Ferrar family to the author (likely Ferdinando Gorges) of a treatise on New England who claimed that 'wee acknowledge our selves specially bound thereunto' to 'build [the Algonquians] houses, and to

[112] James I, 'Basilikon Doron', sig. O2r.   [113] Ibid.
[114] Walter Ralegh [compiled Robert Vaughan], *Remains of Sir Walter Ralegh* (1657; Wing R180), sigs. G1or, G12r.
[115] John Brinsley, *A consolation for our grammar schooles* (1622; STC 3767), sigs. A3r–A3v.
[116] Ibid.

provide them Tutors for their breeding'.[117] Teaching the Irish and Native Americans English and Latin would 'reduce them all . . . to a loving civility, with loyall and faithfull obedience to our Soveraigne, and good Lawes, and to prepare a way to pull them from the power and service of Sathan'.[118]

From the pulpit, the preacher William Crashaw advocated Brinsley's educational methods, while Crashaw's friend the young minister Alexander Whitaker went to Virginia himself to set up a school in Henrico in 1611.[119] In 1619, the Virginia Company allocated a committee to oversee an English college at Henrico, placing Dudley Digges, John Danvers, Nathaniel Rich, and John Ferrar in charge.[120] Anonymous benefactors across England contributed to this cause, including an individual who styled themselves 'Dust and Ashes' and contributed a staggering 550l. towards the school, promising a further 450l. if the colony sent indigenous children to England to be educated.[121] Nicholas and John Ferrar's father, Sir Nicholas, bequeathed 300l. to the college at his death in 1620, requesting at least ten Algonquian children be educated at his expense.[122] Patrick Copland, Scottish chaplain to the East India Company, became a free member of the Virginia Company after dedicating himself to this project. In 1622, after sending a manuscript copy to the Virginia Company, Copland published a catalogue of the 'gentlemen and marriners' who ventured funds for this 'pious worke'.[123] Copland listed nearly 150 names from a range of social backgrounds, including merchants, sailors, pursers, stewards, surgeons, and carpenters who donated sums ranging from 1s to 30l. Copland's efforts raised 100l. 8s 6d and, unlike joint-stock investments, contributors expected no economic return, seeking instead to take part in 'instructing of the children there, in the principles of Religion, civility of life, and humane learning'.[124]

A London committee in 1621 discussed further appeals by Copland to build a school in Charles City, Virginia, based on the funds he had collected. Tellingly, the council decided there was a greater need 'of a school than of churches' to introduce 'the principles of religion, civility

---

[117] *A briefe relation of the discovery and plantation of New England*, sig. E3r.
[118] Brinsley, *A consolation for our grammar schooles*, sig. A3v.   [119] Ibid., sig. Av.
[120] Quoted in Robert Hunt Land, 'Henrico and Its College', *The William and Mary Quarterly*, 18 (1938), 453–98, at 475.
[121] Letter from Dust and Ashes, 22 February 1620, in *Memoir of Reverend Patrick Copland: Rector Elect of the First Projected College in the United States*, ed. Edward N. Neill (New York: Charles Scribner, 1871), 22; Letter from Dust and Ashes, 30 January 1622, in ibid., 41.
[122] Land, 'Henrico and Its College', 483.
[123] Patrick Copland, *A declaration how the monies . . . were disposed* (1622; STC 5726), sig. Ar.
[124] Ibid., sig. A3v.

of life, and human learning'.[125] Education, the council determined, was where 'both church and commonwealth take their original foundation and happy estate'.[126] To the same purpose, Harvard College in Massachusetts, founded in 1636 – less than ten years after the foundation of the Massachusetts Bay Company – received the first English printing press in North America in 1638. The charter of 1650 aimed for the 'education of the English & Indian youth of this Country in knowledge and godlines'.[127] Rather than being relegated to decorum alone, civility through conversion and education was to be the foundation of a civil, transatlantic polity, and would nourish pupils into accepting their prescribed places in society.

State and Estate

The state's concern with conformity and obedience highlights shared attitudes towards authority in England and its colonies at a time when these were governed by the same men. Framed as a pious work that would bring those 'savage, and to be pittied *Virginians*' into the folds of English civility, as Richard Crakanthorpe preached at Paul's Cross in 1608, the aim of plantation was to allow for 'a new BRITTAINE in another world ... together with our English'.[128] The crossover between these domains of rule made plantation and estate management an important indicator of the successful flourishing of English civil society. Just as the microcosm of the body paralleled the body politic, so a gentleman's plantation was connected to the harmony of the state and imperial expansion. As one author expressed, referring to Newfoundland, the merits of plantation were two-fold. Firstly, '[t]his countrey, which hitherto hath only served a den for wilde beasts, shal not only be repleat with Christian inhabitants, but the Savages ... may in time be reduced to Civilitie'.[129] Secondly, a sustained presence in Newfoundland would cause 'an Iland every way as bigge and spacious as *Ireland* ... to be brought to bow under the waight of his royall Scepter'.[130] By articulating plantation estates, and the associated responsibility of office-holding and governance, as locked in a relationship with the

---

[125] 'A meeting of the committee', 30 October 1621, in *Memoir of Reverend Patrick Copland*, 32.

[126] Ibid.

[127] 'The Charter of 1650', in *The Development of Harvard University since the Inauguration of President Eliot, 1869–1929*, ed. Samuel Eliot Morison (Cambridge, MA: Harvard University Press, 1930), 6.

[128] Richard Crakanthorpe, *A sermon at the solemnizing of the happie inauguration* (1609; STC 5979), sigs. D2r–D2v, D3v.

[129] T. C., *A short discourse of the New-found-land* (Dublin, 1623; STC 4311), sigs. A4r–v.

[130] Ibid., sig. A4v.

state, pro-colonial gentlemen sought to create 'a new BRITTAINE in another world' in a tangible way.

Plantation is so profoundly engrained in the American story that it is easy to forget that methods of planting colonies were a response to a process already under way in England, one that saw vast changes in attitudes to the English landscape. The Italian treatises on civility, so influential in the Renaissance, were never fully applicable to the English gentry, who retained a 'quasi-urban' mode of life that connected their social and political life in London to their estates in the localities.[131] As the author Barnabe Rich pointed out in *Foure bookes of offices* (1606), the Roman historian Livy had praised Marcus Cato for 'his knowledge [which] was absolute both in urbanitie and husbandrie'.[132] To gentlemen who endorsed plantation, urbanity and husbandry need not be antithetical. Quite the opposite, for a '[s]tates-man' gained renown through his mastery of civility and rhetoric, enabling him to manage his estate and public affairs in a way that related to 'the greatnesse of the whole Empire'.[133] Humanist scholarship, disseminated by print, made classical pastoral works including Virgil's *Georgics* more readily available, contributing to 'a culture of active estate management involving experience'.[134]

The proliferation of maps and surveys drew on the language of the common good while exhibiting malleable, at times contradictory ideas about the relationship between public and private good, in schemes often coming at the expense of common land.[135] Domestic projects used the same language found in colonial literature. The enclosure of forests, for example, would be 'good for the commonwealth', with 'plantation' bringing 'inhabitants to a civil and religious course of life'.[136] Projectors consistently spoke of the dignity of the plough, and the call of work for the poor, coalescing with a paternalist discourse that was also apparent in overseas plantation.[137] At the same time, profiteering seemed to stand at odds with traditional concepts of nobility. Moral literature and

---

[131] Bryson, *From Courtesy to Civility*, 281.

[132] Barnabe Barnes, *Foure bookes of offices* (1606; STC 1468), sig. G2v. For an example of Jacobean gentlemen applying Cato to private study, see 'Catoes Distinctions concerninge manners, in English'.

[133] Barnes, *Foure bookes of offices*, sigs. G3r.

[134] Michael Leslie and Timothy Raylor, 'Introduction', in *Culture and Cultivation in Early Modern England: Writing and the Land*, ed. Michael Leslie and Timothy Raylor (Leicester: Leicester University Press, 1992), 1–14, at 7.

[135] Ibid., 3.   [136] Quoted in Slack, *The Invention of Improvement*, 61.

[137] Bushnell, *Green Desire*, 55.

parliamentary debates lamented the eroding divisions in social status that accompanied the successes of merchant projectors.[138]

Though moralists wrote scathing denunciations of the privatization of land and the exploitation of resources by the elite, projectors benefitted from expanding literature about surveying and estate management.[139] These works reflected economic but also ideological shifts in landholders' relationships with their estates, where gentlemen were encouraged to intimately know the conditions of the land they owned.[140] Surveyors were called upon to use mathematical precision and the language of the law to re-configure traditional tenurial relationships.[141] From the sixteenth to the eighteenth centuries, landed properties – estates – went from being described as collections of rights and incomes to expanses of private, controlled land.[142] In *The compleat surveyor* (1653), William Leybourn recommended that gentlemen place surveys of their estates in their private chambers, where visual iconographies of land, gardens, and family crests 'will be a near Ornament for the Lord of the Manor . . . so that at pleasure he may see his Land before him, and the quantity of all of every parcell thereof'.[143]

The libraries and studies where gentlemen were encouraged to hang their surveys were often where they also kept their globes and cosmographies, reinforcing the connection between estate management and expansion overseas. In drawing and publishing detailed maps of English counties, as of the colonies, the surveyors John Norden and John Speed indicated an interest in charting regional boundaries that related domestic cartography to imperial aspirations.[144] The frontispiece to Aaron Rathbone's *The surveyor in foure bookes* (1615) depicted a gentleman with his large estate behind him, standing in a cultivated landscape with a globe at his side while trampling the satyr-like 'folk' figures of popular lore.[145]

---

[138] Mervyn James, *Family, Lineage and Civil Society: A Study of Society, Politics and Mentality in the Durham Region, 1500–1640* (Oxford: Clarendon, 1974), 93.

[139] Andrew McRae, 'To Know One's Own: Estate Surveying and the Representation of the Land in Early Modern England', *Huntington Library Quarterly*, 56 (1993), 333–57.

[140] Joan Thirsk, 'Making a Fresh Start', in *Culture and Cultivation in Early Modern England*, 15–34, at 26–7.

[141] McRae, 'To Know One's Own', 355. See also Charles E. Orser, *An Archaeology of the English Atlantic World, 1600–1700* (Cambridge: Cambridge University Press, 2018), chapter 2.

[142] *Estate Landscapes: Design, Improvement, and Power in the Post-medieval Landscape*, ed. Jonathan Field and Katherine Giles (Woodbridge: Boydell, 2007), 10.

[143] William Leybourn, *The compleat surveyor* (1653; Wing L1907), sig. Nn2r.

[144] Hollis, 'The Crown Lands and the Financial Dilemma in Stuart England', 442.

[145] Aaron Rathborne, *The surveyor in foure bookes* (1615; STC 20748), frontispiece.

This image appeared between the columns of arithmetic and geometry, the latter topped with a globe labelling America, Europe, and Africa.

To land-holding gentlemen, plantation was a justifiable form of land management that established regional ascendancy and godly authority. 'The Country is now also Described & drawne into Mapps & Cardes', wrote John Davies to Cecil from Ireland. 'The use & Fruit of this Survey ... will discourage & disable the Natives henceforth to rebell against the Crowne of England'.[146] To Davies, plans for Ireland extended naturally to colonizing America: 'the most Inland part of Virginia is yet unknowne' and must be treated, Davies continued, with the same rigour as Ireland, 'whereas now we know all the passages, have penetrated every thickett & fast place, have taken notice of every notorious Tree or Bush; All w[hi]ch will not only remayne in our knowledge & memory during this Age; but being found by Inquisitions of Record, & drawn into Cardes & mappes ar discovered & layd open to all posteritie'.[147] Davies' words, however, highlight the predatory nature of such revelation, where landscapes seemed to come alive, becoming 'notorious', subject to 'inquisitions', and 'layd open' to intrusion.

Architecture, like cartography, could embody values of intervention and surveillance. The earliest English surveying manual, *The boke of surveying and improvements* (1523) translated the French 'surveyour' into 'Englysshe as an overseer'.[148] Jacobean architecture imposed a verticality on the landscape that reflected drastic changes in rural economies and landscapes following the rise of industries like coal mining in the North East, where quick profits led aspiring members of the gentry to physically assert their status through building.[149] The 'great re-building' of the late sixteenth and early seventeenth centuries reflected the increased national consciousness apparent after the Reformation and its ensuing re-distribution of Church property.[150] The enclosure of landscapes found a parallel in the architectural enclosure of stately homes, where open halls were replaced by private bedrooms and dining rooms that restricted access to select members of the

---

[146] Sir John Davies to the Earl of Salisbury, 24 August 1609, Hatfield House, CP 127/133r.
[147] Ibid., f. 133v.   [148] Quoted in McRae, 'To Know One's Own', 336.
[149] David Levine and Keith Wrightson, *The Making of an Industrial Society: Whickham, 1560–1765* (Oxford: Clarendon, 1991); Green, *Building for England*. For a discussion of the politics of architecture and its relationship to taste and economic growth, see Jules Lubbock, *The Tyranny of Taste: The Politics of Architecture and Design in Britain, 1550–1960* (New Haven, CT: Yale University Press, 1995).
[150] Matthew Johnson, *English Houses, 1300–1800: Vernacular Architecture, Social Life* (New York: Routledge, 2010), 109–10.

household and their guests.[151] Formidable two- or three-storey houses with high gables added to the visibility of estates, enabling those who had access to the private chambers and galleries on the upper floors to look over their grounds. Though completed in the mid-seventeenth century, some of the earliest elite houses in English Barbados, St Nicholas Abbey and Draxe Hall were built in the Jacobean style. Since planters oversaw their own workforces, these high structures enabled them to dine and socialize while keeping an eye on their sugar plantations.[152] These developments happened gradually, but they indicate distinct architectural changes that shaped household relationships, reflecting the immense inequality and social exclusion perpetuated by buildings and their positionality to surrounding landscapes.[153]

During the Jacobean colonization of Ireland, colonists targeted the structures previously built by the Gaelic nobility, supplanting more feudal or military manifestations of power, such as castles with forts, turrets, and narrow windows, with houses modelled after English estates.[154] In using the language of civility to praise the efforts of the Irish elite who conformed to English architectural styles, the English asserted their commitment to a larger cultural and political hegemony centred largely on London.[155] The earliest permanent architecture in Bermuda was the governor's state house of 1620, built in stone and modelled after Inigo Jones' Italianate architecture for the Jacobean nobility.[156] John Smith included an image of the state house, alongside other dominant architecture, in *The generall historie of Virginia,* its columned entryway and walled grounds allowing the building to operate as something more than just defence. The state house exuded a sense of classical authority and permanence, contrasted against the thatch roofs, small timber-framed houses, and mud huts used by workers and enslaved peoples. It was 'in the Governours newe house' in 1621 that a wedding took place between an Englishman and an Algonquian

---

[151] Ibid., 103.

[152] Russell Menard, *Sweet Negotiations: Sugar, Slavery, and Plantation Agriculture in Early Barbados* (Charlottesville: University of Virginia Press, 2006), 104.

[153] Johnson, *English Houses, 1300–1700*; James Walvin, *Slavery in Small Things: Slavery and Modern Cultural Habits* (Chichester: John Wiley & Sons, 2017), 'Stately Homes and Mansions: The Architecture of Slavery'.

[154] James Lyttleton, *The Jacobean Plantations of Seventeenth-Century Offaly: An Archaeology of a Changing World* (Dublin: Four Courts Press, 2013), 58.

[155] Ibid., 162; Jane Ohlmeyer, *Making Ireland English: The Irish Aristocracy in the Seventeenth Century* (New Haven, CT: Yale University Press, 2012).

[156] Jarvis, *In the Eye of all Trade*, 507 n49.

woman who had formerly travelled to London with Pocahontas, where the guests revelled in a 'fashionable and full manner' in attempts to illustrate the possibilities of settled and refined society in a prosperous plantation.[157]

Through their estates, gentlemen expressed their status while using plantation management as a stated means of extending the authority of the state. In 1611, echoing the complaints of many gentlemen who had gone to colonize Ireland, Henry Goldfinch petitioned Cecil for his losses. He had 'a Reasonable estate in England', Goldfinch wrote, but had 'ventered the same to plant him selfe uppon her late Ma[jest]ies landes in Ireland'.[158] Because this venture had required 'building, planting, Inhabitting, & maintayning' land, he had lost upwards of 2,000l.[159] Goldfinch's petition conveyed his belief in a protected relationship between elite landholders and the Crown. He had used his estates to perform duties for the state, Goldfinch wrote, implying that his assets should be protected, locked as they were in a reciprocal relationship of fidelity and trust between obedient gentlemen and the world of Westminster.

Richard Norwood had successfully divided and mapped all of Bermuda by the mid-1610s, but it was the gentry's rising commitment to Virginia that established a particularly powerful relationship between overseas estates and metropolitan conceptions of political responsibility. When the Virginia Company's gentry faction gained ascendancy over its rivals in 1619, its members sought to restore the colony's ailing reputation by modelling colonization more closely on the traditional values of land-holding. The General Assembly of 1619 gathered in the church at Jamestown, where the establishment of common law reflected this change in the colony's direction and ushered a new phase in its development. Rather than using the colony as a trading outpost or a base for piracy against other European powers, as the Earl of Warwick and Thomas Smythe advocated, gentry leaders of the London council expressed disdain for unregulated private enterprise and placed greater emphasis on land-holding and settlement.[160] Although some scholars have hailed the first meeting of the General Assembly as the democratic beginnings of the American nation, the view from England was somewhat different. The establishment of English systems of law and jurisdiction exhibited a clear effort to divide and classify land and to establish hierarchical authority that

---

[157] *Historye of the Bermudaes or Summer Islands. Edited, from a MS in the Sloane Collection, British Museum*, by J. Henry Lefroy (London: Hakluyt Society, 1882), 294.
[158] Henry Goldfinch to the Earl of Salisbury, before December 1611, Hatfield House, CP Petitions 300.
[159] Ibid.   [160] Walsh, *Motives of Honor, Pleasure, & Profit*, 40–4.

would ensure its maintenance and enable the London council to retain oversight.

In reality, the rise of planter society in colonial Virginia depended on both private and public enterprise, the circulation of goods, the explosion of the tobacco market, and exploitation at all levels of society. But to pro-imperial gentlemen in London, the rise of plantations would be ensured by protecting elite authority and yoking the colony to the governing mechanisms of the polity. When the colonial administrator John Pory arrived in Jamestown in 1619, he expressed a sense of isolation at its remoteness, but he also saw Virginia as offering the 'rudiments of our Infant-Commonwealth'.[161] Though it was 'nowe contemptible', Pory wrote to the ambassador Dudley Carleton, 'your worship may live to see [it] a flourishing Estate'.[162] Pory's letter reflected a sense of connection to England and its global interests. Though he looked back wistfully at his travels through the Continent to Constantinople, Pory embraced his role as company secretary, and returned to Virginia to serve as a commissioner in the 1620s. In requesting 'pamphletts and relations' of events at home, Pory connected the world of manuscript and print circulation and information-sharing in London to the fledgling polity in America.[163] When corresponding with Carleton, who was serving as ambassador in the Netherlands after time in Venice, Pory wrote as a friend but also as one officeholder writing to another, conveying a shared sense of urbanity that emerged from service to the state.

In 1620, a set of instructions and ordinances published by the Virginia Company celebrated how 'the Colony beginneth now to have the face and fashion of an orderly state'.[164] This was due to the successes of those men of 'good quality' who had demonstrated 'sufficiency' and who were charged with 'the government of those people' in the colony.[165] Political service and land management operated together, since the governor had established order by dividing the colony, demarcating public land and 'private Societies' while ensuring the maintenance of these allotments through 'necessary Officers'.[166] The publication included a list of the company's hundreds of investors, who ranged from James' secretary of state and other prominent courtiers to companies and guilds including the Grocers, Skinners, Goldsmiths, and Merchant Taylors. The investors consisted of a close network of alliances with friends and family – fathers, brothers, sons, cousins, and wives. More than 50 were esquires, and nearly 100 were

---

[161] John Pory to Dudley Carleton, 30 September 1619, in *Narratives of Early Virginia, 1606–1625*, ed. Lyon Gardiner Tyler (New York: Charles Scribner, 1907), 282.
[162] Ibid.   [163] Ibid., 286.
[164] Council for Virginia, *A declaration of the state of the colonie*, sig. Bv.   [165] Ibid.   [166] Ibid.

knights. Southampton, Theophilus Howard, second Earl of Suffolk, Thomas West, Lord de la Warr, and several other members of the nobility had contributed more than 150l. each, as had affluent merchants and MPs like Walter Cope, Robert Johnson, and Thomas Smythe. The amounts invested do not necessarily indicate levels of commitment or interest in and of themselves, but the publication of names held them publicly accountable for their subscriptions, and, by extension, to the structure of colonization that underpinned these lists.

The Virginia Company ordinances were particularly concerned with delineating the roles and responsibilities of the councillors who convened in London. These men were expected to 'faithfully advise in all matters tending to the advancement and benefit of the *Plantations*: and especially touching the making of *Lawes* and Constitutions, for the better governing as well as the *Company* here, as also of the *Colonie* planted in Virginia'.[167] The responsibility to govern plantations imbued gentlemen with a sense of political duty alongside an expectation of profit. Martin's Hundred, one of the earliest plantations to emerge from the policy revisions to Virginia Company land grants in 1618, was also one of the plantations most closely connected to gentlemen in the Virginia Company. Edwin Sandys wrote that he had a general commitment to Virginia, but 'toward Southampton & Martins Hundred in particular'.[168] Of a sample list of thirty-four colonists who arrived at Martins Hundred in September 1623, fifteen were from London, and about a third were gentlemen.[169]

London councillors were expected to meet regularly to discuss colonial governance, usually on Wednesday afternoons, and were responsible for sending 'choise men, borne and bred up to labour and industry' to the Chesapeake.[170] 'They shall also according to the first institution and profession of this *Companie*, advise and devise to the utmost of their powers, the best meanes for the reclaiming of the *Barbarous Natives*; and bringing them to the true worship of God, civilitie of life, and vertue'.[171] Gentlemen were to secure the success of the colony by overseeing land grants and distribution as well as regulating elections and offices, and demonstrating competent record-keeping that would assist metropolitan oversight. While four ordinances in the council's instructions pertained to trade, and three to establishing a college, a significant eleven pertained to

---

[167] Ibid., sig. B3r.
[168] Ivor Noël Hume, *The Archaeology of Martin's Hundred* (Philadelphia: University of Pennsylvania Press, 2001), 31.
[169] Ibid., 88.   [170] Council for Virginia, *A declaration of the state of the colonie*, sig. Br.
[171] Ibid., sig. B3v.

land.[172] These entrenched systems of indentured servitude to plantation management, and reiterated the right of company and Crown to extract revenues from any gold and silver mines that might be discovered.

To those in charge of sustaining early hundreds and plantations, the language of effacing savagery met with practical, material efforts to convey order. In the 1620s, ordinances in Virginia sought to prevent any person residing in Virginia to wear gold or silk in their apparel, 'excepting those of the Counsill And heads of Hundreds and plantations and their wyves & Children'.[173] While the company insisted that colonists must 'frame, build, and perfect' houses to ensure their survival, gentlemen also arrived with objects that reflected their aspirations as colonial leaders.[174] Along with book clasps and drug jars, fragments of glass vessels and Ming porcelain have been excavated from Martin's Hundred and Jamestown: fragile, precious objects that indicate attempts to reflect the status and lifestyle gentlemen enjoyed in England. The 1624 inventory of George Thorpe's estate in Virginia, one of the earliest of its kind, is illuminating. Kept in the vast collection of Chesapeake plantation papers owned by the MP John Smyth of Nibley, the inventory consists in large part of apparel: a lined velvet cloak, a black silk grosgrain suit, a black satin suit, silk garters, pantofles, velvet jerkins, gloves, and russet boots.[175] Along with clothes, Thorpe's most expensive objects were featherbeds, pillows, gilt bowls, and silver cutlery. Land and the material culture of plantation that gentlemen sought to cultivate – those 'healthfull Recreations' and demonstrations of civil authority – helped to link the 'Adamantine chaines' of 'Societie' across the Atlantic, from Martin's Hundred to the Middle Temple.[176]

*

From Francis Bacon's *The Advancement of Learning* (1605) to Michael Drayton's *Poly-Olbion* (1612), Jacobean oeuvres often placed geography at the centre of the national imagination, employing horticultural language that related cultivation to virtue.[177] This served to frame colonization as a natural extension of the civilizing project while offering a practical method of carrying it out. As early as the 1590s, George Chapman's

---

[172] Ibid., sigs. D3v–E2v.   [173] Quoted in Hume, *The Archaeology of Martin's Hundred*, 23.
[174] ibid., 88, 187.
[175] Inventory of George Thorpe estate, 1624, Smyth of Nibley Papers, New York Public Library, MssCol 2799.
[176] George Chapman, 'De Guiana, Carmen Epicum', in Lawrence Kemys, *A relation of the second voyage to Guiana* (1596; STC 14947), sig. A4r.
[177] Bernhard Klein, *Maps and the Writing of Space in Early Modern England and Ireland* (Basingstoke: Palgrave, 2001), 152.

celebratory verses on Guiana viewed the civilizing project – 'Riches with honour, Conquest without bloud' – as contingent on subduing Native Americans while simultaneously creating a society joined through land management and building.[178] The English Atlantic was one where '[a] world of Savadges fall tame before them' but also where leisure made 'their mansions daunce with neighborhood', conveying an Arcadian world of palaces and temples that evoked the sensual delights of elite gardens.[179]

Though couched in language of lush abundance and technical innovation, in pleasing cultivation rather than brutal conquest, 'planting' involved a recognition of violent supplanting. It took a translation of the French writer Michel de Montaigne's essays by the second-generation Italian migrant John Florio to puncture the ideologies of colonization. The Tupinambá in Brazil 'are even savage, as we call those fruites wilde, which nature of hir selfe ... hath produced', Montaigne wrote. '[W]hereas indeede, they are those which our selves have altered by our artificiall devises, and diverted from their common order, we should rather terme savage ... we have bastardized [true virtues], applying them to the pleasure of our corrupted taste'.[180] Prevailing discourse written by English policy-makers and colonial promoters, however, celebrated the pleasures of plantation without expressing fears that it 'diverted' from virtue and order. Unlike Montaigne's praise of a benign Eden, the English continually conveyed the exploitation of nature as essential to their civil designs and to strengthening their state, where civility involved not just the urban but a specific connection to the localities.

Arriving in Barbados in 1631, the Essex gentleman Henry Colt expressed frustration at the behaviour of the young Englishmen he encountered on the island. Even as he struggled to navigate Barbados' alternative 'societye' and its adapted codes of conduct, Colt's sense of responsibility lay in upholding the traditional virtues embodied in the upright and committed gentleman, and he condemned the lack of husbandry that sullied the reputation of pleasure-seeking colonists.[181] Ideas of savagery and cultivation suffused his articulations of colonial responsibility. 'You are all younge men, & of good desert', Colt wrote, yet '[y]our grownd & plantations shewed whatt you are ... What digged or weeded for beautye? All are bushes, & long grasse, all thinges caryinge the

---

[178] Chapman, 'De Guiana, Carmen Epicum', sig. Av.   [179] Ibid., sig. A4r.
[180] 'Of the Canniballes', John Florio translation of Michel de Montaigne, in *The essayes or morall, politike and millitarie discourses of Lo: Michael de Montaigne* (1603; STC 18041), sigs. K3r–v.
[181] 'The Voyage of S[i]r Henrye Colt Knight', 65.

face of a desolate & disorderly shew to the beholder'.[182] An ordered plantation manifested the ability to subjugate territories and those 'naked Indians paynted red, & feathers in their heads' who lived in them.[183] Cultivation, and enjoying the fruits of the soil that industrious plantation yielded, would ensure the success of future enterprises. When Colt rebuked his idle peers, he mirrored the language of domestic surveying literature: 'doe but consider what you are owners of'.[184]

[182] Ibid., 66–7.   [183] Ibid., 96.   [184] Ibid., 67.

CHAPTER 2

Colony as Microcosm
Virginia and the Metropolis

Forty-two years after the 1607 establishment of James Fort, John Ferrar –
London merchant, MP, and former deputy of the Virginia Company –
reflected on the colonial enterprises to North America in which he had been
so invested. One of the most poignant aspects of Ferrar's annotations,
scrawled in the margins of the colonist William Bullock's later text on
Virginia, were his commentaries on policies towards the Chesapeake
Algonquians. He conformed to tropes of savagery when he deemed them
'a good loving harmelesse peopell [who] dwelt in Villages togeather yeat
went Naked', but he also referred to them in the past tense, as if they had
irrevocably disappeared.[1] English policy-makers' express desire to 'civilize'
the Powhatans and other groups in the early seventeenth century had
seemed, at least to Ferrar, to be a genuine aim, but this goal had already
proven unattainable by the end of James' reign. Where Bullock's text
suggested the English might quell Algonquian power by turning *werowances*,
or regional leaders, into royal favourites, bestowing them with titles and
jewel-embellished ribbons, Ferrar noted in his marginalia that this

> was the Deliberation of the Counsell and Company 30 yeares a goe in the
> time of the Government heere of that Most Noble Earle of Southampton
> and all this and much more determined and Ordered for the Civilizinge of
> the Indians as a matter of the greatest consequence.[2]

Ferrar regarded the frequent and dynamic exchanges between the English
and Algonquians as a distinct part of the early colonial project, and of the
Virginia Company's vision under Edwin Sandys and the Earl of
Southampton's direction.

---

[1] John Ferrar's marginalia is reproduced in full in the online appendix to Peter Thompson, 'William
Bullock's "Strange Adventure": A Plan to Transform Seventeenth-Century Virginia', *The William
and Mary Quarterly*, 61 (2004), 107–28. https://oieahc-cf.wm.edu/wmq/Jan04/ThompsonWeb.pdf.
[2] Ibid.

The '[c]ivilizinge of the Indians as a matter of the greatest consequence' was related to personal virtue and political identity on both
sides of the Atlantic. Throughout the Jacobean period, interest in
Virginia and its indigenous inhabitants pervaded political discourse.
Newsletters, rumours, and diary entries about Pocahontas, the knight-
ing of new governors, or the king's decision to send weapons to
colonists appeared in the midst of news about Spanish threats, dis-
graced courtiers, and parliamentary affairs. The lead up to, and dissolution of, the Virginia Company in 1624 was a messy, drawn out, and
highly personal affair. Members gave each other the lie, brawled along
the Royal Exchange, and were placed under house arrest, some of them
losing their tempers in front of the king. The survival of Virginia was
important to men in both houses of Parliament, who fought bitterly to
keep the company and their colonial interests alive. The successes of
conversion – whether by exposing Algonquians to Protestant doctrine,
or transforming plantation landscapes into profitable industries –
implicated the honour of policy-makers and their capacity to govern.
The trial-and-error nature of early colonization exhibits a clear connection between events in Virginia and decision-making in London.

Focussing on political friendships and practices of statecraft, such as
counsel and collecting news, this chapter places Jamestown and Anglo–
Algonquian relations within Jacobean political culture, raising attention to
Virginia's formative role in developing articulations of an imperial polity.
Protestant statesmen, including the king himself, developed their conceptions of governance and civility through specific responses to issues of
orthodoxy and conformity provoked by the colonial experience By the
1620s, though the Virginia Company had failed as a joint-stock enterprise,
the colony had played a considerable role in shaping metropolitan articulations of empire, including the responsibility of the English state to
maintain it.

Jamestown in London

The first English voyages to Virginia – especially the 1607 arrival of
Godspeed, Susan Constant, and *Discovery* – are well documented. So are
the hardships endured by the 104 colonists who, fearing attacks from
the Spanish, established a fort along the brackish waters of the James
River, where disease contributed to the high death rates further
effected by hunger, cold, and conflict with the Powhatans, and with
some groups who had resisted incorporation into the Powhatan

confederacy.[3] When Christopher Newport, a veteran of Atlantic sea voyaging, arrived at Jamestown with the second supply of settlers in 1608, the original colonists were reduced to thirty-eight. By James' death in 1625, the population had been in flux, pending between extinction and stability, for eighteen years, surviving almost exclusively through its tobacco exports and the bounty of indigenous groups. Eleven governors had attempted to impose a functioning society through a mix of martial law and common law, in regimes that alternated from stabilizing to brutal. The year 1619, with the abolishment of martial law and the implementation of English common law, brought a renewed interest among London backers in establishing diverse industries in the region and reaping the fruits of more settled plantation.

Since the Virginia Company ended with bankruptcy and dissolution in 1624, the impact of Jacobean colonial interest on domestic politics often seems to die with it. Jamestown continues to occupy an ambiguous place in the American and English imaginary. Virginia has been viewed by some as the 'birthplace' of the United States, by others as the shameful precursor to the godly colonies of New England with its myths of the sanctified beginnings of America.[4] In decentred Atlantic histories, Jamestown is 'another outpost on the margins of expanding European influence … a minor player'.[5] Bernard Bailyn's *The Barbarous Years* focusses on the brutality evident in some Anglo–Powhatan encounters, while Karen Ordahl Kupperman concentrates on moments of intercultural exchange and mediation that highlight the richness of Algonquian life but tend to diminish the active role London councillors and the Crown played in overseeing early colonization.[6]

---

[3] J. Frederick Fausz, 'An "Abundance of Blood Shed on Both Sides": England's First Indian War, 1609–1614', *The Virginia Magazine of History and Biography*, 98 (1990), 3–56; Edmund S. Morgan, *American Slavery, American Freedom: The Ordeal of Colonial Virginia* (New York: W. W. Norton, 1975); Bernard Bailyn, *The Barbarous Years: The Peopling of British North America: The Conflict of Civilizations, 1600–1675* (New York: Knopf, 2012); Helen C. Rountree, *The Powhatan Indians of Virginia* (Norman: University of Oklahoma Press, 1989); Martin H. Quitt, 'Trade and Acculturation at Jamestown, 1607–1609: The Limits of Understanding', *The William and Mary Quarterly*, 52 (1995), 227–58; J. Frederick Fausz, 'The Invasion of Virginia: Indians, Colonialism, and the Conquest of Cant: A Review Essay on Anglo–Indian Relations in the Chesapeake', *The Virginia Magazine of History and Biography*, 95 (1987), 133–56; Kupperman, *The Jamestown Project*.

[4] James Horn, *A Land as God Made It: Jamestown and the Birth of America* (New York: Basic Books, 2005); Karen Ordahl Kupperman, 'The Founding Years of Virginia – and the United States', *The Virginia Magazine of History and Biography*, 104 (1996), 103–12.

[5] Mancall, 'Introduction', 13; Horn, *A Land as God Made It*; Kupperman, 'The Founding Years of Virginia'.

[6] George Wyatt, 'A Letter of Advice to the Governor of Virginia, 1624', ed. J. Frederick Fausz and Jon Kukla, *The William and Mary Quarterly*, 34 (1977), 104–29, at 115; Karen Ordahl Kupperman,

Ongoing excavations at the Jamestown archaeological site and invaluable work by colonial historians have brought detailed insight into the plight of Jacobean colonists and their struggles with the neighbouring Powhatans, but by this point a disconnect has already occurred. The narrative has travelled with the colonists to the shores of the Chesapeake, where their relationship with those in London – those who saw themselves in charge of the enterprise – has been sidelined. The death rates in early Virginia were so high that there could be more company councillors in London than there were settlers in Jamestown.[7] What did councillors do with the information colonists sent them, and how did these accounts, riddled as they were with failures, uncertainties, embellishments, and accusations, affect the way the London council regarded not only colonial conditions, but also the necessity of government more widely? In his meticulous study of the dissolution of the Virginia Company, Wesley Craven acknowledges that 'the events which made of Virginia the first royal colony [brought] many of the considerations which later dictated an attempt to bring all colonial settlements in a more closely knit and better administered unit under the direct supervision of the Crown', but he concludes that colonization remained a mostly economic enterprise, a statement supported by Jack P. Greene and Kenneth Andrews.[8] It is difficult to sustain this view when Algonquians are integrated more fully into the picture. Establishing the presence of Native Americans in Jacobean political thought brings the English civilizing project back into political decision-making. To indigenous peoples, colonization was always political.

In many ways, the colony's failures kept Virginia alive in metropolitan debate. Policy-makers grappled with devastating death rates, colonists' frequent complaints about provisioning, fears of Spanish attacks, regional warfare, and rumours of colonial mismanagement. In 1612, John Digby informed Dudley Carleton from Madrid that the Spanish were 'discontented' by rumours that the English 'council of state' was handling affairs in North America.[9] 'I informed Your Majesty how urgently these [people] are pushing forward with establishing themselves in Virginia', pressed the Spanish ambassador Pedro de Zuñiga from London, adding, several weeks

Indians and English: Facing Off in Early America (Ithaca, NY: Cornell University Press, 2000); Kupperman, *The Jamestown Project.*

[7] Wesley Frank Craven, *Dissolution of the Virginia Company: The Failure of a Colonial Experiment* (New York: Oxford University Press, 1932), 296.

[8] Ibid., 335.

[9] John Digby to Dudley Carleton, 20 October 1612, in *Calendar of State Papers: Colonial, Vol. 1*, 14.

later, that 'everyone [is] exerting themselves to give what they have to so great an undertaking'.[10] A deeply committed John Ferrar, who named his daughter Virginia after the company's dissolution, frequently commented on his 'great employments in the Virginia Plantations & Company' with Edwin Sandys and the Earl of Southampton.[11] To Sandys, colonial affairs were a matter of state business, to be prioritized alongside discussions of free trade and impending war in Europe. 'I will spend most of this week', Sandys noted in 1622, 'in writing to Virginia'.[12] Issues of government were inherent in company affairs, since those who went to Virginia went as English subjects. The royal investigation of 1623 set out to determine 'whether the sending of so many people hath ... been a means to cast away the lives of many of his majesty's Subjects'.[13] One of the reasons James felt compelled to intervene directly in Virginian affairs was because so many English men and women had perished.

The interest of statesmen in and around Whitehall was critical to the survival of the colony, but also to forging the sense of personal investment that gentlemen conveyed when they gathered news about Virginia. This adds another layer to the metropolitan colonial interest that Andrew Fitzmaurice uncovers in *Humanism and America*. Fitzmaurice finds that fears of corruption and luxury, and the recurrent rhetoric of civic-mindedness, pervaded Virginia Company literature in this period.[14] His study brings the dynamism of Jacobean intellectual thought to life by situating expansionist debates within humanist political theory. While discussions of the *vita activa* feature heavily in Fitzmaurice's book, civility receives less of a focus. Manuscript sources from Virginia, alongside imaginative literature and the material culture of the metropolis, broaden the framework supplied by print propaganda and intellectual thought and suggest a depth of colonial interest that went beyond political rhetoric, inflecting gentlemanly concepts of honour in ways that influenced how they socialized and behaved.

As Chapter 1 argued, policy-makers' shifting policies towards coloniza-tion and settlement brought with them a sense of responsibility towards governance and oversight. When he hastily scrawled his initial impression

---

[10] Pedro de Zuñiga to Philip III, 1 April and 12 April 1609, in *The Jamestown Voyages under the First Charter, 1606–1609: Vol. 2*, ed. Philip L. Barbour (London: Hakluyt Society, 1969), 158–9.

[11] John Ferrar, 'A Life of Nicholas Ferrar', in *The Ferrar Papers*, ed. B. Blackstone (Cambridge: Cambridge University Press, 1938), 20–1; 'The Ferrar Papers at Magdalene College, Cambridge (Continued)', *The Virginia Magazine of History and Biography*, 11 (1903), 41–6, at 42.

[12] Edwin Sandys to John Ferrar, 23 September 1622, Ferrar Papers, FP 416.

[13] Quoted in Craven, *Dissolution of the Virginia Company*, 272.

[14] Fitzmaurice, *Humanism and America*, 68.

of the Chesapeake in a letter, the gentleman William Brewster praised the landscape as an 'Infynyt treasuor', so long as 'the kings Maj[esty]' could find a way to control this 'moste Statlye, Riche kingdom' by conquering it.[15] Over the course of the early seventeenth century, the bays, rivers, and lands that Brewster had acclaimed became better known in metropolitan discourse. Gentlemen envisaged political spaces in relation to coordinates of the James River, and phonetically spelled out Algonquian place names and Powhatan groups: 'Chicepeiake', 'Kiskiack', 'Weromocomoco', 'Pamunkie'.[16] What another gentleman called 'the London colonie' was indeed the project of a number of gentlemen who viewed colonization as a legitimate arena for their political ambitions.[17] This helps to make sense of John Donne's attempt to become secretary of Virginia in 1609, for example, which is often considered an eccentric footnote in the poet and clergyman's otherwise illustrious career. Struggling to find political advancement after the disastrous decision to marry Anne More in secret, the poet's bid for secretary was perhaps desperate, but it was not arbitrary. Donne's unsuccessful attempts to occupy an administrative colonial role, like the more successful William Strachey or John Pory, suggest that politically minded gentlemen, whether aspiring members of the gentry or younger sons of prominent families, turned to America as a means of advancement from very early on. Without an appreciation of the place of Virginia in metropolitan political culture, the gentlemanly investment in colonization seems random or outlandish, obscuring the role of colonization in shaping developing concepts of political thought and activism prior to the English civil wars.

Converting Savagery

This section relates the religious ideals of Protestant authorities to developments in Virginia and to theological discourses about conformity in England. The providential framework through which gentlemen viewed plantation involved a rigorous demand for religious orthodoxy that also served to advance their political and civil aspirations. The Virginia Company charters proclaimed the conversion of Native Americans as the primary aim of colonization. Desiring to make 'a Virginian ... thy Neighbour, as well as a Londoner' presented an inclusive vision of

[15] 'A p[a]rt of a letter of William Brewster gent fro[m] Virginia', 1607, Hatfield House, CP 124/17r.
[16] Ibid.; John Hagthorpe, *Englands-exchequer* (1625; STC 12603), sig. E3v; Thomas Dale to the Earl of Salisbury, 17 August 1611, in *Jamestown Narratives*, 554.
[17] Thomas Holland to the Earl of Salisbury, 30 October 1609, Hatfield House, CP 128/24r.

community that nonetheless required indigenous assimilation.[18] To policy-makers, creating a transatlantic polity hinged on a Protestant civility that demanded confessional allegiance to Church and state. Anglican preachers in London supported James' vision of *imperium* as a monarchical project. In *A good speed to Virginia* (1609), Robert Gray actively propounded the use of force in conversion and settlement, anticipating the more stringent governmental policies of the 1620s.[19] 'All Politicians doe with one consent', Gray said, 'holde and maintaine, that a Christian king may lawfullie make warre uppon barbarous and Savage people, and such as live under no lawfull or warrantable government, and may make a conquest of them'.[20]

These discourses held political as well as spiritual weight. In his dedication to members of the Virginia Company, Gray wrote that he preached his sermon from Sithes (now Sise) Lane in London. This was in or near the residence of John Ferrar, where the Virginia Company held its meetings, and where Ferrar frequently received letters from his friends in Jamestown.[21] Authorized colonial intelligence from secretaries and councillors arrived at the Ferrar household in letters sealed with impressed wax stamped with their signet rings, several of which have been found at the Jamestown site, including Strachey's.[22] The sermons delivered by ministers like Gray, therefore, did not just operate as vague endorsements of the colonizing mission, but within this nexus between Protestant theology and colonial decision-making, between company affairs in London and the latest news arriving from Virginia to 'my very worthie frend M[aste]r John Ferrar, at his house in St Sithes Lane'.[23]

The same year that Gray declared conquest to be a legitimate project of the civil state, the clergyman William Symonds, who later edited John Smith's *Map of Virginia* (1612), compared the English to the Israelites wandering through the wilderness on their way to the Holy Land. Symonds likened the Algonquians to the idolatrous gentiles who opposed the Israelites, providing obstacles to God's designs for his chosen people. In their struggles to find the Promised Land, the Israelites 'were cursing and killing enemies', Symonds said, who were 'no better than Canibals' and those Atlantic 'savages' the

---

[18] Quoted in Thomas Festa, 'The Metaphysics of Labour in John Donne's Sermon to the Virginia Company', *Studies in Philology*, 106 (2009), 76–99, at 92.

[19] Robert Gray, *A good speed to Virginia* (1609; STC 12204), sig. C2v.

[20] Ibid., sig. C4r. On conquest theory, see Pagden, *Lords of All the World*.

[21] 'The Ferrar Papers. At Magdalene College, Cambridge (Continued)', *The Virginia Magazine of History and Biography*, 10 (1903), 414–18, at 415.

[22] William Strachey's signet ring, pre-1611, Jamestown Rediscovery, JR-424.

[23] 'The Ferrar Papers. At Magdalene College, Cambridge (Continued)', 415.

English currently faced.[24] 'I should more admire Virginiea with these inhabitants', Alexander Whitaker wrote from Jamestown in 1611, 'if I did not remember that Egypt was exceedingly fruitful, that Canaan flowed with milk and honey before Israel did overrun it, and that Sodom was like the garden of God in the days of Lot'.[25] The lessons of the Old Testament reminded the English that 'in a strange Countrey, we must looke for enemies'.[26] In such circumstances, force was called for and in many cases encouraged. 'Here then is a *warrant*', Symonds urged, 'that where godly men are constrained to encounter with cursers, such as are the Priests of the Gentiles, it is Gods ordinance to bring a curse upon them, and to kill them'.[27] As in Ireland, the 'problem' of idolatry could not be isolated from politics: 'as it is a greate sinne, soe it is allsoe a matter of most dangerous consequence'.[28]

Whitaker expressed a vivid interest in the power of Algonquian rituals (Figure 3). He described an almost dream-like world saturated with harvest and rain dances, fire, the sound of rattles, and the rustling of plants. Yet those who participated in these formidable customs 'tossed smoke and flame out of a thing like a censer', and the '[i]mage of their god' that Whitaker sent to the London council resembled to him 'a deformed monster', a term also used to describe the pope.[29] Whitaker believed the rituals indicated the Powhatans' ability to contemplate holy matters, however misguidedly, and anticipated sharing the gospel with them.[30] This could not be done without initial violence, as governors like John Smith and Thomas Dale indicated when they openly reported the devastation of Algonquian places of worship. English responses to encountering these holy places were rife with mistrust and unease, and the violence against Powhatan buildings and objects was not unlike the iconoclasm practised against Catholic churches in England into the 1640s, where destroying images was spurred by biblical imperative and often considered a political act of reform.[31] 'We Beate the Salvages outt of the Island burned their howses ransaked their Temples, Tooke downe the Corpes of their

---

[24] William Symonds, *Virginia. A sermon* (1609; STC 23594), sig. Gv.
[25] Alexander Whitaker to William Crashaw, 9 August 1611, in *Jamestown Narratives*, 550; Whitaker, *Good newes from Virginia*, sig. G2v.
[26] Symonds, *Virginia. A sermon*, sig. Gv. [27] Ibid., sig. G2r.
[28] 'The Judg[e]m[en]t by way of p[ro]testacon of the Archb[isho]pp and Bishopps of the Realme of Ireland', 23 January 1624, British Library, Add MS 12496, f. 340r.
[29] Whitaker to Crashaw, in *Jamestown Narratives*, 550. [30] Ibid.
[31] On iconoclasm, see John Walter, '"Abolishing Superstition with Sedition"? The Politics of Popular Iconoclasm in England, 1640–1642', *Past & Present*, 183 (2004), 79–123; Natalie Zemon Davis, *Society and Culture in Early Modern France: Eight Essays* (Stanford, CA: Stanford University Press, 1975), 152–88; Margaret Aston, *The King's Bedpost: Reformation and Iconography in a Tudor Group Portrait* (Cambridge: Cambridge University Press, 1993).

Figure 3 John White, 'A festive dance', c.1585–93. This detail of a dancing figure
shows the fluidity and naturalism of the artist's sketches, and his attention to
Algonquian patterns of life. Courtesy of the British Museum/© The Trustees of the
British Museum.

deade kings from their Toambes', reported George Percy, younger brother
to Henry Percy, the ninth Earl of Northumberland, 'and Caryed away
their pearles Copp[er] and bracelets wherew[i]th they doe decore their
kings funeralles'.[32] To Percy, the brutality of reform, of destroying sacred
spaces and viscerally extracting jewellery from the dead, was a natural
product of purging idolatry.

On 29 November 1618, the newly appointed governor of Virginia,
George Yeardley, dined with James at one of the king's royal residences
and hunting lodges in Newmarket. The account of this dinner exhibits
James' keen preoccupation with non-conformity in Virginia and England.

---

[32] 'George Percy's "Trewe Relacyon"', 245.

Sitting with Prince Charles, the Duke of Buckingham, and other members of the king's Privy Council, Yeardley explained his aims for colonization directly to the king, where 'for a long hower and a halfe [the king] reasoned w[i]th him a lone & onely of Virginia'.[33] Concerns with orthodox behaviour and establishing civil structures occupied an ample part of this extraordinary record of the king's conversation. James asked 'what inclination the savages had to Christian religion, and how many of them had bine converted or christened'.[34] To James, the conversion of the Powhatans was closely tied to the need for English conformity. He enquired after the 'quality of our ministers in Virginia', and 'wished that both now & heereafter they would ever conforme themselves to the church of England, & would in no sorte (albeit soe farre from home) become authors of Novelty or singularity', promising that English ministers who returned from service in Virginia would be well preferred upon their return.[35] James further 'commanded that o[u]r churches should not bee built like Theaters or Cockpitts, but in a decent forme, & in imitation of the churches in England'.[36] James' view towards building English spaces might also be situated within long-standing strategies, in the early Church, of depriving local geographies of their 'pagan' sanctity by transforming them into sites of Christian worship.[37]

Conformity to the Church of England, already seen in the company's ordinances against Powhatan *quiakros* or religious men and in the need to establish English sacred spaces, continued to figure large in the success of the enterprise, while non-conformity began to be articulated in relation to Algonquian unorthodoxy. Experiences in Virginia became a means of accentuating the dire situation of religion within England, describing a society as imperilled as that of the Algonquian Chesapeake. To worship the devil was 'to sacrifice to him [along] with the poore Virginians, and the Heathenish Savages', wrote Stephen Jerome in 1614, warning his congregation to take 'heede of this cursed course, and Satanicall practice in thy sicknesse'.[38] Those who were 'worse then the *Indians*, in some of their blinde and idolatrous sacrifices' were dangerous because they 'impoverished the church' and 'impoverished the common-wealth', becoming little better than cannibals who 'devoured the people of God'.[39] 'Surely the

---

[33] 'A report of S[i]r Yeardlyes going Governor to Virginia', 5 December 1618, Ferrar Papers, FP 93.
[34] Ibid.
[35] Ibid. John Ferrar drew a hand pointing to the words 'authors of Novelty or singularity' in the margin of his copy, reminding himself to 'note this well'.
[36] Ibid.   [37] Walsham, *The Reformation of the Landscape*, 40–1.
[38] Stephen Jerome, *Moses his sight of Canaan* (1614; STC 14512), sigs. Gg5v–Gg6r.
[39] Thomas Adams, *The blacke devil* (1615; STC 107), sig. Kv.

Devill is the same here, that he is in the Indies', warned the theologian and
MP Francis Rous, 'bee yee weary of your gods, O yee Heathen Christians,
and serve the true God'.[40] The English might, 'in scorne . . . term [them]
Savages', but 'the worse thou callest them, the worse thou callest thy
selfe'.[41] Expansion and conformity were both tied to Protestantism, for
the English could hardly participate in converting other peoples if they
were 'idolatrous' themselves. Further, because Catholicism and Spanish
designs for a universal monarchy were so entwined in the eyes of Protestant
polemicists, English Catholics were often accused of being opponents to
English designs in North America. 'The papists', preached the colonial
promoter William Crashaw to the Virginia Company, 'approve nothing
that *Protestants* undertake'.[42]

Whitaker in Virginia and Robert Cushman in New England sent
manuscripts of sermons to friends in England, who used contemporary
examples from the colonies to emphasize the need for English values in
their congregations. Travel news seemed to confirm the assumption that
godlessness would taint even 'civilized' subjects whose exposure to the
wilderness eventually led to disorder:

> It is reported, that there are many men gone to that other Plantation in
> *Virginia*, which, whilest they lived in England, seemed very religious,
> zealous, and conscionable; and now they have lost even the sap of grace,
> and edge to all goodnesse . . . It is indeede a matter of some commendations
> for a man to remove himselfe out of a thronged place into a wide wildernesse
> [but] having [his] owne lusts . . . his substance is nought.[43]

The title of Cushman's sermon was indicative. It was preached 'in an
assemblie of his Majesties faithfull subjects', contrasted against those who
had failed to uphold Protestant English virtues. When John Hagthorpe,
a gentleman poet from County Durham, faced the possibility of migrating
to America with his family if his financial conditions did not improve, he
demonstrated a detailed knowledge of current geographies. The English in
Virginia were:

> exposed to their treacherous Enemies so that they cannot goe hunt in the
> woods, nor travell in safety, but with greater numbers . . . Whereas, if they
> had setled themselves, some of them in *Pamunkie River*, they might have

---

[40] Francis Rous, *The diseases of the time* (1622; STC 21340), sig. E6r.   [41] Ibid., sig. E5v.

[42] Crashaw, *A sermon preached in London*, sig. H2v. See also Hagthorpe, *Englands-exchequer*, sig. Ev.

[43] Robert Cushman, *A sermon preached at Plimmoth in New-England* (1622; STC 6149), sig. C2r. On
English concerns over deformity and sinfulness, see Alexandra Walsham, *Providence in Early
Modern England* (Oxford: Oxford University Press, 2001).

lived secure fro[m] the salvages, there being but 8. mile at the head, betwixt it and *James* River, as in an Iland.[44]

Hagthorpe also included a story of an English gentleman in Virginia who had survived the Powhatan attack of 1622. Having held 'no correspondency or commerce with the salvages, [he] scaped free and untoucht', since 'the Salvages did not know his house as they did the rest'.[45] Intolerance brought with it a certain safety.

James' dinner conversation and the writings of ministers suggest that a concern with civility and advancing Protestantism entailed underlying preoccupations with Englishness itself. Civility was a strategy for inclusion, but inclusion into a society with carefully prescribed rules. To 'make a great nation' in Virginia, preached Symonds, the English must 'keepe them to themselves'.[46] Fears of cultural ambiguity were not merely rhetorical. Detractors used evidence of the failures of civility as a slur against English colonization. An informant wrote to the Spanish king Philip III in 1612 that 'I have been told by a friend, who tells me the truth, that ... Englishmen after being put among [the Algonquians] have become savages'.[47] 'If he desire to know what Civilizers of people' Protestants were, asserted the Jesuit John Floyd in a caustic response to a sermon by Crashaw, 'let him goe to *Virginia*, where he may find one of the two or three Ministers that went thither, become savage, not any Savages made Christians by their meanes'.[48] Addressing the gentlemen of the Inns of Court, Floyd ruthlessly criticized the men who held their own civility in such high regard when Virginia existed as a glaring example of English failings to keep savagery at bay. Without the ability to control a regression to savagery, the monarch exposed his weakness in failing to secure the obedience of his subjects.

Events in Jamestown between 1607 and 1622 served as constant, often harrowing reminders that the idealism of Elizabethan visions of America and hopes of converting Native Americans were repeatedly undercut by the difficulties of establishing 'a new BRITTAINE in another world'.[49] The brutal winter of 1609/10, with its 'Starving Time' that reduced Jamestown from 500 to 60 men and women, reminded the company that for all its hopes for profit, the survival of the colony was by no means assured.

---

[44] Hagthorpe, *Englands-exchequer*, sig. E3v.   [45] Ibid.   [46] Symonds, *Virginia. A sermon*, sig. F2r.
[47] Flores (Zuñiga) to Philip III, 1 August 1623, in *The Genesis of the United States: A Narrative of the Movement in England, 1605–1615: Vol. 1*, ed. Alexander Brown (Boston, MA: Houghton Mifflin, 1890), 572.
[48] John Floyd, *Purgatories triumph over hell* (St Omer, 1613; STC 11114), sig. Bb3r.
[49] Crakanthorpe, *A sermon at the solemnizing of the happie inauguration*, sig. D3v.

Colonists and councillors alike saw many of the events in the colonies as a struggle for the preservation of English values among an onslaught of horrors. A sense of the physicality and frailty of human beings emerged from discourses describing broken bodies and bursting hearts. Recalling his time in Jamestown in a letter to his nephew Algernon Percy in 1624, George Percy recorded the harrowing litany of miseries that struck the colonists. Though Percy movingly described the hardships suffered by those in the fort, he showed little sympathy for those who 'cryeinge owtt we are starved, [w]e are starved' went through the marketplace claiming 'there was noe god', noting that they were killed by Algonquians that same day in a clear manifestation of divine punishment.[50] Those who cared only for their own safety, like the group of men who attempted to flee to nearby Kecoughtan, similarly found just ends when they were found 'slayne w[i]th their mowthes stopped full of Breade, beinge donn as itt seamethe in Contempte and skorne'.[51] To Percy, as to the governors who imposed martial law on the colony, those who failed to create a conforming polity by abandoning their duty to the commonweal deserved punishment to the point of death. Fears of abandoning civility were so strong that such actions seemed entirely justified, as Strachey iterated when he published Dale's laws in London. 'Contending with all the strength and powers of my mind and my body', Strachey wrote, 'I confesse to make [Virginia] like our native country', a transformation only possible through an active and ruthless policy towards disorderly or self-seeking behaviour.[52]

In the highly charged politics of colonial settings, cultural fluidity often seemed to offer a direct challenge to orthodoxy. Colonists at the first general assembly of elected representatives that met in the brick church in Jamestown in 1619 took considerable pains to uphold the ordinances of London councillors. On 4 August, the council called a captain forward on charges of speaking 'unreverently & maliciously ag[ain]st this present Governor whereby the honour & dignity of his place & person, and so of the whole Colonie, might be brought into Contempte'.[53] This was Henry Spelman, one of John Smith's boy interpreters who had first arrived in the colony in 1609. The wayward nephew of the antiquarian Henry Spelman, Henry lived with an adopted Powhatan family and wrote a short

---

[50] 'George Percy's "Trewe Relacyon"', 251.   [51] Ibid., 247.

[52] William Strachey, *For the colony in Virginea Britannia. Lawes divine, morall and martiall* (1612; STC 23350), sig. G4v.

[53] 'A Reporte of the Manner of Proceeding in the General Assembly', in *Journal of the House of Burgesses of Virginia*, ed. Henry Read McIlwaine and John Pendleton (Richmond: Virginia State Library, 1915), 15.

manuscript account of Algonquian ways of life. Brought before the assembly in 1619, Spelman denied many of the accusations made by fellow interpreter Robert Poole, but not that he had informed Opechancanough, a regional leader and the younger brother of the paramount ruler, Wahunsenacah/Powhatan, that 'w[i]thin a yeare there would come a Governor greater than this that nowe is in place', which the assembly decided 'hath alienated the minde of Opochancano from this present Governour, & brought him in much disesteem', bringing 'the whole Colony in danger of their Slippery designes'.[54]

This was a serious charge, and copies of the inquest were preserved in the private papers of several members of the London council. The treachery was reinforced by the use of a specific object: Spelman was accused of manipulating diplomatic encounters by using a portrait medal of King James. The assembly deliberated 'several & sharpe punishments', including death, but eventually inclined towards sympathy for twenty-four-year-old Spelman.[55] Having mediated between powerful members of the Powhatan confederacy and English settlers a decade, the council may have been sensitive to Spelman's forced exclusion from English society, where the very traits that made him un-English – for example, speaking regional dialects – were an important asset in negotiations. Nonetheless, his actions were attacked as profoundly disloyal. The assembly degraded Spelman of his captaincy and indentured him to Yeardley for seven years. Neither did the council refrain from a final biting remark: that Spelman, when hearing his sentence and failing to show appropriate gratitude or remorse, acted 'as one that had in him more of the Savage then [*sic*] of the Christian'.[56]

When the assembly derided Spelman as a 'savage', the reproach indicated how far political success depended on a refusal to sympathize with indigenous cultures. Spelman's reluctance, on an earlier occasion, to offend his companion Iopassus, when pressed by Captain Argall to enquire into his religion, was one thing; it was another to report to Opechancanough, as he was said to have done, that 'S[i]r George should be but a *Tanx wiroans*, that is, a petty governor not of power to doe any thing'.[57] In this instance, Spelman framed English political offices in relation to Algonquian ones. He depicted Governor Yeardley in Powhatan terms, as a *tanx wiroans*, just as Opechancanough became elevated in status to a king. Spelman's

---

[54] Ibid.
[55] Ibid. A sentence Spelman never fully carried out; he died in a trading expedition in 1623.
[56] Ibid.
[57] 'Copie of the Examinations of Robert Poole touching H. Spilman', 13 July 1619, Ferrar Papers, FP 113.

familiarity with 'the Indian language' and his willingness to speak to the Powhatans about English affairs became 'p[re]judiciall to the State in generall'.[58]

Spelman is but one example. The other interpreter involved in the inquest, Robert Poole, was accused by John Rolfe of 'being even turned heathen' in 1620, by which Rolfe meant his negotiations were not done for the good of the colony and were therefore treasonous.[59] Though colonists trusted Poole less than Spelman, his power to undermine the colony through over-close association with Algonquian groups made the accusation especially damaging to English interests. Reverend Jonas Stockham deeply mistrusted this fluidity, reporting that 'we have sent boies amongst [the Powhatans] to learne their Language, but they return worse than they went'.[60] 'I am no States-man', Stockham professed, 'but I can find no probability by this course to draw them to goodnesse ... till their Priests and Ancients have their throat cut'.[61]

Stockham's ruthless but commonplace opinion indicates the raw concerns over savagery that dominated the early Jamestown years. Councillors were inundated with letters that catalogued the effects of degeneration and misgovernment, providing stark confirmation of how easily government floundered without strict regulation. 'Our second shipp is returned out of the partes of Virginia', Ferdinando Gorges reported from Plymouth in 1608, referring to the Sagadahoc colony in Maine.[62] The men meant to be establishing St George's fort for the Virginia Company were idly 'devidinge themselves into factions, each disgracinge the other, even to the Savages, the on[e] emulatinge the others reputation amongst those brutish people'.[63] Encounters between 'exceeding subtill' Native Americans and the colonists 'whose conversation, & familiarity, they have most frequented' blurred the lines between peoples that the English had gone to draw.[64]

The English, after all, had not ventured to America 'to make Savages and wild degenerate men of Christians, but Christians of those Savage, wild degenerate men'.[65] Raising young Powhatans who were then to return to their communities as representatives of English civility would 'prove also of great strength to our people against the Savages', turning them into 'fitt Instruments to assist afterwards in the more generall conversion of the heathen people'.[66] This strategy was apparent in one of the watercolours by

[58] John Rolfe to Edwin Sandys, January 1620, Ferrar Papers, FP 151.   [59] Ibid.
[60] Reverend Jonas Stockham, reported in Smith, *The generall historie*, sig. T2v.   [61] Ibid.
[62] Ferdinando Gorges to the Earl of Salisbury, 7 February 1608, Hatfield House, CP 120/66r.
[63] Ibid.   [64] Ibid.   [65] Purchas, *Purchas his pilgrimes*, sig. M6r.
[66] 'Instructions to the Governors for the tyme beinge & Counsell of state in Virginia', 1621, Ferrar Papers, FP 285.

John White, painted during or shortly after his time in Roanoke in 1585, which portrayed the young daughter of a local *werowance* holding an Elizabethan doll of a woman in a dress. This is the only image of White's that directly exhibited the English presence in Virginia. Looking up at her mother, the girl seemed to be conveying a sense of longing, as if hoping to become less like her mother and more like the object in her hand.

The young, unmarried, often poorer travellers who sailed from London to Virginia must have seemed especially vulnerable to abandoning English ways of life in the absence of community and traditional family units. Writers on either side of the Atlantic specifically framed their concerns over degeneration in terms of savagery's power to undermine English structures, especially among those of lower status. 'Marvell not if honest and understanding Christians be so hardly drawne over to these places, as namely into *Virginia*', wrote the schoolmaster John Brinsley, 'where as there are in the same so manifold perils, and especially of falling away from God to Sathan, and that themselves, or their posterity should become utterly savage, as [Algonquians] are'.[67] Intermarriage between Native Americans and the English, Symonds believed, 'may breake the neck of all good success'.[68]

Meanwhile, gentlemen including Percy and Thomas West, Lord de la Warr, strove to maintain veneers of civility and sociability, importing clothing, furniture, drinking vessels, and jewellery at huge personal expense. In the midst of starvation and armed conflict, colonial officials kept sealed records in carved chests and used desks and tables. Excavations at Jamestown have uncovered objects ranging from gold rings to lace shirts and military sashes, imported Continental and Chinese drug jars to a finely wrought silver grooming tool shaped like a dolphin. Five extant goffering irons, the hollow iron tubes used to crimp and shape ruffs, speak to gentlemanly concerns with appearance but also with the time, preparation, and servant labour needed for such status display. The rich archaeological findings at Jamestown offer material evidence of how gentlemen sought a semblance of their lives and routines in England, where displays of hierarchy were seen as essential to implementing stability. Objects not only spoke to status, but also helped to effect the refining qualities of civil society, whereby gentlemen might begin to participate in the lives of leisure and cultivation that they had envisaged colonization would make possible.

---

[67] Brinsley, *A consolation for our grammar schooles*, sigs. A2v–A3r.
[68] Symonds, *Virginia. A sermon*, sig. F2r.

When Yeardley arrived in Jamestown in 1619, he proudly fashioned himself as the harbinger of a more concertedly English polity characterized by gentlemanly refinement. Yeardley's governorship replaced martial law with what the council in London hoped would be 'a Magna Charta', laws and ordinances that would 'not be chested or hidden like a candle under a bushell' but available for reference by any members of the colony.[69] At the same time, Yeardley's instigation of the common law did not prevent the advancement of private interests. The law was never intended to be common to all, and the renewed colonial enthusiasm among the English elite in 1619, including the king, revealed that gentlemen viewed this new phase in Jamestown's development as an opportunity to enhance their own civil lives as much as to ensure the rights of English colonists. The gentry in the Virginia Company pursued plantation models that would establish recognizably English landscapes through industry and settlement, while projecting a model of civility that specifically pandered to the tastes of the elite. Yeardley's arrival in Jamestown sent a new wave of enthusiasm for colonization, with his backers expressing the belief that 'yf you would ever beginne a plantation – nowe is the tyme'.[70]

James and his councillors specifically seem to have viewed the colony as a place for elite pleasure and sociability. James 'layde a strict com[m]ande upon Sir George . . . in all p[ar]tes of Virginia to cherish up silkewormes, & to plant and preserve Mulberie trees', a project that reflected the king's interest in domestic silkworm cultivation.[71] Around the time when James had begun to commission the Banqueting House in London, which involved an elaborate grotto and 'privy cellar' for his drinking parties, the king pressed for 'the planting of vines' in Virginia, not only because wine would bring a profitable trade, but also for purposes of sociability: 'pretious liquour' would 'drawe much good company to come & live there'.[72] Theodore de Bry's engraving of Virginia captured these fantasies of gentlemanly sociability, conveying men fishing and hunting, the landscape populated by horses, dogs, birds, and stags.[73] Near the centre of the image,

---

[69] 'A report of S[i]r Yeardlyes going Governor to Virginia', FP 93.

[70] Ibid.; John Chamberlain to Dudley Carleton, 28 November 1618, The National Archives, SP 14/103, f. 170v.

[71] 'A report of S[i]r Yeardlyes going Governor to Virginia', FP 93; Bonoeil, *His Majesties gracious letter to the Earle of South-Hampton*. As the king's silkworm expert, Bonoeil was charged with caring for the royal mulberry trees.

[72] 'A report of S[i]r Yeardlyes going Governor to Virginia', FP 93.

[73] The images from de Bry's *Americae pars decima* (Oppenheim, 1619) that pertained to English colonization were collated by Thomas Millet in his 'Tracts of America, trades, &c', *c.*1619 – 1625, Folger Shakespeare Library, MS V.b.335.

an English gentleman in a ruff and hat stood with his right foot gracefully forward, a hawk perched on his wrist.

Following the king's discussion with Yeardley, James' courtiers proposed further schemes. Francis Bacon offered to find a means of securing a monopoly on tobacco for the Atlantic companies, while the Earl of Lincoln resolved to send 'some of his best horses ... to sett up a Race [track]'.[74] The extractive refinement of elite plantation is evident in the planter David Thomson's letter to Thomas Howard, Earl of Arundel, from Massachusetts, asking whether Arundel had received the sample 'of graye marble I found in this countrie neere to Naemkeek [Naumkeag]'.[75] Thomson was clearly pandering to Arundel's well-known interest in architecture and collecting antique marbles. 'I have seene a Tobacco pype of a transparent stone lykest in my simple judgem[en]t to pure whyte Alabaster,' Thomson wrote, perhaps alluding to the quartz quarries outside Jamestown that Algonquians excavated to make crystal arrowheads.[76] Thomson also referred to Arundel's desire to know 'what places in the Countrey Vynes would thrive'; but these hopes of growing vines and acquiring marble depended on confronting the 'greater and greater multitudes of Salvages' they 'daylie discover in the countrie'.[77] The civility that colonial promoters envisaged in Virginia involved Protestant orthodoxy but also the social refinement that reform would make possible.

London and the Attack of 1622

The dangers of tolerating Algonquians appeared at the fore of public debate in London in the summer of 1622. On the morning of 22 March, between 500 and 600 men from an alliance of Algonquian groups led by Opechancanough attacked the English plantations along the James River. Having visited and dined with the English, as they were accustomed to doing, these *mecaûtea* or *muckquompaûog*, warriors or fighters, engaged in hand-to-hand combat against male and female colonists, using whatever was most readily available to them, from table knives to farming tools.[78]

[74] Ibid.

[75] Davis Thomson to the Earl of Arundel, 1 July 1625, in *The Life, Correspondence, and Collections of Thomas Howard, Earl of Arundel*, ed. Mary F. S. Hervey (Cambridge: Cambridge University Press, 1969), 502.

[76] Ibid. Quartz crystal arrowhead, *c.*1617–1630, Jamestown Rediscovery, 2106-JR.

[77] Thomson to Arundel, in *The Life, Correspondence, and Collections of Thomas Howard*, 502–4.

[78] The Algonquian terms used here are intended to offer a more nuanced perspective on the status of those who coordinated the attack. These translations for 'fighters' or 'valiant men' give a better idea

The attack devastated the colony.[79] Those who escaped faced famine and the gruesome task of finding and burying the dead. The death toll, recorded by the English as 347, amounted to around a third of Virginia's English inhabitants. Fledgling industries like iron and glass manufacture were destroyed. The college at Henrico, which had drawn funds from parishes across England, lay wasted, as did countless makeshift churches and houses across the plantations.

The event brought a decisive shift in Anglo–Native American relations, as colonists agonizingly realized they had misjudged their Algonquian neigh-bours, who may have been planning the attack for years. Colonists and councillors in London described the event as a massacre, an invasion of savagery that amounted to betrayal. Responses were highly emotive. The attack, wrote one survivor, killed many and 'burst the heart of all the rest'.[80] The Algonquians' intimate knowledge of English settlements and ways of life had made this more than an impersonal act of war. Yeardley's regime had brought years of relative peace, and colonists had seemed to believe Wahunsenacah, 'King of the savages', would induce his people to be 'faithful subjects of the King of England', with peace prevailing for so many years that 'our people went among [the Powhatans] unarmed and the Savages became so friendly that they often visited . . . and dined with them'.[81]

Strikingly, English writers blamed colonists most heavily for the disaster, viewing the event as proof that accommodation imperilled the civilizing project. Looking back on the time before the event, the colonist George Sandys reported contemptuously that colonists lived 'lyke libertines out of the eye of the magistrate, not able to secure themselves'.[82] Even 'if they had had anie knowledge of the purpose of the Indians, the most part could not possiblie have prevented their treacheries'.[83] One petition to James remarked that 'the Hostilitie w[i]th the Infidells' had largely subsided after 1614, but that 'wee boast not consideringe that itt lulled the English asleepe in too great securitie and consequently gave op[or]tunitie to the late bloody Massacre'.[84]

---

of the web of allegiance between *sachems*, or 'princes', and their 'chiefest warriors'. Williams, *A key into the language of America*, sigs. N4r–v.

[79] Horn, *A Land as God Made It*, 255–8.

[80] William Capps to Doctor Wynston, 1623, in *Records of the Virginia Company, Vol. IV*, ed. Susan Myra Kingsbury (Washington, DC: Government Printing Office, 1935), 38.

[81] 'Voyage of Anthony Chester, 1620', in 'Two Tragical Events', *The William and Mary Quarterly*, 9 (1901), 203–14, at 208–9.

[82] George Sandys to Miles Sandys, 30 March 1623, in *Records of the Virginia Company, Vol. IV*, 70.

[83] Ibid.

[84] 'An answere to a Petition delivered to his Ma[jes]tie by Alderman Johnson in the names of sundry Adventurers and Planters', 7 May 1623, in *Records of the Virginia Company, Vol. III*, ed. Susan Myra Kingsbury (Washington, DC: Government Printing Office, 1933), 395.

Some twenty years later, after the same Opechancanough conducted another, equally destructive attack, authors continued to view the violence as the fault of 'the *English*, [who] by reposing trust and confidence in the *Indians*, gave the opportunity'.[85] The danger lay not in Algonquian might itself, but in English mismanagement: 'there is no danger in them, except you give them weapons, and stand still whilst they destroy you'.[86]

As Londoners reported and discussed the news in following weeks, the event not only seemed to prove the indigenous refusal to be incorporated into English systems of law, but raised serious questions over English competence. This must have seemed especially relevant in the aftermath of the outbreak of the Thirty Years' War in Europe, at a time when the supposed effeminization of the English elite also came under pointed critique. The frontispiece to Samuel Ward's *Woe to drunkards* (1622), published the same year as the attack, visually rendered this concern in a narrative that attributed idleness and overindulgence to declining English honour and strength. The oft-cited Ciceronian lament, 'O maners, O tymes', appeared under images that contrasted the martial chivalry of previous eras against a panoply of distinctly Jacobean courtly fashions including ribbons and garters, heeled shoes with rosettes, lace cuffs, and tobacco pipes.[87]

Tobacco directly related courtly fashions to the imperial project, but other objects in Ward's woodcut, including Venetian glassware and dice, have also been excavated at Jamestown. Like tobacco, gaming was not confined to the elite, but the costliness of several of the surviving objects suggests gentlemen owners. The 'serpent glass' resembled the finely crafted objects gentlemen collected for their cabinets, and the ivory dice set them apart from those made from bone or lead.[88] These material glimpses of shared elite tastes between court and colony help explain the urgency of the reproaches that related moral degeneration to incompetence abroad. Although exaggerated, criticisms of the colonists focussed on the dangers of allowing martial ability to decay, damaging the fabric of domestic order. Hopes for a refined gentility uniting the English polity across the Atlantic could not precede the necessary eradication of savagery that must come first. To John Chamberlain, indulging Native Americans had sown the seeds for such an incalculable disaster. It was the 'disgrace and shame as

---

[85] William Bullock, *Virginia impartially examined, and left to publick view* (1649; Wing B5428), sig. C2v.
[86] Ibid.   [87] Samuel Ward, *Woe to drunkards* (1622; STC 25055).
[88] Serpent glass fragments, c.1608–10, Jamestown Rediscovery, 7860-JR; dice, 4221-JR, 4865-JR, 4866-JR, 6629-JR, 6623-JR.

much as the loss' that made the event so lamentable, for 'no other nation would have been so grossly overtaken'.[89] The ramifications of poor management in other parts of James' *imperium* affected the reputation of England and the honour of those who governed it.

The year 1622 marked a decisive shift in English colonial policy-making. For all the professed interest in assimilating indigenous peoples, the English recognized the fundamental incompatibilities of acculturation. 'Before the last Massacre', commented Nathaniel Rich, 'o[u]r Colonyes were almost made subjectes to the Savages', forced into a state of quasibondage because of their dependence on Algonquian goods.[90] The shock of the assault made tolerance suddenly seem unfathomable. In cataloguing the ills besetting the plantations, the Earl of Warwick noted that it was hardly a surprise that 'the savages . . . took the advantage', a result of 'o[u]r owne p[er]fidiouse dealing w[i]th them & the supine negligence in letting those furious wild people to grow uppon the[m] & to delude them with faire shewes'.[91] Colonial governors addressed this accusation of 'too great securitie' by noting the contradictions in the policies themselves. 'Whereas in the beginning of your L[et]res . . . you pass soe heavie a Censure uppon us', protested the distraught governor Francis Wyatt, with George Sandys, '[a]s yf we alone were guiltie, you may be pleased to Consider what instructions you have formely given us, to wynn the Indyans to us by a kinde entertayninge them in o[u]r howses'.[92] To the council in London, the 'unwelcome newes, that had beene heard at large in Publicke Court, that the *Indians* and [the English] lived as one Nation' with 'the Salvages as frequent in their houses as themselves' was nothing less than scandalous.[93] Reports circulated that Jamestown was in 'pieces', and 'the market-place, and streets, and all other spare places planted with Tobacco'.[94]

Behind anxieties over the English and Algonquians living as 'one Nation' lay a central problem in the civilizing project. 'Civilizing' without violence took time, and the attack had brought serious doubts about Algonquians' ability or willingness to submit to English rule. The English were 'stupid' for believing peace was a means of 'winning the

---

[89] John Chamberlain to Dudley Carleton, 13 July 1622, The National Archives, SP 14/132, ff. 55r–v.
[90] 'Draft of Instructions to the Commissioners to Investigate Virginia Affairs', 14 April 1623, in *Records of the Virginia Company, Vol. IV*, 118.
[91] Nathaniel Rich, 'Draft of Instructions to the Commissioners to Investigate Virginia Affairs', 14 April 1623, in ibid., 118.
[92] 'Council in Virginia. Letter to Virginia Company of London', 20 January 1623, in ibid., 10.
[93] Smith, *The generall historie*, sigs. R2v.   [94] Ibid., sig. Vv.

Savages to Civilitie'.[95] 'Not being content with taking life alone, [the Algonquians] fell after againe upon the dead', reported the Virginia Company secretary, Edward Waterhouse, 'defacing, dragging, and mangling the dead carkasses into many pieces, and carrying some parts away in derision, with base and bruitish triumph'.[96] Waterhouse did see one good in the attack: the English were now free to apply greater force against resistance. They were set 'at liberty by the treacherous violence of the Savages' for 'right of Warre, and law of Nations' allowed them to 'invade the Country, and destroy them who sought to destroy us'.[97] Widely referenced in London, Waterhouse's tract equated savagery with rebellion, a view that seemed to confirm that, as with the Gaelic Irish he had encountered in Ulster twenty years before, 'savages' and English authority were irreconcilable, and conquest justified.

Ballads, poems, treatises, and letters written in 1622 encouraged subjects to actively condemn those who refuted English values and indulged savagery, projecting it as a danger to the polity as a whole. The colonists who allowed 'those furious wild people to grow upon the[m]' must now draw more distinct bounds or risk losing the largest and most promising colony the English possessed.[98] The call for bloodier initiatives against Algonquians legitimized larger-scale colonial violence as a necessity that would preserve the values of English civil society. In 1623, a broadside circulated a poem written by a 'gentleman in that colony' that celebrated conquest.[99] 'Good newes from Virginia' (not to be confused with Alexander Whitaker's 1613 work of the same name) turned the events of 1622 into a ballad that reinforced the 'savage treacheries' of the 'savage foe'.[100] The poem disseminated colonial news to a wider audience, exalting colonists as heroic figures:

> Bould worthy Sir *George Yardly*
> Commander cheife was made . . .
> Against the King Opukingunow,
> against this savage foe . . .
>
> Stout Master *George Sands* upon a night,
> did bravely venture forth;
> And mong'st the savage murtherers,
> did forme a deed of worth.

[95] Edward Waterhouse, 'A Declaration of the State of the Colony', 1622, in *Records of the Virginia Company, Vol. III*, 553.
[96] Ibid., 551.   [97] Ibid., 556.
[98] Rich, 'Instructions', in *Records of the Virginia Company, Vol. IV*, 118.
[99] 'Good newes from Virginia, 1623', reproduced in *The William and Mary Quarterly*, 5 (1948), 351–8.
[100] Ibid., 353.

For finding many by a fire,
to death their lives they pay:
Set fire of a Towne of theirs,
and bravely came away . . .

The Kings of Waynoke, Pipskoe,
and Apummatockes fled:
For feare a way by *Charles* his Towne,
not one dares show a head.[101]

The verses displayed an awareness of particular Algonquian groups of the
Chesapeake, but local names were invoked only to be razed. Those who
listened to or sang the words were invited to accept the actions of colonists,
and to join in the call to take action against the Powhatans.

Interest in the attack filled diaries and personal letters. The Inns of
Court student William Wynn wrote to his father on 12 July 1622: 'In
Virginia, the savages have by a wile come (as they weare wont) to traffique
into our English howses', where they had subverted the bonds of trust and
ushered war in the locus of English domesticity, the plantation house.[102]
The very tools of English civility – eating utensils and farming and gardening tools – had been stolen or taken as trophies, just as Wahunsenacah had
confessed to John Smith that he had seen the 'carkasses, the dispersed
bones of their and their Countrey men' in the lost colony of Roanoke, and
proved this by showing Smith the utensils his men had recovered from the
site.[103] Simonds d'Ewes, another law student at the Inns, recorded on
7 July 1622 that '[f]rom Virginia wee had exceeding badd newes for the
inhumane wretches wee had given peace too thus long, conspired together
[the colonists] were slaine chieflye in St Martins Hundred'.[104] D'Ewes'
focus on Martin's Hundred is telling. The plantation may have affiliated
with Richard Martin, a Virginia Company member and a respected figure
at the Inns of Court, and suggests a connection between members of the
Inns and their endorsement of plantation, explored at greater length in
Chapter 5.

Six weeks later, d'Ewes added that he was 'partaker of an exact discourse
of the massacre as I may learne it of our men in Virginia', though he
deferred from commenting on the event until he could 'gett the thing it
selfe' through further reading.[105] D'Ewes appears to have actively engaged
with Virginia affairs, exhibiting a desire to gather intelligence about events

---

[101] Ibid., 353–5.
[102] Quoted in 'Notes', *The Virginia Magazine of History and Biography*, 68 (1960), 107–8.
[103] Purchas, *Purchas his pilgrimes*, sig. Mmmmmmmm2r.   [104] 'Notes', 107–8.   [105] Ibid., 107.

in the colony. As in debating other current, sensational affairs, news from Virginia seemed to lend political currency, reinforced by the sense of solidarity in referring to 'our men in Virginia'.[106] The Cambridge reverend Joseph Mead, an avid collector and writer of news, received information of the attack around the same time. He wrote on 13 July that 'this week ill newes come from Virginia (which every man reports that come to London)', that 'the Indians ... fell upon [the colonists] & beat out their braines scarce any escaping'.[107] As well as indicating the pervasiveness of the news in metropolitan discourse, Mead's comments also placed the Chesapeake within the networks of information exchange within and beyond London.

Several lost works, surviving only as brief notes in the Stationers' Register, serve as a reminder that the works on the attack that do survive may only skim the surface of London responses. As Mead noted, news of the English deaths seemed on the lips of all those 'that come to London', and only a small sample of impressions remains. The Stationers' company registers approved a ballad titled 'Mourning Virginia' for print on 10 July 1622, days after the news reached the metropolis.[108] By the following summer, Henry Herbert, master of the revels, licensed 'A Tragedy of the Plantation of Virginia' for the Curtain Theatre.[109] Though these titles indicate little about the content of these texts, Herbert would hardly have approved a play that disparaged English involvement in the Chesapeake at a critical moment in its survival, and the 'tragedy' of Virginia presumably recounted the deaths of the English at the hands of Algonquians. It is uncertain whether the play ended with bloody resolutions, though elaborate and gruesome spectacles were certainly regular features of Jacobean tragedy. Even as Herbert licensed the play, he did so under the condition that its high level of profanity be purged first.

'Our Royal Empire': Sovereignty over Savagery

The attack brought the urgency of Virginia Company mismanagement to the fore, with competing factions blaming the policies of the other for the

---

[106] Ibid.

[107] 'The Indian Massacre of 1622: Some Correspondence of the Reverend Joseph Mead', ed. Robert C. Johnson, *The Virginia Magazine of History and Biography*, 71 (1963), 408–10, at 408.

[108] Catherine Armstrong, 'Reaction to the 1622 Virginia Massacre: An Early History of Transatlantic Print', in *Books between Europe and the Americas: Connections and Communities, 1620–1860*, ed. Leslie Howsam and James Raven (Basingstoke: Palgrave 2011), 23–41, at 30.

[109] Claire Jowitt, *Voyage Drama and Gender Politics, 1589–1642: Real and Imagined Worlds* (Manchester: Manchester University Press, 2003), 202.

colony's dire circumstances. A distressed John Ferrar equated the physical carnage with the heated atmosphere of the London courts, where he held the attack against colonists' bodies to be less damaging than its effects on the honour of the London council. 'Wee have hadd a Massacre . . . no lesse unexpected nor daungerous then yo[u]rs, p[er]happs more', Ferrar wrote to Francis Wyatt, 'the execuc[i]on beinge not uppon mens bodyes . . . butt uppon the Honour Creditt & reputac[i]on of those . . . whereon under God the Colloneys life seemeth to depend'.[110] Both the colonists' relationship to the Powhatans, and the resentments between opposing company factions, could be described the same way: 'the tearmes betwixt us and them are irreconcilable'.[111] The disagreements and resentments grew so impassioned that members of the company ultimately appealed to the king to arbitrate, despite the potential damage such an action might cause to their private interests.

Colonists' struggle in America did not only affect the king's image as sovereign over indigenous peoples, but also brought into question his ability to care for his own subjects. After fifteen years of the Virginia Company's relative freedom in managing overseas affairs, with successive charters granting the corporation increasing power, the royal investigation of 1623 allowed James to proclaim his sovereignty over his subjects more forcefully. The king asked his privy councillors to carry out investigations that involved travelling to Virginia and confiscating company papers from private households by force. Considering the 'faction and distraction among them, being followed on both sides w[i]th much eagernes and animositie', James forbade the House of Commons to intervene, promising 'to rid them of the thornie business touching Virginia'.[112] The king, Chamberlain reported, would no longer rely on the Lower House to debate the matter, but intended to bring the business under his direct oversight.

To James, as to many observers, the company had proven incapable of governing itself, much less managing colonial affairs, without his direct interference. The very structure of a joint-stock company endowed it a republican potential that did not sit comfortably with the Privy Council. Captain John Bargrave accused Edwin Sandys of harbouring a 'malicious heart to the Government of a Monarchy', though his insistence that Sandys

---

[110] 'Coppie of a Letter to S[i]r Frauncis Wyatt and M[aste]r George Sandys', 18 December 1622, Ferrar Papers, FP 437.
[111] 'The Generall Assemblies Replie to those foure propositions made unto them by the Commissioners', 20 March 1623, The National Archives, CO 1/3, f. 48r.
[112] John Chamberlain to Dudley Carleton, 30 April 1624, The National Archives, SP 14/163, f. 110r.

proposed a 'popular Government' in Virginia did not seem to be taken seriously, even by Sandys' opponents.[113] Nonetheless, Sandys admitted that if the king disapproved of the company's government, he would need to change its joint-stock system. 'These Plantations, though furthered much by your Majesty's grace', Sandys pointed out, were upheld by private adventurers who would naturally fail to take interest in 'the regulating and governing of their own business [if] their own votes had been excluded'.[114] Joint-stock companies were well suited for advancing commercial interests, but the territorial control and land management required to affix Virginia to the English polity was a different matter.

After years of admonishing the Virginia council for its disagreements and poor handling of affairs, James finally 'reserved of the whole cause to his own hearing'.[115] James seemed to have exerted considerable effort in overseeing the disputes, receiving petitions from colonists and their representatives in London and ordering Ferrar to bring all Virginia Company patents, invoices, and account books to the council chamber, to be securely kept by the keeper of the council chest.[116] The king commissioned drafts of a new charter for Virginia. 'There is a Commission of Privy Counsellors and others appoynted to advise upon a fit Patent to be given to the Company of Virginia [at] last being overthrowne', Francis Nethersole reported to Dudley Carleton.[117] 'The Reformation intended as I heare is that there shall be a Company for trade, but not for Government of the Countrey of w[hi]ch his Ma[jes]ty will take care'.[118] Nethersole added that the 'popularitie of the Gover[n]ment' had 'beene also o[ver]throwne' as it was 'displeasing to his Ma[jes]ty'.[119]

Tensions ran high. In his invective against the merchant Thomas Smythe, Edward Sackville, fourth Earl of Dorset, 'caried himself so malapertly and insolently that the k[ing] was faine to take him downe soundly and roundly'.[120] Several months later, the Earl of Warwick and William Cavendish, second Earl of Devonshire, were reported to have gone to France to duel over the affair.[121] The gentleman Robert Bing was excluded from the Virginia commission in March 1623 because he had displayed 'saucy conduct before the Council table, and offensive behaviour to Lord

---

[113] Craven, *Dissolution of the Virginia Company*, 277.   [114] Ibid., 284.

[115] The King to the Speaker of the House of Commons, 28 April 1624, The National Archives, SP 14/163, f. 106r; Chamberlain Carleton, 30 April 1624, SP 14/163, f. 110r.

[116] Meeting at Whitehall, 26 June 1624, The National Archives, PC 2/34, f. 344v.

[117] Francis Nethersole to Dudley Carleton, 3 July 1624, The National Archives, SP 14/169, f. 19r.

[118] Ibid.   [119] Ibid.

[120] Chamberlain to Carleton, 19 April 1623, The National Archives, SP 14/143, f. 30.

[121] Chamberlain to Carleton, 26 July 1623, The National Archives, SP 14/149, f. 64.

Southampton'.[122] He would be released from Marshalsea prison only after giving satisfaction to Southampton, for '[t]he business in hand is weighty and serious'.[123] James took the final measures necessary to assume clearer control of his colony in 1624, after pressuring the Virginia Company to surrender its patent.[124] Colonization, 'this worthie action reserved by the Devine providence', was to 'bee perfected and Consumate, by his Royall hands'.[125] Colonization seemed to hinge on the stabilizing presence of the civilizing sovereign who alone could now bring order to the disarray in the courts, as to the colony itself.

Policies towards and experience among the Powhatans figured large in domestic debates over the colony's fate. The deprivation of the 1609 Starving Time was attributed partly to an inability to trade successfully for corn. Members of the company cited the nightmarish conditions of Thomas Dale and Thomas Gates' martial regimes to remind their audiences that 'some were driven through unsufferable hunger unnaturally to eate those things w[hi]ch nature most abhorrs, the flesh . . . of o[u]r owne Nation as of an Indian digged by some of his grave after he had lyene buried three dayes . . . wholly devoured'.[126] Others 'put themselves into the Indians hands though o[u]r enemies, and were by them slayne'.[127] The events in 1622 crystallized the idea that the 'trecherous enemy the Savadges' helped to bring about the 'ru[i]ne of o[u]r state', though the governor and the council tried 'their uttermost and Christian endeavo[u]rs in prosecuting revenge against the bloody Savadges . . . employeinge many forces abroad for the rootinge them out'.[128] The dissolution of the Virginia Company forced discussions about sovereignty to be articulated in relation to the reality of events in Jamestown.

In this way, correspondence that survives from the Virginia Company years – letters, commissions, reports, even poems directly naming members of the council – serves a distinct role in how subjects articulated political ideas. These actively influenced how the king came to project his conception of an imperial polity. Quentin Skinner argues that modern ideas of the

---

[122] Attorney General [Thomas] Coventry to Secretary [Edward] Conway, 25 July 1624, in *Calendar of State Papers: Colonial, Vol. 1*, 65.

[123] Ibid.; 'Upon the humble submission of Robert Bing, gentleman', 25 March 1623, The National Archives, PC 2/31, f. 635r.

[124] Lord President [Henry] Mandeville to Secretary Conway, 17 October 1623, The National Archives, SP 14/153, f. 87.

[125] Governor Wyatt and Council of Virginia to the Privy Council, 17 May 1626, in 'Documents of Sir Francis Wyatt, Governor', *The William and Mary Quarterly*, 8 (1928), 157–67, at 166.

[126] 'A copy of a Brief Declaration of Virginia in the first 12 years', 1624, Ferrar Papers, FP 532.

[127] Ibid.   [128] Ibid.

state derive less from the evolution of legal theories than from the early histories, advice books, and mirror-for-princes literature emerging from the political turmoil of Italian city states in the late medieval period.[129] These tracts were concerned with how rulers might obtain honour and renown while promoting their subjects' well-being, and sought to relate regional particularities to more abstract ideas of statecraft. This view of political power, Skinner contends, as personal and open to counsel operated not unlike the absolute monarchy propounded by the Stuarts in early seventeenth-century England, where the powers of government were often considered inseparable from the character and will of the king.[130] Skinner argues that such thinking developed specifically from advice manuals and treatises in Europe, incorporating reactions against ideologies of popular sovereignty that sprang from the religious wars in France. While the influence of European political works should not be downplayed, a case might also be made for the letters that came to the attention of the king and the Privy Council as a result of the early colonial projects. The Virginia Company's struggles and ultimate appeal to James called for solutions that would benefit the common good, articulated in language that corresponded to that observed by Skinner. However coincidental, it is notable that John Chamberlain associated the Virginia Company quarrels with those of the Ghelphs and Ghibellines, supporters of competing claimants to political authority in the northern city states of medieval Italy.[131] In invoking a historical example of public dispute over political authority, Chamberlain emphasized how debates about the colonies had become important issues of state, bringing quarrels into the streets and the Royal Exchange.

Gentlemen in London articulated political disintegration as a specific consequence of Powhatan agency, drawing on their knowledge of events to impart political advice. George Wyatt's letter to his son Francis contained many of the stylistic devices characteristic of Elizabethan and Jacobean political counsel. 'Let the severitie of justice not let blud too m[uch] that it cause not a Consumption in the body too weake alreddy', Wyatt urged, adding, 'State secrets and Hopes are safest kept [in] one bosome'.[132] At the same time, the letters have a distinctly novel element in their engagement

[129] Quentin Skinner, 'The State', in *Political Innovation and Conceptual Change*, ed. Terence Ball, James Farr, and Russell L. Hanson (Cambridge: Cambridge University Press, 1989), 90–131, at 96.
[130] Ibid., 103.
[131] John Chamberlain to Dudley Carleton, 26 July 1623, The National Archives, SP 14/149, f. 64r.
[132] George Wyatt, 'A letter of advice', 116.

with the Powhatans. Wyatt adapted well-known attitudes towards rule and government by applying them to a world that had not been part of the English governing landscape even twenty years before. 'Your brow of Providence is to looke with Janus two waies', Wyatt wrote, 'on your owen Countrimen Christians, and on the Salvage Infidels'.[133] Opinions towards those 'salvages' bore on how stability and authority might be justified and achieved. Caution, Wyatt wrote, was '[t]he first Military precept your Barbarians have tought you now'.[134] These were hard lessons, he acknowledged, and only knowledge of the land and its peoples would prompt his fair-minded son to take the necessary initiatives to strengthen the vulnerable colony. Francis, Wyatt urged, must learn to be less trusting, and to respond to devastation with force.[135] Wyatt's advice to form a permanent militia to protect the area from attack sprang from a need to fight savagery: 'your Militia ... will searve you against suche an Enimie ... the wilde and fierce Savages'.[136] This corroborated the views of other commentators, who specified that only after colonists implemented what 'may be aptly termed a Militarie intendencie' would the colony 'tie Virginia as fast to England as if it were one terra firma with itt'.[137]

Similarly, George Percy's 'Trewe Relacyon', also written in 1624, used the specific conditions he had experienced in Jamestown to expound more generally on conduct. As Mark Nicholls has suggested, Percy's 'Relacyon' read like a letter of advice. Written to counsel and to guide, it emphasized the morality and deference to authority 'entirely appropriate to a narrative fashioned by an older generation for the instruction – and improvement – of the young'.[138] This reinforces the notion that those who wrote about colonization saw it as a clear parallel to, or even a didactic tool for, the civilizing initiatives within England itself. The experiences wrought among the uncertainty and hardships of that 'new' world were not incidental, even to those who never travelled there, but a comprehensive part of a widening English identity. The behaviour of *all* English subjects, contrasted against but also compared unfavourably to those 'savages' in America, was part of an overarching project that sought to promote deference and submission within the English realm and its dominions.

This is not to imply that all letters by counsellors and governors from Jamestown were specifically written to advise policy-makers on abstract matters of state, but that one substantial consequence of the struggles and

---

[133] Ibid., 114.   [134] Ibid.   [135] Ibid., 118.   [136] Ibid., 120–1, 125–7.
[137] 'Right ho[nora]ble I have tendered to my Lord President . . .', 9 Dece[m]b[er] 1622, British Library, Add MS 12496, f. 433r.
[138] 'George Percy's "Trewe Relacyon"', 237.

debates over Virginia was to force a better articulation of the transatlantic polity, and to do so in ways that put these ideas more concretely into motion. Privy councillors specifically asked for details on how the colony 'now stands in respects of the Salvages'.[139] When Francis Wyatt wrote to the London assembly describing how the colony might be secured in 1623, and again the following year, he did so in direct response to its specific requests for information.[140]

The 'Discourse of the Old Company', written in 1625, serves as a final example. Composed by defeated members of the company after the loss of its charter, the discourse acknowledged that Virginia's best hope for survival now rested in the king's direct control. Old members of the company used the document largely as a space to defend and to justify their actions against the slanders brought about by the company's fall, and the Sandys–Southampton faction specifically called to mind 'those Twelve yeares Governm[en]t' between 1607 and 1619 to paint a picture of stunning failure in the absence of strict metropolitan oversight. Members described the destitution, poor defences and resource control, martial law, few women, 'doubtfull Termes' with the Powhatans, and severe restriction of 'their Lib[er]ties, being violently deteyned as serv[an]tes' to conclude that nothing but the king's 'Royall authoritie' would work for the good of everyone involved.[141] A dedicated London council, acting in the interest of the state while protecting the private interests of English subjects, would enable 'by his Ma[jes]ties Royall authoritie, w[i]th consent of Parliament, bothe Plantac[i]ons might be annexed to the Imperiall Crowne of this Realme'.[142]

Only strict royal and parliamentary control would allow Virginia to truly be incorporated into the unique governing system of the English state in ways that would benefit monarch and subject alike. When overseen by 'Royall authoritie, w[i]th consent of Parliament', the 'Imperiall' polity would promote economic activity that deployed traditional systems of indentured labour, land management, and governance to achieve expansion and longer-term settlement. The articulation of kingly participation depended on the management of savagery:

---

[139] 'The general Assemblies answer to those Propositions made by the Com[m]issioners to be p[re]sented to the lords of his Ma[jes]ties most hono[ura]ble privy Counciel', 20 March 1623, British Library, Add MS 62135(II), f. 211r.

[140] See, for example, the letters between the General Assembly of Virginia and the Privy Council commissioners, March 1624, in *Calendar of State Papers: Colonial, Vol. 1*, 28–9.

[141] 'Discourse of the Old Company', April 1625, in *Records of the Virginia Company, Vol. IV*, 519–21.

[142] Ibid., 546.

The wounds w[hi]ch since that great wound of the Massacre, it hath more lately receaved, from their hands whom it least beseemed, are still so wide & bleedinge, that unlesse his Ma[jest]ie, and yo[u]r Lo[rdship]ps as deputed from him, shall vouchsafe to apply a Soveraine hande for the healing of them, *wee are resolute of opinion*, that it is impossible, the Plantation carried as formerly by private persons, should either prosper or long subsist.[143]

Heavily involved with the royal investigation, the privy councillor Julius Caesar collected reports from his brother-in-law John Martin, then in Virginia, who suggested that members of the nobility be appointed 'by his Ma[jes]ties counsel and company two seates, the first in Opuhankanos Island in Pamaunkey river ... The second at Okanahone River' to better control Algonquians and other colonists.[144] The internal disputes, the significance of the 'wound of the Massacre', and news from the colony prompted James and his councillors to involve themselves in colonization in more active and intrusive ways. As the lawyer Thomas Floyd wrote in 1600, the chief purpose of monarchy – the 'royal estate of an empire or government' – was to avoid the 'sturdy stormes of pinching misery' and dissent, and the aftermath of the attack called for a forceful manifestation of royal sovereignty.[145] 'We humbley refer unto your Princely conscideration', the assembly wrote to James in 1624, '[i]nvokinge that divine and supreame hand to p[ro]tect us'.[146]

Despite James' persistent belief in a monarch's absolute authority, the Virginia Company had not, in its early stages, been a domain where the king had sought to impose his authority with any real force. The early 1620s must therefore be seen as a decisive moment in which the English Crown recognized its responsibilities towards overseas settlements for the first time.[147] In his capacity as lord chancellor, Francis Bacon wrote to investors in 1620 to inform them that the king had instructed him to apply renewed energy to recovering the debts due to the Virginia Company for the advancement of plantation.[148] The honour of the state was involved, Bacon wrote, and the enterprise could not be allowed be fail. In 1623, Samuel Purchas attributed the successful flourishing of an imperial polity

143   Ibid., 530. Emphasis added.
144   John Martin to Julius Caesar, [1622?], British Library, Add MS 12496, f. 436r.
145   Thomas Floyd, *The picture of a perfit common wealth describing aswell the offices of princes* (1600; STC 11119), sig. B10v.
146   'The answere of the general assemblie in Virginia to King James', 16 February 1624, Ferrar Papers, FP 527.
147   'A report of S[i]r George Yeardlyes going Governor to Virginia', FP 93.
148   Francis Bacon to an adventurer for Virginia, November 1620, Ferrar Papers, FP 193.

to the king's 'singular, masculine, reall, regall, absolute [power] over his own', framing the triumph of the civilizing project in distinctly masculine and royal terms.[149] In 1624, Captain Bargrave wrote to the Duke of Buckingham about draft proposals given to the king, 'whoe promiseth to read it himself, this being the sole and onely safe and profitable way to plant Virginia'.[150] Following his father's death in March 1625, Charles immediately affirmed that he would maintain the plantation as he did the rest of his dominions, expressing his belief that joint-stock companies were good for business but dangerous to the state. Virginia would 'immediately depend upon Our Selfe, and not be committed to any Company or Corporation', Charles proclaimed, 'to whom it may be proper to trust matters of Trade and Commerce, but cannot bee fit or sage to communicate the ordering of State-affaires'.[151]

*

By the 1620s, the presence and possibility of America was woven into the lives of those who were committed to advancing the civil life of the realm and the reputation of their nation. Viewing plantation through the lens of metropolitan oversight reveals how deeply Virginia's fortunes had become related to Protestant providentialism and the honour of imperially minded gentlemen. The 'care that I have of this plantation', Richard Martin wrote in 1610, is a '[f]ire that doth not onlie burn in mee, but flames out to the view of everyone'.[152] The colonial intelligence addressed to London gentlemen was often the result of this active desire to stay informed. '[L]et me understand', Martin told Strachey, praising his faithfulness as an intelligencer and urging him to 'deale Clearly w[i]th me'.[153] It was 'the direction & protection of Godes divine providence' that would allow the English to 'shine as the starres in the firmament', and colonists and councillors alike were 'partakers of this promisse [sic]'.[154]

James' eventual decision to involve himself directly in Virginia Company debates is significant. Firstly, it suggests that by acknowledging 'that worke w[hi]ch wee have begunne', the king was prepared to assume responsibility for Virginia, and that his interference was the result of the letters and petitions presented to him and his Privy Council from 1619

[149] Samuel Purchas, *The kings towre* (1623; STC 20502), sig. D6r.
[150] Captain John Bargrave to the Duke of Buckingham, October 1624, The National Archives, SP 14/173, f. 150r.
[151] Quoted in Horn, *A Land as God Made It*, 279.
[152] Richard Martin to William Strachey, 14 December 1610, Folger Shakespeare Library, MS V.a.321, f. 62r.
[153] Ibid., f. 63r.   [154] Ibid., ff. 62v–63r.

onwards.[155] Secondly, James' increased attention to America suggests that the king recognized that addressing affairs in the colony was crucial to settling the tensions wrought between competing visions of government and civil society held by members of the elite in his own realm. The Earl of Warwick had attributed the miseries that had befallen those in the colony 'p[ar]tlie through want of good gov[ern]ment and direccons both here and there', and the new patents were to be confirmed by acts of Parliament that provided stronger measures of oversight from London.[156] The process through which this occurred fostered a more nuanced dialogue about the realities of what political expansion actually involved.

In advocating 'the civilizinge of the Indians as a matter of the greatest consequence', the Virginia Company had encouraged gentlemen to view their own civil self-awareness through the intimate conditions of encounter. While Bermuda and Newfoundland often entered debates over commodities like tobacco, fish, and ambergris, prolonged interaction with the Powhatans necessarily involved discussions of subjugation and rule, forcing complex articulations of English civility. Some might be 'discouraged from this worthy enterprise, by raylers and scoffers', wrote the keeper of the king's silkworms, John Bonoeil, but such men were 'next a kinne, indeed, to the hatefull Savages, enemies herein to God, their King, and Country'.[157] Bonoeil's text read like a conduct manual, linking colonial support with the appeal of silk cultivation and a disdain for those who derided expansion. Englishmen who mocked the wishes of 'God, King, and Country' were not only uncivil, but also actively *against* the civilizing project. Refinement would come from setting themselves apart: 'there is a naturall kind of right in you, that are bred noble, learned, wise, and vertuous, to direct [the Algonquians] aright, to governe and command them'.[158]

By the time Thomas Hobbes – himself a shareholder in the Virginia Company, where he attended meetings with his patron, William Cavendish, in the 1620s – published *Leviathan* in 1651, he sought to paint a picture of civil government that both conceded to the rights of the people while promoting absolutist political allegiances, reconciled in citizens choosing to 'renounce and transfer' their authority to a guardian of state, the monarch.[159] Without a king, Hobbes maintained, the state

[155] 'Commission to Sir Francis Wyatt', 26 August 1624, in 'Sir Francis Wyatt, Governor: Documents, 1624–1626', ed. Minnie G. Cook, *The William and Mary Quarterly*, 8 (1928), 157–67, at 160.

[156] Nathaniel Rich, 'Notes of Letters from Virginia', May/June 1623, in *Records of the Virginia Company, Vol. IV*, 161.

[157] Bonoeil, *His Majesties gracious letter to the Earle of South-Hampton*, sig. M3v.   [158] Ibid.

[159] Skinner, 'The State', 117.

remained a headless aberration, a government no more effective than those held by 'savages' living outside the structures and institutions that society offered. Hobbes specifically evoked Native American ways of life as examples of lust-driven communities that let nature dominate reason, drawing on tropes about continual warfare that were partly a reflection of the ideas crystallized under James.[160] The many exchanges between London and the Chesapeake not only helped a fledgling colony to stabilize and to develop its distinct identity in its critical early decades. They also exposed a metropolitan sphere that was invariably implicated in the world it had sought to transform.

[160] Thomas Hobbes, *Leviathan* (1651; Wing H2246), 62–3.

CHAPTER 3

Cannibalism and the Politics of Bloodshed

Shipwrecked on St Lucia in 1605, the English passengers of the Guiana-bound ship *Olive Branch* found themselves in open conflict with Carib-speaking peoples. Recording his experiences in an account published in London shortly after his return, the mariner John Nicholl recalled watching his shipmates die. Left 'onely with a companie of most cruell Caniballs', Nicholl felt he and his companions were 'seeing as in a Glasse, the utter ruine and Butcherly murthering of our owne selves, being we made most assured accompt to drinke of the same Cuppe'.[1] What is striking in Nicholl's account, as in most narratives by Englishmen purporting to encounter 'cannibals' first-hand, is the absence of any description of actual man-eating. Failing to describe rituals of consumption, Nicholl was most disturbed by the extremity of violence.

As the English began to engage with Native American groups in the Caribbean and South America, they were prone to reflecting on these experiences 'as in a Glasse' to examine 'our owne selves'. To many Jacobean political thinkers, the state of nature offered the starting point for investigating the origins and functions of the civil state, including the role of the Crown and its agents in mediating conflict.[2] Cannibals were consistently depicted as the enemies of mankind, embodying extreme savagery in a way that allowed policy-makers and moralists to examine the destructive consequences of rejecting the combined authority of the Crown and the Protestant Church.[3] The English pitted cannibal violence, understood to embody raw nature in its most anarchic form, against the ideal subject to explore the nature of society, the need for charity and

---

[1] John Nicholl, *An houre glasse of Indian newes* (1607; STC 18532), sigs. B3r, D2v.
[2] Noberto Bobbio, *Thomas Hobbes and the Natural Law Tradition* (Chicago, IL: University of Chicago Press, 1993), 1.
[3] Pierre d'Avity [tr. Edward Grimeston], *The states, empires, & principalities of the world* (1615; STC 988), sig. Aa2v.

interpersonal amity, and the role of the monarch and the law in maintaining order.

In particular, the prominence of civility as an instrument of reform rendered cannibalism an important term for thinking about violence and the rights of bloodshed. One of Norbert Elias' central assertions in *The Civilizing Process* is that subjects' adherence to the rules of civility 'stands in the closest relationship to the monopolization of physical force' by the monarch.[4] The Crown's drive to civilize its subjects, Elias argues, was an attempt to re-balance social forces within the developing state through internal pacification.[5] This did not negate the need for violence altogether, but it did affect who might legitimately carry out acts of violence, and in what contexts. Elias contends that a consequence of the move from a feudal society to a court-centred administrative regime meant that subjects from the sixteenth century now tended to commit acts of large-scale violence in crisis points like war or conquest.[6] Few historians in the twenty-first century would argue for a neat progression, but Elias' insistence on the centrality of managing violence as a marker of civility is worth examining, particularly as Elias does not consider the drive to 'civilize' through colonization as informing concepts of state power.[7]

The pervasiveness of the cannibal in political discourse was effective precisely because Native Americans were not a metaphor. Although English understandings of indigenous American societies were often flawed or incomplete, the acknowledgement of indigenous practices added weight and urgency to English people's debates about their own civil society. The first part of this chapter establishes how European interactions with America in the sixteenth century revised classical associations of man-eating. The second section argues that examining ideas of cannibalism in debates over Catholic transubstantiation, self-seeking factionalism, and the breakdown of trust helps to situate late Elizabethan and Jacobean anxieties around social change within an imperial framework. The chapter closes by considering the relationship between a subject's physical body and the body politic, where manifestations of tearing apart or breaking bodies resonated with the king's understanding of treason and his right to shed blood for the good of the state. The presence of Native

---

[4] Elias, *The Civilizing Process*, 447; *Weber: Political Writings*, ed. Peter Lassman and Ronald Speirs (Cambridge: Cambridge University Press, 1994), 310. On the shared values of policy-makers who sought to enforce standards of behaviour, see Hindle, *The State and Social Change*, 35.

[5] Mennell, *Norbert Elias*, 66–9.　　[6] Ibid., 55.

[7] For the 'multi-vocality' of civility and the role of duels in complicating Elias' thesis on the monopolization of violence, see Peltonen, *The Duel in Early Modern England*, 11.

Americans in political discourse suggests that domestic articulations of civil society developed alongside, and partly as a result of, a civilizing project that could not be separated from English aspirations in the Atlantic.

English Encounters with Cannibalism

European knowledge of humans eating each other dated to antiquity. The fifth-century BC Greek writer Herodotus was an early chronicler of anthropophagy:

> Beyond the desert the androphagi dwell . . . The [a]ndrophagi have the most savage customs of all men: they pay no regard to justice, nor make use of any established law. They are nomads and wear a dress like a Scythian; they speak a peculiar language; and of these nations, are the only people that eat human flesh.[8]

The recurrent associations between cannibalism and savagery appeared almost universally in subsequent texts. Cannibals were described as living beyond the pale of human civilization, lacking laws and systems of justice, speaking differently, and setting themselves apart by their taste for human flesh. Invoked in philosophical treatises, travel narratives, epic poetry, and political works by Aristotle, Pliny, and Juvenal, man-eating became short-hand for groups like the Scythians that existed on the margins of civil life.[9] In the hierarchy of societies, cannibals occupied the lowest rung of humanity, if indeed they were human at all.

Nonetheless, travel reports and rumours of cannibalism in Brazil and the Caribbean changed pre-existing ideas of man-eating in specific ways. Columbus' term for Caribs provided the linguistic base from which 'canibe' or 'cannibal' likely derived.[10] English writers originally used the Greek term 'anthropophagy' to discuss instances of man-eating, as indicated in the humanist and statesman Thomas Elyot's *Bibliotecha Eliotae* (1542).[11] In the second half of the sixteenth century, clearer distinctions between 'anthropophagy' and cannibalism emerged as a result of European

---

[8] Quoted in William Arens, *The Man-Eating Myth: Anthropology and Anthropophagy* (New York: Oxford University Press, 1979), 10.

[9] Andrew McGowan, 'Eating People: Accusations of Cannibalism against Christians in the Second Century', *Second-Century Journal of Early Christian Studies*, 2 (1994), 413–42, at 426.

[10] *The Four Voyages of Christopher Columbus*, ed. and tr. J. M. Cohen (London: Penguin, 1969), 17, 215; also Arens, *The Man-Eating Myth*, 44. Scholars largely accept Shakespeare's Caliban in *The Tempest* (1611) to be an anagram of this.

[11] Thomas Elyot, *Bibliotheca Eliotae* (1542; STC 7659.5), sig. Dr. Elyot published an earlier version of this dictionary in 1538, where 'anthropophagi' specifically described peoples from Asia. Thomas Elyot, *The dictionary of syr Thomas Eliot knyght* (1538; STC 7659), sig. Gg4v.

exploration. Sebastian Münster's popular *A treatyse of the newe India*, translated by Richard Eden in 1553, described man-eaters as 'people called *Anthropophagi*, which are wont to eate mens fleshe'.[12] These inhabitants 'live al naked' and are 'barbarous and rude', sharing similarities with their classical forbears.[13] André Thevet's *The new found worlde*, translated into English in 1568, depicted a 'Countrey of *Canibals, Anthropophages*, the which regions are comprehended in America, compassed with the Ocean sea'.[14] Though Thevet felt that the word 'anthropophagy' was enough to indicate to readers that certain groups of Native Americans ate human flesh, his work also located the cannibals specifically within the geographic confines of the 'new' world.

Though some continued to use the terms interchangeably, the association between cannibals and America became widely maintained by contemporaries. Richard Eden's translation of another cosmography, Peter Martyr's *De Orbe Novo*, described 'the wylde and myschevous people called *Canibales*, or *Caribes*, which were accustomed to eate mannes flesshe (and called of the olde writers *Anthropophagi*)'.[15] Eden's *Decades* was published before Thevet's book, and the term 'anthropophagy' did not disappear from print after contact with peoples in the Amazon and Caribbean, but his comment does indicate that those living in sixteenth-century England recognized a difference between the 'olde writers' and the recent developments that had endowed Europe with new knowledge about the world and its peoples. Cosmographies, engravings, and woodcuts depicting the 'four parts of the world' often personified America as a cannibal, leg in hand. Unlike stereotypes about Jews or witches eating human flesh in demonic rituals in Europe, 'manhuntyng *Canibales*' were portrayed as fierce and warlike peoples who actively preyed on surrounding groups and were described in political terms: 'invaydynge theyr country, takynge them captive, [and] kyllyng and eatyng them'.[16]

The French Protestant Jean de Léry's account of living among the Tupinambá in Brazil, frequently cited by English writers, showed sensitivity to the lives and social practices of Tupi rituals. Yet he too saw cannibalism as indicative of bloodlust:

[12] Sebastian Münster [tr. Richard Eden], *A treatyse of the newe India with other new founde lands and islandes* (1553; STC 18244), sig. E7r.

[13] Ibid., sig. Piv.

[14] André Thevet [tr. Thomas Hacket], *The new found worlde* (1568; STC 23950), sig. Piir.

[15] Peter Martyr [tr. Richard Eden], *The decades of the newe worlde or west India* (1555; STC 647), sig. A3r.

[16] Ibid.

These barbarians, in order to incite their children to share their vengefulness, take them one at a time and rub their bodies, arms, thighs, and legs
with the blood of their enemies ... When the flesh of a prisoner, or of
several ... is thus cooked, all those who have been present to see the
slaughter performed gather joyfully around the *boucans*, on which they
gaze with a furious and covetous eye, contemplating the pieces and members
of their enemies.[17]

Readers of Samuel Purchas' *Purchas his pilgrimes* (1625) could have read
Léry's account in English for themselves, as well as other instances of
cannibalism appearing in the narratives of exploration that Richard
Hakluyt and Purchas collected from travellers. There were descriptions
of 'many ... killed in Chila, whom the Savages flaied and eate, hanging up
their skinnes in their Temples'; the Spanish who, in 1535, escaped drowning
only to be 'eaten by the savages'; unrest in Hispaniola and Cuba when 'the
Savages did rise against' Columbus and his crew.[18] While these accounts
often recounted the experiences of the French or Spanish, the English
insinuated that they had also encountered cannibal societies. In his voyage
to Guiana, Walter Ralegh described 'those Canibals of Dominica' and
Trinidad who navigated the islands through which 'our ships passe
yearly'.[19] Francis Drake's voyage through the West Indies in 1585 included
the violent death and 'savage kind of handling [of] one of our boyes' from
whom the inhabitants had 'taken his head and his heart, and had strangled
the other bowels about the place, in a most brutish and beastly manner'.[20]
Although many explorations were described in the past tense, cannibals
remained living, contemporary beings in these sources, engaged with in the
present tense: 'abhominable' men who 'eate mans flesh'.[21] The parallel
existence of those peoples made them a threatening reality.

This association between Native American violence and the term 'cannibal' is reinforced by English distinctions between consuming flesh out of
necessity and as an indicator of ferocity. The fear of moral and even
physical disintegration into savagery became chillingly relevant after the

---

[17] Jean de Léry, *History of a Voyage to the Land of Brazil*, tr. Janet Whatley (Berkeley: University of
California Press, 1992), 126–7.

[18] Richard Hakluyt, *The discoveries of the world from their first original ... Briefly written in the Portugall
tongue by Antonie Galvano* (1601; STC 11543), sigs. H4v, M2r, F2v; Richard Hakluyt, *The principal
navigations, voyages, traffiques and discoveries of the English nation* (1598–1600; STC 12626a).

[19] Walter Ralegh, *The discoverie of the large, rich, and bewtiful empire of Guiana* (1596; STC 20634), sigs.
D3v, Nv.

[20] Purchas, *Purchas his pilgrimes*, sig. Yy3v. The head and heart may have been taken as trophies and
objects of consumption; see *The Taking and Displaying of Human Body Parts as Trophies by
Amerindians*, ed. Richard J. Chacon and David H. Dye (New York: Springer, 2007).

[21] Purchas, *Purchas his pilgrimes*, sig. Ooo2v.

English attempted sustained colonization first-hand. Hakluyt included an instance of Englishmen in Newfoundland eating each other out of dire hunger in 1536, and the colonist George Percy wrote a description of anthropophagy during the harrowing Starving Time in Jamestown in the winter of 1609/10. A teenage girl's skull and leg bone, uncovered by archaeologists at Jamestown in 2012, indicates multiple, tentative incisions that substantiate Percy's allegations.[22] Forensic investigation found that attempts were first made to open the cranium from the middle of the forehead, followed by blows to the back of the head. Further punctures and markings were made to access not just the brain but to also remove flesh and muscles from the face and leg, evident in the tibia found with the skull in a deposit of snake vertebrae, dog and horse bones, and other food remains dating from the Starving Time.[23] 'And now famin beginneinge to Looke gastely and pale in every face', Percy wrote, survivors had to 'doe those things w[hi]ch seame incredible, as to digge upp deade corpes outt of graves and to eate them. And some have Licked upp the Bloode w[hi]ch hathe fallen from their weake fellowes'.[24] Rumours recounted by John Smith and circulated in London in the 1610s described how a man in Jamestown had killed his pregnant wife and eaten her, offering a stinging indictment of a Protestant enterprise that gained its legitimacy through the promise of 'civilizing' others.[25]

Although the Virginia Company challenged these allegations, no author, even Percy or Smith, referred to English colonial anthropophagy as cannibalism. This suggests that these authors considered connotations of 'cannibal' unsuitable for hunger cases. Writing to Dudley Carleton in 1600, the news writer John Chamberlain reported a story about an adventurer and his crew who were forced to land in Puerto Rico and faced 'such want that they were fain to eate one another'.[26] Tales of starvation on islands or during city sieges likewise avoided the word.[27] The omission of this term in these cases implies that 'cannibal' was closely related to Native American anthropophagy and considered more relevant in describing

---

[22] 'Jane' skull, found in a deposit dating from *c.*1609 to 1610, Jamestown Rediscovery, 8205-JR.

[23] James Horn, William Kelso et al., *Jane: Starvation, Cannibalism, and Endurance at Jamestown* (Williamsburg, VA: Colonial Williamsburg Foundation, 2013). With thanks to Jim Horn and Merry Outlaw for sharing the forensic details and allowing me to view the skull.

[24] 'George Percy's "Trewe Relacyon"', 249.

[25] Rachel B. Herrmann, 'The "tragicall historie": Cannibalism and Abundance in Colonial Jamestown', *The William and Mary Quarterly*, 68 (2011), 47–74.

[26] John Chamberlain to Dudley Carleton, 10 October 1600, The National Archives, SP 12/275, f. 143v.

[27] Hakluyt, *The principal navigations*, sig. L4r; Léry, *History of a Voyage to the Land of Brazil*, 212; Valentine Dale to Lord Burghley, 28 August 1573, The National Archives, SP 70/128, f. 108v.

situations outside of famine. Descriptions of Europeans casting lots to determine whom to eat first reinforced that acts of anthropophagy committed by those suffering from hunger were undertaken reluctantly and under immense strain.

It was the awareness of Tupi and Carib ways of life, though half understood or clouded by assumptions, that provoked Jacobean writers to draw on ideas of cannibalism in their political discourse. For this reason, the scholarly attention to human consumption in medicine or food studies is insufficient to explain anxieties about cannibalism in the early seventeenth century. It is certainly true that medicinal uses of human body parts meant that incorporation might be condoned in particular cases.[28] Pharmacopoeias suggested powdered skull as a cure for 'falling sickness' or fits, and some physicians considered human blood to contain curative properties.[29] Though one scholar deemed it 'inarguable' that 'early modern Europeans ate each other for therapeutic purposes', this statement is tempered by the fact that in such cases, 'eating each other' largely entailed making medicinal use of bodily excretions or pulverized bone, following the medical advice of the physicians Galen and Paracelsus.[30]

As this chapter argues, English ideas about cannibalism often related more to violence than to flesh-eating. John Nicholl's short account of Anglo–Carib conflict on St Lucia offers the fullest account of direct English conflict against groups considered to practise cannibalism. It is far shorter and less ethnographically rich than the accounts of Europeans in Brazil from Léry or the German Hans Staden.[31] The text is useful, however, in that it provides a Jacobean engagement with Native Americans from the Caribbean outside of Hakluyt and Purchas' immense compendia, where Nicholl's slim work was cheaply available to curious readers specifically drawn to news from America. Nicholl situated the English travellers on 'an

---

[28] For an overview, see P. Kenneth Himmelman, 'The Medicinal Body: An Analysis of Medicinal Cannibalism in Europe, 1300–1700', *Dialectical Anthropology*, 22 (1997), 183–203.

[29] Ibid., 197.

[30] Louise Noble, '"And Make Two Pasties of Your Shameful Heads": Medicinal Cannibalism and Healing the Body Politic in "Titus Andronicus"', *English Literary History*, 70 (2003), 677–708, at 681; Richard Sugg, '"Good Physic but Bad Food": Early Modern Attitudes to Medicinal Cannibalism and Its Suppliers', *Social History of Medicine*, 19 (2006), 225–40; Louise Noble, *Medicinal Cannibalism in Early Modern English Literature and Culture* (New York: Palgrave Macmillan, 2011).

[31] While scholars have queried Staden's interpretation of his imprisonment, anthropologists have also used the account to re-construct aspects of tribal practices in Greater Amazonia that are in keeping with current Guarani oral tradition and cosmographical meaning. *Hans Staden's True History: An Account of Cannibal Captivity in Brazil*, ed. Neil L. Whitehead (Durham, NC: Duke University Press, 2008), 123, 128; *The Gift of Birds: Featherwork of Native South American Peoples*, ed. Ruben E. Reina and Kenneth M. Kensinger (Philadelphia, PA: University Museum, 1991).

island of caniballs, or men-eaters in the West-Indyes'.[32] As in many other accounts, the initial, more peaceable exchanges with indigenous groups involved trade, gift-giving, and dining together.[33] As anxieties grew between the English, Caribs, and other European powers, Nicholl described the Caribs as 'most strange and ugly, by reason they are all naked, with long blacke haire hanging downe their shoulders, their bodies all painted with red … which makes them looke like divels'.[34] Other Englishmen who spent more time observing customs in the Caribbean and South America noted that red body paint was not always intended to look threatening. Rather, some indigenous groups liberally applied red earth to their bodies so that 'the Muskitas [mosquitoes] or Flies shall not offend them', while in Algonquian colour symbolism, body paint made from the puccoon root related red to land, mountains, and masculinity, given the colour's associations with copper and therefore virility or high status.[35]

Though quick to associate Caribs with lawless aggression, Nicholl did not claim to witness acts of cannibalism himself. He associated 'cannibals' with anarchic violence, including the tearing and dismembering of bodies, rather than human consumption. In portraying the Caribs as 'cruel and bloodye' enemies who preferred to massacre the English than to provide succour to suffering human beings, Nicholls imparted to his readers an association between excessive violence and unreason.[36] This corresponded to widely current assumptions about the Caribbean, but it also exposed the crew's vulnerability in an environment dominated by Native Americans.

Anthropological approaches to indigenous lifeways can bring new insights to English colonial texts. The anthropologist William Arens critically assesses purported instances of cannibalism in his influential *The Man-Eating Myth* (1979), arguing that most documented cases of man-eating were European misrepresentations, either accidental or intentional, of indigenous beliefs. This prompted a wave of scholarship that re-examined colonial encounters within a larger cultural and literary understanding of the early modern era and economies of power. European scholars argued that cannibalism fascinated writers and travellers because of its relevance to post-Reformation

---

[32] Nicholl, *An houre glasse of Indian newes*, sig. B3r.   [33] Ibid., sigs. B4r, C2v.   [34] Ibid., sig. B3r.

[35] William Davies, 'Captain Thornton's Expedition to the Amazon on Behalf of the Grand Duke of Tuscany, 1608', in *English and Irish Settlement on the River Amazon*, 144; Margaret Holmes Williamson, *Powhatan Lords of Life and Death: Command and Consent in Seventeenth-Century Virginia* (Lincoln: University of Nebraska Press, 2003), 48–53.

[36] Nicholl, *An houre glasse of Indian newes*, sigs. C4r–v.

debates about incorporation, whether in terms of assimilation and submission to authority or in debates about religious rites, notably the Eucharist.[37] Arens' research frequently appeared in post-colonial scholarship that emphasized how imperial powers used ideas about cannibalism to legitimize expansion and subsume 'subaltern' peoples.[38]

Though Arens rightly questions European depictions of Native Americans in the context of expansion, there is some danger in dismissing the 'cannibal' label altogether, or in arguing that the historical reality of cannibalism is unimportant. The tendency in some areas of cultural studies to place too much emphasis on representation can be problematic. It has become commonplace to argue that English perceptions of 'others', however mistaken, matter as much – or even more – than reality, insofar as this can be re-constructed.[39] In the context of colonization, this risks continuing to marginalize indigenous societies by dismissing anthropological practices, inadvertently rendering them incidental to the matter at hand. One of the more positive responses to Arens' work has been to prompt more detailed fieldwork and research by archaeologists and anthropologists. Through the examination of human body parts, skulls, burial pits, and interaction with surviving indigenous groups and their oral traditions, archaeologists have found that the taking and occasionally consuming of human body parts functioned in a range of ways, from obtaining prestige, avenging death, humiliating the enemy, legitimizing political power, transferring attributes to skilled fighters, and assisting in religious

[37] Cătălin Avramescu, *An Intellectual History of Cannibalism*, tr. Alistair Ian Blyth (Princeton, NJ: Princeton University Press, 2009); Neil L. Whitehead, 'Hans Staden and the Cultural Politics of Cannibalism', *The Hispanic American Historical Review*, 80 (2000), 721–51; Janet Whatley, 'Savage Hierarchies: French Catholic Observers of the New World', *The Sixteenth Century Journal*, 17 (1986), 319–30; Janet Whatley, 'Food and the Limits of Civility: The Testimony of Jean de Léry', *The Sixteenth Century Journal*, 15 (1984), 387–400; C. Richard King, 'The (Mis)uses of Cannibalism in Contemporary Cultural Critique', *Diacritics*, 30 (2000), 106–23; Shirley Lindebaum, 'Thinking about Cannibalism', *Annual Review of Anthropology*, 33 (2004), 475–98, at 486.

[38] Stephen Greenblatt, *Marvellous Possessions: The Wonder of the New World* (Chicago, IL: University of Chicago Press, 1991); Frank Lestringant, *Cannibals: The Discovery and Representation of the Cannibal from Columbus to Jules Verne*, tr. Rosemary Morris (Cambridge: Polity, 1997); *Cannibalism and the Colonial World*, ed. Francis Barker, Peter Hulme, and Margaret Iversen (Cambridge: Cambridge University Press, 1998); Peter Hulme, *Colonial Encounters: Europe and the Native Caribbean, 1492–1797* (London: Methuen, 1986); Kelly Watson, *Insatiable Appetites: Imperial Encounters with Cannibals in the North Atlantic World* (New York: New York University Press, 2015).

[39] Bellany and Cogswell, *The Murder of King James I*; Herrmann, 'The "tragicall historie"'; Alessandro Arcangeli, 'Dancing Savages: Stereotypes and Cultural Encounters across the Atlantic in the Age of Exploration', in *Exploring Cultural History: Essays in Honour of Peter Burke*, ed. Melissa Calaresu, Filippo de Vivo, and Joan-Pau Rubiés (Farnham: Ashgate, 2010), 289–326.

ceremonies, shedding light not just on violence but on a host of inter-connected issues.[40]

English writings about 'cannibals' must be treated with appropriate levels of scepticism, but approaching these texts with different questions can offer a starting point for thinking more carefully about English responses to the indigenous Atlantic. Beyond its associations with physical incorporation, the term 'cannibal' in English travel writings appears to have been intended to refer to a range of socio-cosmic beliefs and practices that were fundamental to the ideologies and identities of Tupi and Carib groups. When the Englishman Anthony Knivet spent most of the 1590s in Brazil, he wrote about the many groups he encountered, acknowledging differences between the Tupi-Guarani, Tapuia, and Carib.[41] Knivet encountered these individuals in a variety of situations, sometimes as friends or fellow captives, other times as enemies or sources of profit to be taken and traded into slavery. Knivet spent years among the Tamoio (Tupi), and it would be easy to assume his continual references to 'the cannibals' operated solely as a kind of debasement of Brazilian societies. Yet anthropologists have found that vengeance, with and without cannibalism, was a driving force in Tupinambá warfare in both the pre- and post-contact eras.[42] The word 'Guarani' derived from the word for 'war', and the jaguar was a vital life force, predatory but also an important agent of change and invention.[43] What Knivet and other observers seemed to be describing when they wrote of cannibals or warriors adopting the properties of jaguars

---

[40] James B. Peterson and John G. Crock, '"Handsome Death": The Taking, Veneration, and Consumption of Human Remains in the Insular Caribbean and Greater Amazonia', in *The Taking and Displaying of Human Body Parts*, 547–74, and Richard J. Chacon and David H. Dye, 'Conclusions', in ibid., 630–49, at 632–42; Donald W. Forsyth, 'Beginnings of Brazilian Anthropology: Jesuits and Tupinambá Indians', *Journal of Anthropological Research*, 39 (1983), 147–78; Peggy Reeves Sanday, *Divine Hunger: Cannibalism As a Cultural System* (Cambridge: Cambridge University Press, 1986); Carlos Fausto, *Warfare and Shamanism in Amazonia* (Cambridge: Cambridge University Press, 2012); Beth A. Conklin, *Consuming Grief: Compassionate Cannibalism in an Amazonian Society* (Austin: University of Texas Press, 2001). For anthropological relativism and indigenous responses to English violence, see Christine M. DeLucia, *Memory Lands: King Philip's War and the Place of Violence in the Northeast* (New Haven, CT: Yale University Press, 2018); Andrew Lipman, '"A Meanes to Knitt Them Together": The Exchange of Body Parts in the Pequot War', *The William and Mary Quarterly*, 65 (2008), 3–28.

[41] 'The admirable adventures and strange fortunes of Master Antonie Knivet', in Purchas, *Purchas his pilgrimes*, sigs. Ggggg3r–Iiiiij5v.

[42] John M. Monteiro, 'The Crises and Transformations of Invaded Societies: Coastal Brazil in the Sixteenth Century', in *The Cambridge History of the Native Peoples of the Americas: Vol. 3, South America*, ed. Frank Salomon and Stuart B. Schwartz (Cambridge: Cambridge University Press, 1999), 973–1024, at 986–9; Fausto, *Warfare and Shamanism*, 1.

[43] Fausto, *Warfare and Shamanism*, 4, 187.

was the very real place that vengeance and enmity played in the organization and social coherence of select coastal groups in Brazil.

Cannibalism and the Protestant Polity

When seeking to establish settlements along the Orinoco and Amazon
Rivers, English explorers wrote about and acknowledged Tupi political
hierarchies, spiritual beliefs, and the circulation of enslaved peoples among
groups in Greater Amazonia.[44] Thomas Roe, before he served as an
ambassador in India, first navigated the waterways of Guiana in a canoe.[45]
And from this early moment of exchange, the English began to adapt this
understanding of 'cannibal' violence to describe individuals who chose to
reject the rules of society by behaving outside the bounds of Protestant
orthodoxy. Although it is true that discussions of man-eating emerged
from 'charged contexts for the production of difference', the significance of
the cannibal within English discourse gained its force from the unsettling
notion of similarity.[46] Accounts of English colonists eating their own
countrymen were either denied or defended out of necessity, but a deep
unease about the English capacity for degeneration remained. 'Brutish
Hatred', wrote the translator and sergeant Edward Grimeston in 1621, 'is
more fitting for ravening wolves' than men, better for 'Canniballs and
those monsters which have layd aside all humanity' and invite 'evill into
themselves'.[47] Paralleling Catholic and cannibal behaviour provided
polemicists with an extreme example of savagery, but also with a chance
to expound on the demonstrable consequences of the breakdown of social
order amidst the threat of aggressive Catholic expansion.

  Administered at least once a year at Easter, the Lord's Supper offered
a chance for individuals to come together in reconciliation, serving an
important function in community life by presenting an opportunity to
heal discord in a way that was both spiritually necessary and socially
affirming.[48] Protestant polemicists often accused Catholics of being cannibals who fed on the flesh of their God. Communion was only considered
valid within the established Church, and it was precisely the significance of

---

[44] *English and Irish Settlement on the River Amazon*; Robert Harcourt, *A relation of a voyage to Guiana* (1613; STC 12754); Kemys, *A relation of the second voyage to Guiana*; Nicholl, *An houre glasse of Indian newes*.

[45] John Hemming, *Red Gold: The Conquest of the Brazilian Indians* (Cambridge, MA: Harvard University Press, 1978), 224.

[46] King, 'The (Mis)uses of Cannibalism in Contemporary Cultural Critique', 109.

[47] Nicolas Coeffeteau [tr. Edward Grimeston], *A table of humane passions* (1621; STC 5473), sig. I12v.

[48] Arnold Hunt, 'The Lord's Supper in Early Modern England', *Past & Present*, 161 (1998), 39–83.

the Lord's Supper for both Protestants and Catholics that rendered it a key point of contention. 'The sacrament is numbred amongst the greatest benefits given to us of God in this life,' wrote Christopher Sutton, author of a popular devotional, and there is no reason to doubt that many churchgoers found the experience poignant.[49] The Church of England accentuated the symbolism of the Lord's Supper, meant to provoke inner reflection:

> The divine wordes of blessing doe not *change* or *annihilate* the *substance* of the *bread* and *wine* . . . but it changeth them in *use* and in *Name*. For, that which was before but *common* bread and wine to nourish mens *Bodies*; is, after the *blessing* destinated [*sic*] to an holy use, for the *feeding* of the *Soules* of Christians: and where before they were called but *Bread* and *Wine*; they are now called by the name of those *holy things* which they signifie.[50]

The usefulness of cannibal imagery lay partly in the contrast between corporality and spirituality, false imaginations and true worship. In a union 'made by faith', Protestants must harbour a 'pure and exquisite faith . . . not by the corporall'.[51] Protestant writers depicted Catholics as choosing to enact a sensual version of the Lord's Supper that involved drinking the blood of their Saviour. Tearing 'the heart, wounds, bloud, yea nayles, feete, guts, yea all the parts of Christs humanitie, as though like Cannibals', wrote Stephen Jerome in 1625, was a sort of blasphemy committed by 'Masse Priests & Papists in a blinde devotion'.[52] 'It should be a Christians shame', wrote the Lincolnshire preacher Henoch Clapham in 1609, 'to seeke union with Christ in such a Canibal manner'.[53]

To Protestants, transubstantiation rendered a symbolic act into physical matter, so that Catholics became perpetrators of violence rather than reconciliation. 'If the Canibals are to be abhorred, because they devour and eate mans flesh, their enimies whome they take in the warres', wrote Thomas Lupton, 'are you then much more to be detested, that are not ashamed to eate and devoure . . . the very bodie of Christ your great & high friend?'[54] Faithful Christians abjured violence in favour of love, wrote Thomas Sanderson in 1611, rejecting the 'mysticall and spiritual kind of

---

[49] Christopher Sutton, *Godly meditations upon the most holy sacrament of the Lordes Supper* (1601; STC 23491), sig. F7v.

[50] Lewis Bayly, *The practice of pietie* (1613; STC 1602), sigs. Gg3r–v.

[51] Philippe de Mornay, *Fowre bookes, of the institution, use and doctrine of the holy sacrament of the Eucharist* (1600; STC 18142), sig. Qq3r.

[52] Stephen Jerome, *Englands Jubilee, or Irelands Joyes* (Dublin, 1625; STC 14511.5), sig. M3v.

[53] Henoch Clapham, *A chronological discourse* (1609; STC 5336), sig. Gv.

[54] Thomas Lupton, *A persuasion from papistrie* (1581; STC 16950), sig. Gg3r.

murder and mangling' that came from 'a corporall feeding [like] brutish Cannibals'.[55] Even Herodotus, an early cataloguer of anthropophagy, would find 'this Theophagie . . . incredible' – these 'Theophages (that is, God eaters)' were not like 'the Reader, from whose eyes God of his good-nesse hath removed the veile of superstition'.[56] Sanderson's words implied a sense of complicity against those who acted uncivilly, where membership in Christ's covenant entailed an inclusivity that 'savages' could not share.

Despite the king's attempts to appease the various religious groups who appealed to him for toleration, the Gunpowder Treason of 1605 ruptured James' hopes of keeping his subjects' private conscience separate from political conformity. Following the Main and Bye Plots of 1603, the Gunpowder Treason seemed to confirm what Elizabeth had often claimed, that religion was a mask under which traitors plotted malicious designs. The 'Romish rabble' were 'right Canniballes, lyke to the barbarous people of [America]' for dividing the Church and undermining civil society through violence.[57] Reformers attacked lax church attendance as represen-tative of Catholic subversion, especially in the north, where Guy Fawkes, Thomas Percy, and other conspirators were raised. The recurring refer-ences to tearing raw flesh brought together concerns over civil disobedience and the incivility and unorthodoxy seen to pervade more rural areas of England. Protestantism, obedience to the Crown, and the reformation of manners were all interrelated aspects of the state's civilizing project.[58]

Since the Reformation gave the monarch authority over church and state, issues around the sacraments and acting out one's faith necessarily became tied to concerns over political order. Protestants described Catholics as inviting a warlike mode of life, behaving 'worse than the Canibals & Indies that eat their enimies' because they sought to perpetuate discord in their communities.[59] The act of theophagy was therefore reflec-tive of the more general violence that Protestants believed their Catholic neighbours guilty of, where the torn and broken body of Christ, ripped apart by Christians living in error, symbolized a more general willingness to commit acts of violence that threatened the stability of the state. This extremity seemed to play out most fully in the religious wars in Europe, where religious bloodshed tore apart communities and turned neighbours

---

[55] Thomas Sanderson, *Of romanizing recusants, and dissembling Catholicks* (1611; STC 21711), sig. G3r.
[56] Henri Estienne [tr. Richard Carew?], *A world of wonders* (1607; STC 10553), sig. B3r.
[57] John Nicholls, *The oration and sermon made at Rome* (1581; STC 18535) sig. G6r, and again sig. M8r.
[58] 'Considerations delivered to the Parliament', 1559, Hatfield House, CP 152/96; Richard [Bancroft], Bishop of London, to Robert Cecil, 4 December 1599, Hatfield House, CP 75/15.
[59] William Attersoll, *The badges of Christianity* (1606; STC 889), sig. Y6r.

against each other. In the 1580s, John Foxe deemed the pope 'a cruell Caniball' for encouraging 'troublesome commotions and disordered factions ... wherewith the peace and concorde of Christians is so lamentably shaken and rent asunder'.[60] Forty years later, George Goodwin's Catholic satires made the same associations. Goodwin called 'this powder age' the age of the Catholic '*Flesh-feeder*', teeming with 'Popish *Caniball*[s]' intent on subverting the laws of state.[61] Acting the cannibal became a direct threat against the power of the monarch over his subjects, since these 'bloudy butchers' assumed 'almost a soveraigne power and princely authority' over their own countrymen.[62] As Arthur Marotti notes, the pope's 'politically intrusive ... vision of international order directly conflicted with the kind of political autonomy' that the centrally governed state sought for itself.[63]

The cannibal nature of Catholic belief became incorporated into a broader mistrust of Jesuit radicalism and the question of secular authority. The climate of mistrust towards Jesuits in the 1580s and 1590s was no less prominent under James, despite his promises of toleration. Not all Catholics supported the pope's ordinance that Elizabeth be 'bereved or deprived of hir ... kingdom, and also of all and whatever dominions', but evidence suggests that the Crown's attempts to locate seditions were more than mere paranoia.[64] 'Many Jesuits come into England disguised to meet the King of Spain's ambassador there,' wrote John Hammond to his brother in 1604, and John Chamberlain reported in 1607 that 'there be at least two or three hundred Jesuites priests and friers lately come over, and grow so bold that they go up and downe in some places in their habits'.[65] Catholic families sent their sons to the Jesuit colleges in France and Spain, where impressionable young members of the nobility were exposed to the rigorous Counter-Reformation influence of their Jesuit tutors.[66]

---

[60] John Foxe, *The Pope confuted* (1580; STC 11241), sig. Pr.

[61] George Goodwin, *Babels balm* (1624; STC 12030), sig. Lr; 'That *Feast's* a *Fact*, not of the *Mouth*, but *Minde*', sig. Lv.

[62] Ibid., sig. S4r.

[63] Arthur F. Marotti, *Religious Ideology and Cultural Fantasy: Catholic and Anti-Catholic Discourses in Early Modern England* (Notre Dame, IN: University of Notre Dame Press, 2005), 9.

[64] 'Notes by Burghley relative to the Bull of Pope Pius V, declaring Queen Elizabeth a heretic and deposing her from her regal authority', May 1582, The National Archives, SP 12/153, f. 147r. On the threat Catholics posed, despite their ultimate failure in subverting the regime, see Michael C. Questier, 'Elizabeth and the Catholics', in *Catholics and the 'Protestant Nation': Religious Politics and Identity in Early Modern England*, ed. Ethan Shagan (Manchester: Manchester University Press, 2005), 69–94.

[65] John Hammond to his brother, 28 December 1603, Hatfield House, CP 48/71v; John Chamberlain to Dudley Carleton, 4 August 1620, SP 14/116, f. 88.

[66] Hugh Lee to the Earl of Salisbury, 15 October 1607, Hatfield House, CP 122/129.

Perhaps the most dangerous threat the Jesuits posed was their support of papal deposition, which maintained that subjects possessed the right to commit acts of violence against their monarchs if the pope declared them heretical.[67] William Barlow's sermon at Paul's Cross in 1601 forcefully condemned the teachings and writings of the English Jesuit Robert Parsons, and Jesuits more generally. 'The law of God is straight in this case, it bridels the mouth that it speake not evill of the King, it bindes the hart not to imagine evil against him, and the civil law punisheth with death'.[68] Such intimate language between a subject's duty to his monarch, and the role of the law in punishing disobedience, made cannibalism a potent example of the wrenching effect of factionalism in a community. The clergyman Thomas Wilson wrote in 1614 that:

> Our degenerate and new *Romanes* take a readier way and shorter cut to quit them of their enemies ... by seditions, rebellions, murthers, treasons, stabbing of Princes, blowing up of English parliament-houses, and other such monstrous unnaturall courses ... How far be they from Antichrist, which delight so in the blood of Gods people, [and] in barbarous savage cruelty, such as amongst *Scythians* & Cannibals is not to be heard of?[69]

James also used the figure of the cannibal in 1616 to combat Jesuit claims that Catholic subjects could lawfully depose their monarch.[70] 'A most detestable sentence', James wrote, 'all the barbarous cruelty that ever was among the Canibals ... may passe henceforth in the Christian world for pure clemencie and humanity'.[71] In his rhetorical outrage, James turned to the cannibal and other 'infidels' to express the illicitness of such presumptions, defending himself against those who opposed a king's temporal authority by equating disloyal subjects to 'savages'. James specifically framed physical violence against a monarch as both irreligious and treasonable.

References to cannibalism brought together Protestant fears of an expanding Catholic monarchy with denunciations of Spain's imperial reach. Theodore Herring's thunderous sermon at Blackfriars in 1625 brought these strands together:

> *No marvaile if they who crash their* Saviour *betweene their teeth, make no bones to crush their* Soveraigne. *No marvaile if those* ... GOD-eaters ... *prove* ...

[67] Alexandra Walsham, '"Domme Preachers"? Post-Reformation English Catholicism and the Culture of Print', *Past & Present*, 168 (2000), 72–123, at 81.

[68] William Barlow, *A sermon preached at Paules Crosse* (1601; STC 1454), sigs. B5v–B6r.

[69] Thomas Wilson, *A commentarie upon the most divine Epistle of S. Paul to the Romanes* (1614; STC 25791), sig. Kkkk4v.

[70] James I, *A remonstrance of the most gratious King James I* (Cambridge, 1616; STC 14369), sig. Hh4v.

[71] Ibid., sig. Iiv.

MAN-eaters (*worse then* Cannibals) STATE-devourers. *What may they not doe to advance the* Catholike Cause? *I shall not need to aggravate their Crueltie, Treacherie, their owne* Acts *proclaime it to the World . . . New projects are daily forged on the* Anvills *of the* Jesuites braines . . . *so just is it . . . that their owne tongues and hands, should be the chiefe Heralds to blazon the barbarous and savage disposition of these Blood-suckers to the whole world.*[72]

Commissioned to preach on the twentieth anniversary of the Gunpowder Treason, Herring showed that memories of Catholic plots within the realm had not faded under James. He explicitly drew a connection between Catholic subversion and 'the *slaughter* of the *Indies*', a reference to the popular writings of the Spanish friar Bartolomé de las Casas, who featured often in anti-Spanish discourse.[73] In an inversion of the usual assumptions about cannibalism, the Spanish became more brutal than Native Americans in their wilful denial of human justice. The Spanish camp, rather than indigenous villages, took on the harrowing semblance of a butcher's shop, where leaders kept 'an ordinarie shambles of mans flesh' as a terror tactic to subjugate local populations.[74] In 1626, preaching at Paul's Cross, William Hampton overtly depicted the Spanish as a legion of cannibals: 'Whole Armies of them living sometime like Cannibals, eating nothing but the flesh of Indians'.[75] His use of the word 'shambles' revealed his debt to English translations of Las Casas, but the word also evoked the illegitimacy of a Catholic regime based on unlawful uses of force.

Fears of a Spanish invasion of England appeared obsessively in English discourse into the 1620s. Hampton's appropriation of the Spanish as cannibals, running butchers' camps with body parts as delicacies, sought to impart the frightening possibility of Spanish rule in a domestic realm already prone to faction. 'We have within us, many home-bred and domesticall enemies, who will betray us', Hampton pressed; they will 'joyne hands with this foreign foe, in working our confusion'.[76] South American children starved and killed, families dashed from mountains and forced into mines, men whipped and maimed and driven to anthropophagy, were all manifestations of the 'dreadfull doing of these capitall enemies of mankind' – enemies who were at that very moment warring

---

[72] Theodore Herring, *The triumph of the Church over water and fire* (1625; STC 13204), sig. A5v.
[73] Ibid., sig. Fv.
[74] Bartolomé de las Casas [tr. M. M. S.], *The Spanish colonie, or Briefe chronicle of the acts and gestes of the Spaniardes in the West Indies* (1583; STC 4739), sig. E4v.
[75] William Hampton, *A proclamation of warre from the Lord of Hosts* (1627; STC 12741), sig. Er.
[76] Ibid., sig. D4v.

against fellow Protestants in Europe.[77] John King, preaching at the court in 1608, reminded his audience that the bloody-mindedness of the Spanish extended from America to Christian Europe, fracturing the peace of former times. 'Cruelty is the ensigne and badge of that church', King announced, and 'the diet of the Cannibals'.[78] Generations of cruelty, refined in the theatres of conquest in America, offered an urgent reminder that Catholics, as 'degenerate' Christians, were capable of atrocities that even unconverted souls were incapable of.

Factionalism and Revenge

The visceral language of cannibalism in debates about religion and kingly authority point to enduring Protestant anxieties after the Reformation. Protestant, particularly puritan, writers seemed to detect the vestiges of a lingering and seductive Catholicism everywhere – under floorboards where priests might hide from local authorities, in rosaries and family heirlooms privately kept to commemorate saints, or, most impenetrable of all, in the secrets and longings of the heart. The dangers of Catholicism loomed in fears of non-conformity and in the unsettled legacies of contested theological doctrines.

In condemning the wrongs that came from a disordered society, subjects engaged with ideas of cannibalism in a particular way. They held up the horrors of exocannibalism – the vengeful eating of humans outside one's kin group – to reflect on an especially unnatural form of *endo*cannibalism – not the internal consumption of community members out of love, as one might conceivably categorize a practice like transubstantiation, but out of cruel ill will. The 'civil monster' was one who 'through disorder, and inordinate desires … become unreasonable'.[79] Succumbing to private desire at the expense of the common good showed ingratitude and excess, inducing the perpetrator to live as if he 'devoures in some sort, them of his owne species, society, and bloud. All which the Anthropophages do not. For though they feed on their species … yet they hunt after straungers … observing still some law of society among themselves'.[80]

---

[77] Ibid.
[78] John King, *A sermon preached at White-Hall the 5. Day of November* (1608; STC 14986), sig. Dr. See also Gonzáles de Montes [tr. Vincent Skinner], *The full, ample, and punctuall discovery of the barbarous, bloudy, and inhumane practices of the Spanish Inquisition* (1625; STC 11999), sig. K4v.
[79] *The yonger brother his apology by it selfe* (St Omer, 1618; STC 715), sig. H2v.
[80] Ibid., sigs. H3v–r.

This idea that English cannibals hatefully consumed their own kin displayed a unique adoption of an American trope, challenging assumptions that cannibals were used entirely to 'mark the boundary between one community and its other'.[81] Cicero had described 'fellow-citizens' of the commonwealth as a collective body bound together by social ties, mutual obligation, and common interests. '[W]e are certainly forbidden by Nature's law to wrong our neighbour', Cicero wrote, whereby self-seeking behaviour 'demolishes the whole structure of civil society'.[82] In the playwright Ben Jonson's *The staple of news*, performed in 1625, the cook Lickfinger proposed to go to America to convert cannibals. Desiring to advance 'the true cause', Lickfinger acknowledged that it was 'our *Caniball-Christians*', rather than the '[s]avages', who had to learn to '[f]orbeare the mutuall eating one another,/Which they doe [*sic*], more cunningly, then the wilde/*Anthropophogi*; that snatch onely strangers'.[83] Lickfinger's understanding that indigenous Americans only ate 'strangers', a legal term denoting foreigners, stood in contrast to the broken values of citizenship evident in the incessant rivalries of the play's money-hungry characters.

Since political authority operated through social relationships, various individuals employed notions of cannibalism to criticize neighbours and friends who acted according to their own desires.[84] Peter Lake's study of murder pamphlets indicates that the godly often directly linked social chaos to the failure of household authority figures to promulgate deference, where individual behaviour paralleled larger political anxieties over legitimate rule and the execution of law.[85] The cannibal enters these murder pamphlets too. Upon the discovery of the murdered merchant John Sanders, his servant lamented, '[m]en have no mercy ... they be Caniballes'.[86] The narrator of a 1616 pamphlet commented in an increasingly common trope that 'the Caniballs that eate one another will spare the fruites of their owne babies, and Savages will doe the like', rendering it all the more shocking that the infanticide committed by Margaret Vincent, 'a Christian woman, Gods owne Image', would be 'more unnaturall then

[81] Hulme, *Colonial Encounters*, 86.

[82] Cicero, *On Duties*, tr. Walter Miller (Harvard, MA: Harvard University Press, 1913), 295.

[83] Ben Jonson, *The staple of news* (1631; STC 14753.5), sig. F2v.

[84] Braddick, 'Civility and Authority', in *The British Atlantic World, 1500–1800*, ed. David Armitage and Michael Braddick (Basingstoke: Palgrave, 2002), 113–32, at 114.

[85] Peter Lake with Michael C. Questier, *The Antichrist's Lewd Hat: Protestants, Papists, and Players in Post-Reformation England* (New Haven, CT: Yale University Press, 2002), 79.

[86] *A warning for faire women* (1599; STC 25089), sig. F2v.

Pagan, Caniball, Savage, Beast'.[87] Another text contrasted social order against 'the very Canibals and men-eating Tartars, people devoide of all Christianity and humanity'.[88] The accompanying woodcut displayed two men in the process of dismembering the body. One held the victim's head in one hand while another man pulled out his entrails, drawing unsettling visual parallels between cannibalistic rituals in South America and the acts of uncivil Englishmen. The author appealed to the authority of lawmakers who, as 'his Majesties Deputies and Viceregents', must combat the 'horrid and bloody' behaviour of those who resisted the king's ordinances.[89]

The use of cannibal imagery in these sources shows the flip side of ideal harmony, not in a way that glorified the 'festive yet forbidden pleasures of the world turned upside down', as Lake finds in the inversions of society in murder pamphlets, but by introducing a new paradigm through which to view and uphold norms and values.[90] Unlike the devil, who lurked behind evildoers in woodcuts, enticing them to sin, the dissident who adopted 'savage' behaviour often *became* the cannibal. Those who subverted 'his Majesties authenticall power' were 'blind Cannibals' sinning 'before God in their conscience'.[91] The English cannibal chose to act in accordance with a people who, in the world order explained by moralists, existed outside God's covenant. Acts of oppression and disobedience showed a cruelty 'beseeming rather the savage Cannibals, then any sound hearted Christians', a statement reinforcing the belief that cannibals were not saved but damned.[92]

The juxtaposition between virtue and cannibal malice found further relevance in criticisms of enclosure and the related pursuit of private profit. John Norden's works on surveying were dedicated to landowning gentlemen who wanted to 'see what he hath, where and how it lyeth, and in whose use and occupation every particular is upon the suddaine view'.[93] By 1623, Norden had surveyed 176 manors in attempts to subordinate the landscape to elite oversight. While proponents of enclosure saw the practice as a civilizing project that reformed both landscapes and those who lived on them, the clergyman Thomas Draxe attacked the system for plaguing the labouring poor.[94] 'The Kingdome is weakened', Draxe

---

[87] *A pittilesse mother* (1616; STC 24757), sig. Bv.

[88] *The crying Murther* (1624; STC 24900), sig. A3r. Note the distinction between 'cannibals' and man-eating in other geographical spaces.

[89] Ibid., sigs. A2v–A3r.   [90] Lake, *Antichrist's Lewd Hat*, 129.

[91] John Deacon, *Tobacco tortured, or, the filthie fume of tobacco refined* (1616; STC 6436), sig. Z3v.

[92] Ibid., sig. R4v.

[93] Quoted in Klein, *Maps and the Writing of Space in Early Modern England and Ireland*, 59.

[94] Andy Wood, *The Memory of the People: Custom and Popular Senses of the Past in Early Modern England* (Cambridge: Cambridge University Press, 2013), 343.

asserted in 1613, by 'these cannibal enclosers ... of ill-gotten goods'.[95] Though he himself enabled the process of enclosure in his role as cartographer and surveyor, Norden employed the language of cannibalism in his devotional works to denounce the same. Creditors were voracious in their demand for financial satisfaction, picking at the bones of the indebted as if 'hee would eate his flesh like a Canniball'.[96]

Images of the money-hungry citizen licking up the carnage in his wake evoked a powerful picture of betrayal, one that the merchant Gerard Malynes used in his tract on economics and foreign exchange. The uncivil monster 'gnaweth the poore artificer to the bones, and sucketh out the bloud and marrow from him', he wrote, 'feeding on him most greedily'.[97] Given the emotive nature of credit relations, the breaches of trust in matters of economy were expressed through violent and vengeful behaviour.[98] No one but tyrants, preached John Scull in 1624, including '[c]anibals that eate one another', would treat their neighbours in such a manner, with 'the lesser always beccoming food to the greater, and the stronger prevailing against the weaker'.[99] Scull called for forgiveness as the only way to heal faction, a virtue that seemed to be lacking in a society where no single vision of Christianity unified the realm.

There is also evidence that cannibal language pervaded everyday interactions beyond sermons and written discourse. Accused of being a Catholic and facing a deprivation of arms, the author and soldier Gervase Markham protested that 'he was no more a papist than an atheist or cannibal', explicitly placing the cannibal outside accepted societal values while reinforcing his own place in the commonwealth.[100] A Middlesex deposition included the colourful case of one woman who slandered another by calling her a 'Cannibal whore'.[101] In these instances, those who transgressed social (and perhaps sexual) norms were described as voraciously self-seeking. Though this description did not, presumably, have anything to do with physical violence, it nonetheless continued cannibalism's

---

[95] Thomas Draxe, *The earnest of our inheritance* (1613; STC 7184), sig. Er.

[96] John Norden, *A pathway to patience* (1626; STC 18615), sig. L7v.

[97] Gerard Malynes, *Saint George for England* (1601; STC 17226a), sig. D6v. Léry had also brought usurers into his discussion of Tupi cannibalism in *History of a Voyage to the Land of Brazil*, 132.

[98] Craig Muldrew, *The Economy of Obligation: The Culture of Credit and Social Relations in Early Modern England* (Basingstoke: Palgrave, 1998), 3.

[99] John Scull, *Two sermons* (1624; STC 22123), sig. D3r.

[100] Quoted in *Calendar of State Papers: Domestic, Charles I: 1629–1631*, ed. John Bruce (London: Her Majesty's Stationery Office, 1860), xxii.

[101] 'Introduction', in *London Consistory Court Depositions, 1586–1611: List and Indexes*, ed. Loreen L. Giese (London: London Record Society, 1995), 7–28.

association with excess and vengefulness. Perhaps most intriguingly, these cases suggest that 'cannibal' was a familiar enough frame of reference to appear outside textual modes of discourse, referenced by men and women alike in situations of anger or stress, whether in one's defence of Protestantism, or in slandering members of the community.

These examples present only a selection of the vast range of discourses invoking cannibalism as a symptom of changing social relations. Attention to anxieties over credit and economy help to make sense of the frequency of this metaphor at this particular time, when subjects attacked the lack of trust that caused fellow humans to betray each other. The early modern economy depended on a system of exchanges in which credit and trust were central, where Christian charity and a rejection of open self-interest characterized the ethics of local agreements and contracts.[102] During the reigns of Elizabeth and James, an unprecedented rise in litigation levels profoundly affected community relations.[103] Litigations against individuals who failed to keep their contracts or fulfil their obligations reached a peak between 1580 and 1640, contributing to a sense of fracturing and deceit as well as a significant growth of debt and downward mobility.[104] 'The earth', wrote Thomas Wilson, 'woulde soone be voide for want of men, one woulde be so greedie to eate up another'.[105] This echoed the apostle Paul's letter to the Galatians, that 'if yee bite and devoure one another, take heed ye be not consumed one of another' (Galatians 5:15, KJV).

Litigations often involved attempts to protect private property. The specific presence of the term 'cannibal' in Jacobean critiques of consumption places this 'emerging materialism' and 'souring of interpersonal relations' in the context of expansion.[106] Blood sacrifices and heart-eating were no longer relegated to Mesoamerican societies but to fractured relationships in England, where the impact of expanding trade networks and the

---

[102] Muldrew, *The Economy of Obligation*, 4.

[103] Tim Stretton, 'Written Obligations, Litigations and Neighbourliness, 1580–1680', in *Remaking English Society: Social Relations and Social Change in Early Modern England*, ed. Steve Hindle, Alexandra Shepard, and John Walter (Woodbridge: Boydell, 2013), 189–209; Keith Wrightson, 'Mutualities and Obligations: Changing Social Relationships in Early Modern England', *Proceedings of the British Academy*, 139 (2006), 157–94; Keith Wrightson, *English Society, 1580–1680* (London: Routledge, 1993); Christopher W. Brooks, *Pettyfoggers and Vipers of the Commonwealth: The Lower Branch of the Legal Profession in Early Modern England* (Cambridge: Cambridge University Press, 1986).

[104] Ibid., 3. See also Mark Netzloff, *England's Internal Colonies: Internal Colonialism in Early Modern England* (Basingstoke: Palgrave, 2003).

[105] Thomas Wilson, *The arte of rhetorique* (1553; STC 25799), sig. D2r. Wilson revisited this in *A discourse uppon usurye by waye of dialogue and oracions* (1572; STC 25807), sig. Y2v.

[106] Stretton, 'Written Obligations, Litigations and Neighbourliness', 190.

monopolization of commodities manifested themselves in biting accusations of a possessive ruthlessness that undermined civil bonds. At the very time when the English celebrated their civility as a means of subordinating indigenous peoples and bolstering their own refinement, rising consumption contributed to the very problems of 'cannibal' behaviour that the English accused each other of. As Markku Peltonen discusses in his study on duelling in England, civility operated at the confluence between merchant and courtly society, where the expression of status so essential to elite concepts of honour and authority relied on commercial development and the acquisition of goods.[107] For cannibals to only eat strangers, while the English devoured their native countrymen out of a lust for commodities and wealth, exposed the vindictiveness of the projecting culture that pitted the English against their own.

Savagery and the State

When Francis Bacon expounded on the reasons why man did not eat fellow man, his concerns lay at the intersection between bloodlust and criminality. Man shunned eating man, Bacon maintained, because humanity 'abhorred' it. Further, if witches were anything to go by, cannibalism induced an insatiable appetite that stirred the imagination and encouraged sin. 'Ca[nnibals] (themselves)', Bacon observed, 'eat no Mans-flesh that Dye of Themselves, but of such as are Slaine'.[108] In portraying cannibals as eating only those they killed, Bacon categorized them as murderers. Cannibalism therefore entailed more than one crime against the body. This raises the final aspect of cannibalism discussed in this chapter: how the king and policy-makers in London debated the uses of violence and the legitimate instances in which violence could serve a redemptive or necessary purpose. As James told assize judges in 1616, his subjects' vices 'must be severely punished, for that is trew government', a sentiment that contrasted with the anarchical quality of cannibal violence whereby subjects assumed the power to execute justice themselves.[109]

James frequently expressed his belief that the monarch always acted in the interest of his subjects, his responsibility to govern granted him by God. Appearing in popular devotionals and maxims, conduct books,

---

[107] Peltonen, *The Duel in Early Modern England*, 299–305.
[108] Francis Bacon, *Sylva sylvarum: or A natural historie in ten centuries* (1627; STC 1168), sig. Gg2r.
[109] Quoted in Hindle, *The State and Social Change*, 178.

sermons, and court rulings, the praise of Aristotelian temperance stood in stark contrast to cannibal vengeance, which might immediately serve the individual but detracted from hierarchical authority and arbitration. In 1606, the poet and soldier Barnabe Barnes considered civility a matter of public order, attacking the enemies of the realm who 'disturbe or diabolically roote up the publike State' through a thirst for blood, inducing them like 'canniballes to feed upon the flesh, and to drinke the blood of such noble persons'.[110] The impulsive behaviour that accompanied uncontrolled rage perpetuated sedition, so that he who 'hates the light of government . . . eates like a cannibal'.[111] Laws were a means of regulating the passions of the body politic through reason, so that the enforcement of the law was not seen as excessively harsh but completely necessary.[112]

The carefully prescribed scripts within which Native American captives participated in the narratives of their executions initially seems to resemble denouements on English scaffolds. European prisoners in Brazil, notably Hans Staden and Jean de Léry, portrayed highly ritualized cannibalistic ceremonies that involved specific dialogues between the powerful 'jaguar' warrior and the victim about to be subsumed. The vanquisher who administered the death blow would proclaim his intentions to kill his victim as retribution for previous deaths in war. The prisoner responded by vowing that his friends would avenge him, before '[t]he executioner then strikes him on the back and beats out his brains'.[113] Like Tupinambá rituals, dialogues about martyrdom or repentance adopted by those sentenced to death allowed them some agency to defend their actions, profess their loyalties, or re-enter a sacred covenant that had been broken when they transgressed.[114] However, English discourse consistently described the monarch's exertion of physical power over individuals as fundamentally different from the seeming excess of revenge killings committed by indigenous Americans, which the English directly related to their perceived lack of civility.[115] The condemned on English scaffolds often died verbally re-affirming social and political norms, choosing to restore the relationships they broke in their acts of sin or resistance. Moreover, while the king

---

[110] Barnes, *Foure bookes of offices*, sig. P2r.
[111] Guillaume de Salluste du Bartas [tr. William L'Isle], *Babilon, a part of the seconde weeke* (1595; STC 21662), sig. Cr.
[112] Shagan, *The Rule of Moderation*, 143.   [113] *Hans Staden's True History*, 132–7.
[114] Peter Lake and Michael C. Questier, 'Agency, Appropriation and Rhetoric under the Gallows: Puritans, Romanists and the State in Early Modern England', *Past & Present*, 153 (1996), 64–107, at 69.
[115] George Peckham, *A true reporte, of the late discoveries* (1583; STC 19523), sig. C3v.

re-instated order through bloodshed, English writings observed, Tupi warfare was intended to perpetuate further vendettas.

Michael Foucault addresses the early modern state's publicized control over a subject's body in his *Discipline and Punish* (1975), a text that has been applied to describe a Tudor 'theatre of state' that used violence to reinforce governing ideologies.[116] Foucault's exploration of 'the power exercised on the body ... as a strategy' enables historians to explore contemporary understandings of the moral and physical significance of violence, where the state's display of bodily punishment was often intended to represent the inversion of the intended harm committed against the sovereign.[117] This supports Elias' contention that what changed in the sixteenth century was not the ubiquity of violence, but its transference to other arenas, where subjects consented to the state's authority to punish subjects in order to achieve higher degrees of safety or prosperity, at least in theory. Foucault's theory has its limitations, and scholars have questioned its usefulness for the English context, where lay participation in criminal justice made the display of state power less absolutist than in France.[118] The use of 'cannibal' to discuss litigation and lawmaking does, however, support the findings of legal historians who detected a general willingness among subjects to denounce those who failed to live up to the standards of civility and godly behaviour that county magistrates and metropolitan lawmakers propounded.[119]

The prolonged debates in Parliament over fitting punishments for state crimes indicate the didactic meanings inherent in state-endorsed bloodshed. The House of Commons remained divided over how best to punish the Inner Temple lawyer Edward Floyd in 1621, for example, for his slanders against the princess Elizabeth Stuart and her husband, Frederick of Bohemia. Members discussed varying combinations of physical pain, public humiliation, and imprisonment. What stood out was the need for a punishment that reflected Floyd's transgression, with MPs suggesting 'as many lashes ... as [rosary] beads', 'as many lashes ... as the Prince and

---

[116] Michael Foucault, *Discipline and Punish: The Birth of the Prison*, tr. Alan Sheridan (New York: Vintage Books, 1979); Lake and Questier, 'Agency, Appropriation and Rhetoric under the Gallows', 64; Stephen Greenblatt, *Renaissance Self-Fashioning: From More to Shakespeare* (Chicago, IL: University of Chicago Press, 1980).

[117] Foucault, *Discipline and Punish*, 26.

[118] Lorna Hutson, 'Rethinking the "Spectacle of the Scaffold": Juridical Epistemologies and English Revenge Tragedy', *Representations*, 89 (2005), 30–58; Derek Dunne, *Shakespeare, Revenge Tragedy and Early Modern Law: Vindictive Justice* (Basingstoke: Palgrave, 2016).

[119] Christopher W. Brooks, *Law, Politics and Society in Early Modern England* (Cambridge: Cambridge University Press, 2009), 395.

Princess old', for Floyd to swallow his rosary beads, and for his crucifixes to be pinned to his body.[120] Debates in Parliament and the Star Chamber over appropriate punishments provide the context for Thomas Egerton's extraordinary suggestion in 1605 that the libeller and courtier Lewis Pickering be punished in the manner of 'the Indians by drawing blood out of the tongue and ears, to be offered in sacrifice'.[121] Whether meant in earnest or offered as dry humour after intense debate, Egerton's statement offers a rare glimpse of how indigenous customs might function in dialogue beyond written discourse. Invoked in the law chamber, the notion of sacrificial violence not only indicated Egerton's awareness of America as a cultural referent, but also provided a means through which the habits of American peoples were adapted and engaged with, becoming part of how policy-makers conceptualized their role in prescribing order. At the same time, Egerton's reference to 'Indians', rather than to 'savages' or 'cannibals', differentiated between Native American rites, however crude he believed them to be, and the extreme and anarchic practices of cannibals.

The proceedings following the Gunpowder Treason of 1605 illustrate the clear moral significance ascribed to kingly authority and James' right to regulate the body politic. William Smith's sermon to the king and court following the event described the plotters as cannibals:

> These men were not content with dagger ... and poison for their privie plots [but] a store-house of powder, to the which if all the fire of hell and Purgatorie could have lent & sent but one spark, we had all been consumed ... *praised be to the Lord, who hath not given over for a praye to the teeth of those cursed Cannibals*, who seeing they cannot satiat their mawes with the blood of *Christ*, in their unbloody Sacrament, have sought to ingorge & imbrewe themselves with the blood of Servants.[122]

The reference to cannibalism through transubstantiation allied confessional disputes with political avarice. Those who were hungry enough for 'the blood of *Christ*' would just as happily 'ingorge & imbrewe' themselves with the blood of kings. The physician Francis Herring drew similar themes in his poem against the plot in 1617.[123] The horror of unbridled violence, coupled with false religious justification, contaminated the Lord's

---

[120] 1 May 1621, in *Journal of the House of Commons, Vol. I*, 598–600.
[121] Quoted in Louis A. Knafla, *Law and Politics in Jacobean England: The Tracts of Lord Chancellor Ellesmere* (Cambridge: Cambridge University Press, 1977), 63.
[122] William Smith, *The black-smith: A sermon preached at White-Hall* (1606; STC 22881), sigs. D6r–D7v.
[123] Francis Herring, *Mischeefes mysterie: or, Treasons master-peece, the Powder-Plot* (1617; STC 13247), sig. E3v.

Supper by bringing vengeance to a sacred meal. The oft-published work of
Samuel Garey likewise deemed the Gunpowder plotter Robert Catesby
a cannibal for his actions.[124] The plotters had targeted the 'whole body of
the Parliament house (the head, hart, eyes, braines, and vitall spirits of the
politicke body of the Kingdome)' in an explosion that threatened to leave
the realm headless.[125] In attempting 'the murther of Gods Anointed King',
Catholics proved that 'the very Cannibals are not more thirsty of bloud'
than the realm's own dissidents.[126]

The corporality of treason is evident in these texts, as in the law itself.
When James became king of England, he and Parliament ratified the
medieval definition of treason specified under *25 Edw. III, Stat. 5, c. 2*.[127]
According to this statute, a subject committed treason not against the
related entities of the Crown, the commonwealth, or an abstract state, but
against the person of the king.[128] James regarded his power as embedded in
his personhood, where a subject must naturally defer to his liege lord,
a concept that leading jurists reiterated in *Calvin's Case* (1608). In deeming
those who wished evil on the king 'Romish Cannibals', Oliver Ormerod
appealed to the constraining hand of the law through a visceral mental
image of the destruction awaiting those who broke the sacred bond
between a monarch and his subject:

> Who would ever imagine, that the sonnes of men, could be thus savage . . .
> thus I leave them, wishing that they might be drawne on hurdles from the
> prison to the execution, to shew how they have beene drawne by brutish
> affections: that their privities might be cut off, & thrown into the fire, to
> shewe that they were unworthie to be begotte[n], or to beget others: that
> their bellies might be ripped up, & there harts torne out, & throwne into the
> same fire as being the fountain of such an unheard treacherie; that their
> bodies, having harboured such wicked harts might be cut off from their
> heads and divided into many quartars, as they were in the bodie politique
> divided by treason . . . and that their quarters might be fixed uppon the gates
> of our Cities, and exposed to the eyes of men: that as their nefarious
> attempts were an evil example to others, so their quartered limmes might
> be a heedfull caveat.[129]

As one Spanish Catholic onlooker observed, when the English hanged
Catholics charged with treason, they 'cut open their chest with a knife and

---

[124] Samuel Garey, *Great Brittans little calendar* (1618; STC 11597), sigs. Ddv, Gg3v.
[125] Ibid., sig. Gg4r.   [126] Ibid., sig. Ir.
[127] Lisa Steffen, *Defining a British State: Treason and National Identity, 1608–1820* (Basingstoke:
Palgrave, 2001),9.
[128] Ibid.   [129] Oliver Ormerod, *The picture of a papist* (1606; STC 18850), sig. Tv.

remove their hearts and entrails, and show them to the populace claiming "Here you see the heart of traitor. Long live the King of England"'.[130] The rebellious body opened itself to brutal but calculated correction, and subjects often voiced their opinion that this letting of the 'corrupt blood' from the body of the state differed fundamentally from 'cruell and bloodye Carrebyes' in the Indies.[131] In cases of treason, writers articulated the need for law and violence to operate together. One without the other was weakness or tyranny, whereas the essence of civility lay in balance and control. Though the hanging of dead bodies in public places might appear similar to the practices of human trophy-taking among the Tupinambá, the act was one of restorative justice rather than passion. Litigation and the threat of violence were closely entwined: the law did not staunch violence altogether but decided who was entitled to execute vengeance and define justice.[132]

James' vision of civility as pacification contributed to his disapproval of feuding and duelling. Christianity, with its emphasis on self-control and forgiveness, sat at odds with personal revenge.[133] Duels, James proclaimed, were 'dishonourable to God, disgracefull to the government, and danger-ous to the p[er]sons'.[134] Since they involved a subject's handling of violence rather than the monarch's, feuds and duels were described in language that paralleled cannibalism. Fighting for the sake of personal honour involved a 'bloodthirsty and revenging appetite' that depended on one's 'owne vindictive and bloody humour'.[135] Duels turned 'courage barbarous' and duellers into 'enemies of humane society', meddling in 'an imaginary Honour' that usurped the power of the sovereign.[136] Attacking the conceits

---

[130] From a 1627 book on martyrdom published in Spain, quoted in *The Life and Writings of Luisa de Carvajal y Mendoza*, ed. Anne Cruz (Toronto: Centre for Reformation and Renaissance Studies, 2014), 82.

[131] Nicholl, *An houre glasse of Indian newes*, sig. C4v.

[132] Dunne, *Shakespeare, Revenge Tragedy and Early Modern Law*, 19.

[133] Michel Nassiet, 'Vengeance in Sixteenth and Seventeenth-Century France', in *Cultures of Violence: Interpersonal Violence in Historical Perspective*, ed. Stuart Carroll (New York: Palgrave, 2007), 117–28, at 125.

[134] 'An act to prevent duels and private combats', 28 February 1621, The National Archives, SP 14/119, f. 263r; Proceedings of the Star Chamber, 13 February 1617, The National Archives, SP 13/90, f. 117; John Chamberlain to Dudley Carleton, 22 February 1617, The National Archives, SP 14/90, f. 151. See also Richard Cust and Andrew Hopper, 'Duelling and the Court of Chivalry in Early Stuart England', in *Cultures of Violence*, 156–74, at 157; Markku Peltonen, 'Francis Bacon, the Earl of Northampton, and the Jacobean Anti-duelling Campaign', *The Historical Journal*, 44 (2001), 1–28.

[135] *By the King. A proclamation prohibiting the publishing of any reports or writings of duels* (1613; STC 8490).

[136] Guillaume de Chevalier [tr. Thomas Heigham], *The ghosts of the deceased sieurs* (Cambridge, 1624; STC 5129), sig. D5v.

of his noblemen in 1613, James declared that 'no quarrell of any Subjects can be lawfull, except in defence of their Prince or their Countrey, the revenging of all private wrongs onely belonging to Us'.[137] This stressed that any behaviour contrary to his wishes undermined his desire for domestic peace and expressed a clear belief in the monarch's right to monopolize force.

This sentiment was apparent in Thomas Middleton's *The peace-maker* (1618), a tract whose frontispiece bore the king's own coat of arms. Middleton explicitly envisioned manful behaviour as rejecting physical violence.[138] The text evocatively compared duellers to the bulls and bears in Southwark, fierce in battle but destined for slaughter. 'We stand disobedient and repugnant to our owne just punishment', Middleton wrote, but '*Vengeance* is God's alone; which no man ought to take in hand, but as delivered from his hand; norso [*sic*] to imitate his Majestie and Greatnesse, that does it not but by Authoritie'.[139] *The peace-maker* did not explicitly mention cannibalism, but it drew a connection between behavioural degeneration and American influences. Violence, like tobacco, enchanted young men. 'I thinke the Vapour of the one, and the Vaine-glorie of the other, came into *England* much upon a voyage, and hath kept as close together'.[140]

In many ways, this text complements James' own *A counterblaste to tobacco* (1604), where the king attributed tobacco and the corruption of manners to the breakdown of political order, especially among young gentlemen. Moreover, the Protestant civility advocated in these texts asserted itself against Spanish imperial identities. Before the Anglo–Spanish peace, merchants 'on either side traffiqu't in blood, their *Indian Ingotts* broght [*sic*] home in bloud'.[141] Duelling corrupted the nobility's honour, Middleton wrote, so that 'Pillars at home, that were enforced to be prodigies abroad' risked fracturing 'our *peace* (in her yong plantation)'.[142] Only in becoming temperate 'branches of the great *Olive Tree*' of peace could gentlemen most display their civil qualities, much less transplant them abroad.[143]

---

[137] Ibid.

[138] Thomas Middleton, *The peace-maker* (1618; STC 14387). The tract was so aligned with James' vision of peace that some scholars have ascribed it to the king, though he likely commissioned rather than penned it.

[139] Ibid., sigs. C2r.   [140] Ibid., sig. D2v.

[141] Ibid., sig. Br. These ingots refer to the blocks of gold shipped from South America to Spain for processing.

[142] Ibid., sig. B3v.

[143] Ibid., sig. B3r. The recurring motif of the olive branch is here contrasted against the 'perpetuall deluge of *Blood* and *Enmity*' (sig. A4r), echoing criticisms of Tupi warfare. The olive branch, however, could also represent victory.

In condemning smoking and duelling, James chose to equate false notions of honour to effeminacy and savagery. Similarly, when the Welsh writer and colonial enthusiast William Vaughan urged 'reformed Christians' to 'follow the traces of Gentlemen, & not like unto heathenish Canniballes, or Irish karnes', he contrasted civil behaviour to that of Native Americans and the Gaelic Irish, those groups the English were currently attempting to colonize.[144] Dissenters 'are more savage then the savages of America. They eate men, but they are either strangers, or their enemies: these kill themselves among themselves, kindred, neighbours, friends, conversing together . . . [Native Americans] doe it, not knowing the mischiefe; these doe it, knowing'.[145] Those who spurned the Christian and civic values of an ordered society fell into miserable conditions without a prince to govern them. 'Are you of civil either nature or education?' the civil lawyer John Hayward asked. 'Who under the name of Civilian do open the way for all manner of deceits . . . ? What are you? For you shewe you selfe more prophane then Infidels; more barbarous then Caniballs'.[146]

Hayward's beliefs, supported by James, who granted him a knighthood in 1619, advocated a civil and religious realm where honour was defined not by personal prowess but by submitting to the will and authority of the king. Research on litigations in the Star Chamber and in country courts provide plenty of evidence that the Crown's insistence on overseeing arbitration was gradually becoming effective.[147] Appeals to the king and to local authorities in cases of duels and slander suggest a growing belief in the function of the law. Gentlemen could, and did, appeal to justices of the peace to settle matters of personal honour.[148] Richard Cust's case studies on gentry litigation find that early Stuart gentlemen increasingly subscribed to ideas of honour that celebrated Protestant activism through public service.[149] The value that many subjects placed on the law provided a contrast to the cultures of vengeance seen among the Tupi, but also in Catholic countries like France, where duels and religious persecution

---

[144] William Vaughan, *The golden-grove* (1600; STC 24610), sig. I3r.

[145] Chevalier, *The ghosts of the deceased sieurs*, sig. C6v.

[146] John Hayward, *An answere to the first part of certain conference, concerning succession* (1603; STC 12988), sig. Tr.

[147] Cust and Hopper, 'Duelling and the Court of Chivalry', in *Cultures of Violence*, 163; Dunne, *Shakespeare, Revenge Tragedy, and Early Modern Law*, 20; Steve Hindle, 'The Keeping of the Public Peace', in *The Experience of Authority in Early Modern England*, ed. Paul Griffiths, Adam Fox, and Steve Hindle (New York: Macmillan, 1996), 213–48.

[148] Cust and Hopper, 'Duelling and the Court of Chivalry', 163.

[149] Richard Cust, 'Honour and Politics in Early Stuart England: The Case of Beaumont v. Hastings', *Past & Present*, 149 (1995), 57–94, at 70.

evaded the execution of state justice. The elite became active participants 'in the rhetoric that made law a central part' in changing concepts of civility and refinement, one that subscribed to arbitration and mediation as a means of tempering the behaviour – and the influence – of the 'overmighty'.[150]

Comments on the extremity of cannibal violence in discourse underline the complexities of the Protestant vision of expansion and the civilizing project. On one level, the use of violent language in political discourse might suggest that subjects supplanted the physicality of violence by channelling conflict through rhetoric and slander instead. The gentry's willingness, in many cases, to defer to the law and higher authority signified that humanist morality could effectively shape gentlemanly conduct, and shaming invectives against extreme violence may have served to underscore and codify these ideas.[151] On the other hand, as this chapter has demonstrated, real colonial experiences underpinned the salience of cannibalism as a metaphor. Many of James' subjects resisted his vision of a masculinity that pacified violence altogether. Satirists and puritan MPs often attributed court corruption to an effeminizing luxury that prioritized peace at the expense of military might.[152] Escalating tensions over James' policies in the 1620s led courtiers and MPs to express violence as integral to retaining and expanding their imperial polity. Pro-imperial gentlemen therefore promoted colonization in the Atlantic in ways that both aligned with and at times contradicted the king's own notion of a civil polity and how it would be achieved.

Although subjects attacked certain policies of James', notions of uncontrolled violence ultimately confirmed the necessity of kingly prerogative. None of James' subjects ever referred to the English state itself as cannibalistic. Whereas Protestant writers consistently depicted Spain's monarchy as ravenous and insatiably destructive, they portrayed their state in opposition to the chaotic violence of illegitimate bloodshed, an idea that subjects appeared to have accepted and subscribed to on the whole.[153] The 1613 translation of Montaigne's essays came closest to attacking state measures, but such views do not seem to have been replicated or vocalized by the majority. Montaigne believed that 'the Canibales and savage people'

---

[150] Brooks, *Law, Politics and Society in Early Modern England*, 306, 284.

[151] Cust, 'Honour and Politics in Early Stuart England', 79.

[152] Michelle O'Callaghan, *The 'Shepheards Nation': Jacobean Spenserians and Early Stuart Political Culture, 1612–1625* (Oxford: Clarendon, 2000), 20.

[153] For a discussion on cannibalism and eighteenth-century views of the cruelty of an absolutist state, see Avramsecu, *An Intellectual History of Cannibalism.*

who consumed dead bodies were less savage than those who inflicted torture – 'even in matters of justice, whatsoever is beyond a simple death, I deeme it to be meere crueltie'.[154] Yet English writers never denied the state its right to practise violence through the execution of the law, for the 'mortall plague of Rebellion ... is a sicknesse not to bee cured but by letting blood'.[155] Those who wilfully acted in stubborn error, whether Native American or natural subject, subverted the king's power, becoming 'blind Cannibals in before God [and] their conscience'.[156]

*

Under James, cannibalism – not a staid repetition of an ancient idea, but a response to encounters with Native Americans, and distinct from hunger anthropophagy – began to take a varied role in the expression of civility and governance in England. The influx of thinking politically about cannibalism was a response to a particular historical moment, informed by English experiences in the Atlantic and by changes within the realm itself. The frequent invocation of Carib and Tupi violence in political discourse placed the religious and political uncertainties of post-Reformation England within an emerging imperial polity, one dominated by hopes that America 'may be possessed, planted, and annexed to his Crowne'.[157] This suggests that what contemporaries deemed 'this powder age', the years when the Gunpowder conspiracy lingered powerfully in popular memory, existed within a global vision of authority, partly expressed through a Protestant imperial impulse that held up the horrors of savagery for political ends while de-legitimizing Catholicism.

The physicality of cannibalism lent itself to discussions of the body politic at a time when treason and state violence were closely connected to the physical person of the monarch. Yet ideas around cannibalism were also symptomatic of the troubling effects of the English civilizing project on Atlantic spaces and at home. What often lay behind accounts of cannibal violence was colonial violence more broadly: a series of shifting alliances and conflicts between the English and Native Americans that profoundly altered patterns of mobility, settlement, and the organization of communities. Beyond English descriptions of 'cannibals' lay a rich, uncertain realm of relations that exposed the English to South American and Caribbean

---

[154] 'Of Crueltie', in Michel de Montaigne [tr. John Florio], *Essays written in French by Michael Lord of Montaigne* (1613; STC 18042), sig. X5v.
[155] Quoted in Palmer, 'At the Sign of the Head', in *Cultures of Violence*, 135.
[156] Deacon, *Tobacco tortured*, sigs. Z3v–Z4r.
[157] Harcourt, *A relation of a voyage to Guiana*, sig. K2v.

Figure 4 Blue and red macaw feather headdress from Guiana with small green feathers and hexagonal plaiting at the base. Though the fragility of featherwork makes early modern examples difficult to preserve, this object and its techniques of production illustrate the long-standing importance of feathers in status display and knowledge transmission in Greater Amazonia. By kind permission of the Pitt Rivers Museum, University of Oxford.

mythologies and rituals, and to their material cultures. Objects fuelled the desire for colonial interference and possession, from macaw feather ornaments and iridescent beetles' wings to animal skins and gemstone jewellery (Figure 4). Caribs 'would provide all kinds of delicious fruits', sugar, '[p]arrats, and any thing that they thought we delighted in', Nicholl reported.[158] In applying ideas of cannibalism to the domestic polity to condemn self-serving profiteering, English writers implicitly conveyed that the pursuit of land and global goods had, in effect, generated cannibals rather than destroyed them. Courtiers and merchant projectors, some of those most determined to expand their estates and attain luxury commodities through colonization and trade, were those now devouring the traditional bonds that held the commonwealth together.

From increased enclosure to the rise of litigation, socio-economic changes in the realm impacted individuals on a deeply personal level. This helps to explain why the cannibal metaphor entered discourses

---

[158] Nicholl, *An houre glasse of Indian newes*, sig. C2v; Harcourt, *A relation of a voyage to Guiana*, sig. B4v.

about friendship and betrayal. The popular Pythagorean aphorism 'eat not thy heart' was an appeal to kindness, to a civil society based on community and fellowship. Those who lacked friends with whom to share secrets or unburden themselves were 'devourers of their owne hearts', wrote Ambrose Purchas. 'So great an Enemy to man is this his secret hatred, or aversation [*sic*] to societie, that it causeth him to degenerate ... to become a Caniball'.[159] When Edward Grimeston evoked cannibals as exemplars of hatred and the breakdown of social order, he discussed love as a solution – not marital love, but the bonds of masculine friendship, for 'to banish *Love* from a civill life, and the conversation of men [fills] the whole world with horror and confusion'.[160] In these ways, writers on both sides of the Atlantic advocated a trust-based civil society as an antidote to both actual and metaphorical cannibalism. Those '[h]eathens ... who very bruitishly and cruelly doe dayly eate and consume one another', wrote Robert Cushman from New England, would find reconciliation by the 'peaceable examples' of the English, encouraging 'many of your Christian friendes in your native Countrey, to come to you, when they heare of your peace, love, and kindness'.[161] To Cushman, the solution to cannibalism was a transatlantic society founded on order and harmony, one that negated the uses of violence altogether.

[159] Ambrose Purchas, *Purchas, his paradise* (1635; STC 20501), sig. B2r.
[160] Grimeston, *A table of humane passions*, sig. E3v.
[161] Cushman, *A sermon preached at Plimmoth in New-England*, sigs. Dv–D2r.

CHAPTER 4

Tobacco, Consumption, and Imperial Intent

In December 1624, university tutors in Cambridge made frantic arrangements for a royal visit. Aware of James' personal preferences and keen to avoid his displeasure, the heads of colleges set clear instructions for their students' behaviour. Students were forbidden to smoke anywhere near the king. Any who 'p[re]sume to take any Tobacco in or neere Trinitie Colledge hall' or 'neere any place where his Ma[jes]tie is' faced 'payne of final expelling [from] ye Univ[er]sitie'.[1]

James' dislike for tobacco is well known. He denounced its ruinous effects in *A counterblaste to tobacco* (1604), published shortly after he ascended the English throne. His offhand references to tobacco in subsequent years continued to express his aversion. Proclamations that dealt with the tobacco trade were prefaced by a reminder of how much James detested this 'new corruption' of 'mens bodies and manners'.[2] When he prepared to attend a sermon at St Paul's Cathedral in 1620, desiring to 'stir up others by his princely example', the king ordered that tobacco houses near the west gate of the church be 'pulled downe to the ground and the sellers and vaultes filled up, that there be noe signe left remaining of any such houses or vaultes there'.[3]

Many scholars have dismissed James' distaste for tobacco, and anti-tobacco tracts more generally, as the dull rantings of a pedant set on hampering the inevitable. Smoking, after all, proliferated in Jacobean London.[4] The leaf unfurled its husky, impertinent sovereignty over the

---

[1] 'Orders and Monitions', 8 December 1624, in *Records of Early English Drama: Cambridge, Vol. 1*, ed. Alan H. Nelson (Toronto: University of Toronto Press, 1989), 597.

[2] *By the King. A proclamation to restraine the planting of tobacco in England and Wales* (1619; STC 8622); *By the King. A proclamation concerning tobacco* (1624; STC 8738).

[3] A letter to the Lord Bishop of London and the Dean and Chapter of the Cathedrall Church of St Paule, 23 March 1620, The National Archives, PC 2/30.

[4] Michael Ziser, 'Sovereign Remedies: Natural Authority and the "Counterblaste to Tobacco"', *The William and Mary Quarterly*, 62 (2005), 719–44; Jeffrey Knapp, 'Elizabethan Tobacco', *Representations*, 21 (1988), 26–66; Sandra Bell, 'The Subject of Smoke: Tobacco and Early

metropolis and in port towns in ship barrels and sailors' pouches, grocers' shops and medicine cabinets, becoming an object of mass consumption by the 1630s.[5] Tobacco imports escalated throughout the century, from an estimated 1,250 lbs in 1616 to 500,000 lbs by 1624.[6] At the Inns of Court, gentlemen discoursed about plays and the law at end-of-term suppers that featured the stuff of still life paintings, the tables piled with chickens, figs, 'sugar and spice', almonds, artichokes, oysters, lobsters, and, from the seventeenth century, tobacco.[7] Like its personification in urban wit poetry, tobacco seems to emerge victorious despite its detractors.

This chapter focusses on the tensions between tobacco's appeal and the difficulty smoking presented to authorities concerned with reforming manners and maintaining socio-political order. Tobacco and civility, after all, were not obvious associates. Purloined from Native Americans, widely smoked by sailors and travellers, and largely sourced from the Spanish West Indies, the commodity initially offered an evocative parallel to the smoke and incense of Catholic subversion. By the 1620s, however, many Members of Parliament, and eventually the king himself, used tobacco to articulate a larger commitment to empire, particularly after the outbreak of the Thirty Years' War. Beginning with policy-makers' unease about the disruptive potential of tobacco, this chapter explores the process through which pro-imperial gentlemen navigated their concerns and sought to turn smoking into a legitimate feature of their political culture. Rather than remove the intoxicant from the world of politics, gentlemen used tobacco to express their imperial intent, relating their smoking habits directly to plantation landscapes and the subordination

---

Modern England', in *The Mysterious and the Foreign in Early Modern England*, ed. Helen Ostovich, Mary V. Silcox, and Graham Roebuck (Newark: University of Delaware Press, 2008), 153–69; T. H. Breen, *Tobacco Culture: The Mentality of the Great Tidewater Planters on the Eve of the Revolution* (Princeton, NJ: Princeton University Press, 1985); Morgan, *American Slavery, American Freedom*; Jordan Goodman, *Tobacco in History: The Cultures of Dependence* (London: Routledge, 1993); Peter C. Mancall, 'Tales Tobacco Told in Sixteenth-Century Europe', *Environmental History*, 9 (2004), 648–78.

[5] Beverly Lemire, *Global Trade and the Transformation of Consumer Cultures: The Material World Remade, 1500–1820* (Cambridge: Cambridge University Press, 2018); Alison Games, *The Web of Empire: English Cosmopolitans in the Age of Expansion, 1560–1660* (Oxford: Oxford University Press, 2008); Carole Shammas, *The Pre-industrial Consumer in England and America* (Oxford: Clarendon, 1990); on the agency of plants, see Michael Pollan, *The Botany of Desire: A Plant's Eye View of the World* (New York: Random House, 2001).

[6] James Horn, *Adapting to a New World: English Society in the Seventeenth-Century Chesapeake* (Chapel Hill: University of North Carolina Press, 1994), 6.

[7] Bill for Parliament suppers in Hilary Term, 1612/13, The Middle Temple, MT.7/SUB/1; Termly bills for Parliament suppers, 1618, The Middle Temple, MT.7/SUB/2; Bills for Parliament suppers, 1632/3, The Middle Temple, MT.7/SUB/3.

of indigenous groups. To its proponents in Parliament, the tobacco monopoly that the king granted Virginia and Bermuda in 1624 was an assertion of independence from Spain. English-sourced tobacco became a physical manifestation of a civil society bolstered by the successful flourishing of transatlantic plantation.

Tobacco in England

Ambiguities around tobacco and civility were expressed in discourses about health, the body, and socio-political regulation. How and why individuals smoked mattered to political thinkers who frequently drew parallels between the physical body and the body politic, linking the health of the individual to wider society. Descriptions of the plant's botanical properties and forms of consumption were informed by the contexts of its production and use. Though domestic planting could be lucrative, tobacco brought English consumers into the evocative world of the Chesapeake and the Caribbean. Reports described English travellers sitting 'all night by great Fiers, drinking of Tobacco, with extraordinarie myrth amongst our selves' after interacting with Carib women and collecting tropical fruits, infusing the commodity with potent imaginings of the kind of consumption possible through imperial interference.[8]

Sailors returned with tobacco from the Atlantic voyages captained by John Hawkins from the 1560s, and men and women began to grow, smoke, and sell tobacco with increasing frequency. On a certain level, tobacco was one medicinal herb among many, incorporated by physicians, travellers, writers, and planters into a larger understanding of pre-existing medicines. The merchant John Frampton's translation of the Spanish physician Nicolás Monardes' *Joyfull newes out of the newfound world* included a botanical illustration of the tobacco plant and a section outlining the virtues of tobacco. Monardes offered a detailed explanation of how tobacco healed headaches, toothaches, swellings, and other ailments. Using 'stamped leaves' in particular provided 'mervellous medicinable vertues'.[9] Describing how best to apply tobacco to the body in each of these occasions, he concluded that 'in woundes newly hurte, and cuttes, strokes, prickles, or any other maner of wounde, our *Tabaco* worketh marvellous effectes'.[10]

---

[8] Nicholl, *An houre glasse of Indian newes*, sig. C3r.
[9] Nicolás Monardes [tr. John Frampton], *Joyfull newes out of the newefound world* (1580; STC 18006), sigs. Jv, J3v.
[10] Ibid., sig. Kr.

Numerous physicians in James' reign reiterated this belief.[11] Surviving copies of medicinal treatises show markings and underlining in the pages describing tobacco, where readers jotted down their impressions on tobacco in the margins for easier reference.[12] Physicians often viewed the temperate consumption of tobacco as capable of removing the aches and discomforts inconveniencing people in their day-to-day lives. Tobacco's dry consistency seemed well placed to offset the dampened humours caused by illness, as when the traveller Fynes Moryson wrote of Lord Mountjoy, the lord deputy of Ireland, that tobacco prevented him falling ill, 'especially in Ireland, where the foggy aire . . . doe most prejudice the health'.[13] Edward Reynolds, clerk of the privy seal, wrote a letter to his brother in 1606, hoping some of 'Cosen Bagges tobacco' would help to combat the pains in his chest with which he had been 'freshlye assaulted'.[14] Tobacco offered a practical solution to everyday ailments, including to those who, like Mountjoy or Reynolds, were employed in the service of the state in unfamiliar environments where their bodies might be more vulnerable to disease.

Always keen to benefit from projects and monopolies, James imposed high taxes and attempted to regulate the trade with grants and licences. He granted the Tobacco Pipe Makers of Westminster sole privileges for making and distributing pipes to London, and raised the duties on tobacco by 4,000 per cent, from 2d to 82d per pound.[15] It was perhaps the fluctuating price of duties and the high price of tobacco that prompted subjects to try to grow their own. In the sixteenth century alone, several thousand printed books in Europe began to incorporate images and stories from the Americas, many describing the uses of tobacco and containing botanical illustrations and instructions on how to grow it.[16] James initially approved licences for tobacco cultivation across the British Isles, and surviving letters between policy-makers and merchants testify to a number of individuals growing tobacco since 'a good rent is growne to

---

[11] See, for example, *A new and short defense of tabacco* (1602; STC 6468.5); William Barclay, *Nepenthes, or, The vertues of tabacco* (Edinburgh, 1614; STC 1406).

[12] John Cotta, *A short discoverie of the unobserved dangers of severall sorts of ignorant and unconsiderate practisers of physicke in England* (1612; STC 5833), sig. B3r; Eleazar Duncon, *The copy of a letter* (1606; STC 6164), sig. A4r.

[13] Fynes Moryson, *An itinerary* (1617; STC 18205), sig. Ff3v.

[14] Edward Reynoldes to Owen Reynoldes, 24 February 1606, The National Archives, SP 14/18, f. 169r.

[15] 'Grant to the Tobacco-pipe Makers of Westminster', 30 July 1619, in *Calendar of State Papers: Domestic, 1619–1623*, ed. Mary Anne Everett Green (London: Longman, 1858), 67; 'License to Philip Foote to sell clay for making tobacco pipes', 24 July 1618, The National Archives, SP 14/141; Goodman, *Tobacco in History*, 148.

[16] Mancall, 'Tales Tobacco Told', 670.

the kinge' and proved profitable despite pitfalls.[17] Charged with household management, women grew tobacco in their gardens for medicinal reasons and smoked recreationally. Before the 1619 ban on English-grown tobacco, one acre of English tobacco could yield anywhere from 29l. to 100l. profit, an inviting prospect to a farmer who made around 9l. a year.[18]

Nonetheless, overindulgence through pipe smoking remained a concern. Pipes changed appearances and behaviour: 'men looke not like men that use them'.[19] Those who discouraged tobacco spent a significant amount of ink outlining its adverse effects. Health and disease was still largely understood in relation to the four humours, modelled heavily on the work of the ancient Greek physician Galen. The four complexions – sanguine, phlegmatic, choleric, and melancholic – were believed to affect personality and physical characteristics in ways that related to the four elements, rendering bodily imbalance the root of other disorders.[20] Physicians who discouraged tobacco related the imbalance it caused to the natural humours of the body. Too much tobacco infected 'the braine and the liver, as appears in our Anatomies, when their bodies are opened', showing 'their kidneyes, yea and hearts quite wasted'.[21]

One of the main arguments of the physician who called himself Philaretes was that tobacco not only had physical but also psychological effects. Tobacco was a 'great increaser of melancholy in us', opening the mind to 'melancholy impressions and effects proceeding of that humour'.[22] Melancholic dispositions arose, Philaretes explained, from black bile, corresponding to the element of the earth and caused by the thickness of a patient's blood. The unnatural rising of bile or yellow choler by hot and dry tobacco would form sediment in the blood, producing melancholy. The clergyman and physician Eleazar Duncon drew similar conclusions in his treatise: 'when the blood growth thicke and grosse, the minde is dull and sad'.[23] Melancholy diminished the 'principall faculty of

---

[17] George Carew to Viscount Cranborne, May 1605, Hatfield House, CP 189/81r; Thomas Alabaster to the Earl of Salisbury, 1607, Hatfield House, CP Petitions 1186; 'Remembrances concerning the Public, given to Mr Treasurer', 29 January 1610, The National Archives, SP 63/227, f. 237.

[18] Goodman, *Tobacco in History*, 142. On the process of cultivating tobacco, see Alexis Liebaert and Alain Maya, *The Illustrated History of the Pipe* (Suffolk: Harold Starke Publishers, 1994), 113–20.

[19] Thomas Dekker, *The shomakers holiday* (1600; STC 6523), sig. C3v.

[20] Margaret Healy, *Fictions of Disease in Early Modern England: Bodies, Plagues and Politics* (Basingstoke: Palgrave, 2001), 20.

[21] William Vaughan, *Approved directions for health, both naturall and artificiall* (1612; STC 24615), sig. F8v.

[22] Philaretes, *Work for chimny-sweepers* (1602; STC 12571), sig. F4v.

[23] Duncon, *The copy of a letter*, sigs. A4v–A5r.

the mind' where '*Reason* is corrupted'.[24] The dangers of melancholy had political repercussions, considered especially destabilizing to gentlemen whose minds must be fit to run their estates and to participate in governing the realm. While a healthy man possessed uncontaminated blood and a tempered brain, a mind 'affable, courteous, and civil', a melancholy man was prone to withdrawing from society, making him 'repugnant and contrary'.[25] Quoting Galen, Duncon summarized that 'the best complexions have the best maners'.[26]

The form and function of pipes directly informed attitudes to consumption. Physicians who prescribed tobacco did not necessarily advocate smoking it. Pipe smoking related directly to Native American, specifically North American, practices. For many physicians, consuming leaves through infusions or pastes offered a more 'civil' means of enjoying the benefits of tobacco. Though physicians did recommend the occasional pipe, others called for the 'leaves [to] be ashed or warmed in imbers', and it was the custom of breathing in the 'Nicotian fume' that seemed to most unsettle John Cotta.[27] For burns, one doctor advocated making a 'salve or ointment of Tabacco', since it 'anoynt the griefe, & killeth the malignant heat of any burning or scalding'.[28] Often, boiling or crushing leaves was seen to be the most efficient way to use the plant as a purgative. The sins of pride and contempt for the poor were directly linked to plague in one 1625 pamphlet, but tobacco was not catalogued as one of the country's sins – instead, it was recommended as a panacea against the plague.[29] This was not to be smoked, but 'smelled unto' and followed by a draught of beer and a restorative walk.[30]

As discourses about health, melancholy, and state regulation suggest, the physical body – its 'complexions' and 'manners' – was not easily separated from the body politic, and patterns of consumption altered both. The making and distributing of pipes and boxes, and attempts to grow tobacco in English gardens, can be integrated into Joan Thirsk's discussion of a rising consumer society in early modern England. As Thirsk's work demonstrates, new techniques of manufacture and cultivation in the second half of the sixteenth century brought an increased market for knitted goods, tobacco pipes, buttons, alum, linen, hemp, flax, and earthenware, all of which

---

[24] Robert Burton, *The anatomy of melancholy* (Oxford, 1621; STC 4159), sigs. A6v, C8r.
[25] Duncon, *The copy of a letter*, sigs. G2v–G3r.   [26] Ibid., sig. A4v.
[27] Henry Butts, *Dyets dry dinner* (1599; STC 4207), sig. P5v; Cotta, *A short discoverie of the observed dangers*, sig. B3r.
[28] Henry Lyte, *Rams little Dodeon, a briefe epitome of the new herbal* (1606; STC 6988), sig. Vr.
[29] *The Red-Crosse, or, Englands Lord have mercy upon us* (1625; STC 20823).   [30] Ibid.

stimulated the economy and allowed men, women, and children to sustain a livelihood while acquiring new goods produced in the country.[31] This economy depended in large part on the skilled labour of migrant communities, many of them religious refugees, and on the vitality through which labourers and middling members of society sought to improve their material conditions of living. Policy-makers sanctioned projects that seemed to offer viable solutions to poverty and idleness while bolstering regional and national economies.[32] At the same time, tobacco's association with America invariably contributed to the way that elite and non-elite consumers participated in a burgeoning Atlantic economy.[33] Sailors, smugglers, pedlars, and merchants played vital roles in circulating tobacco, disseminating the plant from ports to localities while also conveying travel news.[34]

Scholars have turned to the effects of intoxication on the body, examining how social practices around tobacco, as with different kinds of alcohol or, later, coffee and tea, developed in ways that resisted or bolstered state authority.[35] By situating consumption within socio-political change, these studies have moved away from the cultural materialist approaches of the late twentieth and early twenty-first centuries that focussed on tobacco's 'sovereignty' or dominance over people and economic markets, where an emphasis on the commodification or fetishizing of luxury goods gave little agency to the behaviour of English subjects.[36] To consider what Arjun Appadurai calls 'the social life of things' presents an opportunity to think about exchange and value in relation to their particular contexts and the politics behind them.[37] This involves an attention to the geopolitics of particular colonies and their relationship to their indigenous inhabitants, as well as a consideration of how metropolitan contexts re-shaped conditions of use.

---

[31] Thirsk, *Economic Policy and Projects*, 7; Slack, *The Invention of Improvement*.

[32] Thirsk, *Economic Policy and Projects*, 18, 32.

[33] See 'Tobacco and the Economy of Empire', in Macmillan, *The Atlantic Imperial Constitution*, 85–111.

[34] Lemire, *Global Trade and the Transformation of Consumer Cultures*; Games, *The Web of Empire*; Orser, *An Archaeology of the British Atlantic World*.

[35] Phil Withington, 'Introduction: Cultures of Intoxication', *Past & Present: Supplement 9* (2014), 9–33, at 20, 14. Also Phil Withington, 'Intoxicants and Society in Early Modern England', *The Historical Journal*, 54 (2011), 631–57; Michelle O'Callaghan, *The English Wits: Literature and Sociability in Early Modern England* (Cambridge: Cambridge University Press, 2007); *A Pleasing Sinne: Drink and Conviviality in Seventeenth-Century England*, ed. Adam Smyth (Woodbridge: Boydell, 2004).

[36] Knapp, 'Elizabethan Tobacco'; Jeffrey Knapp, *An Empire Nowhere: England, America, and Literature from Utopia to the Tempest* (Berkeley: University of California Press, 1992), chapter 4; Susan Campbell Anderson, 'A Matter of Authority: James I and the Tobacco War', *Comitatus*, 29 (1998), 136–63.

[37] *The Social Life of Things: Commodities in Cultural Perspective*, ed. Arjun Appadurai (Cambridge: Cambridge University Press, 1992).

The archaeological concept of a 'commodity chain' is useful for acknowledging the connection between a colonially sourced product and its imperial implications when smoked in England.[38] This began with the raw material grown from carefully cultivated seeds in different colonial environments, whether the Spanish Caribbean or English Bermuda or Virginia. Since the Spanish learned to consume tobacco from Native Americans in Central and South America and the West Indies, they often smoked in the manner of Mesoamericans, using reed pipes, or in the form of 'pudding rolls' or cigars.[39] Gentlemen were attuned to the realities of cultivation and manufacture, and this contributed to ideas of taste. Preferring the leaf tobacco and pipe smoking gleaned from their contact with Algonquians in North America, the English increasingly branded Spanish tobacco as destructive to their merchandizing. Tobacco from the West Indies, as one author complained, was mixed with 'juices' and 'syrops' to alter its colour, and 'in some places they adde a red berry . . . with which the Indians paint their bodies'.[40] Such 'colour and glosse' masked 'rotten, withered, & ground-leaves' that associated Iberian trade with corrupted manufacturing techniques: this 'filthy leafe' was 'solde by the Portugalles residing in London, the same beeing made up in rolles'.[41] The sourcing and packaging of tobacco, and the stamped and engraved boxes in which members of the elite carried cured tobacco leaves, shaped how consumers re-contextualized the commodity and gave it new meanings in metropolitan spaces.

These differences placed Africans and Native Americans within hierarchies of production. Wit literature and pamphlets circulated fictions of 'Indian Tobacco' or 'pure Indian' coming from wilful trade or gift-giving in North America, in contrast to the unfree labour in the West Indies. 'Spanish slaves' on Iberian plantations, maintained one pamphlet advocating domestic planting, dressed their wounds with the same hands they used to produce cheap rolls.[42] Of all the plant illustrations that appeared in a botanical book printed in London in 1571, only one included the depiction of a human, where the head of an African man appeared next to the drawing of tobacco.[43] The African smoked an oversized cigar-like roll that associated tobacco with the enslaved workers on Iberian plantations,

---

[38] Orser, *An Archaeology of the British Atlantic World*, 337.
[39] Marcy Norton, *Sacred Gifts, Profane Pleasures: A History of Tobacco and Chocolate in the Atlantic World* (Ithaca, NY: Cornell University Press, 2008), 171.
[40] C. T., *An advice how to plant tobacco in England* (1615; STC 23612), sig. A4r.
[41] Ibid., sigs. A4r–v.   [42] Ibid., sig. Br.
[43] Pierre Pena and Matthias de L'Obel, *Stirpium adversaria nova* (1571; STC 19595), 252.

perhaps also alluding to the widespread practice among labourers of smoking or chewing tobacco to survive the arduous conditions of plantation life.[44] From the start, gentlemen in England understood tobacco not just in terms of its medicinal properties or as a source of relief from bodily humours; their tastes were rooted in the colonial.

Incivility and Disorder

The economic potential of tobacco vied with authorities' awareness of its circulation by non-elite go-betweens such as sailors, and with the knowledge that the plant came from an Atlantic economy whose labour and production depended on non-Europeans. English anxieties about tobacco in the 1610s and 1620s expressed mistrust over the fluid boundaries between English and Native American bodies. 'Satan visibly and palpably raignes here', the minister Alexander Whitaker reported from Jamestown in 1613.[45] Smoking played an important role in North and South American religious ceremonies and social healing, connecting individuals to spiritual realms in ways that seemed incompatible with the Jacobean state's concern with Protestant conformity.[46] 'The *Tobacco* of this place is good', summarized one explorer who travelled to the Caribbean with Ralegh, 'but the *Indians* [are] *Canibals*'.[47]

Thomas Hariot, polymath and friend of Ralegh's, was among those who praised tobacco for its medicinal qualities.[48] At the same time, Hariot had spent time in Roanoke in the mid-1580s, and his descriptions of indigenous practices highlighted how removed these were from English models of civility. Tobacco, or *vppówoc*, Hariot wrote,

> is of so precious estimation amongst [the Indians], that they thinke their gods are marvelously delighted therwith: Wherupon sometime they make hallowed fires & cast some of the pouder therein for a sacrifice . . . all done with strange gestures, stamping, sometime dauncing, clapping of hands,

[44] On slaves chewing or smoking to prevent exhaustion, see Norton, *Sacred Gifts, Profane Pleasures*, 157. For an allusion to the uses of tobacco in reviving weakened spirits in a bawdier context, see Thomas Nashe's 'The Choice of Valentines' (1592), in which the narrator, suffering from impotence, wishes for 'those hearbes and rootes of Indian soile,/That strengthen wearie members in their toile', in *The Unfortunate Traveller and Other Works*, ed. J. B. Steane (Harmondsworth: Penguin, 1972), 467.

[45] Whitaker, *Good newes from Virginia*, sig. C2r.

[46] Alexander von Gernet, 'North American Indigenous *Nicotiana* Use and Tobacco Shamanism: The Early Documentary Record, 1520–1660', in *Tobacco Use by Native North Americans: Sacred Smoke and Silent Killer*, ed. Joseph C. Winter (Norman: University of Oklahoma Press, 2000), 59–83, at 73.

[47] Kemys, *A relation of the second voyage to Guiana*, sig. E2v.

[48] Thomas Hariot, *A brief and true report of the new found land of Virginia* (1588; STC 12785), sig. C3v.

holding up of hands, & staring up into the heave[n]s, uttering therewithal and chattering strange words & noises.[49]

To detractors, smoking allowed individuals to express a certain contempt for their circumstances or their surroundings in a visual, sensory way that directly related to tobacco's American provenance. As one physician wrote in 1621, the 'vaine dreams and visions, which this fume suggesteth' were akin to the religious ceremonies that 'bewitched' North and South Americans and filled them with 'watonnesse and delight'.[50] For the first time in history, one could 'leave the Americans, and come to our Europeans' to find that the English '(well-neare) use the fume of Tobacco with as much excess as [the Indians] doe'.[51] The tobacco that the Algonquians imbibed in religious ceremonies no longer seemed strange to the English because it was now a widespread custom for a man 'to become of an English-man, a Savage Indian'.[52]

Anxieties over imitating Algonquians knit domestic conformity to concerns over the success of the civilizing project abroad. The London council advocated a complete eradication of Powhatan temples and burial grounds because they were deemed superstitious and prevented Protestantism from taking root. It hardly seemed consistent to indulge in a plant that Algonquians themselves used to mediate the sacred. As one writer reflected, subjects were concerned that those who imbibed tobacco 'did seem to degenerate into the nature of the Savages, because they were carried away with the self-same thing'.[53]

Moralists frequently depicted smokers as deliberately placing themselves outside civil society. As such authors maintained, uncivil behaviour might be expected among the 'savages' of America, but to choose to behave like Native Americans produced a quite different and altogether more serious problem. The '[s]trangers savage Ignorance' was lamentable, but 'wilful Arrogance' far worse.[54] The *Epigrammes and elegies* of John Davies and Christopher Marlowe included a praise of tobacco in the same volume as Marlowe's translation of Ovid's love poetry, as well as passing references to smoking in other poems. Davies referred to tobacco's 'heave[n]ly power',

---

[49] Ibid. For the role of tobacco in indigenous American ceremonies, see Lee Irwin, *Coming Down from Above: Prophesy, Resistance, and Renewal in Native American Religion* (Norman: University of Oklahoma Press, 2008).

[50] Tobias Venner, *A briefe and accurate treatise, concerning, the taking of the fume of tobacco* (1621; STC 24642), sig. B2v.

[51] Ibid., sig. B4v.   [52] Purchas, *Purchas his pilgrimage*, sig. Ooo4r.

[53] William Camden, *Annales the true and royall history of the famous empresse Elizabeth* (1625; STC 4497), sig. P2r.

[54] Josuah Sylvester, *Tobacco battered, & the pipes shattered* (1621; STC 23582a), sig. F4v.

describing its effects as an epiphany-inducing rapture of the senses that would 'clarifie/The clowdie mistes before dim eies appearing'.[55] His praise of its sweet fumes enhanced the exoticism of his heady verses, but Marlowe's own association with tobacco proved somewhat less enchanting. The informer Richard Baines' damning charges presented to the Privy Council against the playwright quoted Marlowe as saying that 'all they that love not tobacco and boies were fooles' in the same indictment that contained Marlowe's apparent penchant for brutality and irreverent quips about Christ and his followers, specifically Protestants.[56]

A libel against Walter Ralegh and other opponents of the Earl of Essex, likely composed after Essex's return from Ireland in 1599, branded the smoking Ralegh with similar language to that used to denounce Marlowe. The libel described the debauchery of Ralegh and his coterie: 'Heele swere by God and worship Devill for gaine/Tobacco boye or sacke to swaye his paine'.[57] Libels often linked individuals and their foibles to political disorder, and tobacco served to reinforce Ralegh's subversive behaviour.[58] The assumption that tobacco was the mark of the rogue manifested itself seventeen years later at Ralegh's death in 1618. On the scaffold, delivering his final words, Ralegh refuted accusations that he encouraged the death of Essex, denying that he 'stood in a window over him when he suffered in the Tower, and puffed out tobacco in disdain of him'.[59] Dying for treason, Ralegh disassociated himself publicly from the idea of tobacco-taking as a gesture of contempt. Yet his need to refute this accusation underlines this association between tobacco and non-conformity, strengthened by stories of the tobacco pouch found in his cell after his execution.[60]

Ralegh, however, was a member of the elite, and his private smoking habits were contrasted to the description by one witness of the 'base and rascal peoples' lining up on the streets throwing 'tobacco-pipes, stones, and mire at him' during his trial.[61] Concerns over regulating smoking were largely a matter of status and social position. Though gentlemen might

---

[55] *Epigrammes and elegies by J. D. and C. M.* [John Davies and Christopher Marlowe] ([London, 1599?]; STC 6350.5), sig. C3v.

[56] David Riggs, *The World of Christopher Marlowe* (London: Faber and Faber, 2004), 327.

[57] 'A dreame alluding to my L of Essex, and his adversaries', 1599, Bodleian Library, Don. C.54, f. 19r–20r, accessible on *Early Stuart Libels* www.earlystuartlibels.net.

[58] Andrew McRae, 'Reading Libels: An Introduction', *Huntington Library Quarterly*, 69 (2006), 1–13, at 1.

[59] *The arraignment and conviction of S[i]r Walter Rawleigh*, sig. E2r. See also 'Sir Walter Raleigh's Imprisonment, Voyage to Guiana, and Execution', in *Criminal Trials, Vol. 1*, ed. David Jardine (London: M. A. Nattali, 1846), 510.

[60] Knapp, 'Elizabethan Tobacco', 37.   [61] 'Sir Walter Raleigh's Imprisonment', 461.

indulge in the pipe in their chambers at the Inns of Court or in their private homes, they condemned the disorders that seemed to arise from tobacco in the hands of the wider population. A debate in the House of Lords in 1621 led to the conclusion that tobacco and ale were now 'inseparable in the base vulgar sort', and inevitably accounted for the 'Idleness, Drunkenness [and] Decay of their Estates' that resulted.[62] The threat lay largely in the fact that tobacco was not only smoked in urban areas, where 'riot and excesse' were expected, but it had 'begun to be taken in every meane village, even among the basest people', remaining outside the regulation of parish authorities.[63] In 1617, the Lord Mayor of London George Bolles issued a proclamation calling for a reformation of abuses in Newgate Prison. He pointed out that 'notorious Mutinies and Out-rages' had been committed by the negligence of the prison guards who allowed their prisoners to become 'drunke and disordered, permitting them wine, Tobacco, [and] excessive strong drinke'.[64] The mayor ordered that gaolers and keepers 'not suffer the taking of Tobacco by the dissolute sort of prisoners in the common gaole' and that 'no Tobacco nor Tobacco-pipes, Candles, or other things to fire their Tobacco be brought to them' so that 'Mutinies and Insolencies may bee prevented'.[65] Tobacco does not seem to have been denied to gentlemen in Newgate, and only to 'the dissolute sort of prisoners', marking 'common' prisoners as those most likely to succumb to uprisings spurred by intemperance and tobacco-taking.

Another set of orders, for Ludgate Prison, indicates similar concerns. Signed by the clerk keeper and numerous bailiffs, it declared that

> sundrie abuses & disorders doe daylie arise in the prison by varietie of prison[er]s selling and retailing of tobacco in the same as namelie occasioning late meetings & sitting up in the night not onelie disquieting theire fellow prison[er]s in the house but by the notice that is taken thereof by the watch and passengers in the street w[hi]ch tendes much to the hindrance of the house by the loose of that charitie w[hi]ch hath usually byn given.[66]

Until 1601, the Ludgate orders pertained to the freedoms allowed a prisoner, the conduct of gaolers, and the disorders caused by drinking.

---

[62] 'Tobacco', 3 May 1621, in *Journal of the House of Commons*, 605; *Know all men by these presents, that wee Thomas Walsingham, William Wythines, and Henrie Sneglar, knight* . . . (1620; STC 9175).

[63] 'A Proclamation to restraine the planting of Tobacco in England and Wales', 30 December 1619, in *Royal Proclamations of King James I, 1603–1625*, ed. James F. Larkin and Paul L. Hughes (Oxford: Clarendon, 1973), 458.

[64] *By the Maior. A proclamation for the reformation of abuses, in the gaole of New-gate* (1617; STC 16727.1).

[65] Ibid.   [66] 'Orders touching Ludgate', 1597–1604, The National Archives, E 215/961.

It is only after this date that tobacco began to appear in rule books as a matter of concern. Those found trafficking tobacco, since the weed 'often breedes contention and debate', were to be fined or 'sitt in the bolts or shackles'.[67] The passage cited also indicates that the disorderly behaviour of tobacco smokers prevented benefactors from donating money to the prison, perhaps believing that those who smoked tobacco did not merit charity.

Authorities also condemned the leisure that smoking encouraged. Natural man should abhor idleness, preached one clergyman in 1595, for sluggards were unproductive and therefore 'as good dead as alive'.[68] Tobacco-taking was not only perilously 'intoxicating', but caused citizens to 'smoake away . . . precious time' better used in diligence.[69] John Deacon wrote in 1616 that those who smoked excessively or wantonly were nothing but 'disordered and riotous persons'.[70] A devotional tract advocating steadfast prayer condemned 'robbers arraigned and judged over night to die the morrow' who smoked tobacco to avoid thinking of their deaths.[71] This must have been a known occurrence during trials and executions. The letter writer John Chamberlain wrote to Dudley Carleton about how 'certain mad knaves tooke tabacco all the way to Tyburn' as they went to be hanged.[72] The length between one's conviction and death was at times very short – Chamberlain noted in 1603 that a captured priest was arrested on the twelfth of February and executed at Tyburn four days later – and spending 'precious time with this filthie weed' was therefore unwise.[73] In terms of gesture, the very act of smoking required the use of the participant's hands to hold the pipe and bring it to his or her mouth to suck in the smoke. This presented an alternative to the gestures of prayerful repentance so often depicted in woodcuts encouraging penitence before death.

Smoke and Treason

The vaulting wordplay and rhetorical embellishments used in anti-tobacco tracts were intended as a means for individuals to confront the consequences that such a commodity might bring, not just to their physical health, but to their behaviour and actions. Robert Bradshaw's unpublished advice treatise 'The way to weldoeing', written some time during James'

---

[67] Ibid.   [68] William Burton, *The rowsing of the sluggard* (1595; STC 4176), sigs. B2v–B3r.
[69] James Hart, *Klinike, or, the diet of the diseased* (1633; STC 12888), sig. Aaa4r.
[70] Deacon, *Tobacco tortured*, sigs. Mv, V2v.
[71] William Innes, *A bundle of myrrhe: or Three meditations of teares* (1620; STC 14091), sig. I4r.
[72] John Chamberlain to Dudley Carleton, 20 October 1598, The National Archives, SP 12/268, f. 141v.
[73] John Chamberlain to Dudley Carleton, 28 February 1603, The National Archives, SP 12/287, f. 58r.

reign, included the story of a captured pirate in Suffolk who 'being redie to dy sayd that the great love he bore unto tobacko was the furst and chef occasion of his overthrow', since the 'importinat delight in taking that harming smoke' propelled him further into drink, excess, women, and eventually 'theverie and manie other disordrs'.[74] 'Iniqitie', Bradshaw concluded, 'shall bring all the earth to a welderness', one that could only be salvaged by good governors.[75] Bradshaw associated poor manners with a tendency to disobedience:

> [Question] What is the reason thinke you that somanie greatwons as well as small creatturs transgress and break the kings laws [?]
>
> [Answer] becaus they wer not brought up in good manors.[76]

James' *A counterblaste to tobacco* (1604) specifically argued that uncivil habits were a danger to the polity. As discussed in Chapter 3, James' view of monarchical authority was intimately related to the human body and to the personal relationship a subject shared with the king as his liege lord. Though frequently overlooked in discussions of James' political rhetoric, *Counterblaste* is a carefully crafted pamphlet with a politically charged core. By yoking 'savage' manners to a disregard of kingly orders, James turned smoking into a manifestation of political disobedience and a challenge to royal prerogative.

Part of the danger, James claimed, was the English willingness to abandon duty for self-gratifying pleasure. The wilful adopting of such a 'savage custom', 'having their originall from base corruption and barbarity', only likened addled Englishmen to 'beastly *Indians*'.[77] James' repetition of 'savage', 'barbarous', 'intemperate', and 'beastly' constructed an image of overwhelming savagery pending over a civil but imperilled realm. Subjects were 'counterfeiting the maners of others to our owne destruction'.[78] Tobacco was a seduction that rendered subjects impertinent, uncommitted to serving the monarch if it stood in the way of 'idle delights, and soft delicacies'.[79]

What lay behind these eccentric hyperboles were attempts to prevent the threats that came from wilful defiance. Though smoke may seem the 'smallest trifle', it was tied to 'greater matters'.[80] The 'maners of the wilde, godless, and slavish *Indians*' were related to the tendency to be 'too easie to be seduced to make Rebellion, upon very slight grounds'.[81] The corrupting

---

[74] Robert Bradshaw, 'The way to weldoeing', [*c*.1612–25], British Library, Royal MS 17 B XIII, f. 70v.
[75] Ibid., f. 91v.   [76] Ibid., f. 7r.
[77] James I, *A counterblaste to tobacco* (1604; STC 14363), sigs. Br–B2r.   [78] Ibid., sig. Cr.
[79] Ibid., sig. A3v.   [80] Ibid., sig. A4v.   [81] Ibid., sigs. Bv, A3r.

nature of tobacco allowed James to use one of his favourite metaphors, that of 'the proper Phisician of his Politicke-Body' who sought to 'purge it of all those diseases' through 'a just form of government, to maintain the Publicke quietnesse, and prevent all occasions of Commotion'.[82] Ultimately, only the king and the tonic of good government could redress society's monstrosities.

Though policy-makers often addressed smoking among the 'lower sort', James especially targeted 'our Nobilitie and Gentrie prodigall', including lawyers and churchmen, who were 'solde to their private delights' and who had become negligent in their duties.[83] The king's express concern with the behaviour of his male elite is significant. The corruption of the body politic began when its authorities failed in their civic duties to uphold the integrity of the household and the state it mirrored. Given the role of the gentry in extending state authority to the localities, their penchant for 'private delights' undermined the fabric of governance. Fears of diluting the civil, Protestant self were expressed as a seductive political menace. More subtle than the threat of war, the pursuit of pleasure would usher its destruction through silken pockets stuffed with West Indian leaves, turning the English, like Native Americans, into 'slaves to the *Spaniards*'.[84] Why doe we not as well imitate [the Indians] in walking naked as they doe?' James asked. '[I]n preferring glasses, feathers, and such toyes … yea why do we not denie God and adore the Devill?'[85]

James' tract was concerned with civil order, but *Counterblaste* also had the foresight to address larger issues over the means of sustaining an imperial polity. The king's attack on luxury did not wholly disparage wealth, and he scorned indigenous Americans for their seeming disregard of precious metals. He did, however, belittle courtiers and gentlemen who exposed themselves to the influence of Native American cultures, condemning 'the first Author [of the] first introduction of [tobacco] amongst us' in a scathing barb against Walter Ralegh.[86] The fashion for smoking had not been introduced by a 'King, great Conqueror, nor learned Doctor' but by a self-seeking man whose allegiances were notoriously slippery, and whose penchant for smoking had been fuelled by his direct exchanges with indigenous groups.[87] The 'two or three Savage me[n]' who had faithfully accompanied Ralegh back to England after his voyage to Guiana had died, James relayed, leaving only their custom alive.[88] The antiquarian William Camden had also drawn a close connection between smoking and Anglo–Native exchange when he credited the Roanoke survivors, Hariot among

---

[82] Ibid.   [83] Ibid., sig. A3v.   [84] Ibid., sig. B2r.   [85] Ibid.   [86] Ibid.   [87] Ibid.   [88] Ibid.

them, as 'the first (that I know of) that brought at their returne into *England*, that *Indian* Plant ... being instructed by the *Indians*'.[89] In reminding his subjects that novelties were the overthrow 'first of the Persia[n], and next of the Romane Empire', James wrote in imperial terms.[90] Decadence would inhibit a transatlantic polity before it even began to flourish.

The association between degeneration and disobedience in other writings continued to engage with the king's views on tobacco as a marker of political subversion. Writers needed only make a small imaginative leap to envision a realm overrun by the puff of smoke to the scourge of gunpowder and fire. Deacon's *Tobacco tortured* (1616) and Josuah Sylvester's *Tobacco battered, & the pipes shattered* (1616) equated tobacco with treason by framing it in a narrative that evoked the Gunpowder Treason of 1605. As Sylvester wrote, there were resonances between the smoke of tobacco and the near-explosions beneath Parliament in 1605, when a group of Catholic subjects took their contempt for princely authority to terrifying extremes. The links between smoking 'heathens' and Catholic dissidents were hardly lost on Protestants concerned with abolishing idolatry. English writers compared Native American smoke and Catholic incense, and the 'savage' fascination with bells, trinkets, and false or misdirected worship: 'The *Divell* that hath so many superstitious conceits wherewith to blindfold the *Papist*, is not unfurnished of vaine impression wherewith to be sot the *Tobacconist*'.[91] Detractors and slanderers of the gospel were seen to 'extoll dumb creatures to the very skies, not much unlike those idolatrous *Indians* who worship the sun'.[92]

To policy-makers, the Catholic plotters' tendency towards savage behaviour had given them the confidence to act against their king. The '*Vanities, Mysterious Mists* of Rome' were equated to that other threat that 'be-smoaked Christendom'.[93] In the plot's aftermath, pamphlets catalogued the execution of Guy Fawkes and other conspirators, where their proclivity for smoking featured as a signifier of their lack of remorse. The imprisoned men were described as impenitently awaiting their trial, where they 'feasted wither their sinnes ... were richly apparelled, fared deliciously, and took Tobacco out of measure'.[94] In their trial, their

---

[89] Camden, *Annales the true and royall history of the famous empresse Elizabeth*, sig. P2r.
[90] James I, *A counterblaste to tobacco*, sig. C4v.
[91] Barnabe Rich, *My ladies looking glasse* (1616; STC 20991.7), sig. C4v.
[92] John Gee, *The foot out of the snare* (1624; STC 11701), sig. Hh2v, also sig. F2r.
[93] Sylvester, *Tobacco battered, & the pipes shattered*, sig. F8r.
[94] T. W., *The arraignment and execution of the late traytors* (1606; STC 24916), sig. B3r.

remorselessness became part of their stubborn idolatry, for they did not seem to pray 'except it were by the dozen, upon their beades, and taking Tobacco, as if that hanging were no trouble to them'.[95] Eleven years after the event, John Deacon made explicit connections between tobacco smoking and the Gunpowder Treason:

> The late disordered enterprise of those our intemperate *Tobacconists*, it was not onely flat opposite to the well-established peace of our soveraigne Lord the King . . . but very rebellious likewise to his kingly soveraigne it selfe, not onely, because they so desperately attempted the wilful breach of his peace, but for that they so *proudly* resisted his kingly power, and did thereby most impudently declare themselves very obstinate, and open rebels against his sacred Majestie.[96]

As 'tobacconists', the plotters' intemperance and arrogance induced them to act treasonably, where imbibing 'Indianized' tobacco subverted the sacred rule of the king.[97]

Anti-tobacco literature often focussed less on tobacco as a disease than a self-induced harm, representing larger concerns about the internal inceptions of social and political disintegration:

> If thou desire to know, and cause demand
> Why such strange monstrous maladies are rife?
> The cause is plaine, and reason is at hand;
> Men like and love this *smokie* kind of life.[98]

James expressed it similarly in 1619:

> [T]o refuse obedience because it is against our mind, is like the excuse of the Tobacco-drunkards, who cannot abstain from that filthy stinking smoake, because forsooth, they are bewitched with it. And this is an excuse for any sinne, they will not leave it, because they cannot leave it.[99]

The seductiveness of disobedience implied that those who took tobacco allowed themselves to be corrupted. To be told by the king himself of the degenerating potential of smoking and to do so anyway made the very act of smoking a possible act of defiance. 'He that dares take Tobacco on the stage,/Dares daunce in pawles, and in this formall age,/Dares say and do what ever is unmeete'.[100] Policy-makers seem to have deemed the combination of tobacco and alcohol especially corrosive. In 1618, James

---

[95] Ibid., sig. B3v.   [96] Deacon, *Tobacco tortured*, sig. V4r.   [97] Ibid., sig. Cv.
[98] Ibid., sigs. Cc2r–v.
[99] James I, *Meditation upon the Lords prayer* (1619; STC 14384), sig. F6v.
[100] *Epigrammes and elegies by J. D. and C. M.*, sig. F8v.

attempted to prohibit alehouses from selling tobacco in an attempt to suppress 'the great disorders daylie used in Ale-houses' that were enhanced by taking the two together.[101]

As concerns raised in Parliament, prison records, and popular print suggest, authorities mistrusted smokers for operating in often public spaces where subversive ideas could be discussed, where 'Indianized' leisure presented 'our Weale publicke deformed'.[102] These spaces were often, but not always, associated with taverns and alehouses. The soldier Barnabe Rich claimed that Jacobean London had 7,000 tobacco shops. Ravaged by seventeenth-century fire and twentieth-century war, London has yielded little archaeological evidence, if any, of the location of such shops, their structural frameworks, or how they functioned in relation to surrounding buildings. These do seem, however, to have been entities that were separate from other shops that sold tobacco. Though it was 'a commoditie that is nowe vendible in every Taverne, Inne, and Ale-house', as well as by apothecaries and grocers, Rich remarked, there was 'a *Cathalogue* taken of all those newly erected houses that have set uppe that Trade of selling Tobacco, in London & neare about London'.[103] Since sellers 'are (almost) never without company, that from morning till night are still taking of Tobacco', these spaces evolved into 'open shoppes, that have no other trade to live by, but by the selling of tobacco'.[104]

Tobacco shops, wrote the satirist John Earle, were 'the Randevous of spitting' where 'communication is smoke', a place, scandalously, where 'Spain is commended and prefer'd before England it selfe'.[105] The reference to Spain may have alluded to Spanish-imported tobacco in England – which, as another author noted, 'cannot but greatly prejudice the Common-weale' – but also to topics of political discourse, including travel news.[106] Published shortly after Rich's description of London's flourishing tobacco shops, a broadside promoting good table manners conveyed authorities' attempts to regulate subjects' manners while also disclosing the particular topics of discourse that tobacco seemed to encourage (Figure 5). Printed by the king's printer Robert Barker in 1615, *Table-observations* grouped tobacco with rumours or stories – perhaps the 'long tales' of travellers returning from Atlantic voyages – and

---

[101] *By the King. A proclamation concerning ale-houses* (1618; STC 8588).
[102] Deacon, *Tobacco tortured*, sig. C3v.
[103] Barnabe Rich, *The honestie of this age* (1614; STC 20986), sig. D4v.   [104] Ibid.
[105] John Earle, *Micro-cosmographie* (1628; STC 7440.2), sig. G10r.
[106] C. T., *An advice how to plant tobacco in England*, sig. Br.

Figure 5 *Table-observations* (1615). By kind permission of the Society of Antiquaries of London.

matters of state, suggesting its links to slander and a dangerous meddling in affairs that went beyond displaying indelicate manners.[107]

According to authorities, tobacco shops were bowers where treasons were whispered and, once spoken, brought into the realm of possibility. The desire to smoke brought subjects to places where they might not otherwise gather.[108] Here were microcosms within the polity where the king did not possess sovereign jurisdiction, where 'a man shall heare nothing but *Destractions*' and 'captious and carping speaches' made with 'taunting tongues', so that 'the wise Surgeons of our State

[107] *Table-observations* (1615; STC 23634.7).
[108] Barten Holyday, *Technogamia: or The marriages of the arts* (1618; STC 13617), sig. Dr.

[must] provide for corrosives and cauterismes against these ugly ulcers'.[109] Tobacco itself was a 'traitour, and doth treason warke' by '*smokie* mists polluting ... [t]hroughout the body every part imbruing'.[110] When James ordered the eradication of the tobacco houses on his route to St Paul's in 1620, he was in many ways exerting his sovereignty over illegitimate or uncivil spaces.

Given its associations with political conversation, it may be that tobacco sellers provided physical sites for public political discourse that prefigured the coffeehouse culture of the mid-seventeenth century. Tobacco sellers created spaces for consumption and discourse at a time when London experienced radical physical alterations, and the shifting spatial topography of the city can offer a category of analysis for the history of civil conversation and political discourse.[111] These new spaces were occupied by unfamiliar odours and social rituals and, unlike alehouses, stemmed directly from English global expansion, reinforced by the wooden Native Americans that might adorn the facades. Like statues of Africans or 'blackamoors', these enticed customers to enter by relating the commodity to the Atlantic world from where the tobacco came.[112] Intent on controlling the flow of news during the heated Parliament of 1614, Francis Bacon and other statesmen conveyed discord and malicious rumour as the enemy of a functioning polity.[113] The Virginia Company used print in its considerable efforts to control 'the malignity of the false' and the 'ignorant rumor, virulent envy, or impious subtilty' that harmed the colonial enterprise, where the abundance of titles promising to offer 'true' or 'sincere' colonial news inveighed against 'those Letters and Rumours [shown] to have beene false and malicious'.[114] These campaigns, though reflecting wider concerns on the part of policy-makers to manage and control information, only fed the vast flow of information that circulated in the metropolis, mingling with the stories of merchants and sailors and fostered by the punchy depth of tobacco itself.

---

[109] William Vaughan, *The arraignment of slander perjury blasphemy, and other malicious sinnes* (1630; STC 24623), sig. Qq4r.
[110] Deacon, *Tobacco tortured*, sigs. Cc2r–v.
[111] *Political Spaces in Pre-industrial Europe*, ed. Beat Kümin (Surrey: Ashgate, 2009); John Schofield, 'The Topography and Buildings of London, ca. 1600', in *Material London, ca. 1600*, ed. Lena Cowen Orlin (Philadelphia: University of Pennsylvania Press, 2000), 296–321; Merritt, *The Social World of Early Modern Westminster*.
[112] For an early mention of the enticing presence of Native Americans on a building's 'frontispiece', see Richard Brathwaite [Blasius Multibibus], *A solemne joviall disputation* (1617; STC 3585), sig. L6r.
[113] Millstone, *Manuscript Circulation and the Invention of Politics*, 69.
[114] Council for Virginia, *A true and sincere declaration* (1610; STC 24832), sig. A3v; Council for Virginia, *A declaration of the state of the colonie*, sig. A3v.

From 'Pagan' Plant to 'Virginia Leaf'

While the state's embeddedness in the reformation of manners at first seemed to provide an obstacle to the endorsement of 'bewitching' tobacco, parliamentary debates over moral regulation and the tobacco trade benefitted from relating the commodity to the colonial. When the Virginia Company's exactions from customs and impositions expired in 1619, the Crown denied the company's petition to extend its privileges.[115] Thomas Cogswell has argued that the ensuing debates around tobacco, both pro and contra, helped to create a 'political vocabulary' around colonial administration, litigation, and free trade that were fundamental to sustaining overseas plantation.[116] This section explores the tobacco debates less through the lens of administration and more through a consideration of policy-makers as consumers, investigating how pro-imperial gentlemen sought to legitimize tobacco smoking by relating the commodity to matters of state. Smoking brought the colonial into the political culture of gentlemen in and around parliament. Unlike the 'impudent upstarts', '[p]agan in beleefe . . . Prodigall in wastfull expence' who puffed their profligate way through the metropolis, the civility of gentlemen smokers came from their ability to relate tobacco to the culture of political participation.[117]

When Edwin Sandys wrote to the Duke of Buckingham in 1620, he presented the survival of the struggling colony in Virginia as a matter of James' personal honour. The subversions of the other factions, Sandys wrote, were a 'derogation of his Ma[jes]ties authoritie, & contrary to his Royall Instructions' as well as a 'dishartning [*sic*] of all Adventurors . . . that [the colony] might not prosper'.[118] Tobacco created a dilemma for Jacobean policy-makers who condemned the habit but supported colonization.

Throughout his reign, James realized the profitability of tobacco but continued to press for other goods that might eventually replace the colonists' dependence on the crop. In a dinner conversation between the king and George Yeardley in 1618, as Yeardley prepared to embark to Jamestown to become its governor, one observer reported that:

---

[115] Macmillan, *The Atlantic Imperial Constitution*, 89.

[116] Thomas Cogswell, '"In the Power of the State": Mr Anys's Project and the Tobacco Colonies, 1626–1628', *English Historical Review* (2008), 35–64, at 63; Macmillan, *The Atlantic Imperial Constitution*.

[117] George Chapman, *Monsieur d'Olive* (1606; STC 4983), sig. B4r.

[118] Edwin Sandys to the Duke of Buckingham, 7 June 1620, in *Records of the Virginia Company, Vol. III*, 295.

His Ma[jes]tie then converted his speech to the matter of Tobacco, w[hi]ch though owte of a naturall antipathy hee hateth as much as any mortall man, yet such is his love to our plantation, as hee is content wee should make our benefit thereof upon certaine conditions: Namely that by too excessive planting of it, we doe neglect planting of corne & soe famish o[ur]selves. For, said his Ma[jes]tie, if our saviour Christ in the gospell saith man liveth not by bread alone, then I may well say, Man liveth not by smoke alone. His Ma[jes]ties other condition was, that wee should dayle indeavour o[ur] selves to raise more ritch and stable commodities ... that by degrees one might growe into contempte, & soe into disuse of yt that fantasticall herbe.[119]

James contrasted tobacco to industries that he viewed as more commend-able foundations for a civil polity, especially silk. Yet the 'disuse of that fantasticall herbe' never occurred. This was not because tobacco's promi-nence was inevitable, or because fears of savagery were merely rhetorical and ultimately too flimsy to dictate policy, but because James, and the MPs who heavily backed the Virginia Company, consciously found ways to reconcile tobacco with both private pleasure and public good.

The tensions between controlling behaviour and endorsing the colony were apparent in debates in the House of Commons in April 1621. Jerome Horsey complained that the 'vile weed' had hardly been present when he first became an MP in the 1590s, and he advocated the complete eradica-tion of the trade.[120] But, Thomas Jermyn contended, resisting Spain and redressing the dire situation in Virginia were more pressing issues. Though he 'loveth Tobacco as ill as any', it was 'fit to be given [to] Virginia'.[121] A substantial number of MPs supported suppressing tobacco altogether, but their desire to 'banish all Tobacco' and 'pull it up by the Roots' because of 'the spoiling of the subjects Manners by it' met John Ferrar's rejoinder that '4,000 English there ... have no Means, as yet, to live' without it.[122] 'Give it some Time', urged the diarist and administrator John Smyth, an investor in the Virginia and Somers Islands companies who had helped to finance settlements in the Chesapeake, 'else we overthrow the Plantation'.[123]

Before John Rolfe, Ralph Hamor, and other colonists in Virginia began sending their own crops to England from the mid-1610s, the English largely consumed Spanish tobacco. They spent an estimated 44,000l. on tobacco

[119] 'A report of S[i]r George Yeardleys going Governor to Virginia', 5 December 1618, Ferrar Papers, FP 93.
[120] 'Tobacco trade', 18 April 1621, in *Journal of the House of Commons*, 579–82.   [121] Ibid.
[122] Ibid.   [123] Ibid.

in 1616, up from 8,000l. when James first ascended the throne.[124] Policy-makers recognized the weakness of this dependence. They were, in essence, investing in a commodity that bolstered a country whose Catholicism was a perceived threat to English activities in the Atlantic, not to mention to England itself. In addition, an estimated 60 per cent of tobacco consumed in England in the 1610s was sold illegally, evading James' customs and inciting numerous proclamations censuring those who thought it fit to ignore the king's laws.[125]

The expiring contract presented opportunities for gentlemen like Thomas Roe to present new projects and monopolies, at a time when the competing aims of plantation in the Virginia Company were contributing to vicious debates about colonial management among London councillors. 'In all contracts', wrote the MP Edward Ditchfield, 'especially of so publique nature, there are two principall qualities thought most consider-able, Justice and Profit'.[126] Ditchfield served on the parliamentary com-mittees for free trade and tobacco impositions with Sandys and saw the failed attempts to set up iron, silk, and wine industries in the colonies as the result of 'sundry misaccidents' that required a serious revision of policy.[127] The failures in Virginia were not the result of a lack of support from English councillors, who 'transported thether at their owne charge, upon the a foresaid hopes and incouragements', but from the 'fatall blow of the Massacrie [of the English in 1622] and the great molestations and disheart-enings of the company and Adventurers'.[128]

The debates conducted in Parliament reveal how deeply entangled colonial and domestic policies had become. Members of Parliament cir-culated copies of the merchant and colonial promoter Edward Bennett's treatise on the damaging effects of trade with Spain. Samuel Purchas referenced Bennett in *Purchas his pilgrimes* (1625), guiding his readers to Bennett's tract and displaying his own awareness of contemporary political debate.[129] 'It may be some man seeing this, will thinke, I am interressed in the *Virginia* Company,' Bennett proclaimed. 'But the Worshipfull of the Company know the contrary. It is the zeale I beare to the good of the State in generall that makes me speake'.[130] The rhetoric of the common good

---

[124] Goodman, *Tobacco in History*, 147.   [125] Ibid.

[126] Edward Ditchfield, *Considerations touching the new contract for tobacco* (1625; STC 6918), sig. A2r. On the rising role of the gentry in expansion and commerce, see Theodore K. Rabb, *Enterprise and Empire: Merchant and Gentry Investment in the Expansion of England, 1575–1630* (Cambridge, MA: Harvard University Press, 1967).

[127] Ditchfield, *Considerations touching the new contract*, sig. A4r.   [128] Ibid., sig. A4v.

[129] Purchas, *Purchas his pilgrimes*, sig. Mmmmmmm6r.

[130] Edward Bennett, *A treatise divided into three parts* (1620; STC 1883), sig. A5r.

met with contentious disagreement from those who preferred Spanish tobacco, but Bennett held firm: 'I defie the perticular gaines that brings a generall hurt'.[131]

Importing tobacco from Spain, Bennett maintained, was the chief cause of scarcity of bullion in England itself. In Parliament, Sandys and Nicholas Ferrar advanced tobacco as a means of salvaging the colony while curbing Spanish power. A petition presented by the Commons and recorded by Ferrar in May 1624 reminded the king that regulations around tobacco were related to much larger state affairs:

> It is generally known, that the West Indies are at this day almoast the onely Fountayne, and Spayne as it were the Cesterne ... But since this weede of Tobacko hath growen into request, they have payde (as their Proverb is) for all our Commodities with Their Smoake; And the rayne of there silver to us ... hath beene in a manner dried upp, to the loss of a Million and a halfe in mony in theese fifteene yeares last past.[132]

This 'miserable' condition had destabilized English trade, with 'mony transformed into a Smoking weed'.[133] The Commons asked James 'that the Importation of Tobacko, may be prohibited from all parts ... save your Majestys Dominions'.[134] Where James had stated in 1604 that 'idle delights' were 'the first seedes of the subversion of all Monarchies', Members of Parliament now deliberately framed tobacco as a marketable commodity under monarchical control.[135]

The royal proclamation following the decision to grant a monopoly on colonial tobacco announced that banning all tobacco not grown in America served the interest of James' loyal subjects in Virginia and 'the rest of our Empire'.[136] Foreshadowing the Navigation Acts of 1651, this was consistent with an emerging 'economy of empire ... determined by reasons of state'.[137] Virginia and Bermuda, James reasoned, 'are yet but in their infancie, and cannot be brought to maturitie and perfection, unlesse We will bee pleased for a time to tolerate unto them the planting and venting of the Tobacco'.[138] Though James built up a language of clemency towards his loyal subjects in the colonies, his dealings with his Privy Council show how concerned he and other members of the elite were

---

[131] Ibid.
[132] 'The Parliamentary Papers of Nicholas Ferrar, 1624', in *Seventeenth-Century Political and Financial Papers*, 89.
[133] Ibid., 90.   [134] Ibid.   [135] James I, *A counterblaste to tobacco*, sig. A3v.
[136] *By the King. A proclamation concerning tobacco.*
[137] Macmillan, *The Atlantic Imperial Constitution*, 107.
[138] *By the King. A proclamation concerning tobacco.*

with finding the best means to regulate importations while also securing high financial returns. The solicitor-general Robert Heath summarized this in a letter to Buckingham: 'the contract for Virginia tobacco ... will be a work both hon[oura]ble & p[ro]fitable if it be well managed'.[139]

In ultimately granting the Virginia Company a monopoly over tobacco in 1624, Parliament and the king acknowledged that though it might be an objectionable commodity, tobacco was also less of a danger than the 'Romish rabble', those 'right Canniballes' who were impeding the flourishing of the Protestant realm both at home and abroad.[140] Several years before, Edward Cecil had commented on the virulent Hispanophobia in England following the outbreak of the Thirty Years' War, telling Parliament he believed 'the Catholique king' represented 'the greatest enimie wee have in respecte of our Religion' and 'the greatest enimie we have in regard of the state'.[141] In terms of Spanish designs for a universal monarchy, 'England is the greatest Impediment in [Philip IV's] way', and Cecil brought home this threat by referencing events in recent memory, where 'the houses of Parliament wherein we nowe sitte doe have a Recorde against them in their unmatchable treason, the powder plott'.[142] He meticulously catalogued the cruelty of Catholics in their various dominions, played out in the Continent's religious wars but soon to affect England too. The outpour of accounts of Spanish horrors in the Indies published in the 1620s further reinforced that this crises was unravelling on a global scale. Investment in colonization projects – including Cecil's own 25l. contribution in 1620 – further connected support for Virginia with actively opposing Spanish rule.[143]

Debates in the Commons indicate MPs' real concerns with regulating behaviour, but also their increased recognition that the desire to check Spanish power was not easily separated from the need to keep Virginia English. The 1622 attack had devastated the resources that colonists had spent years cultivating, including glass and wine industries. Policies towards Algonquians became more punitive. The Virginia Company was bankrupt and in a state of collapse. A wealthier state would be in a position to exercise greater control, while the immediate concern of losing

---

[139] Solicitor General Heath to the Duke of Buckingham, 2 August 1624, The National Archives, SP 14/171, f. 10r.
[140] Nicholls, *The oration and sermon made at Rome*, sig. G6r.
[141] Speech in Parliament [Edward Cecil?], 1621, Hatfield House, CP 130/46r.   [142] Ibid.
[143] See, for example, Thomas Scott, *An Experimentall discoverie of Spanish practices* (1623; STC 22077), sig. E2r; King, *A sermon preached at White-Hall*, sig. Dr; de Montes, *The full, ample, and punctuall discovery of the barbarous, bloudy, and inhumane practices of the Spanish Inquisition*.

a presence in North America, alongside the promise of financial returns to company investments, rendered tobacco an accepted means of strengthening political authority. As the English Protestant polity looked westwards, the king himself acknowledged 'tobacco' as critical to 'our Empire', placing the commodity within the debates about colonial policy and sovereign authority discussed in Chapter 2.

Outside the council chamber, the incorporation of tobacco into elite sociability created new assemblages of goods and demonstrations of taste. Elaborate rituals of consumption served to separate gentlemanly smoking from Native American practices and the habits of the 'lower sort'. The publication of the London poet Anthony Chute's *Tabacco* in 1595 is evidence of how quickly gentlemen integrated tobacco into their wit coteries, where pipes appeared alongside heraldic designs, crowns, laurel leafs, and swords.[144] Personalized tobacco boxes or pouches accompanied other accoutrements including flint, steel, tongs, and pipes.[145] Thomas Dekker included a description of the process of smoking in his humorous mock-conduct manual, *The guls horne-booke* (1609), where 'our Gallant must draw out his Tobacco-box, the ladell for the cold snuffe into the nosthrill, the tongs and priming Iron: All which artillery may be of gold or silver (if he can reach to the price of it)'.[146] Cheaper boxes might be made of wood, while those most likely to endure were wrought with gold, silver, and ivory, often engraved with names, messages, mottos, or the faces of monarchs. A gold tobacco box from the second half of the seventeenth century, engraved with the face of Charles I, materially conveys the weight and importance of tobacco in a gentleman's self-presentation while connecting the object to royalist sympathies.[147] The box's bright metalwork and large size – eight centimetres long and six centimetres wide – suggests it was intended to be visually admired even as it served a practical function.

The tobacco debates in Parliament, in other words, did not happen in isolation. Referencing the quality of tobacco and the importance of provenance in dictating taste, Dekker's text situated tobacco and its associated cluster of goods within a broadening world of circulation and exchange. Though poking fun at fashion-seeking gentlemen lurking around 'the new Tobacco-office, or amongst the Booke-sellers, where [you] inquire who has writ against this divine weede', the humour in the rambling tale of young

[144] Anthony Chute, [*Tabacco*] (1595; STC 5262.5), sig. Av.
[145] Goodman, *Tobacco in History*, 66.
[146] Thomas Dekker, *The guls horne-booke* (1609; STC 6500), sig. Er.
[147] Tobacco box, circa the later seventeenth century, Victoria & Albert Museum, London, Loan: Gilbert. 545:1, 2–2008. Other extant tobacco boxes include M.26–1964, M.695:1.

men loose in London hinged on its recognizability, on the popularity of such shops and booksellers, and on the lively exchange of rumours about overseas interests.[148] Knowing 'what state Tobacco is in towne, better then the Merchants ... gaine Gentlemen no meane respect'.[149]

By creating a colonial monopoly on the trade, the commodity, to the metropolitan English, ceased to be a Native American one. Re-packaging an indigenous plant as a marker of colonial intervention allowed gentlemen to reconcile two seemingly conflicting things: intoxication and industry, pleasure and political good. John Smith commented that the average English planter in Virginia was 'applied to his labour about Tobacco and Corne' and that colonists no longer 'regard any food from the Salvages, nor have they any trade or conference with them'.[150] By the 1620s, Smith claimed, Algonquians were completely absent from the process of growing, cultivating, and trading tobacco with the English. Tobacco was an herb 'whose goodnesse and mine owne experience' induced Ralph Hamor to praise the 'pleasant, sweet, and strong' qualities of his 'owne planting'.[151]

Since the 'languishing state of the colonies' relied on metropolitan support of their only successful industry, gentlemen could frame tobacco less as an idle luxury than a 'taste of necessity'.[152] Having removed the plant from its biggest danger – that it was produced and smoked by 'savages' who exhibited behaviour unbefitting English subjects – it became possible to accept tobacco into society with more ease while continuing to advocate moderation and industry. Instead of a 'pagan' plant, tobacco was a 'Virginia leaf', grown by enterprising Protestant planters whose industriousness kept the colonies alive. This allowed Protestant policy-makers to distinguish their colonial efforts against Spain's *encomienda* system, endorsing Virginia as a stronghold against the extractive cruelty seen to characterize Spain's imperial aims and coercive labour force.

Yet under the harmonious fictions and the weighty language of public good expressed in parliamentary debate, the demand for tobacco

---

[148] Dekker, *The guls horne-booke*, sig. D2r.   [149] Ibid., sig. Er.

[150] John Smith, *The true travels, adventures, and observations of Captaine John Smith* (1630; STC 22796), sig G2v.

[151] Ralph Hamor, *A true discourse of the present state of Virginia* (1615; STC 12736), sig. Fv.

[152] James I to Solicitor General Heath, 2 July 1624, in *Calendar of State Papers: Colonial, Vol. 1*, 63; Orser, *An Archaeology of the British Atlantic World*, 376. On luxury, see Trentmann, *Empire of Things*; Sarah M. S. Pearsall, 'Gender', in *The British Atlantic World, 1500–1800*, 2nd ed., 133–51, at 144–5; John Sekora, *Luxury: The Concept in Western Thought, Eden to Smollet* (Baltimore, MD: Johns Hopkins University Press, 1977); Craig Muldrew, 'From Commonwealth to Public Opulence: The Redefinition of Wealth and Government in Early Modern Britain', in *Remaking English Society*.

necessitated greater labour forces than colonists could sustain on their own. From Bermuda, Nathaniel Butler reprimanded London councillors' unreasonable requests for tobacco, particularly when life on the island remained precarious. The plantations were plagued by infestation and suffering from poor management, and the 'Ilands . . . continually require trimmeinge'.[153] 'All the negroes left', Butler wrote, 'let them be delivered to the right honourable the Erle of Warwick . . . as his lordship himselfe shall direct', for he did not know how to provide for them.[154] It was the whims of gentlemen in London and the 'charge' to himself that most aggravated Butler: 'Informe me then, I beseech you . . . how are your negroes to be kept from going naked?'[155]

*

Over the course of James' reign, moral concerns over tobacco's capacity for inducing bodily and even spiritual corruption were subordinated to the greater need for economic prosperity and security against other European powers. MPs' attempts to regulate tobacco expressed concerns at how subjects might behave and what they might talk about when they met to smoke, relating tobacco to anxieties over social unrest and managing political news and rumour. In many ways, gentlemen could endorse an American intoxicant while continuing to disparage its use among the 'common sort' because the practice of smoking developed alongside the theories and policies about plantation, authority, and the law discussed in previous chapters. Intent on maintaining traditional systems of hierarchy and deference and grappling with the perceived dangers of tobacco on the body politic, pro-colonial gentlemen drew on broader ideas about civility to articulate refinement through industrious cultivation, one that resisted assimilation and operated independently from indigenous manufacture.

In the contested political climate of the 1620s, amid the laughter, heckling, and scribbling that enlivened Parliament sessions and tavern sociability, gentlemen used economic debates about tobacco to bring colonization into this theatre of dispute and mediation. Political pressures and personal desires informed the speeches of those who stood before the Commons to make a case for the value of tobacco in sustaining an English America. 'All our riches for the present doe consiste in Tobacco', John Pory reported to his friends from Jamestown in 1619. To John and Nicholas Ferrar, Sandys, and other Virginia Company supporters in Parliament, to

---

[153] *Historye of the Bermudaes or Summer Islands*, 219.   [154] Ibid., 211.   [155] Ibid., 219.

fail to support the tobacco monopoly was to abandon the colonial enterprise and their friends who had gone to carry it out.

The performance of civility, if correctly handled, could be enhanced
rather than damaged by incorporating tobacco within it. '[T]his smokes
delicious smack' evoked 'Westerne winds' and the 'fertile earth ... of
plenteous corne', bringing colonial aspirations into the households,
taverns, and council chambers where gentlemen debated politics.[156]
Though sourced from Native Americans whose practices were thousands
of years old, tobacco 'is thought a gentleman-like smell'.[157] Tobacco, pipes,
and finely wrought boxes made from costly materials became part of an
assemblage of goods that displayed the wealth of gentlemen while exhibiting their access to colonial trades and intelligence. As the next chapter
explores, these Atlantic 'things' fuelled gentlemanly sociability while operating in dialogue with political treatises, conduct manuals, and wit
literature.

The gentry's support of the colonial monopoly is indicative of their
imperial intent. According to the oral history of the Virginia Mattaponi,
John Rolfe married Pocahontas primarily to access the secret knowledge
about curing and processing tobacco, information that Powhatan religious
leaders or *quiakros* carefully guarded but might share with trusted members
of their communities.[158] The English nonetheless continued to describe
Native Americans as a 'scattered people' and 'ignorant', voicing their
responsibility to 'discover the country, subdue the people, bring them to
be tractable civil and industrious, and teach them trades that the fruits of
their labours might make us recompence'.[159] This idea of making *them* civil
and industrious to benefit *us* went to the heart of metropolitan ideas about
the making of a successful polity, where gentlemen sought to establish an
infrastructure of plantation industry intended to enhance the civil identities of those who governed.

---

[156] John Beaumont, *The metamorphosis of tabacco* (1602; STC 1695), sigs. Dr, D3v.
[157] *Epigrammes and elegies by J. D. and C. M.*, sig. C4r.
[158] Linwood 'Little Bear' Custalow and Angel Daniel 'Silver Star', *The True Story of Pocahontas: The Other Side of History* (Golden, CO: Fulcrum, 2007), 73–4.
[159] Smith, *A map of Virginia*, sig. Lr.

CHAPTER 5

Wit, Sociability, and Empire

Onlookers described the social world of the metropolitan elite as a glittering and at times poisoned menagerie, inhabited by peacocks, swans, chameleons, and monkeys. Young, 'new-fangled' gentlemen flitted '[i]n silken sutes like gawdy Butterflies' along the Thames, travelling from Whitehall to Southwark to frequent plays or to woo lovers.[1] Satires derided the mix of pleasure-seeking and political pretensions found among urban gentlemen who lived around the four Inns of Court. Impetuous, beautifully attired, status-driven: these men were ruthlessly 'in contempt of poorer fates' and '[p]uft up by conquest'.[2] The political aspirants who navigated the 'sinewes of a cities mistique body', as John Donne's narrator complained in 'Satire I', were status-obsessed officeholders and young members of the gentry, who 'did excell/Th'Indians, in drinking [their] Tobacco well' and who sought the goods that 'schemes' and global intervention produced.[3]

While scholarship remains attuned to the way manners created modes of urbanity through which politics was discussed and accessed, little has been made of the influence of colonization on metropolitan civility, particularly among a demographic of young men intent on establishing state careers.[4] At the Inns of Court, gentlemen were encouraged to respond creatively to debates about the political realm and civil society through plays, masques, and the circulation of verse. In 1572, the MP John Hooker compared the House of Commons to a theatre, where, like civility, politics was performed and put on display.[5] What happened to these performances when American objects and representations of Native peoples came into them?

---

[1] Edward Guilpin, *Skialetheia. Or, A shadowe of truth* (1598; STC 12504), sig. B4r.
[2] Ibid., sig. A3v. [3] *Poems, by J[ohn]. D[onne].* (1633; STC 7045), sigs. Tt3r, Tt4v.
[4] Ian Warren, 'The English Landed Elite and the Social Environment of London, 1580–1700: The Cradle of an Aristocratic Culture?', *English Historical Review*, 126 (2011), 44–74, at 46.
[5] Chris R. Kyle, *Theatre of State: Parliament and Political Culture in Early Stuart England* (Stanford, CA: Stanford University Press, 2012), 1–2.

As Noah Millstone argues, attention to political culture should include language and ideas as well as material culture and the social meaning of objects that emphasize 'use, purpose, and strategy' – in other words, that demonstrate how beliefs functioned in practice.[6] This final chapter examines how the Inns as institutions fostered spaces of masculine sociability where gentlemen came to behave and view themselves as colonizers. Understanding how gentlemen incorporated America into their social habits and performances challenges the idea that civility was 'essentially rhetorical', or that sociability and taste were disconnected from political decision-making and a detailed knowledge of colonial conditions.[7]

As Donne himself exemplified, moving beyond the sumptuous imagery of America in his wit poetry composed at Lincoln's Inn in the 1590s to sitting on the Virginia Company council and preaching a sermon in support of colonization in 1622, here was a generation who came of age with America. This demographic complicates the scholarly tendency to see the language of civic duty and common good as overwhelmingly driving Jacobean expansion.[8] In the realm of political thought, such rhetoric did dominate, but the making of an imperial polity also involved concerted efforts to make colonization a fashionable element of English political culture for the first time. By negotiating the bounds of excess and control, gentlemen praised plantation through carefully calibrated expressions of wit that simultaneously served to exclude those who failed to meet accepted standards of behaviour and taste. By promoting their civilizing project through colonial intervention, gentlemen developed and modified their own ideas of civility, one that was increasingly contingent on endorsing empire.

The Taste for Expansion

The seventeenth century saw the development of a London 'season' caused by two major factors: first, the development of London-based political, legal, and administrative institutions; and second, the city's rise in trade and a global economy that made London the centre of commercialized leisure.[9] The Inns of Court were affected by both. Admissions rose steeply in this period, with the sons of gentry increasingly seeking to polish their education through an immersion into London society. The Inns partly

[6] Millstone, *Manuscript Circulation and the Invention of Politics*, 15.
[7] Thomas, *In Pursuit of Civility*, 255.
[8] Fitzmaurice, *Humanism and America*; Rabb, *Jacobean Gentleman*.
[9] Warren, 'The English Landed Elite and the Social Environment of London', 44.

served as a 'finishing school' while offering a place to establish political connections essential to establishing a career in government.[10] The training in law, whether or not members of the Inns were ever called to the bar – many were not – endowed members with the rudimentary basics that statesmen like Thomas Elyot had advocated since the sixteenth century for those who sought government positions.[11] The impact of metropolitan life on large numbers of the gentry who had previously spent much of their time in the provinces was substantial, and manifested itself partly through changing codes of behaviour and sociability among the elite.[12]

As early as the fifteenth century, chief justice John Fortescue stressed that the education that young men received at the Inns went beyond the study of law, providing 'nurseries' where the courtly arts and government patronage might be obtained.[13] Inventories show that the most valuable goods gentlemen brought with them from Oxford or Cambridge to London were apparel and books, including cosmographies.[14] In their pursuit of refined civility, Inns members in the early Stuart period disparaged the lower branches at the Inns of Chancery, not because these students lacked learning but because their education often served as a form of apprenticeship.[15] Members of the lesser gentry or country merchant families made up the 'lower branch' of the legal profession, usually trained at one of the eight Inns of Chancery that prepared them to become justices of peace, sheriffs, and clerks.[16]

Scholars have examined the unique dramatic and literary environment of the Inns, where gentlemen were encouraged to think about the law and government through creative refraction.[17] Entertainments, spectacles, and literary output at the Inns were a mandatory feature of formal education, often intersecting with 'devices' and performances at court.[18] While Paul

---

[10] David Lemmings, *Gentlemen and Barristers: The Inns of Court and the English Bar, 1680–1730* (Oxford: Clarendon, 1990), 5.
[11] Brooks, *Pettyfoggers and Vipers*, 161.
[12] Warren, 'The English Landed Elite and the Social Environment of London', 45.
[13] Brooks, *Pettyfoggers and Vipers*, 161.
[14] Inventory of M[aste]r Smith's apparel and books at Cambridge and Gray's Inn, 1603, The National Archives, SP 12/288, f. 52r.
[15] Brooks, *Pettyfoggers and Vipers*, 181.   [16] Ibid., 2.
[17] *The Intellectual and Cultural World of the Early Modern Inns of Court*, ed. Jayne Elisabeth Archer et al. (Manchester: Manchester University Press, 2011); Wilfred R. Prest, *The Inns of Court under Elizabeth I and the Early Stuarts, 1590–1640* (London: Longman, 1972); Paul Raffield, *Images and Cultures of Law in Early Modern England: Justice and Political Power, 1558–1660* (Cambridge: Cambridge University Press, 2004); *Inns of Court*, ed. Alan H. Nelson and John R. Elliott (Cambridge: D. S. Brewer, 2010); Jessica Winston, *Lawyers at Play: Literature, Law, and Politics at the Early Modern Inns of Court* (Oxford: Oxford University Press, 2016).
[18] Raffield, *Images and Cultures of Law*, 87.

Raffield emphasizes, perhaps overly so, the Inns' constitutionalism and critique of the monarchy, Jessica Winston demonstrates that the Inns provided contested spaces where gentlemen passionately defended 'the necessity of political dialogue' and where they 'broadened participation in that dialogue, making themselves figuratively and perhaps even literally, in terms of the performance space, central to conversations'.[19] As Winston points out, the influence of the Inns as institutions operating within the political nation did not lie just in members' interest in the law or literature, but in their political connections and their strong sense of duty.[20] The Inns were places where Members of Parliament, justices of the peace, lawyers, poets, magistrates, and courtiers all mingled, exchanged ideas, and, as Michelle O'Callaghan demonstrates, drank, ate, and discoursed together.[21] Sociability involved the meeting between friends but also the networks of associations, both professional and informal, that perpetuated specific codes of behaviour and led to charged moments of social interaction and political debate.[22] The terms 'company', 'society', or 'fraternity' suggested an associational politics of participation that involved constructing boundaries to include and exclude, and concerns over civil behaviour propagated at this time should be understood partly as a response to this competitive atmosphere.[23]

Jacobean satirists frequently lampooned Inns gentlemen for caring more about social status than their studies. At times, critiques of ostentation hardly seem exaggerated. Looking back on his time at the Middle Temple in the 1620s, Edward Hyde, later Earl of Clarendon, admitted that 'the License of those Times ... was very exorbitant'.[24] Writers mocked the Inns man who 'takes Tobacco, and doth weare a locke,/ And wastes more time in dressing then [*sic*] a Wench'.[25] 'Initiated in a Taverne', members soon learned what was truly important in university and then the city: velvets, tennis, books about honour tied with silk strings, and wit 'which may doe him Knights service in the Country hereafter'.[26] Matthew Carew, a civil lawyer trained on the Continent, complained to Dudley Carleton in 1613 that one of his sons cared only for 'houndes and hawkes' while the other 'is of the Midle [*sic*] Temple, where

---

[19] Winston, *Lawyers at Play*, 187.   [20] Ibid., 51.   [21] O'Callaghan, *The English Wits*.
[22] Phil Withington, 'Company and Sociability in Early Modern England', *Social History*, 32 (2007), 291–307.
[23] Ibid., 302.
[24] Quoted in Will Tosh, *Male Friendship and Testimonies of Love in Shakespeare's England* (Basingstoke: Palgrave, 2016), 100.
[25] *Epigrammes and elegies by J. D. and C. M.*, sig. B4r.
[26] Earle, *Micro-cosmographie*, sigs. E8r–9r.

he hath a chamber and studye, but I heare studieth the law very litle'.[27] This was the poet Thomas Carew, eighteen at the time and seemingly inclined to use his education for somewhat less principled reasons than serving the commonwealth.

On the other hand, the sometimes unruly behaviour at the Inns was often less a rejection of discipline than an attempt to preserve and define it in other spheres. The term 'civil' brought together 'the political and the social, the personal and the public within a common framework of order'.[28] Members styled themselves as active proponents of a '"civilizing" agency' and promoted an ethos of responsibility towards government and the law, all in a cosmopolitan environment through which good manners were cultivated.[29] What was law, the Gray's Inn lawyer Henry Finch wrote, but the '[a]rt of wel ordering a Civil Societie'?[30] Portraits commissioned by students portrayed them with formal demeanours that appear to reflect their attempts to separate themselves from those enrolled at the Inns of Chancery. Nicholas Hilliard's portrait miniature of Francis Bacon is one example, painted in 1578 when Bacon resumed his studies at Gray's Inn following his tour of Europe. Clad in simple black attire, his head held high and framed by a large ruff, Bacon cast an elegant but haughty gaze towards the viewer, while a Latin inscription declared the mind to be worthier of illustration than the face.[31]

Given members' self-referential commitment to civility, their deep enthusiasm for colonization strongly suggests that expansion increasingly served as a manifestation of their own civil interests. While it is not the intention to downplay the importance of the law in the education of gentlemen at the Inns, little extant evidence suggests that gentlemen used the law to pursue colonization in particularly innovative ways. If anything, the law is strangely absent in benchers' fascination with the Atlantic. Bacon, in his essay 'On Plantations', made no mention of the lawfulness of expansion. Commonplace books belonging to law students were filled with poetry, diary entries, and litigation terms and cases, but interests in Native Americans and America appear in the first two forms rather than the latter. The Virginia Company had repeatedly stated that territorial expansion in the Atlantic was lawful because it involved converting 'infidels'; because the English were not coming to conquer, but to trade; and due to the concept of *res nullius*, that 'there is roome sufficient in the

---

[27] Sir Matthew Carew to Dudley Carleton, 25 February 1613, The National Archives, SP 14/72, f. 71r.
[28] Bryson, *From Courtesy to Civility*, 73.   [29] O'Callaghan, *The English Wits*, 13.
[30] Henry Finch, *Law, or a discourse thereof* (1627; STC 10871), sig. Br.
[31] Portrait of Francis Bacon by Nicholas Hilliard, 1578, National Portrait Gallery, NPG 6761.

land . . . for them, and us'.[32] Further, the company claimed, the Powhatans had already violated the 'law of nations' by using English 'ambassadors' poorly, and '*Powhatan*, their chiefe King, received voluntarilie a crowne and a scepter, with a full acknowledgement of dutie and submission'.[33] Rather than drawing on the law to justify expansion, gentlemen seemed to accept the justifications laid out in the charters of joint-stock companies, and used America and its peoples to construct their social and political identities in other ways.

Scholarly discussions of English civility remain curiously void of the influence of imperial aspirations and discourses about 'civilizing' others on its development. Anna Bryson remarks on the significance of John Dickenson's translation of Aristotle's *Politics* (1598), which included mention of the uncivil 'savages' of America, but her study only allows for a fleeting acknowledgement that colonization must have influenced ideas of civility and savagery.[34] Nonetheless, from the later Elizabethan era gentlemen at the Inns advanced a civility that related to imperial intervention. In 'The Prince of Love', the elaborate Christmas revels at the Middle Temple in 1597/8, gentlemen channelled their devotion to Queen Elizabeth by proclaiming her power to soften and refine men: 'She, by uniting mens hearts unto her, hath made herself a mind-subduing Conqueror . . . civilizing her subjects, whom in the past accounted barbarous'.[35] The author, likely Bacon, espoused the classical ideas of honour with imperial might, specifically relating successful expansion to the civilizing power of the monarch. '[B]y your Exploits and Victories . . . you shall find a sweet Respect into the Adventures of your youth . . . you shall eternize your Name, and leave deep Foot-steps of your Power in the World'.[36]

The networks of patronage at the Inns helped to turn such spectacles into reality. Fuelled by the travel reports they acquired at nearby printers' shops and privy to colonial intelligence through their connections to court and Parliament, gentlemen were well placed to apply their political aspirations to expansionist projects. The physical spaces of the Inns – gardens, private chambers, libraries, halls, chapels – provided places of study, deliberation, and performance. Bacon's close affiliation with Gray's Inn,

---

[32] *A true declaration of the estate of the colonie in Virginia* (1610; STC 24833), sig. B3v.
[33] Ibid., sig. B4r.   [34] Bryson, *From Courtesy to Civility*, 51–2.
[35] Rudyerd, *Le prince d'amour*, sig. B6r. See also Rudyerd's notes on the event, 'Benjamin Rudyerd's account of the joint revels of the Middle Temple and Lincoln's Inn', 1597, The Middle Temple, MT.7/RUD/1.
[36] Rudyerd, *Le prince d'amour*, sig. Fr.

where he lived and built expansive gardens, involved meeting with projectors and other colonial enthusiasts. He likely met with Ralegh in the Gray's Inn gardens to discuss Ralegh's Guiana ventures, and William Strachey, who went to Virginia as secretary, dedicated his 'Historie of the Travaile into Virginia Britannia' to Bacon in 1612. Strachey offered himself to Bacon's service because he was 'bound to your observance, by being one of the Graies-Inne Societe', where '[y]our Lordship ever approving yourself ... of the Virginia Plantation, being from the beginning (with other lords and earles) of the principal counsell applyed to propagate and guide yt'.[37]

In his dedicatory epistle to Francis Walsingham in the first edition of *The principal navigations* (1589), Richard Hakluyt credited the Middle Temple as the place where his interests in colonization were first ignited. Writing in the mystical language of revelation, Hakluyt recalled the moment, as a boy in his cousin's chambers in the Middle Temple, when he first gazed upon a cosmography and heard of the opportunities that lay in the uncharted realms beyond England. This left a deep impression on Hakluyt, for his cousin's discourse was 'of high and rare delight to my yong nature'.[38] Sermons that endorsed colonization were entrenched in this world of reading and exploration. The churchmen enlisted to support the Virginia Company in its 1609 campaign had Inns connections. William Crashaw, for example, was preacher at the Middle Temple, where he helped to collect and publish news from North America and Bermuda. Crashaw retained close links to fellow Middle Templar Henry Wriothesley, third Earl of Southampton, who acquired much of Crashaw's vast library before becoming treasurer of the Virginia Company.

The literary scholar Michelle O'Callaghan finds that wit coteries in Jacobean England were closely related to members' associations with the Virginia Company, especially at the Middle Temple and Lincoln's Inn.[39] Men who spent much of the year in the localities came to London on business and to sit in Parliament, meeting in taverns and public houses to discuss current events in a convivial atmosphere in which literature and politics easily and often converged. The 'sireniacal gentlemen' who met at

[37] William Strachey, *The Historie of Travaile into Virignia Britannia*, ed. R. H. Major (London: Hakluyt Society, 1949), xli; Mark Nicholls and Penry Williams, *Sir Walter Raleigh: In Life and Legend* (London: Continuum, 2011), 288.

[38] Richard Hakluyt, *The principall navigations, voiages and discoveries of the English nation* (1589; STC 12625), sig. *2r.

[39] O'Callaghan, *The English Wits*, 4.

the Mermaid tavern on Bread Street in the early 1600s included lawyers, courtiers, and business associates who encouraged colonization. Robert Phelips, John Hoskyns, John Donne, Francis Bacon, Christopher Brooke, and Richard Martin were among those who served the London company in various legal capacities and had clear vested interests in Virginia. They were encouraged by patrons including Southampton, Robert Cecil, and the financier and MP Lionel Cranfield, first Earl of Middlesex, who had connections with City merchants and offered major financial support for Atlantic expeditions.[40] The playwrights Ben Jonson, Francis Beaumont, and John Fletcher also met at the Mermaid, and brought America, Native Americans, and tobacco to the popular stage.[41] These men also collaborated on court masques and City pageants, suggesting a cross-over between ideas of America and its peoples as they were depicted in various spaces, and to different audiences.

Viewing themselves as the arbiters of taste, gentlemen helped to set the foundations for what a well-ordered 'Civill Societie' might entail in an imperial context. Their role was especially important after Cecil and James' eldest son, Henry, both died in 1612. Cecil and Henry were two of the most influential colonial patrons of the time, and, until James' renewed interest in the Virginia colony in the late 1610s, members of the Inns helped to keep colonial interest alive. George Chapman's *The memorable masque* (1613), featuring members of the Inns dressed as 'Virginians', allowed Richard Martin and other investors to employ the politically charged symbolism of the performance to present a utopian colony at an uncertain moment in its future, enabling affiliates of the company to make pointed political comments to an aristocratic audience.

Inns members sought intelligence on overseas voyages and copied travel reports into their commonplace books. Individuals kept themselves informed on Ralegh's attempts at colonizing South America by transcribing Ralegh's accounts 'selected out of S[i]r Walter Raleighes first booke of his discoverie of Guyana'.[42] One anonymous transcriber chose to note the customs of the indigenous inhabitants who fiercely resisted foreign powers: they were 'wont to make war upon all Nations, and especially w[i]th the

---

[40] Ibid., 16.

[41] Gavin Hollis, *The Absence of America: The London Stage, 1576–1642* (Oxford: Oxford University Press, 2015), 28–30.

[42] Ralegh's Guiana Voyages, 1618, British Library, Sloane MS B 3272; 'An abstract of diverse memorable thinges, worth the noting, selected out of S[i]r Walter Raleighes first booke of his discoverie of Guyana', after 1595, British Library, Sloane MS B 3272; 'Miscellaneous letters from Sir Walter Rawleighe', 1611–18, British Library, Add MS 29598.

Caniballs'.[43] These groups separated the skin from the bones of their dead, taking the former to 'hang it in the Casiq[ue]s howse that died, and deck his scull w[i]th feathers of all colours, & hang all his goldeplates about the boanes of his armes, thighs, and legges'.[44] These reports seem to describe what anthropologists now acknowledge was a practice of memorializing the dead among certain groups.[45]

Inns gentlemen also expressed interest in the short-lived Amazon Company in 1619. Of the thirteen original adventurers, roughly a third were trained at Gray's Inn, Lincoln's Inn, or the Inner Temple. James knighted three members at some point in their careers, and they contributed 500l. to the original 2,500l. collected for the company's first voyage.[46] Investment in the Amazon Company brought together the interests of Inns members and court patrons. These South American projects were 'an adventure and a chaunce at hazarde', wrote the lawyer John Hayward to his friend Nicholas Carew in an enthusiastic note written at Inner Temple in 1617.[47] Disenchanted courtiers, aggravated by the Spanish ambassador Gondomar's proximity to James and the Duke of Buckingham's pro-Spanish policies, supported intervention in Guiana partly to challenge Catholic interests. Related to this, the support of the Amazon Company may reflect attempts on the part of Ralegh's supporters to sustain his imperial projects after his trial and execution in 1618. While merchants had largely steered clear of Ralegh's final Guiana voyage, backing for his ventures at the Inns had remained strong. 'I praye let us heare from you to morrowe, and let mee receave my dyrections from you for w[i]thout yt I shall doe nothinge more,' Hayward had written to Carew, urging him to invest in Ralegh's undertaking. 'I coulde wishe you were in towne, for I feare mee you will gette no monye, but you must adventure'.[48]

Gentlemen also directly involved themselves first-hand in voyages of discovery. In 1582, Richard Madox, an Oxford fellow at All Souls, embarked on a voyage overseen by Martin Frobisher and Francis Drake to establish spice trades, in a route that eventually took Madox to Sierra

---

[43] 'An abstract of diverse memorable thinges', f. 7r.　　[44] Ibid.

[45] James B. Peterson and John G. Crock, '"Handsome Death": The Taking, Veneration, and Consumption of Human Remains in the Insular Caribbean and Greater Amazonia', in *The Taking and Displaying of Human Body Parts*, 547–74.

[46] 'The preamble for subscription to the Amazon company, with the signatures of the original thirteen adventurers', 6 April 1619, in *English and Irish Settlement on the River Amazon*, 194–5. The affiliated members were John Danvers (Lincoln's Inn), Robert Rich (Inner Temple), Edward Cecil (Gray's Inn), and Nathaniel Rich (Gray's Inn).

[47] John Haywarde to Nicholas Carew, 12 February 1617, Folger Shakespeare Library, MS V.b.288.

[48] Ibid.

Leone and Brazil.[49] Madox's diary seemed to have been intended for readership, probably by the courtiers who invested in the voyage. These included Francis Walsingham, William Cecil, and the Earl of Warwick, all of whom were members of Gray's Inn. With its Latin and Greek references, veiled allusions and pseudonyms, and recordings of seditious behaviour, Madox's diary was both private record and government report, and offers one example of the way university-educated gentlemen participated in projects for expansion in America beyond collecting second-hand information.[50] Better known for his later travel to India, the Middle Templar Thomas Roe commanded an expedition to Guiana in 1611, encouraged by Ralegh, Cecil, and Prince Henry. Accounts written into the 1630s, including Henry Colt's from Barbados in 1631, are in many ways the results of the vogue for planting apparent at the Inns in the 1580s and 1590s. Colt had been admitted to Lincoln's Inn in 1596 and, before the systems of slavery irrevocably changed plantation systems, colonization remained in the hands of those Colt considered 'gentlemen of note' – 'younge men, & [of] good desert' who must find ways to rein in the 'quarrelsome conditions of your fiery spiritts' by serving the commonwealth abroad.[51]

Sociability and table talk brought colonization into networks of literary production. The poems and epigrams about America by Chapman, Donne, and Michael Drayton, some of them likely shared over dinners in City taverns, were informed by an awareness of their associates' experience abroad. Around 1610, a W. S., perhaps William Strachey, wrote a letter asking to borrow money, desperate not to miss the opportunity to 'meete w[i]th some Frendes at dinner [who are] returned from Virginia'.[52] Chapman's poem 'De Guiana' (1596), Drayton's 'To the Virginian Voyage' (1606), and tobacco poems like John Beaumont's *The metamorphosis of tabacco* (1602) or Raphael Thorius' *Hymnus tabaci* (1626) must be situated within this milieu of gentlemanly sociability, where verses were privately circulated, read aloud, and discussed over wine and tobacco. 'De Guiana' was Chapman's contribution to Lawrence Kemys' *A relation of the second voyage to Guiana* (1596), a voyage 'perfourmed' under the direction of Ralegh.[53] Under the rhetoric of easy imperialism, Chapman and his readers were aware of the more complex process of colonization

[49] 'The Diary of John Walker', 7 December 1582, in *An Elizabethan in 1582: The Diary of Richard Madox, Fellow of All Souls*, ed. Elizabeth Story Donno (London: Hakluyt Society, 1976), 326.
[50] Ibid., 21, 59.   [51] 'The Voyage of S[i]r Henrye Colt Knight', 65.
[52] W. S. to [unknown], *c.*1610, Folger MS V.a.321, f. 60r.
[53] Kemys, *A relation of the second voyage to Guiana*, frontispiece.

that included interactions with Arawaks and Caribs. While the land itself offered itself willingly to the English, Chapman extolled, the English must actively bring 'what heretofore savage corruption held/in barbarous *Chaos*'.[54] '*America*, A merry K, *Peru*', wrote the water poet John Taylor to his friend, the fellow 'sireniacal' Thomas Coryate, '*Virginia* of thy worth doth onely heare,/And longs the weight of thy foot-steps to beare:/Returne thee, O returne thee quickly than,/And see the mighty Court of *Powhatan*', a reference to Pocahontas' father.[55]

A later poem by Drayton, 'To Master George Sandys Treasurer for the English Colony in Virginia' (1626), concluded by asking after 'noble *Wyats* health', referring to the governor Francis Wyatt, who was just finishing his term as first royal governor.[56] In asking about 'descriptions of the place' and 'our people there', Drayton exhibited an awareness of actual happenings on the ground. John Donne, in privately circulated manuscripts in the 1590s, may have eroticized the American landscape in 'Elegy XIX – To His Mistress Going to Bed', but he also sought the position of treasurer for the Virginia Company in 1609. This post demanded conformity to the dominant Protestant attitude that sought to convert Algonquians, but also to 'civilize' them according to English customs, a stance Donne publicly promoted as dean of St Paul's in his sermon to the Virginia Company in 1622. Colonization, Crashaw had insisted in 1610, 'is not only a lawfull, but a most excellent and holie action, and, as the case now stands, so necessarie, that I hold every man bound to assist', an appeal gentlemen responded favourably to.[57]

The Material Atlantic

In August 1586, Francis Drake returned from his raids on the Spanish West Indies and 'came into the Middle Temple Hall at dinner time', where benchers filled the hall with applause and greeted him 'with great joy'.[58] Drake enjoyed a privileged status at the Inns despite having begun his career as a seafaring apprentice. Fragments of the 'Drake lantern', ostensibly from Drake's ship *The Golden Hind*, continue to hang in Middle

---

[54] Kemys, *A relation of the second voyage to Guiana*, sig. Av.

[55] John Taylor, *All the workes of John Taylor the water-poet* (1630; STC 23725), sig. Gg6r.

[56] Michael Drayton, *The battaile of Agincourt … Elegies upon sundry occasions* (1627; STC 7190), sig. Bbv.

[57] Crashaw, *A sermon preached in London*, sig. C4v.

[58] *The Middle Temple Records, Vol. 1: 1501–1603*, ed. Charles Henry Hopwood (London: Butterworth & Company, 1904), 285–6.

Temple Hall, where an oak desk said to contain part of the ship's deck also survives. When Drake made his dramatic entrance at Middle Temple Hall that late summer evening, he had been to South America but also to Roanoke, bringing back its struggling colonists.

The excitement of Drake's return was undoubtedly linked to Drake's flamboyant opposition of the Spanish and, related to this, to the acquisition of goods. The commodities that circulated in Drake's own ships, and those he intercepted in the West Indies and South America, connected the Americas to England in a tangible way. These ships were conduits to the circulation of precious commodities that the English sought as demonstrations of their own prestige, from pearls to precious metals.[59] Objects were intended to carry out the civilizing project of empire on multiple levels, from the material wealth they brought into England to the 'civilizing' effect English objects were believed to have on Native Americans. The baskets and red featherwork presented by the coastal Miwok to Drake in California were contrasted against the wrought silver items that the English brought with them overseas. Drake's ships were equipped with provisions 'for ornament and delight', such as silver table utensils and 'all sorts of curious workmanship' so that 'the civilitie and magnificence of his native country' might be 'more admired'.[60] To the English, showcasing metal-wrought objects to Native Americans expressed a covetable English civility while establishing trade links that would benefit the 'kingdome here at home' and build indigenous Americans' dependence on European goods.[61]

Objects brought back by captains and merchants helped to establish the relationship between American landscapes and the metropolis. Recounting Drake's trip to western North America, one report described that '[t]his country our General [Drake] named *Albion*, and that for two causes; the one in respect of the white bancks and cliffes, which lie towards the sea; the other, that it might have some affinity, even in name also, with our own country'.[62] The particular things that Drake brought with him into the Middle Temple from his Atlantic voyages are unknown. Whether he carried Native American artefacts with him or not, other Atlantic things played a role in gentlemanly self-presentation. Thomas Hariot, who returned to England from Roanoke with Drake, was credited with helping to make tobacco a popular pastime among the elite, but his drawings and notes about Algonquians, at least those that survived the voyage back, may

---

[59] Orser, *An Archaeology of the British Atlantic World*, 186.
[60] Francis Fletcher, *The world encompassed by Sir Francis Drake* (1628; STC 7161), sig. A6r.
[61] Ibid., sig. Lr.   [62] Ibid., sig. L2v.

also have been shared or circulated prior to him publishing versions of his *Briefe and true report*. John White's watercolours, still acclaimed for their elegant naturalism, paid remarkable attention to Algonquian facial expressions and details (see Figure 3). These were also, however, presentation items. Copies were made and were likely intended for display, visible to select members of the pro-imperial coteries of which Ralegh and his friend Henry Percy, ninth Earl of Northumberland, were patrons.

Objects and visual displays of colonial knowledge shaped gentlemanly responses to colonization. The spaces of the Inns, like some portraits, may be seen as amassing and exhibiting 'consumption constellations' that served to endorse the visual appeal of colonial intervention through a series of interconnected objects.[63] Gentlemen used these environments to promote colonization through specific assemblages of material culture, including globes, cosmographies, travel compendia, pearl jewellery, drawings and engravings, and tobacco pipes and boxes. The Middle Temple Library's terrestrial and celestial 'Molyneux globes' raise attention to how such objects connected gentlemen to their imperial aspirations in a physical way. These globes, created in 1592, were subsequently modified to contain updated information that reflected Ralegh and Drake's voyages in the Atlantic. As on maps, gentlemen updated the coastlines of their globes based on changing cartographic knowledge, where subtle overlayers of paint display ongoing attempts at cartographical precision.[64] The commissioner of the globe is unknown, but the globe maker, Emery Molyneux, was affiliated with John Dee and Ralegh's circle in London and accompanied Drake on his circumnavigation.[65]

Gentlemen quickly began to use and display the objects that came to them from America, drawing on iconographies and representations of Native peoples in their writings and performances. The Middle Temple lawyer Edward Phelips was not amused when benchers complained in 1613 that one gentleman refused to return his costume from the Virginian masque.[66] 'Lett m[aste]r peters presently come unto me', Phelips scrawled underneath the complaint, 'for I hold his deniall very strange'.[67] The

[63] Orser, *An Archaeology of the British Atlantic World*, 359.
[64] Lesley B. Cormack, *Charting an Empire: Geography at the English Universities, 1580–1620* (Chicago, IL: University of Chicago Press, 1997); Helen M. Wallis, 'Further Light on the Molyneux Globes', *The Geographical Journal*, 121 (1955), 304–11; Susan Maxwell, 'Thomas Cavendish's Visit to Puná Island in 1587', *The Mariner's Mirror* (103), 136–49, at 147.
[65] Cormack, *Charting an Empire*, 126–7.
[66] Petition by the benchers of the Middle Temple to Sir Edward Phelips, 1614, The Middle Temple, MT.7/MAA36r.
[67] Ibid.

surviving petition does not specify which costume Peters seemed so intent on retaining, but it very well may have been one of the fifty 'Virginian' habits worn by the 'civillest' gentlemen of the Inns and 'imitating Indian worke' and motifs, including embroidered suns and feathers 'compast in Coronets, like the Virginia Princes'.[68]

'Coronets' or feather headdresses were a recurring symbol of indigene-ity, appearing in emblems, cosmographies, and fashion books derived from earlier Continental works and from more recent accounts of English travel. Henry Peacham, a writer and illustrator at Prince Henry's court, used a South American headdress to invite a reflection on personal honour in his 1612 emblem book (Figure 6). Peacham's engravings were of his own invention, and he depicted an 'Indian Diadem' suspended over water, framed by Italianate grotesques that were given an American bent with the inclusion of a turkey. To gain acclaim, the verses went, '[w]e pick from others praises here and there,/So patch herewith an Indian Diadem/Of Parrats feather'.[69]

Intriguingly, Peacham's verses seemed to demonstrate some knowledge of the function of feathers in bestowing honour upon the wearer who earned them. To accumulate undeserving accolades was akin to wearing 'Plumes indeed, whereto we have no right'.[70] Peacham perhaps gleaned his information from accounts of English travel to Greater Amazonia. The shading of the feathers in the emblem suggests a multi-coloured headdress, such as were prized by indigenous leaders, and the woven basketry plaiting at the base is strikingly similar to that of surviving featherwork from Guiana (compare to Figure 4). Despite the English awareness of the value of such objects, the appearance of featherwork in cabinets of curiosity or in performances also indicates a willingness to disregard their super-natural force.

At the Middle Temple, perhaps as a result of Pocahontas and other Algonquians coming to London in 1616, English 'Virginians' were accused of wearing their hair in imitation of Powhatan religious men.[71] 'I have heard Sir Thomas Dale and Master Rolph say', Samuel Purchas recounted, that this fashion 'was first by our men [worn] in the first plantation ... borrowed from these savages – a fair unlovely generation of the lovelock, Christians imitating savages, and they the devil!'[72] In 1628, William Prynne also attributed lovelocks to Algonquians. Prynne had entered Lincoln's Inn

---

[68] George Chapman, *The memorable masque of the two honourable Houses or Innes of Court* (1614; STC 4982), sig. Br.

[69] Henry Peacham, *Minerva Britanna, or A garden of heroical devises* (1612; STC 19511), sig. Eev.

[70] Ibid. [71] Tomocomo, 'Interview in London (1617)', in *Jamestown Narratives*, 881. [72] Ibid.

Figure 6 Henry Peacham, *Minerva Britanna, or A garden of heroical devises* (1612), featuring a head ornament from South America. Used by permission of the Folger Shakespeare Library.

in 1621, at a time when authorities were clamping down on the more gaudy sartorial displays of wayward students insistent on wearing long boots and growing their hair. Prynne's attempt to promote civil deportment seems directly informed by the Algonquian Tomocomo's earlier presence in London. 'A Virginian comming into England', Prynne recounted, had 'blamed our English men for not wearing a long locke as they did: affirming the God which wee worship to bee no true God, because hee had no Love-locke'.[73] 'Our sinister, and unlovely Love-lockes, had their generation, birth, and pedigree from the Heathenish, and Idolatrous

---

[73] William Prynne, *The unlovelinesse, of love-lockes* (1628; STC 20477), sig B3v.

Virginians', Prynne alleged.[74] They, in turn, 'tooke their patterne from their Devill Ockeus: who visually appeared to them in forme of a man, with a long black Locke on the left side of their head . . . so that if wee will resolve the generation of our Love-lockes . . . the *Virginian Devill Ockeus* will proove to be the natural Father'.[75] Whether a connection actually existed between Native American hairstyles and the English adoption of the fashion, Purchas and Prynne's criticisms were remarkably detailed, condemning metropolitan styles by drawing on Algonquians' socio-cosmic beliefs and their physical presence in England.

The way that gentlemen expressed their identities by appropriating Native styles and commodities carried important implications for the relationship between empire and polity. Their urbanity included an element of the subversive or playfully reckless that did not actually oppose civility but rather seemed to sharpen its complexity. Such civility was differentiated from English interactions with other territories because it involved appropriating goods and styles from colonial environments that the English sought to control. While late Elizabethan satires critiqued opulence as eroding masculine strength – the courtier with 'golden bracelets wantonly . . . tied' and '[t]wo Indian pearles . . . pendant at his eares' was 'himselfe in nothing but in name' – gentlemen in London related such luxuries to the successes of geopolitical exploitation.[76] Praising the precious minerals he sourced in Guiana in 1595, Ralegh reported a gemstone containing the 'strange blush of a carnation', 'which being cut is very rare'.[77] Ralegh's promise that 'there are not more diamonds in the East Indies than are to be found in Guiana' specifically related to his aspirations to 'govern that country which I have discovered and hope to conquer for the queen'.[78]

This link between consumption and subordination also meant effeminizing highly skilled warriors in metropolitan discourse, despite their undergoing the intensely challenging *huskanaw* coming-of-age ritual. The Virginia Company investor Walter Cope praised the pearls in Virginia but disdained Wahunsenacah/Powhatan for 'stately marchinge w[i]th a great payre of buckes hornes fastened to his forhead, not knowinge what esteeme we make of men so marked'.[79] By comparing him to a cuckold, Cope reduced Wahunsenacah's display of power into a symbol of bawdy humour.

[74] Ibid., sig. B2v.   [75] Ibid.
[76] J[ohn]. H[arington]., 'Of a courtier effeminate', in *Englands Parnassus* [compiled Robert Allott] (1600; STC 378), sigs. Z7v–8r.
[77] Walter Ralegh to Robert Cecil, 13 November 1595, in *Calendar of the Manuscripts of the Most Honourable the Marquis of Salisbury, Vol. 5*, 457.
[78] Ibid.   [79] Walter Cope to the Earl of Salisbury, August 1607, Hatfield House, CP 124/18.

Meanwhile, the painted bearskins the Powhatans offered to John Smith, the product of much labour and technical refinement, were deemed 'toyes'.[80]

Pearls are so pervasive in Elizabethan and Jacobean portraits that they can become almost invisible, but these also served as 'imperial blueprints'.[81] As luminous gems with potent mythological associations with the sea and carnality, they were increasingly viewed as the currencies of maritime power and global trade.[82] Colonists in the Chesapeake and Bermuda frequently commented on the abundance of oyster beds. Ralegh's 1588 portrait, like Elizabeth's 'Armada' portrait of the same year, was rife with pearls that played into the duality of their appeal as emblems of purity and sensuality while directly associating the display of these goods to a burgeoning English Atlantic.[83] One of the largest pearls in Elizabeth's portrait pended from a weighty gem, tied with a pink ribbon and hanging suggestively below her waist. Lest anyone remain unsure of the statement of Atlantic intent, Elizabeth's hand lay on a globe, specifically on the Americas.

The large, double-pearl earring in Ralegh's portrait may draw the eye first, but nearly all his attire contained clusters and waves of pearls. From the double-stringed bracelet to his breeches and belt, rows of pearls were set on black cloth that heightened their brilliance while pandering to Elizabeth's favoured colour combination, white and black. Portraits of Drake and Hawkins also featured globes and a multitude of pearls, Hawkins' in the form of a bracelet, his hand wrapped around a captain's sash with silver spangles similar to the one excavated in the grave of Captain William West in Jamestown. The objects gentlemen possessed and conspicuously displayed were not neutral expressions, but promoted a masculine Protestant civility that related imperial participation to expressions of status and authority of rule.

Political historians have traced the rise of the 'information state' in the late Elizabethan and early Stuart eras, where the practice of politics involved 'the collecting, interpreting, manipulating, and disseminating of information as a primary mode of exercising and maintaining power'.[84]

---

[80] 'The proceedings of the English colonie in Virginia (1612)', in *The Jamestown Voyages under the First Charter, Vol. 2*, 408; Williamson, *Powhatan Lords of Life and Death*, 250.

[81] Molly Warsh, *American Baroque: Pearls and the Nature of Empire, 1492–1700* (Chapel Hill, NC: University of North Carolina Press, 2018), 194.

[82] Ibid.

[83] Elizabeth I, unknown artist [English school], 1588, National Portrait Gallery, NPG 541; Walter Ralegh, unknown artist, 1588, National Portrait Gallery, NPG 7. See also John Hawkins, unknown artist [English school], c.1581, Royal Museums Greenwich, BHC2755.

[84] Nicholas Popper, 'An Information State for Elizabethan England', *The Journal of Modern History*, 90 (2019), 503–35, at 503.

This involved 'the material conditions of governance' through attempts to physically collect and manage news and record-keeping.[85] The material politics of the state also involved the access to and display of global goods. When Nicholas Saunders, a country gentleman, noticed a pedlar wearing what seemed to be 'an Indian hatt' with a 'Jewell fittar for a greater parsonage then that party of now hath it', he wrote to Cecil to explain what he had seen, believing this 'rare and riche thing' to have belonged to a West Indian ruler and brought back on Drake's ship.[86] Saunders described the hat with intricate detail, relating its 'beaten plates of gould' intermingled with pearls, which he believed unfit for a man who 'caryed a pack at his back about the countrey'.[87] This curious story raises intriguing questions about the acquisition and distribution of American or indigenous-inspired objects in rural areas of England. Saunders' observations also show how assumptions about social status and access to goods were rooted in the political.

The Sociability of Smoking

The stereotypes of the Inns man in the early seventeenth century depicted him as enamoured with the 'Indian weed'. 'His Recreations . . . are his only studies (as Plaies, Dancing, Fencing, Taverns, and Tobacco)'.[88] Epigrams described preened, ruffled, and velvet-clad creatures who expressed themselves through oaths and rituals of intoxication. Moralists complained that gentlemen were at times so uncivil that it seemed 'their Progenitors had beene some Cumanian [Cumaná] Indians', and they were encouraged to 'resume spirits truly English' to avoid becoming a 'degenerating posteritie'.[89] Visitors to London noticed that 'the English are constantly smoking tobacco', and their descriptions specifically related this practice to the physical spaces in and around the Inns of Court.[90] From there, it was only a short walk to the Thames, where gentlemen were daily reminded of their imperial aspirations: 'Upon taking the air down the river, the first thing that struck us, was the ship of that most noble pirate, Sir Francis Drake, in which he is said to have surrounded this globe of earth'.[91]

---

[85] Ibid.   [86] Nicholas Saunders to Robert Cecil, 30 June 1596, Hatfield MS, CP 41/97r.   [87] Ibid.
[88] Francis Lenton, *Characterismi* (1631; STC 15463), sig. F5r.
[89] Purchas, *Purchas his pilgrimage*, sig. Oooo4r.
[90] *Paul Hentzner's Travels in England, during the Reign of Queen Elizabeth*, tr. Horace, Earl of Orford (London: Edward Jeffrey, 1797), 30.
[91] Ibid., 33.

Chapter 4 ended with an analysis of how the tobacco debates in parliament created new clusters of consumption and assemblages of goods involving questions of taste and access.[92] This section explores how tobacco informed the colonially inflected civility of those gentlemen through their social performances and literary production in and around the Inns of Court. While wine 'doth the wits refine', intoxication had found a new contender now that 'this our age an other worlde hath founde'.[93] Satires conjured changing modes of sociability through smoking, evoking friends who crossed each other in the streets and carried their conversations 'unto his Chamber [for] the best *Tobacco* that he ever dranke'.[94] American-sourced tobacco was preferred over tobacco from other territories: 'All that which others fetcht, he doth abhor/His grew upon an Iland never found'.[95] As Jessica Winston argues, a 'vital relationship' existed between civil affairs and leisure at the Inns, where states of play informed attitudes towards governance and served to extend the legitimate spaces where political discourse could operate.[96] The introduction of tobacco within these spaces of literary production helped to bring America in conversation with the political nation.

Their own superior civility, gentlemen claimed, allowed them to smoke without degenerating into the savagery they condemned in others. Still in his teens, the budding poet John Beaumont, a member of the Inner Temple alongside his young brother the playwright Francis, published a mock encomium that spun an elaborate, heroic tale of 'this precious herbe, Tabacoo' whose heavenly properties transformed and inspired its partakers.[97] Beaumont introduced this sweet 'nymph' with a history of her own, one ancient, pastoral, and divine. The Nymph was a civilizer of men: had gods and philosophers known her, the fluency of good rhetoric would have been rendered obsolete, with tobacco compelling the 'rule uncivill throng' to '[a]n order'd Politike societie'.[98] In Beaumont's verses, tobacco contained civilizing properties that propelled civil society. The poem distinguished between refined, discerning gentlemen and London gulls who imbibed inferior strains of tobacco merely for fashion's sake. In praising 'thou great God of Indian melodie', Beaumont conjured the

---

[92] The terms 'assemblages' and 'clusters of consumption' were discussed at the 'Intoxicants, Space, and Material Culture' workshop at the Beinecke Library, Yale University, in April 2018, particularly in Benjamin Breen and Mark Peterson's presentations.

[93] *Epigrammes and elegies by J. D. and C. M.*, sig. C3v.

[94] Samuel Rowlands, *The letting of humors blood in the head-vaine* (1613; STC 21397), sig. A5r.

[95] Ibid.   [96] Winston, *Lawyers at Play*, 217.

[97] Beaumont, *The metamorphosis of tabacco*, sig. A3r.   [98] Ibid., sig. D4r.

heady, golden-hued plant of the Americas as a fitting intoxicant for urbane gentlemen, a sentiment underscored by the ten commendatory verses written by friends in Beaumont's Inns network.[99] These poems celebrated the 'Americk Ile', but they did so in expressions of wit directed 'To the white Reader'.[100]

Though Beaumont's poem contained a streak of youthful resistance to authoritarian control, his description of the 'circles of a savage round', and of Virginian religious men and 'the valleyes of Wingandekoe ... in the North part of *America*', appears to directly reference the engravings of Algonquians by Theodore de Bry that appeared in Hariot's influential and oft-cited 1590 edition of his *Briefe and true report*.[101] The closing stanzas framed the commodity within current events. Native Americans, with 'savage rites, and manners fear'd', possessed a plant whose glories they did not fully comprehend, and must yield to 'the walles of *Albions* cliffie towers'.[102] 'In the farre countries, where *Tabacco* growes', the Nymph's guiding hand would lead the English to assert their presence 'over *Virginia* and the *New-found-land*' and '[tame] the savage nations of the West'.[103] To Beaumont, the glorification of an indigenous commodity nevertheless justified the subjugation of America through the subordination of nature and an interference in Spanish affairs.

Such sentiments reached their most outrageous extremes in the London-based physician and poet Raphael Thorius' *Hymnus tabaci*, published in Latin in 1626, but written as early as the 1610s. In Thorius' poem, Bacchus led a legion of merrymakers to conquer Native Americans by teaching them to smoke. Submerged in the dark bower of a cannibal cave, mirroring a canto from *The Odyssey*, Bacchus encouraged its denizens to learn to drink and smoke in good company, for only through sociability with others could they assume 'a civil garb smooth'd by urbanity'.[104] The element of transformation, of turning nature into what was artificial and civil, was a crucial marker between Thorius' 'savage' inhabitants and 'enlightened' civilizers. 'Eat not the Leaf', Bacchus warned the cannibal, 'there's danger in it raw'.[105]

Like the gentlemen who wrote, shared, and read these poems, Bacchus articulated that 'to live the life of men' involved discoursing with friends and partaking in social pleasures, luring cannibal creatures into grace. It was Idmon, famed for his wit, who braved the fiercest cannibal king and

---

[99] Ibid., sig. Bv.   [100] Ibid., sigs. B2v, A4r.

[101] Ibid., sigs. Bv, Cr; Hariot, *A briefe and true report of the new found land of Virginia* (1590).

[102] Beaumont, *The metamorphosis of tabacco*, sig. E3v.   [103] Ibid.

[104] Thorius, *Hymnus tabaci*, sig C4v.   [105] Ibid., sig. Bv.

told him, 'our manners are not *steep*'d in *blood*, but *wine*'.[106] This fraternity of civilizers would come to '[s]*ophisticate* by *Art*, but naturall'.[107] Here, the taste for colonial-sourced tobacco may have reinforced or encouraged gentlemen to act out their imperial pursuits through social performance. Verses commanding readers to '[t]ake up these lines Tabacco-like unto thy braine,/And that divinely toucht, puffe out the smoke againe' brought poetry to the service of action, encouraging consumption while bringing attention to the content of the verses themselves.[108]

Richard Brathwaite, a member of Gray's Inn since 1609, also entrenched the appeal of expansion within the rituals of masculine conviviality in *A solemne joviall disputation* (1617), a small octavo conducive to easy sharing and circulation. Brathwaite's text was divided into two parts. The first was a translation of a Continental drinking treatise, the second half an addition devoted entirely to tobacco. This latter part, 'The Smoaking Age', framed the metropolitan gentleman as one informed by the world of expansion and discovery beyond him (Figure 7). Decades before the arrival of the first coffeehouses in England, Brathwaite conjured the microcosm of the tobacco shop as a political space, where men could meet to smoke, speak to travellers, and discuss state affairs. Much of the humour in Brathwaite's discourse relied on probing the tensions between the pleasures of smoking and the duties of state, between expected conduct and long-standing concerns over the perils of degeneration through the exposure of 'savage' influences. The author's invented acquaintance, the 'Bermudan' Boraccio Fumiganto, discussed his resolve to 'worke wonders among the wilde *Irish*' by reducing 'all those bogs, and marishes [*sic*] to plots of *Tobacco*', a ludicrous project that jabbed at Jacobean schemes that purported to benefit both state and private purse.[109]

Brathwaite included a lengthy lament by a cantankerous Father Time who echoed prevalent anti-tobacco polemic by asking why men now preferred 'an herbes vapour' over 'their countries renowne; Commonweales success; or publike managements of state'.[110] This seems to have been an extension of the comic rhetoric around tobacco apparent at the Inns from the 1590s. The Christmas revels at the Middle Temple in 1597/8 included a speech where the orator instructed his audience to 'examine the Complots of Politicians from the beginning of the world to this day . . . It is apparent it was not Tabacco [that caused them] . . . to conclude, Tabacco is not guilty of

---

[106] Ibid., sig. C3r.   [107] Ibid., sig. Er.
[108] B. H., 'To the white Reader', in Beaumont, *The metamorphosis of tabacco*, sig. A4r.
[109] Richard Brathwaite, *A solemne joviall disputation* (1617; STC 3585), sig. G5v.
[110] Ibid., sig. M6v.

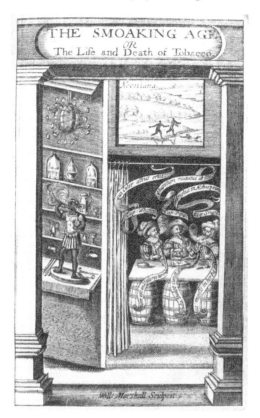

Figure 7 'The Smoking Age' engraving included in Richard Brathwaite, *A solemne joviall disputation* (1617). The shop interior offers a space of urban sociability underpinned by global consumption and production. By kind permission of the University of Liverpool Special Collections and Archives.

so many faults as it is charged withal'.[111] The inclusion of tobacco in the speech may have been a response to Ralegh's own links to the Middle Temple and his recent voyage to Guiana, but it also brought tobacco into the folds of humanist discourse. Woven within discussions about the 'Ramus Method' and Roman eloquence, even mock celebrations of misrule could not disentangle tobacco from its inherent performativity or the world of 'states', 'politicians', and 'poets'.[112]

[111] 'The *Fustian* Answer made to a *Tufftaffata* Speech', printed in Anthony Arlidge, *Shakespeare and the Prince of Love: The Feast of Misrule in the Middle Temple* (London: Giles de la Mare, 2000), 144.
[112] Ibid.

Beyond the comic effect achieved by mimicking the dominant rhetoric against smoking, the exaggerated capacity for tobacco to undermine civil society allowed Brathwaite to bring his readers into complicity, set against other Englishmen as well as other peoples. The pleasures of smoking would not corrupt cities or deprave youth, the text implied, because its readers were, through their own virtuosity, reconciling pleasure with virtue by transforming tobacco into an acceptable component of civil society. The frontispiece to *A solemne joviall disputation* depicted smoking as a suitable pastime for the elite. Gentlemen sat around a tavern table, their pipes serving as conduits to poetic inspiration and civil discourse while revellers of humbler status performed jigs in an alehouse below. Historians and literary scholars often discuss this image, 'The Lawes of Drinking', in relation to sociability, but the accompanying engraving for 'The Smoking Age' in the second half of the volume deserves equal attention. It is one of the only known depictions of what appears to be an English tobacco shop, or of a designated space, set behind curtains, where men went to smoke. Food is noticeably absent, the table filled instead with pipes, leaf tobacco, and what appears to be a tobacco box. While this is no certain indication of what London tobacco shops actually resembled, and mirrors popular Dutch engravings and paintings of the time, the advice in the text placed the practice within physical spaces of sociability. Putting a '[b]lackamoore' fishing for Caribbean pearls, or 'a Virginia-man . . . upon the Frontespice [*sic*] of thy doore' would beguile students to enter the shop, relating tobacco directly to its colonial source.[113]

Brathwaite's text was printed in 1617, a year after the second Earl of Warwick deliberately began sending skilled Angolan labourers to Bermuda to cultivate tobacco and dive for pearls.[114] A fertile landscape inhabited by dark-skinned figures adorned the wall behind the three smoking gentlemen in 'The Smoking Age' engraving, over which appeared the word '*Necotiana*'. In the microcosm of the shop, gentlemen positioned them-selves quite literally against Native Americans and Africans, and against the Spanish-style pudding tobacco smoked by the classicized African figure. Framed by columns and adorned with quotes from Ovid's *Metamorphoses*, the image turned ancient verses about the harvest of the earth into a praise for a new global pastoral, a life of leisure and political participation related to the world beyond and to social relations in urban spaces. Literary licence and a knowledge of colonial affairs worked together to imagine a sociability underpinned by imperial intervention and plantation industry. As in

[113] Brathwaite, *A solemne joviall disputation*, sig. L6r.   [114] Guasco, *Slaves and Englishmen*, 200.

Beaumont's *Metamorphosis of tabacco*, Brathwaite's civility quelled savagery through linguistic sophistication and a moderate worldview, even as he seemed to celebrate the fanciful disorder intoxicants might provide.

Performing Masculinity in an Age of Colonization

Though he had addressed his *Counterblaste to tobacco* to all his subjects, James' special emphasis on 'able, yong, strong, healthful men' put new forms of consumption at the heart of questions over political behaviour.[115] One's identity was 'the product of social interaction', and although manhood and patriarchy were not always aligned, the hierarchical structure of Protestant England heavily influenced articulations of honour, shame, and social status.[116] Beyond the bravado of masculine conviviality and the friendships that were often defined in relation to, or against, men's relationships with women, gentlemen also thought about themselves in relation to those they sought to colonize. Questions over identity and belonging were not always as explicitly professed as they were by Anthony Knivet when he lived among the Tupi in 1590s Brazil ('I sat downe remembring my selfe in what state I was, and thinking what I had beene'), but the jewellery, books, doublets, beds, and other personal items that gentlemen brought with them to the colonies, often impractically and at great expense, offer some clues as to their fears of losing what made them who they were when separated from home.[117]

The confluence between personal conduct and colonial engagement is evident in Jacobean conduct manuals and commonplace books that interspersed poems about tobacco or reports of New England *sachems* alongside libels or reflections on friendship.[118] Edward Hoby, a member of the Middle Temple and later a courtier at James' court, kept a commonplace book that exhibited an active interest in affairs in America. He included numerous transcriptions of news from North and South America, including a tract by George Popham, future leader of the short-lived Sagadahoc colony in Maine. Hoby's commonplace book also held his correspondence with his good friend George Carew, who advanced colonization in Ireland and eventually Virginia, and copies of specific instructions for discovering

---

[115] James I, *A counterblaste to tobacco*, sig. A4v.
[116] Shepard, *Meanings of Manhood in Early Modern England*, 6, 11.
[117] Purchas, *Purchas his pilgrimes*, sig. Hhhhh5v.
[118] Commonplace book, [begun 1620s], Beinecke Library, Osborn b197, ff. 85–6; Cosmographical commonplace book, early to mid-seventeenth century, Beinecke Library, Osborn b337.

and cataloguing areas of North America.[119] This would partly be achieved through discovering the 'statutes conditions apparell and manners of foode, w[hi]ch of them be men eaters ... what manner they arme and order them selves in warres and who oure friendes or enemies [are] to each other of them'.[120]

The letters Hoby copied were attentive not just to acquiring new territories, but also to the customs of indigenous peoples, their political systems, and how best to govern them. Hoby collected this information between adages on civility, interspersing travel reports with reflections on sociability and conduct. 'There be fowre thinges in the world most needfull', Hoby wrote, 'and the same ofte most hurtfull. witt, and wordes; drinck, and Company'.[121] Commonplace books compiled seemingly disparate material and encouraged comparison or contrast by nature of those inclusions in one bound entity, so that Hoby's interest in America and his reflections on sociability operated together to frame his thinking about himself in relation to the world. As in the colonies themselves, gentlemen in England constructed their masculine selves partly in relation to their imperial ambitions.

Could collections of printed works have achieved a similar effect? James' *Counterblaste*, for example, re-appeared in the 1616 edition of the king's *Workes*. The tract sat chronologically between *The Trew Law of Free Monarchies* (1598) and *A Discourse of the Maner of the Discoverie of the Powder-Treason* (1605). However incidentally, this may have reinforced associations between tobacco-smoking, gunpowder, and treason that appeared in multiple texts in the 1610s. An extant copy of Josuah Sylvester's poems, printed in London around the same time, bound his *Tobacco battered; & the pipes shattered* with other verses, including translations of the poems of the Huguenot Guillaume de Salluste, sieur du Bartas, and musings on mortality dedicated to the Earl of Southampton.[122] Readers contemplated the corrupting dangers of tobacco alongside such works as *Auto-Machia: or, The Self-Conflict of a Christian*, a translation of the Latin verses by the anti-Catholic poet George Goodwin that reflected on the inconsistencies of the human heart. *Auto-Machia* opened with a powerful commitment to coming to terms with oneself: 'I *Sing not PRIMA, nor the Siege of TROY* ... *I sing my Self: my* Civil-Warrs *within:/*

---

[119] Sir Edward Hoby's commonplace book, 1582–96, British Library, Add MS 38823, ff. 1r–5v; also ff. 5v–8r, 93r–94v.

[120] Ibid., ff. 1r–v.   [121] Ibid., f. 26r.

[122] Josuah Sylvester, *Tobacco battered; & the pipes shattered*, bound with Sylvester, *The maiden's blush ... From the Latin of Fracastorius* (1620; STC 11253) in the copy at the Huntington Library, call number 22318.

The Victories *I howrely lose and win*'.[123] Here, secret temptations and desires vied to demean virtue: 'my Minde divine, My Bodie brute by Birth/O! what a Monster am I, to depaint ... halfe-Savage, halfe a Saint'.[124]

Reading *Tobacco battered* alongside these other poems shifts Sylvester's tract from mere polemic or hyperbole to a more sensitive portrayal of the tensions between personal desire and public duty, between the lure of sin and the importance of virtue. Sylvester's poem is rarely considered beyond its strong anti-tobacco stance, likely written to pander to James' sensitivities, but his work also criticized the devastations that colonization unleashed. It is perhaps commonplace to encounter concerns that '[d]ebaucht behaviour' and '[d]amn'd *Libertinism*' through smoking turned Christians into 'heathens', for 'the *Conscience* ... /*This* Indian *Weed doth most molest*'.[125] But Sylvester also insisted that it should be 'question'd ... Whether Discoverie of *AMERICA*,/That *New-found World*, have yeelded to our Ould/More Hurt or Good'.[126] In doing so, Sylvester lamented the misfortunes that befell Native Americans and Englishmen through disease, violence, and greed. Although more concerned with using indigenous peoples to critique the policies of Spain than to argue for Native American rights, Sylvester's verses were nevertheless some of the few that explicitly lamented that 'for *Christians*/It had been better, and for *Indians* ... that the Evill had still staid at home'.[127] His concerns over tobacco were wrapped up in 'conscience', 'behaviour', and displays of masculinity. 'We shoot Manners', Sylvester wrote in his dedication to the Duke of Buckingham, to 'save the Men'.[128]

Alongside Sylvester's other poems, notably his translation of du Bartas' *The colonies*, the critique of disordered conquest becomes a particular anxiety related to personal honour. In Parliament or the Inns' 'smirking wit of all-male society', gentlemen fiercely prized their intellect, but they were also aware of its dangers.[129] This might present a physical danger, as when James sought to assert his royal prerogative by imprisoning outspoken MPs in the Parliaments of 1614 and 1621, but it was also linked to individual conscience. We write satires, Donne wrote, 'and we look that the world shall call that *wit*; when God knowes that that is in great part, self-guiltinesse, and we do but reprehend those things which we our selves have done, we cry out upon the illness of the times, and we make the times ill'.[130] In the troubled world of failed responsibility, literature contained

---

[123] Ibid., sig. L3r.   [124] Ibid., sigs. L4r, L5r.   [125] Ibid., sigs. Hv, F6r.   [126] Ibid., sig. F6v.
[127] Ibid.   [128] Ibid., sig. F4v.
[129] Wayne A. Rebhorn, *The Emperor of Men's Minds* (Ithaca, NY: Cornell University Press, 1997), 96.
[130] Quoted in ibid., 90.

hints of an unease about colonization rarely seen elsewhere. '*Ambition* which affords thee Wings,/To seek new Seas beyond Our Ocean's Arms,/For Mounts of Gold', wrote Sylvester, 'Shal not preserve thy Carcass from the Wormes'.[131] The '*pleasure*' of tobacco that '[b]esots thy Soule, intoxicates thy Sense' would tear laurels from 'mighty Conquerors'.[132] What was at stake was the individual and an entire country, for the 'Worlde it Selfe is dying and decaying ... The Sphears are distun'd', and 'the choicest ... *British Gallants*' go forth in 'brave *Deseignes* to do their Country honor' only to perish in the process.[133]

The disenchantment of later Jacobean politics and James' inflation of titles led to vehement critiques of those who sought honour through corrupt means. Beyond the 'infinite sweet sinnes' that moralists denounced as 'Libertine Feasts, worse then *Pagan* Adulteries', gentlemen sought to find ways to imbue worldly pleasures with the language of virtue.[134] As Bryson finds in her study on civility, although 'libertine' entered English usage at the end of the sixteenth century, Jacobean gentlemen never reached the levels of anarchic excess found in the libertinism of the later seventeenth century.[135] Nonetheless, civility was undergoing a point of change. By invoking Native Americans to present the glories of conquest to the king, or deriding their peers for behaving like 'savages', gentlemen were not renouncing colonization but expressing the necessity of rule and promoting themselves as ideal colonizers. They were turning the Atlantic into a recognized component of gentlemanly urbanity, related to their conception of what civil society was and how it might be advanced.

In their verses and political writings, gentlemen drew on America to celebrate the civilizing power of urban sociability in a performative way. The two masques featuring American motifs staged by members of the Inns brought their odes to cultivated refinement to Whitehall, offering different but complementary approaches to the colonial support demonstrated within the Inns themselves. The imperial designs expressed in masques allowed gentlemen to perform their ideals of improvement in full view of the king and the nobility. George Chapman's *The memorable masque* (1613) and *The maske of flowers* (1614), of unknown authorship but commissioned at great personal expense by Francis Bacon, were institutional and collective statements of support for colonization, allowing

---

[131] *All the small workes of that famous poet Josuah Sylvester* (1620; STC 23575.5), sig. I5r.   [132] Ibid.
[133] Ibid., sig. Hh6r.   [134] Thomas Adams, *The gallants burden* (1612; STC 117), sig. H3v.
[135] Bryson, *From Courtesy to Civility*, 243, 247.

gentlemen to articulate their own status by advancing a graceful masculinity that defined itself partly against the savagery it purported to subdue.

Scholars have recognized that Chapman's masque, performed for the marriage of James' daughter Elizabeth to Frederick V, Elector Palatine, exhibited the interests of those who had been associated with Prince Henry's court.[136] On the night of 15 February 1613, an ensemble of fifty 'Virginians' paraded along the Strand and spilled into James' tiltyard, moving through the galleries and circling an extra lap around the tilting yard. Their faces, wavering through the illuminated spaces made by rows of fiery torchbearers, were 'of olive collour', their hair 'blacke & lardge, waving downe to their shoulders', and they moved in an incandescent swirl of sun-embroidered cloth and 'high sprig'd feathers'.[137] These performers were not Native Americans but members of the Middle Temple and Lincoln's Inn, where they presented a lavish and triumphant civility while bringing imperial agendas to the court.[138] The king commended Edward Phelips and Richard Martin, both shareholders of the Virginia Company, for their role in organizing the spectacle.

Paul Raffield describes masques and revels at the Inns as enactments of 'a traditional code of manners or honour as the basis of ideal governance', concerned primarily with questions of kingly authority and its tensions with the law and its constitution.[139] *The memorable masque*, however, might be seen less as exhibiting a 'traditional code of manners', than a willingness on the part of gentlemen to advance a vision of governance that did not eschew, but subordinated, the exoticism of America to English political life. Bringing emblems of indigeneity like feather headdresses into metropolitan political spaces in modified forms, using costumes and sets made by local craftsmen, placed colonization in the hands of those who professed to know the difference between savagery and mimesis. A speech from St George's, Bermuda, urged colonists not to 'shame themselves' by disgracing the colony, for this would be 'after that fashion as if one of you should walke through Cheapside at noone day, all to be bepainted and stuck with feathers like an Americane, wher he may be sure [not just] to be

---

[136] Patricia Crouch, 'Patronage and Competing Visions of Virginia in George Chapman's "The Memorable Masque" (1613)', *English Literary Renaissance*, 53 (1986), 673–707; Hollis, *The Absence of America*.

[137] Chapman, *The memorable masque*, sigs. Br–v. For an idea of the immense cost undertaken by the Inns, and the difficulties in repaying these debts, see the taxation records in *The Middle Temple Documents Relating to George Chapman's* Memorable Masque, ed. Tucker Orbison (Oxford: Malone Society, 1983); Records relating to the Whitehall masque, 1612/1613, The Middle Temple, MT.7/MAA.

[138] Chapman, *The memorable masque*, sig. B3v.   [139] Raffield, *Images and Cultures of Law*, 1.

looked at, but laught at'.[140] While the unthinking imitation of indigeneity invited ridicule, gentlemen used performances to play out the civilizing narrative they advocated in their colonial projects. American motifs and commodities, in the right contexts, had a place in the imperial polity.

The printed account of Chapman's masque included detailed descriptions of the gentlemen's appearance and 'Indian habits'. The chief masquers wore apparel embroidered with suns, covered in gold and '[r]uffes of feathers, spangled with pearle and silver . . . like the Virginian Princes they presented'.[141] These gentlemen were differentiated within their own ranks from the torchbearers, who assumed a 'humble variety' of the costumes to exhibit 'the more amplie, the Maskers high beauties . . . and reflected in their kinde, a new and delightfully-varied radiance on the beholders'.[142] Through the masque, students demonstrated their ability to transform the perceived savagery of America through superior artifice. This 'art', visible in the costumes themselves as in the behaviour of the wearers, presented a symbiotic relationship between appearance and cultivation. The masquers' apparel demonstrated the dual nature of the elite's civilizing project, where 'civilizing' Native Americans would serve to radiate and enhance the civility of gentlemen at home. The '[b]ody expresseth the secret fantasies of the minde', Brathwaite wrote.[143]

Chapman's careful attention to the performers' physical appearance suggests that gentlemen at the Inns fashioned themselves both in relation to aristocratic courtliness and against the presumed brutishness of unrestrained nature. Arriving on an island 'in command of the Virginia continent', the masque featured Capriccio, a self-styled man of wit who embodied the archetypal foolish Jacobean gallant or the 'Italianate' Englishman.[144] Not unlike Beaumont's differentiation between fops and urbane gentlemen who tastefully flirted with licence but remained committed to moral uprightness, members poked fun at the stereotypes of their own wit culture while ultimately disassociating themselves from those who sought riches without honour. In their dedication to honour and the law, the 'Knights of the Virgine Land' adhered to the neo-chivalric ideas of expansionist valour that had characterized Prince Henry's court, where Chapman had served the prince and written him a funeral elegy that explicitly related Henry's virtue to his colonial interests.[145] Capriccio and his band of foolhardy global travellers, dressed

---

[140] Historye of the Bermudaes or Summer Islands, 196.
[141] Chapman, The memorable masque, sigs. A4v–Br.   [142] Ibid., sig. B2r.
[143] Brathwaite, The English gentleman, sig. B3r.   [144] Chapman, The memorable masque, sig. D2v.
[145] George Chapman, An epicede or funerall song (1613; STC 4974), sig. D3v.

as ruff-clad baboons, had crudely 'cut out the skirts of the whole world' in search of riches but remained overshadowed by the grace of Eunomia, 'the sacred power of Lawe'.[146] The costumes, together with the American motifs, separated the principal masquers from the uncivil adventurers in the anti-masque who proved unfit to bear the responsibilities of colonization.

The masque of flowers, performed at Whitehall on 6 January 1614, featured Kawasha, the 'chiefe' god recounted by contemporary histories of Virginia and depicted pictorially in the 1590 edition of Hariot's *A briefe and true report*.[147] Presented by the gentlemen of Gray's Inn, the performance celebrated the wedding of the king's favourite, Robert Carr, first Earl of Somerset, to Lady Frances Howard. Bacon filled the hall with flowers that metamorphosed into 'beautiful youths' with the onset of spring.[148] On either side of Banqueting House stood the temples of Silenus (Wine), and Kawasha (Tobacco), where the two contended for superiority in the anti-masque. Kawasha appeared '*borne upon two* Indians *shoulders*', 'his body and legges of Olive colour stuffe, made close like the skinne, bases of Tobacco-colour stuffe cut like Tobacco leaves' and holding a pipe the ludicrous size of a harquebus.[149]

The masque contained an elaborate garden setting featuring a globe, where cultivation and industry were celebrated in both a colonial and a domestic context, and where the transformation of wild nature represented an essential component of English civility. Through the flower boys, nature was transformed into the human – 'your verdure to fresh bloud' – and the restoration celebrated in terms of James' civilizing power.[150] 'Britain' became 'fit to be,/A seate for a fitt Monarchie'.[151] Like *The memorable masque*, the performance undoubtedly revealed prejudices against indigenous peoples, as Raffield notes, but it also enabled gentlemen to propound a complex civility that praised the cultivation of artifice over raw nature while also envisioning a refinement found on the other side of empire.[152] The good-humoured battle for sovereignty between Silenus and Kawasha, ultimately, was hardly a battle at all. The two figures operated on the same stage, inviting less a polarity than a reconciliation: a world in which the 'old' successfully incorporated and accommodated the 'new'.

---

[146] Chapman, *The memorable masque*, sigs. Ev, E4v.
[147] Hariot, *A briefe and true report of the new found land of Virginia* (1590), sig. D2r; Smith, *The generall historie*, sig. Hh4v.
[148] John Coperario, *The maske of flowers* (1614; STC 17625), sig. A4v.   [149] Ibid., sig. B3r.
[150] Ibid., sig. C3r.   [151] Ibid., sig. C4r.   [152] Raffield, *Images and Cultures of Law*, 147.

The Passions of Empire

Gentlemen operated in a society with deeply entrenched ideas of youth as prone to folly. The Jacobean writer Owen Felltham wrote that his 'passions and affections are the chief disturbers of my civil state', a belief that harked back to the writings of Augustine.[153] 'Yong men', wrote the soldier Barnabe Barnes, are 'much subject to vicious affectations and pleasures of nature; to passions and perturbations of the minde, so distracted with heat of youth'.[154] This final section explores how literature and sociability invoked the senses to urge imperial participation, allowing colonial promoters to turn the desire for knowledge and possession into a political good.

As Kevin Sharpe observes, political theorists often denounced the passions while acknowledging that all individuals, including the monarch, were subject to them.[155] Frequent denunciations of the passions only highlighted their ubiquity. 'Some yeares ago ... I was requested by divers worthy gentlemen', wrote Thomas Wright, in *The passions of the minde in generall* (1604), 'to write briefly some pithie discourse about the passions of the minde: because (as they said) they were things ever in use ... yet never well taught'.[156] Wright described the passions as fundamentally related to civility and political conduct. To engage with the passions was to learn control, but also to channel the senses for good so that gentlemen might know 'how to behave our selves when such affections possess us ... and the fittest means to attain religious, civil, and gentlemanlike conversation'.[157]

Rather than the temperance advocated in prescriptive literature, the verses gentlemen penned in the 1610s and 1620s used the senses to draw readers into the pleasures of conquest. The poetry and travel writing that compared America to a naked woman might be understood in this light. Beaumont and the colonist Luke Gernon described America as a 'nymph', as did Hakluyt in his translation of Peter Martyr's *Decades* (1587): 'no terrors ... would ever tear you from the sweet embraces of your own Virginia, that fairest of nymphs'.[158] 'Nymph' conformed to gentlemanly fantasies of the sensuous personifications of desire, but the word also invoked Greco-Roman mythologies that bound these creatures to

[153] Kevin Sharpe, 'Virtues, Passions and Politics in Early Modern England', *History of Political Thought*, 32 (2011), 773–98, at 775–6.
[154] Barnes, *Foure bookes of offices*, sig. Q3v.
[155] Sharpe, 'Virtues, Passions and Politics in Early Modern England', 775.
[156] Thomas Wright, *The passions of the minde in generall* (1604; STC 26040), sig. A2r.   [157] Ibid.
[158] Quoted in Jorge Cañizares-Esguerra, *Puritan Conquistadors: Iberianizing the Atlantic, 1550–1700* (Stanford, CA: Stanford University Press, 2006), 60.

geographical places, further relating them to nature and territorial bounty. Ralegh famously praised Guiana for having 'yet her Maydenhead, never sackt, turned, nor wrought'.[159] The fantasies of penetration were clear, climaxing with the triumph of imperial possession. Guiana's earth had 'not beene torne, nor the virtue . . . of the soyle spent', 'the mines not broken', 'never entred by any armie of strength, and never conquered or possessed'.[160] Ralegh's description seduced readers towards imagining a greater intimacy with the 'new' world. This world might not yet be possessed by the English, but metaphor enabled an aspiration to be imagined as physically present and attainable. In 'To the Virginian Voyage' (1606), Drayton drew on sumptuous imagery to allure the reader into endorsing the first settlement in Virginia, using language that built up the notion of a country ripe for picking – 'kiss', 'entice', 'enflame', 'delicious', 'luscious', and 'subdued'.[161]

Conditioned by stylistic conventions and crafted to flatter the wit of authors and audience alike, verses entwined desire, even lust, with calls to political action. Aristotle's own discussions of the passions appeared most prominently in his *Art of Rhetoric*, where he frequently considered emotions and desires in how people were inclined to behave.[162] Aristotle did not consider impetuousness to be wholly destructive. Youth made men brave, and the young 'are ready to desire and to carry out what they desire . . . they are fond of their friends and companions, because they take pleasure in living in company'.[163] Though heavily gendered and eroticized, the colonial in wit poetry referenced friendship and pleasure while maintaining a political and geographical edge. The lawyer Gernon's description of Ireland specifically utilized the imagination as a tool for visualizing colonial settlement. 'Your imagination transports yourself into Ireland . . . I will depaynt her more lively and more sensible to your intelligence'.[164] Gernon followed this with his explicit and lengthy description of the soil as a teenage girl, a 'nymph' 'that hath the green sickness for want of occupying . . . Her flesh is a soft and delicate mould of earth . . . Betwixt her legs, she hath an open harbour . . . she wants a husband. She is

---

[159] Ralegh, *The discoverie of the large, rich, and bewtiful empire of Guiana*, sig. N4v.   [160] Ibid.

[161] Michael Drayton, 'To the Virginian Voyage' (1606), in *The Oxford Book of English Verse, 1250–1900*, ed. A. T. Quiller-Couch (Oxford: Clarendon, 1919), 171–3.

[162] Aristotle, *Art of Rhetoric*, tr. John Henry Freese (Cambridge, MA: Harvard University Press, 1926).

[163] Ibid., 247–9. Conduct manuals echoed Aristotle, as in Thomas Hoby's translation of Castiglione's *The Courtier*: 'the sins . . . of man in youthfull age is . . . sense'. Thomas Hoby, *The courtyer of Count Baldessar Castilio* (1561; STC 4778), sig. U2v.

[164] Luke Gernon, 'Discourse of Ireland (1620)', in *Illustrations of Irish History and Topography, Mainly of the Seventeenth Century*, ed. Litton C. Falkiner (London: Longman, 1904), 349.

not embraced, she is not hedged and ditched'.[165] 'Soil', 'hedge', 'ditch' –
even in its most exalted crescendos, Jacobean literature conveyed the
physical reality of landscapes and the desire for cultivated order. When
Samuel Purchas called upon readers to 'survay' the bounties of the
Chesapeake while playing on virgin/Virginia, he referenced the technolo-
gies of seeing: those economies of mapping, anatomizing, enclosing, and
gazing that fundamentally involved dynamics of power.[166]

Rituals of sociability were acts of persuasion that implicated participants within a budding imperial system. Imagining the intoxicating
splendour of a lush and yet-unravished America was often facilitated by
the literal intoxication of tobacco on the senses. The powers of intoxication, in Beaumont's words, 'set'st forth with truth, fictions,
Philosophie', envisioning a transformation of America before it had
happened, and drawing little distinction between 'truth' and
'fiction'.[167] Wits explicitly connected smoking and conviviality to
both the glories of the imagination – the '[c]rown'd Bowls to add
quick Spirits unto men' – and to the colonial context, a world populated by cannibals, heady tobacco, and 'affrighted *Indians*'.[168] In this
way, imagining and valorizing colonization became an integral means of
beginning to achieve it. Inviting tobacco to enter the body enabled
gentlemen to see the possibilities of empire spread before them, where
the '*inventing Power* shines forth, & now descries/The worlds large
Fabrick to the mentall eyes./The eternall *Species* now do *naked* stand/
In comely order'.[169] To sing the pastoral '*Georgicks* of *Tabaco*' was to
acknowledge the necessity of plantation, one that hinged on an English
model of civil conviviality.[170]

Moralists and colonial promoters exhibited an awareness that the senses
were important tools in advancing plantation. Poetry written in the first
person encouraged readers to participate in the glories of expansion: 'While
through the worlds ... wilderness/I, th'olde, first Pilots wandring House
address:/While (*Famous* DRAKE-*like*), coasting every strand,/I doe discover many a *New-found-Land*'.[171] Virginia Company propaganda repeatedly appealed to the youthful desire for honour and distinction. Advancing
the glory of God in Virginia, Robert Gray preached in 1609, would

[165] Ibid., 350.
[166] Purchas, *Purchas his pilgrimes*, sig. Mmmmmmm4v; Hulse and Erickson, 'Introduction', in *Early
Modern Visual Culture*, 1–14, at 2.
[167] Beaumont, *The metamorphosis of tabacco*, sig. A4v.   [168] Ibid., sigs. B2v, B3v.
[169] Ibid., sig. B6v.   [170] Thorius, *Hymnus tabaci*, sigs. Er, E2v.
[171] Josuah Sylvester, *Du Bartas his devine weekes and workes* (1611; STC 21651), sig. Z8r.

perpetuate 'the immortalitie of your names and memory, which, for the advancement of Gods glorie, the renowne of his Majestie, and the good of your Countrie, have undertaken so honorable a project'.[172] To bring glory to God and to the realm, wrote the colonial promoter George Peckham, 'noble youthes couragiously this enterprise discharge'.[173] The value of emotion is evident in Samuel Purchas' 'Virginias Verger' (1625). As the church historian Alec Ryrie argues, Protestantism was a religion that involved reason and feeling. If properly disciplined, the passions need not always be restrained.[174] To Purchas, virtue and godliness were not necessarily at odds with personal advancement or even sexual fulfilment. Though he heavily criticized the profiteering nature of earlier colonial projects, he drew his readers' interest by appealing to the 'Twinnes of . . . Profit and Pleasure'.[175] Look upon Virginia, Purchas urged, and

> view her lovely lookes (howsoever like a modest Virgin she is now vailed with wild Coverts and shadie Woods, expecting rather ravishment then Mariage from her Native Savages) survay her Heavens, Elements, Situation; her divisions by armes of Bayes and Rivers into so goodly and well propor-tioned limmes and members; her Virgin portion nothing empaired . . . and in all these you shall see, that she is worth the wooing and loves of the best Husband.[176]

Though re-directing the wits' celebration of illicit amorous encounters towards marriage, Purchas used the language of carnal sensuality to legit-imize possession. 'Luxuriant wantonnesse' served to inspire good, while '*Virginia* was violently ravished by her owne ruder Natives, yea her Virgin cheekes dyed with the bloud' of murdered English colonists.[177] Sustained English interference would engender prosperity. God had 'enriched the Savage Countries, that those riches might be attractives to *Christian* suters, which there may *sowe spirituals and reape temporals*'.[178] Purchas stressed that hopes for America should involve spiritual fruition, not just gold and silver; but gardening and husbandry did not mean frugality.[179] Rather, God had given Virginia abundance 'to allure and assure our loves' by providing woods and rivers, wine, silk, 'the bodies of Natives servile and serviceable', '[t]obacco, and other present improvements as earnest of future better hopes'.[180] These goods were precisely those James and his

---

[172] Gray, *A good speed to Virginia*, sig. A3v.   [173] Peckham, *A true reporte*, sig. §ir.
[174] Ryrie, *Being Protestant in Reformation Britain*, 18–19. See also *Puritanism and Emotion in the Early Modern World*, ed. Alex Ryrie and Tom Schwanda (Basingstoke: Palgrave, 2016).
[175] Purchas, 'Virginias Verger', in *Purchas his pilgrimes*, sig. Mmmmmmmm4v.   [176] Ibid.
[177] Ibid., sig. Mmmmmmmm2v.   [178] Ibid.   [179] Ibid., sig. Mmmmmmmm3r.
[180] Ibid., sig. Nnnnnnn2v.

courtiers recommended when they backed George Yeardley's governorship at the end of 1618.

Purchas' critique of the 'partialities to friends and dependants, wilfull obstinacies, and other furious passions [that] have transported men from *Virginias* good and their owne' may well have targeted overenthusiastic gentlemen in London.[181] But his text also reveals commonalities between the promises of godly reformers and the hopes of colonists themselves. In 1614, the planter John Rolfe wrote a letter to the governor of Jamestown, Thomas Dale, asking permission to marry Pocahontas. It is 'not for transitory and worldly vanities, but to labour in the Lords vineyard, there to sow and plant', Rolfe maintained, that he sought to promote the word of God through whatever means necessary.[182] When writing to colonial authorities, Rolfe framed his desire as one of selfless devotion. His pure motivations should 'clean [me] from the filth of impurity ... [I do so] not from hungry appetite'.[183] This was not quite the euphoric celebration of abandon seen in the discourses of urbane wits, but neither does it seem that Rolfe was shunning his desires. Rather, Protestant duty, his desire to 'civilize', and his confessed 'agitations', 'passions of my troubled soule', and even transcultural 'love' had become part of how he articulated 'the honour of mine country'.[184] Pocahontas had sparked in him 'perturbations and godly motions, which have striven within me ... many passions', bringing about 'fervent praiers' that allowed him to 'performe the dutie of a good Christian'.[185] A civil society based on cultivation and husbandry both indulged and channelled certain passions, echoing Francis Bacon's belief that 'to set affection against affection and to master one by another' was 'of special use in moral and civil matters'.[186] As Albert Hirschman argues, statesmen like Bacon offered radical revisions to sixteenth-century moral philosophy by suggesting that the passions had a place in spurring virtue.[187] Colonial promoters' discussion of luxury in the context of expansion and godly plantation – where 'Profit and Pleasure' were 'twinnes' – helped stimulate political discourses about the place of public good and private gain in civil society.

Inns members drew on the passions to urge revisions to colonial policy. Escalating anti-Algonquian sentiment in the 1620s were conveyed through a sense of personal grief and loss. In the months following the 1622 attack,

[181] Ibid., sig. Mmmmmmm3r.
[182] John Rolfe to Sir Thomas Dale, 1614, in *Narratives of Early Virginia*, 242–3.   [183] Ibid., 243.
[184] Ibid., 239–41.   [185] Ibid., 242–3.
[186] Quoted in Albert O. Hirschman, *The Passions and the Interest: Political Arguments for Capitalism before Its Triumph* (Princeton, NJ: Princeton University Press, 1977), 22.
[187] Ibid.

Christopher Brooke, an established lawyer at Lincoln's Inn and heavily involved with the Virginia Company, wrote a poem advocating the eradication of Native American ways of life. Brooke's appeal to apply unmitigated force against the Powhatans was startlingly genocidal compared to the extant writings of many of his peers. Rather than emerging from prejudice alone, Brooke's views were informed, indeed intensified, by his access to letters and news from Virginia. He wrote his poem, Brooke acknowledged, because he felt devastated by the loss of several close friends, especially the MP and Middle Templar George Thorpe, who had gone to Virginia in 1620 to build an Algonquian school.

Brooke sensationalized the attack in order to condemn political instability, viewing excessive violence towards the Algonquians as the essential outpour that would create a temperate polity. The Algonquians were '[s]oules drown'd in flesh and blood' and '[e]rrors of Nature', but he also reserved blame for the English themselves:

> Yee are call'd Christians in the common voice,
> But are yee so in Essence, and in choice
> From vnbaptized Soules? And do your hearts
> Performe in Manners, Life, and Act, those parts
> That really confirme you?[188]

This '[e]xample', written in the blood of their friends and fellow countrymen, should be 'printed in your hearts, and understood'.[189] Invoking his friends by name and drawing parallels between broken physical bodies and threats to the body politic, Brooke urged 'gentle' Francis Wyatt and George Sandys to respond more powerfully to their grief. Violence, and the emotions that compelled acts of forceful subjection, would help sustain the imperial polity at a critical moment.

Finally, the language that often passionately urged colonization in the 1620s was likely influenced by subjects' dissatisfaction with James' policies and personal behaviour. Gentlemen at the Inns conveyed a sense that the king's own appetites were too subversive to guarantee the safety and prosperity of the realm. 'It cannot be denied but that he had his vices and deviations', the Middle Templar Simonds d'Ewes wrote in his diary following James' death in March 1625.[190] Libels denounced political

---

[188] Christopher Brooke, 'A Poem on the Late Massacre in Virginia (1622)', reproduced in facsimile form in *The Virginia Magazine of History and Biography*, 72 (1964), 259–92, at 275–9, 285.

[189] Ibid.

[190] *The Autobiography and Correspondence of Sir Simonds d'Ewes, Vol. 1*, ed. James Orchard Halliwell (London: Richard Bentley, 1845), 263, 265.

disorders as manifestations of James' 'deviations', where his lust for male favourites, his Hispanicized and Catholic court, and the corruption of offices and titles came under attack. 'The Five Senses', an audacious political libel based on verses in Ben Jonson's 1621 masque, 'The Gypsies Metamorphosed', criticized the king's political weaknesses through his social and sexual behaviour. 'Seeing' involved the captivation of youthful beauty, while the king's 'false frends' and 'after supper suits' to privy councillors equated hearing with flattery and deceit.[191] 'Tasting' evoked the forbidden fruits of 'the Cand[i]ed poyson'd baites/Of Jesuites', excess 'wyne that can destroye the braine', and 'the daingerous figg of Spaine'.[192] Smooth-skinned youths embodied 'Feeling', where the 'moyst palme' of a favourite's hand led the king to 'things polluted'.[193] 'Smelling' conjured the smoky altars of Catholic idolatry and the 'whoreish breath' of the king's 'Ganimede', a daring reference to the king's love for boys.[194]

Partly in response to the climate of court corruption, many gentlemen framed the pleasures of America as a God-given consequence of virtuous behaviour, a world that could be subordinated in a way that would enrich their own civil mores and reinforce their authority. Though they flirted with subverting established norms in their poetry, gentlemen remained aware of the precariousness of colonial conditions and agreed with moral authorities who associated the rejection of Christian, usually Protestant, values with degeneration. Without godly order, polities would become 'a Chaos, every Monarchie an Anarchy', preached Matthew Stoneham in 1608.[195] 'Let Theologie die, and no policie can live ... at this day [this] is proved among the rude & naked Indians in the Westerne parts of the world'.[196] James' belief in a monarch's absolute prerogative had never been popular with members of the Inns, and the king came under increasing attack in the Parliaments of 1621 and 1624.[197] Despite accusations of social climbing or effeminacy, wits projected their colonial support as acting on traditionally masculine and more acceptable pursuits: honour, land, martial ability, and, through the personification of the American landscape, sex with women. The imperial polity was to be a well-governed world effectively kept in good order through cultivation,

[191] 'The Five Senses', c.1621–3, Bodleian Library, Malone 23, Early Stuart Libels www .earlystuartlibels.net. See also Henry Wotton's 'Ode to the Queen of Bohemia', in Commonplace book: poetical and legal, c.1623–40, Huntington Library, mssHM 46323, f. 10v.
[192] 'The Five Senses'.   [193] Ibid.   [194] Ibid.
[195] Matthew Stoneham, Two sermons of direction for judges and magistrates (1608; STC 23290), sig. B5r.
[196] Ibid., sig. B5v.   [197] The Autobiography and Correspondence of Sir Simonds d'Ewes, 188.

but one elevated by fraternal sociability and friends with whom to enjoy the bounties such a world brought forth.

*

Though moral literature, Continental treatises, and classical translations all served to prescribe civil behaviour, colonization generated new fashions and codes of conduct. As Anna Bryson finds, the humanist emphasis on civility re-structured the principles of elite behaviour and mapped concepts of socio-political order onto standards of conduct and the body itself.[198] In her conclusion, she observes that bodies 'controlled and refined' involved a self-valuation against savagery that partly 'developed in response to the challenge presented by the discovery of the New World'.[199] Bryson's conclusions deserve more than an afterthought, but they also require some modification. By relating expansion to their aspirations for political participation and civil refinement, gentlemen specifically framed the civil body as one that benefitted from an interaction with and the subordination of indigenous America. By the early seventeenth century, the 'challenge' of defining civility in relation to America emerged from intent and entanglement, not the 'discovery' of something unexpected or intellectually problematic.

This chapter took a relational approach to political culture, emphasizing the importance of networks in and around the Inns of Court and examining the interplay between texts, performances, and objects that shaped individual self-presentation. Poems and masques, portraits, and commonplace books that reflected interests in colonial projects did not just provide a backdrop to a wider context of global expansion, but became active components in effecting the civilizing project of a burgeoning imperial polity. Brought into the context of social gatherings and masculine performance, from masques to dinners in private chambers, artefacts from America influenced sociability and involved judgements about the places from where they came. Dressing up like Native Americans to enact colonization at court, writing verses that glorified the pacification of 'savages' through refined conviviality, and modifying practices around tobacco created a complicated politics of appropriation that sought to destroy or devalue some artefacts, such as indigenous-worked animals skins or terracotta pipes, while taking and re-contextualizing others. Even as high-ranking London councillors berated merchants in New England for 'robbing natives of their furs', American commodities

---

[198] Bryson, *From Courtesy to Civility*, 277–8.   [199] Ibid.

appeared with increasing frequency in the expenditures of gentlemen seeking 'a new black beaver hatte for mie self' and 'tobacco'.[200] The demand for Atlantic things reinforced a need for sustained intervention.

Encouraged to respond creatively and provocatively to questions about governance and civility, Inns gentlemen grappled with the moral responsibilities of colonization. They used their writings and performances to test the bounds of accepted behaviour, to imagine interactions with indigenous groups, to find acceptance among peers, and to shame or exclude others. '*Society* is of such power', Brathwaite warned, that the pressure to belong turned saints into serpents.[201] Despite the mood of disenchantment or uncertainty expressed in wit poetry, gentlemen ultimately found ways to reconcile their vision of civil society to their expansionist agendas. As the king came under increasing attack for his pacifist policies, they pursued a more aggressive vein of colonization than James had called for when he directed 'all the planters to deale gently & favourably w[i]th the Indians . . . by faire means and good example of life'.[202] The stated intent of 'civilizing' Native Americans that appeared in state discourses and charters did not operate beyond, but within, changing codes of behaviour in London, where political decision-making and sociability fuelled each other.

---

[200] 'Minutes of the Council of New England', 17 December 1622, in *Calendar of State Papers: Colonial, Vol. 1*, 35; *A briefe relation of the discovery and plantation of New England* (1622; STC 18483), sig. B3r; 'A book of receipts and expenditures of William Petre', 1597 – 1610, Folger Shakespeare Library, MS V.a.334, ff. 79r–v, 95v, 123v.

[201] Brathwaite, *The English gentleman*, sig. B3r.

[202] 'A report of S[i]r Yeardlyes going Governor to Virginia', FP 93.

Conclusion

In a collection of satires printed in 1621, the poet George Wither rejected the imperial-mindedness of statesmen around him. What of '*America's* large Tract of ground?' Wither asked, '[a]nd all those Isles adioyning, lately found?'[1] He spurned the wealth of America and Spain, Wither wrote, for had not Greece and Rome, and more recently the Ottoman Empire, shown the inevitability of decline? The frontispiece to *Wither's motto* depicted a man enjoying pastoral simplicity, wrapped in a floral mantle and crowned with laurels, reclining against the pillar of fortitude and constancy. Disdaining luxury and leaving the 'savages' in the background to war on their own, the figure impudently pushed the world itself away with a toe.[2]

Although he seemed to reject the expansionist designs of men in the metropolis, Wither could not rebuff the ambitions of his peers without invoking the Atlantic. His depiction of England as a realm that lay apart from or untouched by the world beyond seemed rather like an Eden, blissfully pastoral but irrecoverable. As a member of Lincoln's Inn, Wither came into contact with a number of gentlemen who promoted expansion. Some of his closest friends were staunch colonial supporters, including the lawyer Christopher Brooke and the poet Michael Drayton, whose *Poly-Olbion* (1612) celebrated the military prowess of 'Great Britaine'.[3] To many Protestants, colonization and the subordination of the natural world in other territories were not peripheral but central to their understanding of reform. However critical of court corruption and the 'vanities' of the gentry, Wither himself wrote dedicatory verses in 1628 to the colonist and poet Robert Hayman, a fellow member of Lincoln's Inn, encouraging him to sing the praises of English muses 'e'en from these uncouth shores' of North America.[4]

---

[1] George Wither, *Wither's motto* (1621; STC 25928.7), sig. D3v.
[2] Ibid., '*The Explanation of the* Embleme'.   [3] Drayton, *Poly-Olbion*, sig. Av.
[4] Hayman, *Quodlibets*, sig. A4r.

Significantly, gentlemen often positioned themselves as those best equipped to undertake and oversee colonial initiatives. In practice colonization required the efforts of vast numbers of people. The merchants, captains, sailors, and male and female labourers who travelled to the early plantations were critical to the survival of the English presence abroad, and to the circulation of material goods across the Atlantic. The purpose of this book has been to apply pressure to the political realm: to probe the causes and consequences of imperial intent in Jacobean England, and to put a nascent colonial-mindedness back into the study of English civility and into the consciousness of the ruling elite in the seventeenth century.

The projects under James differed from the joint-stock companies incorporated under Elizabeth because they involved large-scale migration and settlement. Unlike trade-based and ambassadorial activities with Eastern territories, colonization sought to transform America into a 'new England', a 'new Britain', a 'Nova Albion'. Land was essential to the English civilizing project, both in physically securing territorial expansion and in giving gentlemen a stake in it. Ireland and America were both part of the civilizing designs of the political elite, but their distinct geographical conditions and local populations led to vastly different experiences on the ground, as in the metropolitan imaginary. The sheer size of American territories, and the discourses of abundance, wealth, and exoticism they engendered, placed the North and South American continents into a dialogue about the global status of the English. Experiences in the Chesapeake led policy-makers and projectors to envisage large-scale plantation industries as a means of producing the goods and financial capital that would allow them to contend with India or Persia. Guiana, not Munster, would bring to 'London a Contratation house [*casa de contratación*, house of commerce] of more receipt ... then there is now in civill [Seville] for the West Indies'.[5]

The young men educated at Oxford and Cambridge in the later sixteenth and early seventeenth centuries were the first to grow up with the possibilities of creating an empire beyond the British Isles. Compared to their actual territorial holdings, English imperial claims were greatly inflated. Scholars have viewed the celebrations of empire in the works of Hakluyt and Purchas as aspirational rather than reflective of the state's priorities.[6] Yet this was the generation who 'first learned ... from the

---

[5] Ralegh, *The discoverie of the large, rich, and bewtiful empire of Guiana*, sig. O2r.
[6] Canny, 'The Origins of Empire: Introduction', in *The Oxford History of the British Empire: Vol. I*, 1-32, at 5.

Indians' and who viewed 'the Civilizinge of the Indians [as] a matter of the greatest consequence'.[7] As the governor Nathaniel Butler complained to the Earl of Warwick from Bermuda in 1620, gentlemen in London spent a great deal of time discussing Atlantic affairs: 'I have heard some of them-selves saye that they have every daye spent twelve houres in studying the courses that concerne the Plantations'.[8] The way the English responded to colonizing indigenous peoples does not dilute what Norbert Elias called 'the process of becoming'.[9] Quite the opposite – this process involved English Atlantic designs. The English engagement with America was not a 'discovery' in which the English simultaneously 'discovered' themselves. Investigating the early colonial moment reveals a conscious effort at making.

These findings contain several implications for the study of James' reign. Firstly, this calls for a re-assessment of James' own relationship to his subjects' expansionist schemes and to Virginia in particular. When compared to more fully fledged articulations of empire following Cromwell's Western Design, James' involvement seems minimal. Yet the king helped to develop the Crown's sense of responsibility towards colonial schemes, partly through his long-standing commitment to the idea of the monarch as a civilizing force. A 1620 portrait of James by the court painter Paul van Somer, commissioned directly by the king and still held in the Royal Collection, depicts the king in a different light than many better-known representations (Figure 8). James' self-presentation is more dynamically regal than his other portraits and offers a visual corrective to his seemingly passive attitude to power and indeed to empire. Rather than sitting on a chair or reclining with one elbow resting on a table, James stands in the centre with a strong sense of presence, holding his orb and sceptre and wearing his coronation robes and a closed imperial crown. Banqueting House, still under construction at the time, appears complete through the window beyond. The portrait exhibits James' belief in order, seen in his acceptance of his role as monarch and in the Palladian principles of the neoclassical architecture behind him. When the colonist Henry Colt described a mountain on the Caribbean island of Nevis in 1631 as 'high above the rest . . . like the banquettinge house att Whitehall over the other buyldinges', he used Banqueting House as a point of reference and a place of memory

---

[7] *Thomas Platter's Travels in England*, 170–1; John Ferrar's marginalia in the online appendix to Thompson, 'William Bullock's "Strange Adventure"'.

[8] Governor Nathaniel Butler to the Earl of Warwick, 9 October 1620, in *The Rich Papers*, 187.

[9] Elias, *The Civilizing Process*, 303.

Figure 8 Portrait of James I by Paul van Somer, 1620. Courtesy of the Royal
Collection Trust/© Her Majesty Queen Elizabeth II 2019.

that connected colonists to institutions at home, in some ways demonstrating the success of elite building projects in promoting civil ideologies.[10]

James viewed his empire as extending beyond the British Isles. He
approved of colonial projects, endorsed the conversion of indigenous
peoples, and drew on America to articulate political ideas in such writings
as *A counterblaste to tobacco*. James also engaged directly with essential
questions of plantation and its relationship to government from 1619,
around the time he commissioned the aforementioned portrait. As the

---

[10] 'The Voyage of S[i]r Henrye Colt Knight', 84.

king declared over dinner in late 1618, 'this is the first day that ever I began hartely to love Virginia, & from this day forwarde I will ever protecte and defend ytt'.[11] James' attempts to reinforce monarchical sovereignty in debates about colonial government in the 1620s were not abstract but a direct response to Virginian affairs. When Charles I declared that 'the territories of Virginia, the Somers Islands, and New England shall form part of his empire, and the government of Virginia immediately depend upon himself', he specifically invoked the judicial decisions made by his father.[12]

Innovations in print helped to stimulate expansionist discourse. Referring to later discourses around East India Company print, Miles Ogborn discusses the formation of 'a colonial marketplace' of ideas.[13] While it may be too early to find evidence of a 'colonial marketplace' in an Elizabethan and Jacobean 'public sphere' in Ogborn's sense, debating America brought issues around territorial expansion into domestic discussions over trade, war, religion, and statecraft. The Protestant state's endorsement of colonization in polemic and prescriptive literature encouraged subjects to view their providentialism from a colonial perspective. Allusions to colonial events increasingly framed calls to piety and reform while familiarizing readers with America as a topic of fashionable conversation. Scholars now know a good deal about the Virginia Company's use of print, but much is left to be done on the production and reception of colonial texts, from their role in fostering a sense of shared transatlantic identities among confessional communities to the influence of particular printers and engravers on disseminating colonial news.

At the same time, humanism encouraged gentlemen to rigorously challenge older forms of knowledge in their pursuit of the *vita civile*.[14] Statesmen debated the direction of colonization by drawing on Native American intelligence, the experience of colonists, and the assistance of indigenous guides.[15] Alongside rumours and manuscript reports, travel narratives presented a range of often conflicting material that served to spur important debates about empire and polity. Colonies became

[11] 'A report of S[i]r Yeardlyes going Governor to Virginia', FP 93.

[12] Charles I, 'Proclamation for settling the plantation of Virginia', 13 May 1625, in *Calendar of State Papers: Colonial, Vol. 1*, 73.

[13] Miles Ogborn, *Indian Ink: Script and Print in the Making of the East India Company* (Chicago, IL: University of Chicago Press, 2007), 203.

[14] Aysha Pollnitz, *Princely Education in Early Modern Britain* (Cambridge: Cambridge University Press, 2015).

[15] Martin D. Gallivan, *James River Chiefdoms: The Rise of Social Inequality in the Chesapeake* (Lincoln: University of Nebraska Press, 2003), 12.

microcosms for fierce disputes in London about company management, the division of land, and policies of conversion or settlement. These exposed inherent rifts in domestic opinions about structures of government and the extent of monarchical power over English institutions.[16]

The outpour of goods and of discourses about America in London became part of the debates on political authority that scholars have seen as a defining feature of the early Stuart era. Rarely concerned solely with the colonies themselves, texts purporting to offer a 'true relation' of overseas affairs involved the articulation of a range of political ideas, from the nature of monarchical authority to the necessity of governors and general assemblies in managing state interests in invaded territories.[17] Colonial news contributed to discussions about the authority of Parliament and the Crown, and about the relationship between the government at Whitehall and the commercial world of the City.[18] As chapters have argued at various points, the practicalities of financing and managing early colonization – from tobacco debates in Parliament to the catastrophes around the dissolution of the Virginia Company – impelled statesmen to draw on their imperial ambitions to contest the balance of power between Crown and Parliament to varying levels of success.

Print functioned within this broader political culture of patronage and institutional networks. The prefatory poetry in colonial texts and pro-tobacco literature exhorted readers to 'go, and Subdue', or to take example from 'industrious *Hakluit*,/Whose Reading shall inflame/Men to seeke Fame', encouraging readers to contribute to colonial projects through a collective sense of participation.[19] Members of Parliament referenced their friends by name in printed discourses that urged reform and increasingly articulated the survival of the colonies as a national imperative.[20] The gentlemen who created elaborate rituals around smoking and performed empire in their social spaces, who formulated projects in the gardens and walks at the Inns or who sat on colonial councils, contributed to the process through which consumption, sociability, and politics worked

---

[16] These issues are discussed in *Virginia 1619: Slavery and Freedom in the Making of English America*, ed. Paul Musselwhite, Peter C. Mancall, and James Horn (Chapel Hill: University of North Carolina Press, 2019); Alexander B. Haskell, *For God, King, and People: Forging Commonwealth Bonds in Renaissance Virginia* (Chapel Hill: University of North Carolina Press, 2017).

[17] For example, 'The Platforme of the government, and Divisions of the Territories in Generall', in *A briefe relation of the discovery and plantation of New England*, sig. D4v.

[18] Ogborn, *Indian Ink*; Popper, 'An Information State for Elizabethan England'; Pollnitz, *Princely Education in Early Modern Britain*.

[19] Drayton, 'To the Virginian Voyage', 171–3.

[20] Brooke, 'A Poem on the Late Massacre in Virginia (1622)', 259–92.

together to negotiate responses to political problems.[21] In doing so, they opened up new spaces for political debate, and not only in the colonies themselves. The tobacco houses discussed in Chapter 4, for example, can be seen as prefiguring the emergence of coffeehouses as political spaces where subjects met to discuss global politics and economies. Gentlemen therefore used a range of interlocking media, from cheap print to poems to letters, to encourage colonial participation and to put pressure on their peers to accept colonial responsibility.

Policy-makers' willingness to engage with colonization highlights the imperial intent evident among the gentry and the nobility. Parliamentary historians have acknowledged the growing Protestant interest in overseas affairs that began in the later part of Elizabeth's reign and escalated in the seventeenth century, much of it related to trade.[22] Their commercial interests, however, did not prevent gentlemen from demonstrating a commitment to the civilizing project that linked these interests to responsibilities of state. Richard Martin's 'great desyre' for English success in Virginia, that '[f]ire' that 'flames out to the view of every one' related the hope of gain to other forms of investment: 'long and hazardous voyages' in the service of plantation were framed as personal and providential acts of fulfilment.[23] Without this context, the demise of George Thorpe, described in a throwaway line in an overview of the House of Commons ('the Powhatans slaughtered him'), seems unfortunate, even random.[24] Projecting Thorpe as a senseless victim of indigenous brutality in another part of the world does little to elucidate his commitment to Protestant expansion, a zeal powerful enough to induce him to settle in Virginia himself. Neither does this brief statement sufficiently situate Thorpe within escalating Anglo–Algonquian conflicts that informed virulent debates in 1620s London. 'I desire you, & conjure you', Martin implored William Strachey, to write from Virginia 'that thereby I may be truly able to satisfy others, & to direct my counsells' to those at home.[25]

The chapters in this book offered perspectives into how aspirations to colonize America became imbedded in the civil identities of the governing elite. Chapter 1 introduced the project of colonization through elite

---

[21] On how negotiation influenced institutional change, see Braddick, *State Formation in Early Modern England*, 437.

[22] Thomas Cogswell, 'The Human Comedy in Westminster: The House of Commons, 1604–1629', *Journal of British Studies*, 52 (2013), 370–89; Rabb, *Jacobean Gentleman*.

[23] Martin to Strachey, 14 December 1610, Folger MS V.a.321, ff. 62r–v.

[24] Cogswell, 'The Human Comedy in Westminster', 376.

[25] Martin to Strachey, Folger MS V.a.321, f. 63r.

patronage and the attitudes towards nature and plantation that informed expansion. It sought to explain why individuals in Parliament, the royal court, and the courts of Anne of Denmark and Prince Henry staked a claim in American plantation when its economic benefits were still uncertain and when treatises on trade remained far more optimistic about establishing connections with Europe and the East.[26] Much of this can be understood through the long-standing relationship between estate management and service to the state. Disdaining mercantile profiteering, which they viewed as offering immediate returns at the expense of longer-term stability, gentlemen considered overseas plantation as extensions of their rising interests in managing and surveying their own lands. Merchants subscribed to this rhetoric, where trade and polity fulfilled each other: 'a worthy enterprise and of great consequence, [Virginia is] much above the Marchants levell and reach', wrote Robert Kayll in 1615. 'And in sure regard of the great expenses ... I could wish, that as many of the Nobility and Gentry of the land have willingly embarqued themselves in the labour, so the rest of the Subjects might be urged to help to forme and bring forth this birth, not of an infant, but of a man; nay, of a people, of a kingdom'.[27]

Chapter 2 examined the influence of 'this birth', a fledgling Virginia, on Jacobean political culture. Prior to mass migration, the Jamestown–London connection offers a case study into the intimacy of the early colonial moment, where the private reflections shared between friends and family about colonial conditions strengthened the commitment to colonize at home. George Percy's elegant descriptions of Powhatan adornment expressed wonder at the beauty of Algonquian featherwork and claw jewellery, but he also catalogued acts of iconoclasm, brutal warfare, and anthropophagy among the English that served as urgent reminders of the fragility of civility and the necessity of uncompromising governance. From Percy's 'Relacyon' to John Bonoeil's treatise on silkworm cultivation, gentlemen viewed the civilizing project in America as a project of refinement, one that related the transformation of new landscapes to their own aspirations for service and distinction. This chapter also traced the influence of Algonquian political action on the colony and metropolitan discourse, including the ways in which Londoners responded to Native

---

[26] 'For the *Bermudas*, we know not yet what they will do; and for *Virginia*, we know not well what to do with it', Robert Kayll, *The trades increase* (1615; STC 14894.8), sig. D3r.

[27] Ibid.

agency, and ended with a discussion of the function of colonial intelligence as a form of political counsel.

Chapter 3 investigated the relationship between violence and civility, placing post-Reformation debates about orthodoxy and civil society within the context of Atlantic exploration. As litigation cases rose and the state's civilizing project seemed to be effectively diminishing outbursts of physical violence in England, writers also began to draw on ideas of indigenous cannibalism to criticize domestic socio-economic changes to an unprecedented degree. This reflected the English exposure to Native American belief systems in the Caribbean and South America, but it also reveals contradictions at the heart of the civilizing project, where accusations of cannibal behaviour served to critique the extractive nature of Jacobean projects and increasing disputes over private property. Though the English conveyed a sense of vulnerability when exposed to Native American violence, they also continued to endorse a world of sociability and consumption that hinged on colonial interference and economic exploitation. The English pursuit of civility can only be framed as a story of declining violence when colonial spaces are considered peripheral rather than central to the political realm.

Chapter 4 examined imperial intent and changing attitudes to consumption through policy-makers' endorsement of the tobacco trade. By using tobacco debates in Parliament to express support for plantation and the Protestant cause at the onset of the Thirty Years' War, gentlemen turned a subversive American commodity into a 'luxury of necessity'. The merchant and economic writer Thomas Mun, in a tract later published by his son, lamented the 'unnecessary wants' of 'Silks, Sugars, Spices, Fruits, and all others' that 'hath made us effeminate' and 'unfortunate in our Enterprises'.[28] To colonial endorsers in Parliament, their values rooted in a sense of history and pedigree, an empire in America was not the problem but the solution. Trading enterprises would become more successful not only as a result of merchandizing, but through elite regulation and the establishment of hierarchies that could manage the potential for degeneration and disobedience. '[C]ivility and knowledge do confirm and not effeminate good and true spirits', Thomas Roe professed, as he sought marble statues, coral, and gems for his patron, the Earl of Arundel.[29]

---

[28] Thomas Mun, *England's treasure by forraign trade* (1664; Wing M3073), sigs. Nv–N2v.

[29] Thomas Roe to the Earl of Arundel, 7 January 1621, in David Howarth, *Lord Arundel and His Circle* (New Haven, CT: Yale University Press, 1985), 88.

The final chapter drew together many of the strands underpinning this book by addressing the role of sociability and Atlantic 'things' in shaping behaviour and envisioning what an imperial polity looked like. Within the formative institutions of the Inns of Court, gentlemen used their literary outputs and political performances to claim colonization as a largely masculine enterprise set against Catholicism and the debasement of the king's own court. Gentlemen learned to behave as colonizers in the social spaces of the metropolis where they circulated pro-imperial poetry and discussed colonial intelligence, fuelled by the actual intoxication of the senses through tobacco. Within these settings, clusters of consumption allowed for a complex self-fashioning that both disdained violence and celebrated conquest, turning the fruits of empire into manifestations of providential favour.

Objects played an active role in shaping civility and social distinction in an imperial polity. This was evident in what gentlemen brought with them to places like Jamestown. From writing utensils and paper for record-keeping to the large chests with locks and keys intended to preserve them, glass drinking cups to Chinese porcelain, the 'need of society' was embedded in the use of, and accessibility to, certain objects.[30] The place of American objects in elite sociability in London is perhaps even more revealing. As discussed in the Introduction, access to foreign goods was indicative of widening global networks of trafficking and exchange that reached far beyond America. In terms of wealth and financial possibility, European exports and spices, textiles, and porcelain connecting England to Eastern trades dominated the marketplace. In a vast, interconnected world of ships and agents, objects acquired by cultural go-betweens in their travels were often valued in ways that related to the personal experience of travel and encounter.[31] Nonetheless, colonial goods – shells, feathers, carved bone and claws, beaver furs – conveyed particular associations to metropolitan gentlemen. These exhibited proof of an alluring world exist-ing just beyond 'those petty English plantations in the savage islands in the West Indies' and evoked verdant landscapes waiting to be exploited through English industry, settlement, and rule.[32]

---

[30] The term 'need of society' is a seventeenth-century one, here adopted from Cary Carson, 'Banqueting Houses and the "Need of Society" among Slave-Owning Planters in the Chesapeake Colonies', *The William and Mary Quarterly*, 70 (2013), 725–80.

[31] Lemire, *Global Trade and the Transformation of Consumer Cultures*.

[32] Francis Wyatt and the Council of Virginia to the Privy Council, 6 April 1626, in *Calendar of State Papers: Colonial, Vol. 1*, 79.

The acquisition and circulation of things is accompanied by the echoes of what do not survive. Dyed animal skin clothing, anthropomorphic terracotta pipes, or quartz crystal arrowheads might appear in cabinets of curiosities, but they were not incorporated into elite ideas of refined sophistication the way Chinese porcelains or Indian calicos were. Wampum belts, viewed by indigenous groups as living, sacred objects that signified pacts of friendship and co-existing but non-interfering worldviews, were valued insofar as they might be used as monetary currency or as contracts of indigenous submission. Algonquian tombs, religious artefacts, or pearls believed to have been artlessly worked were consistently deemed less precious to Englishmen than sassafras or chunks of ambergris.

The emotional and spiritual power of eagle or parrot feathers, if not their beauty and lustre, were lost on those who appropriated ceremonial objects. Mantles and featherwork in London often served as material tokens of ostensible submission. 'The robe of the King of Virginia' in the collector and gardener John Tradescant's collection reputedly came from the ceremonial 'crowning' of Wahunsenacah, who in fact refused to willingly bend a knee to the English.[33] Francis Drake took the 'peeces of the shels of pearles', bone, and red feathers presented to him by the Miwoks in California as proof that they revered him as a god.[34] When Nicholas Saunders wrote to Cecil about the pedlar wearing what he took to be an artefact from the West Indies, he understood the object to have been stolen or taken in battle: a captain who had gone 'w[i]th S[i]r Frauncys Drake in the last voyadge ... tould me that there was such a hatt taken in that action of an Indian king'.[35] For some Brazilian groups, the word for nudity translated as 'without feathers' or 'without earrings'.[36] To be stripped of such objects was to be socially incomplete, as one Tupi man iterated in 1613 when he regarded his enslavement 'without paint and with no feathers fastened to my head or on my arms or wrists' as worse than death.[37] South American featherwork or Algonquian 'crowns' in the metropolis were not just curiosities; some were spoils of war. Taking objects and depriving individuals of their

[33] John Tradescant, *Musaeum Tradescantianum* (1656; Wing T2005), 47.
[34] Fletcher, *The world encompassed by Sir Francis Drake*, sigs. K4r–v. Fletcher's intelligence was known to Hakluyt and appeared in part in Hakluyt's *The principall navigations* (1589).
[35] Nicholas Saunders to Robert Cecil, 13 July 1596, Hadfield House, CP 42/40r.
[36] Kenneth M. Kensinger, 'Why Feathers?', in *The Gift of Birds*, xix–xxi, at xxi.
[37] Hemming, *Red Gold*, 39.

traditions reinforced political authority and contributed to the material politics and particular aesthetics of civility that accompanied empire.

What emerges from this study is the instrumental role that political friendships and social habits played in furthering and normalizing colonization in intersecting public and private spaces. Some of Ralegh's last words on the scaffold were to his friend the Earl of Arundel, who had boarded Ralegh's ship before his departure to Guiana. Ralegh recalled how Arundel 'took me by the hand, and said you would request one thing of me, which was, that whether I made a voyage good or bad, I should not fail, but to return again'.[38] When the brothers Edward and Thomas Hayes sought to further 'the business of planting Christianitie among heathens' in 1606, they informed Robert Cecil that regardless of his support, they planned to circulate copies of their proposal in Parliament, and to 'div[er]s o[u]r frendes, members of the same'.[39] These were not just court-centred friendships; they stemmed from a number of institutional affiliations and confessional or family alliances that suggest more permeable and overlapping boundaries.

Michelle O'Callaghan argues that the rise of friendship manuals and the language of love and trust between men encoded values that helped to define 'the class identity of gentlemen' from the later sixteenth century.[40] These values also served the political culture of imperial participation by conveying a particular vision of transatlantic masculine sociability whose fraternal bonds were influenced by the language of wit coteries. Strachey was 'a fytt *Achates* for such an *Aeneas*' as Lord de la Warr, Martin wrote, referring to the faithful traveller and companion to Virgil's classical hero.[41] When Drayton wrote a poem to send off his friend George Sandys to Virginia, he praised Sandys' resolution to continue translating Ovid's *Metamorphoses* on the banks of the James River, and urged Sandys to 'impart your skill/In the description of the place, that I,/May become learned in the soyle thereby'.[42] Drayton linked a knowledge of husbandry to plantation but also to the 'industry' of literary composition, one with distinctly classical resonances: 'Let's see what lines Virginia will produce;/

---

[38] Quoted in *The Life, Correspondence, and Collections of Thomas Howard, Earl of Arundel*, 150.

[39] Edward and Thomas Hayes to the Earl of Salisbury, 1606, Hatfield House, CP 119/6r.

[40] Michelle O'Callaghan, 'The Duties of Societies: Literature, Friendship and Community', in *Renaissance Transformations: The Making of English Writing, 1500–1650*, ed. Margaret and Tom Healy (Edinburgh: Edinburgh University Press, 2009), 97–111, at 99.

[41] Martin to Strachey, Folger MS V.a.321, f. 62r.

[42] Drayton, 'To Master George Sandys *Treasurer for the English Colony in* Virginia', sig. Bbv.

Goe on with Ovid . . . /Intice the Muses thither to repaire,/Intreat them gently, trayne them to that ayre'.[43]

As Chapter 3 demonstrated in relation to cannibalism, discourses about the violent rupturing of civil society often expressed factionalism as a personal attack against humanist models of friendship, and against the bonds created by shared living in the *vita civile*. This reflected early modern political theories about authority stemming from the ordered patriarchal state, but it also suggests that male friendships were integral to how gentlemen understood the relationship between colonization and state-building. One manuscript treatise from the 1620s thus insisted that investing in Virginia would 'marrye Virginia to the Soveraignetie of England', but that the best means to do so would be to 'spurre on manie that have good estates in England to plant there, and to drawe their freindes [*sic*] and kindred w[i]th them'.[44] Friends were 'apt instrumentes' to 'farther our pollitick end of houlding Virginia to England'.[45]

This understanding of male friendship as an instrument of expansion recognized all three elements of Aristotle's theory of friendship, where trusted bonds between men served a political necessity, reflected a greater good, and provided a source of pleasure.[46] When colonial promoters described friendship as a part of how colonization might be effected, they viewed this relationship as a political necessity but also as a component of the ideal society they wished to create. Before the arrival of larger numbers of women in America, gentlemen celebrated male friendships as an essential means of securing political control while simultaneously enjoying relationships that reflected the highest forms of civility in Greco-Roman thought. The colonist Robert Cushman, writing for audiences in New England and London in 1621, argued that self-love was anathema to plantation, whereas 'the sweetnesse of true friendship' ensured its success.[47] Cushman's title promised to discuss the importance of friendship alongside 'the state of the Country, *and condition of the SAVAGES*', thereby linking the civilizing function of masculine relationships to the development of plantation. Cushman opened his text with a quote from Romans 12:10 advocating brotherly love, and urged that men must be of one heart, echoing classical

[43] Ibid., sig. Bbr.
[44] John Bargrave, 'A treatise shewing howe to erect a publique and increaseing Treasurie for Virginia', *c*.1622 [?], Huntington Library, mssHM 962, f. 5v.
[45] Ibid.
[46] John M. Cooper, 'Aristotle on the Forms of Friendship', *The Review of Metaphysics*, 30 (1977), 619–48.
[47] Cushman, *A sermon preached at Plimmoth in New-England*, title page.

discourses about perfect friendship uniting hearts as one.[48] This fraternal view of the world marked the language of transatlantic civility and the values of gentlemen planters long after the Jacobean era.

It is tempting to dismiss such literature as evocative but inconsequential, unrelated to the brutal business of effecting empire. Fantasies of bloodless conquests and pleasure gardens seem far removed from evidence of colonists licking the blood off dead Native Americans for sustenance, or reports of soldiers shooting Algonquian women in the rivers of the Chesapeake. But what often allowed opulent colonial imaginings to intermingle with the fraught knowledge of colonial conditions was, in the end, civility itself. Gentlemanly celebrations of their own refined sense of self and nation defined the English civilizing project, underpinned by the belief that to 'be a man' required demonstrations of subordination and control.

By 1628, the writer and Newfoundland colonist Robert Hayman could position himself on the cusp of a more integrated colonial world united by friendships between men in London and America. The generational aspect explored at various points in this book emerges strongly in Hayman's narrative. Hayman had been inspired to explore the world beyond England after an encounter with Francis Drake in his boyhood, where Drake bestowed on him an orange and a kiss. Hayman's publication contained a mix of poems encouraging plantation intermixed with memories of his time and friendships at the Inns of Court, referencing Wither, Drayton, and the colonist George Calvert, who had served as James' secretary of state.[49] Dedicated to King Charles, Hayman focussed less on the logistics of plantation management and more on cultivating a transatlantic society sustained through close personal ties. The colonial promoter William Vaughan penned the prefatory verse, 'To my deare Friend and Fellow-Planter', and Hayman composed verses 'To a worthy Friend, who often objects to the coldnesse of the Winter in Newfoundland', and 'To the right Honourable Sir *George Calvert*, Knight, late Principall Secretary to King *JAMES* ... and Lord of Avalon in Newfound-land'. These poems created a world that was recognizably English – and elite – but also influenced by life in America. With its references to nymphs and muses, West Indian iguanas and wooded plantations, the tract envisaged a hybrid, shared environment between gentlemen on both sides of the Atlantic. While some men sought to evade the

---

[48] Ibid., sig. Dv. On male friendship, see Thomas MacFaul, *Male Friendship in Shakespeare and His Contemporaries* (Cambridge: Cambridge University Press, 2009); Tosh, *Male Friendship and Testimonies of Love in Shakespeare's England*.

[49] Hayman, *Quodlibets*, sig. Iv.

challenging duties of colonization, such behaviour was 'lamentably strange to me', and '[i]n the next age *incredible*'twill be'.[50] By the next generation, Hayman believed, England and America would be fully engrained, a disconnect between them impossible to fathom.

*

England in the 1620s stood poised on the brink of large-scale change. Those 'petty English plantations' in the Caribbean that Francis Wyatt mentioned in 1626 were soon to become lucrative sites for sugar and tobacco.[51] Thousands of men and women settled in North America in the 1630s in waves of migration that drastically changed the demographics of earlier colonization. The recorded presence of Africans in the English Chesapeake in 1619 numbered around twenty, but the concentration of these Africans on certain plantations is indicative, suggesting a correlation between forced African labour and the estates' status-conscious owners.[52] A defence of slavery appeared at the start of a 1638 pamphlet about a hurricane on St Christopher's (St Kitt's) by the London 'water poet' John Taylor, who maintained that forced servitude was a productive condition whereby 'savages' became 'civil', a means through which many nations had been 'happily brought to Civility'.[53] While freedom made 'barbarous' nations licentious cannibals, 'being conquer'd and overcome [taught] the laudable Experience of Tillage and Husbandry'.[54] While not 'all are civiliz'd' in the world, Taylor concluded, such as 'in *America*, and in divers Islands adjacent', the English were well-poised to do unto others as 'more civiller Nations did conquer, tame, and teach us'.[55] England as a once-conquered island, fit for conquering, was by now an ingrained component of political rhetoric, one that gained particular force from recent expansion and the entrenched assumptions behind such victories.

By the mid-seventeenth century, the development of plantations and the formation of an English colonial elite were well underway. The beginnings of the 'great houses' era from the 1640s to the 1660s, characterized by formidable building projects such as William Berkeley's Green Spring plantation in Virginia, connected the gentlemanly 'need of society' to

---

[50] Ibid., sig. G4v.

[51] Wyatt and the Council of Virginia to the Privy Council, in *Calendar of State Papers: Colonial, Vol. 1*, 79.

[52] List of names living in Virginia, 16 February 1624, in ibid., 57. On the gentry's willingness to use African labourers from early on and on the calculated absence of positive law regarding enslaved Africans in Virginia, see John C. Coombs, 'The Phases of Conversion: A New Chronology for the Rise of Slavery in Early Virginia', *The William and Mary Quarterly*, 68 (2011), 332–60, at 338.

[53] John Taylor, *Newes and strange newes from St. Christophers* (1638; STC 23778.5), sig. A3v.

[54] Ibid., sig. A4r.   [55] Ibid., sigs. A4r–v.

rising consumption, forced labour, and estate-building in North America and the Caribbean.[56] When gentlemen in the mid-seventeenth century praised the production of tobacco and silk, ordered landscapes, and industrial diversification as a means of contending with the luxuries of Persia, they were celebrating the civil order that earlier projectors and statesmen had envisaged from the start.[57] In their aspirations for colonial participation and display, governors like Berkeley showed themselves to be a product of this early imperial moment. Born two years after James' accession to the throne, and as a participant in the literary culture of the Middle Temple in the late 1620s, Berkeley was shaped by the networks of colonial enthusiasm engendered in the metropolis, where gentlemen had articulated the importance of land management and the subjugation of other peoples as vital to their projects and as desirable components of status.

As George Wither knew when he wrote his satires, here was a realm that increasingly understood itself by looking outward. Within a vast array of interlocking global interactions, colonization impelled policy-makers to think about themselves as rulers of other territories and peoples, and committed the Crown and Parliament to colonial management in America. Shortly after the publication of Wither's book, George Wyatt, proud father to the Virginia governor Francis, corresponded from the Kentish countryside with his son on Algonquian stratagems of war and collected verses written by the parish vicar lauding Francis' virtuous duty abroad. Employing the metaphor of the beehive so popular in Elizabethan and Jacobean notions of the perfect commonwealth, the elder Wyatt now included a new emphasis in this model of industry and governance. For good or ill, those armed to defend the realm and protect its orthodoxies – 'skild and resolvd to fight' – now faced new directions, reflected in the closing lines of Wyatt's poem: 'To gather Wax and Hony to their Hive ... To drink thos Nectars gladdinge God and men ... Their young broode, they in colonise [colonies] out send'.[58] To

---

[56] Carson, 'Banqueting Houses and the "Need of Society"', 725–80. Coombs discusses the correlation between expanding plantations and the beginnings of institutionalized slavery in 'The Phases of Conversion', 353.

[57] Warren M. Billings, 'Sir William Berkeley and the Diversification of the Virginia Economy', *The Virginia Magazine of History and Biography*, 104 (1996), 433–54; 'A Memorandum of the Virginia Plantation' [undated], The Hartlib Papers, 61/5/1A-2B www.dhi.ac.uk/hartlib/; Meeting of divers Adventurers of Martins Hundred at Sir John Wolstenholme's, 1 November 1624, Ferrar Papers, FP 1365.

[58] George Wyatt, untitled and undated [early seventeenth century], British Library, Add MS 62135 (II), f. 331r.

Wyatt, the colonies offered fragrant '[n]ectars' that benefitted the hive, and the agents who would bring about domestic prosperity were young men like his son, committed to affairs of state. The dissolving bounds between societies and peoples that occurred as a result of colonization, however, transformed the English realm far more than it succeeded in assimilating those who lived beyond it.

Bibliography

Manuscripts and Archives

Beinecke Rare Book & Manuscript Library, New Haven
Osborn b197
Osborn b337

British Library, London
Add MS 12496
Add MS 29598
Add MS 34599
Add MS 38823
Add MS 62135(I & II)
Add MS 73085
Egerton MS 2087
Royal MS 17 B XIII
Royal MS 18 A XI
Sloane MS 1622
Sloane MS 1768
Sloane MS B 3272

British Museum, London
BM 1870,0514.1176–79
BM 1906,0509.1–16
BM 1931,1114.625
SL, 5270.1–6

Edinburgh University Library
Laing MS III 283

Ferrar Papers, Cambridge
FP 93
FP 113
FP 151
FP 193

FP 285
FP 415
FP 416
FP 437
FP 527
FP 532
FP 1365

Folger Shakespeare Library, Washington, DC

V.a.321
V.a.334
V.b.335
V.b.288
X.c.45
X.c.54

Hatfield House, Hatfield

CP 41
CP 42
CP 48
CP 67
CP 75
CP 87
CP 112
CP 119
CP 120
CP 122
CP 124
CP 127
CP 128
CP 130
CP 152
CP 189
CP 196
CP Petitions 300
CP Petitions 1186
CPM I 12

Huntington Library, San Marino

mssHM 78
mssHM 962
mssHM 1648
mssHM 46323

Jamestown Rediscovery, Jamestown

424-JR

656-JR
2106-JR
2961-JR
3077-JR
3078-JR
3397-JR
3734-JR
4049-JR
4221-JR
4438-JR
4865-JR
4866-JR
5696-JR
6629-JR
7420-JR
7423-JR
7783-JR
7819-JR
7860-JR
8204-JR
8205-JR

Middle Temple, London
MT.3/MEM/3
MT.3/MEM/7
MT.7/MAA/4
MT.7/MAA/36
MT.7/RUD/1
MT.15/TAM/12

The National Archives, Kew
CO 1
E 215
PC 2
SP 12
SP 13
SP 14
SP 53
SP 63
SP 70

National Portrait Gallery, London
NPG 7
NPG 541
NPG 4032
NPG 6761

Royal Collection, London

RCIN 404446

Victoria & Albert Museum, London

545:1, 2–2008
622–1882
E.371–1926
M.26–1964
M.695:1
P.5–1917

Printed Primary Sources

Adams, Thomas, *The blacke devil* (1615; STC 107).

The gallants burden (1612; STC 117).

Alexander, William, *An encouragement to colonies* (1624; STC 341).

Aristotle, *Art of Rhetoric*, tr. John Henry Freese (Harvard, MA: Harvard University Press, 1926).

The arraignment and conviction of S[i]r Walter Rawleigh (1648; Wing A3744).

Attersoll, William, *The badges of Christianity* (1606; STC 889).

The Autobiography and Correspondence of Sir Simonds d'Ewes, Vol. 1, ed. James Orchard Halliwell (London: Richard Bentley, 1845).

d'Avity, Pierre [tr. Edward Grimeston], *The states, empires, & principalities of the world* (1615; STC 988).

Bacon, Francis, *The essays, or councils, civil and moral, of Sir Francis Bacon* (1696; Wing B296).

Sylva sylvarum: or A natural historie in ten centuries (1627; STC 1168).

Barclay, William, *Nepenthes, or, The vertues of tabacco* (Edinburgh, 1614; STC 1406).

Barlow, William, *A sermon preached at Paules Crosse* (1601; STC 1454).

Barnes, Barnabe, *Foure bookes of offices* (1606; STC 1468).

Bartas, Guillaume de Salluste du [tr. William L'Isle], *Babilon, a part of the seconde weeke* (1595; STC 21662).

Bayly, Lewis, *The practice of pietie* (1613; STC 1602).

Beaumont, John, *The metamorphosis of tabacco* (1602; STC 1695).

Becon, Richard, *Solon his follie, or a politique discourse* (Oxford, 1594; STC 1653).

Bennett, Edward, *A treatise divided into three parts* (1620; STC 1883).

Bonoeil, John, *His Majesties gracious letter to the Earle of South-Hampton* (1622; STC 14378).

Bradford, William, *Of Plymouth Plantation, 1620–1647: The Complete Text*, ed. Samuel Eliot Morison (New York: Knopf, 1952).

[with Edward Winslow] *A relation or journall of the beginning and proceedings of the English plantation settled at Plimoth* (1622; STC 20074).

Brathwaite, Richard, *The English gentleman* (1633; STC 3564).

    A solemne joviall disputation (1617; STC 3585).

Brereton, John, *A briefe and true relation of the discoverie of the north part of Virginia* (1602; STC 3611).

    A briefe relation of the discovery and plantation of New England (1622; STC 18483).

Brinsley, John, *A consolation for our grammar schooles* (1622; STC 3767).

Brooke, Christopher, 'A Poem on the Late Massacre in Virginia (1622)', reproduced in *The Virginia Magazine of History and Biography*, 72 (1964), 259–92.

Bruce, John, ed., *Calendar of State Papers: Domestic, Charles I: 1629–1631*, (London: Her Majesty's Stationery Office, 1860).

Bullock, William, *Virginia impartially examined, and left to publick view* (1649; Wing B5428).

Burton, Robert, *The anatomy of melancholy* (Oxford, 1621; STC 4159).

Burton, William, *The rowsing of the sluggard* (1595; STC 4176).

Butts, Henry, *Dyets dry dinner* (1599; STC 4207).

By the King. A proclamation concerning ale-houses (1618; STC 8588).

By the King. A proclamation concerning tobacco (1624; STC 8738).

By the King. A proclamation prohibiting the publishing of any reports or writings of duels (1613; STC 8490).

By the King. A proclamation to restraine the planting of tobacco in England and Wales (1619; STC 8622).

By the King. Whereas at the humble suit and request of sundry our loving and well disposed subjects . . . (1621; STC 8660).

By the Maior. A proclamation for the reformation of abuses, in the gaole of New-gate (1617; STC 16727.1).

C. T., *An advice how to plant tobacco in England* (1615; STC 23612).

Camden, William, *Annales the true and royall history of the famous empresse Elizabeth* (1625; STC 4497).

Carew, Thomas, *Coleum Britanicum. A masque at White-hall* (1634; STC 4618).

de las Casas, Bartolomé [tr. M. M. S.], *The Spanish colonie, or Briefe chronicle of the acts and gestes of the Spaniardes in the West Indies* (1583; STC 4739).

Chapman, George, *An epicede or funerall song* (1613; STC 4974).

    The memorable masque (1614; STC 4982).

    Monsieur d'Olive (1606; STC 4983).

de Chevalier, Guillaume [tr. Thomas Heigham], *The ghosts of the deceased sieurs* (Cambridge, 1624; STC 5129).

Chute, Anthony, [*Tabacco*] (1595; STC 5262.5).

Cicero, Marcus Tullius, *On Duties*, tr. Walter Miller (Harvard, MA: Harvard University Press, 1913).

    Tusculan Disputations, tr. A. E. Douglas (Warminster: Aris and Phillips, 1990).

Clapham, Henoch, *A chronological discourse* (1609; STC 5336).

Coeffeteau, Nicolas [tr. Edward Grimeston], *A table of humane passions* (1621; STC 5473).

Colonizing Expeditions to the West Indies and Guiana, 1623–1667, ed. V. T. Harlow (Surrey: Ashgate, 2010).

The Complete Poems of John Donne, ed. Robin Robbins (Harlow: Longman, 2010).

Coperario, John, *The maske of flowers* (1614; STC 17625).

Copland, Patrick, *A declaration how the monies . . . were disposed* (1622; STC 5726).

Corona Regia, ed. Winfried Schleiner and Tyler Fyotek (Geneva: Librarie Droz, 2010).

Cotta, John, *A short discoverie of the unobserved dangers of severall sorts of ignorant and unconsiderate practisers of physicke in England* (1612; STC 5833).

Council for Virginia, *A declaration of the state of the colonie and affaires in Virginia* (1620; STC 24841.4).

A true and sincere declaration (1610; STC 24832).

Crakanthorpe, Richard, *A sermon at the solemnizing of the happie inauguration* (1609; STC 5979).

Crashaw, William, *A sermon preached in London before the right honorable the Lord Lawarre* (1610; STC 6029).

Criminal Trials, Vol. 1, ed. David Jardine (London: M. A. Nattali, 1846).

The crying Murther (1624; STC 24900).

Cushman, Robert, *A sermon preached at Plimmoth in New-England* (1622; STC 6149).

Davies, John, *A discourse of the true causes why Ireland was never entirely subdued* (1612; STC 6348).

Deacon, John, *Tobacco tortured, or, the filthie fume of tobacco refined* (1616; STC 6436).

A declaration for the certain time of drawing the great standing lottery (1616; STC 24833.8).

Dekker, Thomas, *The guls horne-booke* (1609; STC 6500).

The shomakers holiday (1600; STC 6523).

Digges, Thomas, *Foure paradoxes, or politique discourses concerning militarie discipline* (1604; STC 6872).

Ditchfield, Edward, *Considerations touching the new contract for tobacco* (1625; STC 6918).

'Documents of Sir Francis Wyatt, Governor', *The William and Mary Quarterly*, 8 (1928), 157–67.

Donne, John, *Fiftie sermons* (1649; Wing D1862).

Poems, by J[ohn]. D[onne]. (1633; STC 7045).

Draxe, Thomas, *The earnest of our inheritance* (1613; STC 7184).

Drayton, Michael, *The battaile of Agincourt . . . Elegies upon sundry occasions* (1627; STC 7190).

Poly-Olbion (1612; STC 7226).

Duncon, Eleazar, *The copy of a letter* (1606; STC 6164).

Earle, John, *Micro-cosmographie* (1628; STC 7440.2).

Eburne, Richard, *A plaine path-way to plantations* (1624; STC 7471).

An Elizabethan in 1582: The Diary of Richard Madox, Fellow of All Souls, ed. Elizabeth Story Donno (London: Hakluyt Society, 1976).

Elyot, Thomas, *Bibliotheca Eliotae* (1542; STC 7659.5).
  The dictionary of syr Thomas Eliot knyght (1538; STC 7659).
Englands Parnassus [compiled Robert Allott] (1600; STC 378).
English and Irish Settlement on the River Amazon, 1550–1646, ed. Joyce Lorimer
  (London: Hakluyt Society, 1989).
Epigrammes and elegies by J. D. and C. M. [John Davies and Christopher Marlowe]
  ([London, 1599?]; STC 6350.5).
Estienne, Henri [tr. Richard Carew?], *A world of wonders* (1607; STC 10553).
Everett Green, Mary Anne, ed., *Calendar of State Papers: Domestic, 1619–1623*,
  (London: Longman, 1858).
The Ferrar Papers, ed. B. Blackstone (Cambridge: Cambridge University Press,
  1938).
'The Ferrar Papers. At Magdalene College, Cambridge (Continued)', *The Virginia
  Magazine of History and Biography*, 10 (1903), 414–18.
'The Ferrar Papers at Magdalene College, Cambridge (Continued)', *The Virginia
  Magazine of History and Biography*, 11 (1903), 41–6.
Finch, Henry, *Law, or a discourse thereof* (1627; STC 10871).
Fletcher, Francis, *The world encompassed by Sir Francis Drake* (1628; STC 7161).
Floyd, John, *Purgatories triumph over hell* (St Omer, 1613; STC 11114).
Floyd, Thomas, *The picture of a perfit common wealth describing aswell the offices of
  princes* (1600; STC 11119).
Ford, John, *A line of life* (1620; STC 11162).
The Four Voyages of Christopher Columbus, ed. and tr. J. M. Cohen (London:
  Penguin, 1969).
Foxe, John, *The Pope confuted* (1580; STC 11241).
Gardiner, Edmund, *Phisicall and approved medicines* (1611; STC 11564.5).
Garey, Samuel, *Great Brittans little calendar* (1618; STC 11597).
Gataker, Thomas, *Maskil le-David* (1620; STC 11655).
Gee, John, *The foot out of the snare* (1624; STC 11701).
*The Genesis of the United States: A Narrative of the Movement in England,
  1605–1615: Vol. 1*, ed. Alexander Brown (Boston, MA: Houghton Mifflin,
  1890).
Gilpin, Bernard, *A godly sermon preached in the court at Greenwich* (1581; STC
  11897).
'Good newes from Virginia, 1623', reproduced in *The William and Mary Quarterly*,
  5 (1948), 351–8.
Goodwin, George, *Babels balm* (1624; STC 12030).
Gray, Robert, *A good speed to Virginia* (1609; STC 12204).
Guazzo, Stefano [tr. George Pettie], *The civile conversation* (1581; STC 12422).
Guilpin, Edward, *Skialetheia. Or, A shadowe of truth* (1598; STC 12504).
Hagthorpe, John, *Englands-exchequer* (1625; STC 12603).
Hakluyt, Richard, *The discoveries of the world from their first original … Briefly
  written in the Portugall tongue by Antonie Galvano* (1601; STC 11543).
  The principall navigations, voiages and discoveries of the English nation (1589; STC
  12625).

The principal navigations, voyages, traffiques and discoveries of the English nation (1598–1600; STC 12626a).

Hamor, Ralph, *A true discourse of the present state of Virginia* (1615; STC 12736).

Hampton, William, *A proclamation of warre from the Lord of Hosts* (1627; STC 12741).

Hans Staden's True History: An Account of Cannibal Captivity in Brazil, ed. Neil L. Whitehead (Durham, NC: Duke University Press, 2008).

Harcourt, Robert, *A relation of a voyage to Guiana* (1613; STC 12754).

Hariot, Thomas, *A briefe and true report of the new found land of Virginia* (1588; STC 12785).

A briefe and true report of the new found land of Virginia (1590; STC 12786).

Hart, James, *Klinike, or, the diet of the diseased* (1633; STC 12888).

Hayman, Robert, *Quodlibets . . . composed and done at Harbor-Grace in Britaniola, anciently called Newfound-land* (1628; STC 12974).

Hayward, John, *An answere to the first part of certain conference, concerning succession* (1603; STC 12988).

Herring, Francis, *Mischeefes mysterie: or, Treasons master-peece, the Powder-Plot* (1617; STC 13247).

Herring, Theodore, *The triumph of the Church over water and fire* (1625; STC 13204).

Historye of the Bermudaes or Summer Islands. Edited, from a MS in the Sloane Collection, British Museum, by J. Henry Lefroy (London: Hakluyt Society, 1882).

Hobbes, Thomas, *Leviathan* (1651; Wing H2246).

Hoby, Thomas, *The courtyer of Count Baldessar Castilio* (1561; STC 4778).

Holyday, Barten, *Technogamia: or The marriages of the arts* (1618; STC 13617).

Illustrations of Irish History and Topography, Mainly of the Seventeenth Century, ed. Litton C. Falkiner (London: Longman, 1904).

'The Indian Massacre of 1622: Some Correspondence of the Reverend Joseph Mead', ed. Robert C. Johnson, *The Virginia Magazine of History and Biography*, 71 (1963), 408–10.

Innes, William, *A bundle of myrrhe: or Three meditations of teares* (1620; STC 14091).

James I, *A counterblaste to tobacco* (1604; STC 14363).

Meditation upon the Lords prayer (1619; STC 14384).

A remonstrance of the most gratious King James I (Cambridge, 1616; STC 14369).

The workes of the most high and mightie prince, James (1616; STC 14344).

Jamestown Narratives: Eyewitness Accounts of the Virginia Colony: The First Decade: 1607–1617, ed. Edward Wright Haile (Champlain, VA: Roundhouse, 1998).

The Jamestown Voyages under the First Charter, 1607–1609, Vol. 1, ed. Philip L. Barbour (Cambridge: Cambridge University Press, 1969).

The Jamestown Voyages under the First Charter, 1606–1609: Vol. 2, ed. Philip L. Barbour (London: Hakluyt Society, 1969).

Jerome, Stephen, *Englands Jubilee, or Irelands Joyes* (Dublin, 1625; STC 14511.5).

Moses his sight of Canaan (1614; STC 14512).

Johnson, Robert, *The new life of Virginea* (1612; STC 14700).

Nova Britannia (1609; STC 14699.5).

Jonson, Ben, *Ben Jonson, his Case is altered* (1609; STC 14757).

The staple of news (1631; STC 14753.5).

Jourdain, Silvester, *A discovery of the Barmudas* (1610; STC 14816).

Journal of the House of Burgesses of Virginia, ed. Henry Read McIlwaine and John Pendleton (Richmond: Virginia State Library, 1915).

Journal of the House of Commons: Vol. 1, 1547–1629 (London: His Majesty's Stationery Office, 1802).

Kayll, Robert, *The trades increase* (1615; STC 14894.8).

Kemys, Lawrence, *A relation of the second voyage to Guiana* (1596; STC 14947).

King, John, *A sermon preached at White-Hall* (1608; STC 14986).

Know all men by these presents, that wee Thomas Walsingham, William Wythines, and Henrie Sneglar, knight ... (1620; STC 9175).

Lenton, Francis, *Characterismi* (1631; STC 15463).

Léry, Jean de, *History of a Voyage to the Land of Brazil*, tr. Janet Whatley (Berkeley: University of California Press, 1992).

Leybourn, William, *The compleat surveyor* (1653; Wing L1907).

The Life, Correspondence, and Collections of Thomas Howard, Earl of Arundel, ed. Mary F. S. Hervey (Cambridge: Cambridge University Press, 1969).

The Life and Writings of Luisa de Carvajal y Mendoza, ed. Anne Cruz (Toronto: Centre for Reformation and Renaissance Studies, 2014).

London Consistory Court Depositions, 1586–1611: List and Indexes, ed. Loreen L. Giese (London: London Record Society, 1995).

Lupton, Thomas, *A persuasion from papistrie* (1581; STC 16950).

Lyte, Henry, *Rams little Dodeon, a briefe epitome of the new herbal* (1606; STC 6988).

Malynes, Gerard, *Saint George for England* (1601; STC 17226a).

Martyr, Peter [tr. Richard Eden], *The decades of the newe worlde or west India* (1555; STC 647).

[tr. Richard Eden], *The history of travayle in the West and East Indies* (1577; STC 649).

Memoir of Reverend Patrick Copland: Rector Elect of the First Projected College in the United States, ed. Edward N. Neill (New York: Charles Scribner, 1871).

The Middle Temple Documents Relating to George Chapman's Memorable Masque, ed. Tucker Orbison (Oxford: Malone Society, 1983).

The Middle Temple Records, Vol. 1: 1501–1603, ed. Charles Henry Hopwood (London: Butterworth & Company, 1904).

Middleton, Thomas, *The peace-maker* (1618; STC 14387).

Monardes, Nicolás [tr. John Frampton], *Joyfull newes out of the newe founde worlde* (1580; STC 18006).

de Montaigne, Michel [tr. John Florio], *The essayes or morall, politike and millitarie discourses of Lo: Michael de Montaigne* (1603; STC 18041).

Essays Written in French by Michael Lord of Montaigne (1613; STC 18042).

de Montes, Gonzáles [tr. Vincent Skinner], *The full, ample, and punctuall discovery of the barbarous, bloudy, and inhumane practices of the Spanish Inquisition* (1625; STC 11999).

de Mornay, Philippe, *Fowre bookes, of the institution, use and doctrine of the holy sacrament of the Eucharist* (1600; STC 18142).

Moryson, Fynes, *An itinerary* (1617; STC 18205).

Mun, Thomas, *England's treasure by forraign trade* (1664; Wing M3073).

Münster, Sebastian [tr. Richard Eden], *A treatyse of the newe India with other new founde lands and islandes* (1553; STC 18244).

Narratives of Early Virginia, 1606–1625, ed. Lyon Gardiner Tyler (New York: Charles Scribner, 1907).

Nashe, Thomas, *The Unfortunate Traveller and Other Works*, ed. J. B. Steane (Harmondsworth: Penguin, 1972).

A new and short defense of tabacco (1602; STC 6468.5).

Newfoundland Discovered: English Attempts at Colonization, 1610–1630, ed. Gillian T. Cell (London: Hakluyt Society, 1982).

Nicholas Ferrar: Two Lives, ed. J. E. B. Mayor (Cambridge: Macmillan, 1855).

Nicholl, John, *An houre glasse of Indian newes* (1607; STC 18532).

Nicholls, John, *The oration and sermon made at Rome* (1581; STC 18535).

Norden, John, *A pathway to patience* (1626; STC 18615).

'Notes', *Virginia Magazine of History and Biography*, 68 (1960), 107–8.

Ormerod, Oliver, *The picture of a papist* (1606; STC 18850).

The Oxford Book of English Verse, 1250–1900, ed. A. T. Quiller-Couch (Oxford: Clarendon, 1919).

Paul Hentzner's Travels in England, during the Reign of Queen Elizabeth, tr. Horace, Earl of Orford (London: Edward Jeffrey, 1797).

Peacham, Henry, *Minerva Britanna, or A garden of heroical devises* (1612; STC 19511).

Peckham, George, *A true reporte, of the late discoveries* (1583; STC 19523).

Pena, Pierre and Matthias de L'Obel, *Stirpium adversaria nova* (1571; STC 19595).

de la Perrière, Guillaume, *The mirrour of policie* (1598; STC 15228.5).

Percy, George, 'Trewe Relacyon', in 'George Percy's "Trewe Relacyon": A Primary Source for the Jamestown Settlement', ed. Mark Nicholls, *The Virginia Magazine of History and Biography*, 113 (2005), 212–75.

Philaretes, *Work for chimny-sweepers* (1602; STC 12571).

A pittilesse mother (1616; STC 24757).

Proceedings in Parliament, 1614, ed. Maija Jansson (Philadelphia, PA: American Philosophical Society, 1988).

Prynne, William, *The unlovelinesse, of love-lockes* (1628; STC 20477).

Purchas, Ambrose, *Purchas, his paradise* (1635; STC 20501).

Purchas, Samuel, *The kings towre* (1623; STC 20502).

   Purchas his pilgrimage (1613; STC 20505).

   Purchas his pilgrimes (1625; STC 20509).

Ralegh, Walter, *The discoverie of the large, rich, and bewtiful empire of Guiana* (1596; STC 20634).

The history of the world (1614; STC 20638).

[compiled Robert Vaughan] *Remains of Sir Walter Ralegh* (1657; Wing R180).

Rathborne, Aaron, *The surveyor in foure bookes* (1615; STC 20748).

Records of Early English Drama: Cambridge, Vol. 1, ed. Alan H. Nelson (Toronto: University of Toronto Press, 1989).

Records of the Virginia Company, Vol. III, ed. Susan Myra Kingsbury (Washington, DC: Government Printing Office, 1933).

Records of the Virginia Company, Vol. IV, ed. Susan Myra Kingsbury (Washington, DC: Government Printing Office, 1935).

The Red-Crosse, or, Englands Lord have mercy upon us (1625; STC 20823).

Rich, Barnabe, *Faultes faults, and nothing else but faultes* (1606; STC 20983).

The honestie of this age (1614; STC 20986).

My ladies looking glasse (1616; STC 20991.7).

The Rich Papers: Letters from Bermuda, 1615–1646, ed. Vernon A. Ives (Toronto: University of Toronto Press, 1984).

Roberts, R. A., ed., *Calendar of the Manuscripts of the Most Honourable the Marquis of Salisbury, Vol. 5, 1591–1595*, (London: Her Majesty's Stationary Office, 1894).

Rous, Francis, *The diseases of the time* (1622; STC 21340).

Rowlands, Samuel, *The letting of humors blood in the head-vaine* (1613; STC 21397).

Royal Proclamations of King James I, 1603–1625, ed. James F. Larkin and Paul L. Hughes (Oxford: Clarendon, 1973).

Rudyerd, Benjamin, *Le prince d'amour; or the prince of love* (1660; Wing R2189).

Sainsbury, Noel W., ed., *Calendar of State Papers: Colonial, America and West Indies, Vol. I, 1574–1640*, (London: Longman, 1860).

ed., *Calendar of State Papers: Colonial, East Indies, China and Persia, Vol. 6, 1625–1629*, (London: Her Majesty's Stationery Office, 1884).

Sanderson, Thomas, *Of romanizing recusants, and dissembling Catholicks* (1611; STC 21711).

Scott, Thomas, *An Experimentall discoverie of Spanish practices* (1623; STC 22077).

Vox populi (1620; STC 22100.2).

Scull, John, *Two sermons* (1624; STC 22123).

Seventeenth-Century Political and Financial Papers: Camden Miscellany XXXIII, Camden Fifth Series Vol. 7, ed. David R. Ransome (London: Royal Historical Society, 1996).

'Sir Francis Wyatt, Governor: Documents, 1624–1626', ed. Minnie G. Cook, *The William and Mary Quarterly*, 8 (1928), 157–67.

Smith, John, *The generall historie of Virginia, New-England, and the Summer Iles* (1624; STC 22790).

[ed. William Symonds] *A map of Virginia* (Oxford, 1612; STC 22791).

The true travels, adventures, and observations of Captaine John Smith (1630; STC 22796).

Smith, William, *The black-smith: A sermon preached at White-Hall* (1606; STC 22881).

Speed, John, *The theatre of the empire of Great Britaine* (1612; STC 23041).

Spenser, Edmund, *A View of the State of Ireland*, ed. Andrew Hadfield and Willy Maley (Oxford: Blackwell, 1997).

Stafford, Robert, *A geographicall and anthologicall description of all the empires and kingdomes* (1618; STC 23136).

Stoneham, Matthew, *Two sermons of direction for judges and magistrates* (1608; STC 23290).

Stow, John, *The survey of London* (1633; STC 23345.5).

Strachey, William, *For the colony in Virginea Britannia. Lawes divine, morall and martiall* (1612; STC 23350).

   The Historie of Travaile into Virignia Britannia, ed. R. H. Major (London: Hakluyt Society, 1949).

Sutton, Christopher, *Godly meditations upon the most holy sacrament of the Lordes Supper* (1601; STC 23491).

Sylvester, Josuah, *All the small workes of that famous poet Josuah Sylvester* (1620; STC 23575.5).

   Du Bartas his devine weekes and workes (1611; STC 21651).

   The maiden's blush … From the Latin of Fracastorius (1620; STC 11253).

   Tobacco battered, & the pipes shattered (1621; STC 23582a).

Symonds, William, *Virginia. A sermon* (1609; STC 23594).

T. C., *A short discourse of the New-found-land* (Dublin, 1623; STC 4311).

T. W., *The arraignment and execution of the late traytors* (1606; STC 24916).

Table-observations (1615; STC 23634.7).

Taylor, John, *All the workes of John Taylor the water-poet* (1630; STC 23725).

   Newes and strange newes from St. Christophers (1638; STC 23778.5).

Thevet, André [tr. Thomas Hacket], *The new found worlde* (1568; STC 23950).

Thomas Platter's Travels in England 1599: Rendered into English from the German, tr. and ed. Clare Williams (London: Jonathan Cape, 1937).

Thorius, Raphael, *Hymnus tabaci* (1626; STC 24033).

   [tr. Peter Hausted] *Hymnus tabaci* (1651; Wing T1040).

Tomkis, Thomas, *Lingua: or, The combat of the tongue* (1607; STC 24104).

Tradescant, John, *Musaeum Tradescantianum* (1656; Wing T2005).

A true declaration of the estate of the colonie in Virginia (1610; STC 24833).

'Two Tragical Events', *The William and Mary Quarterly*, 9 (1901), 203–14.

Vaughan, William, *Approved directions for health, both naturall and artificiall* (1612; STC 24615).

   The arraignment of slander perjury blasphemy (1630; STC 24623).

   The golden-grove (1600; STC 24610).

Venner, Tobias, *A briefe and accurate treatise, concerning, the taking of the fume of tobacco* (1621; STC 24642).

Walkington, Thomas, *The optick glasse of humors* (1607; STC 24967).

Ward, Samuel, *Woe to drunkards* (1622; STC 25055).

A warning for faire women (1599; STC 25089).

Waterhouse, Edward, *A declaration of the state of the colony* (1622; STC 25104).

Whitaker, Alexander, *Good newes from Virginia* (1613; STC 25354).

White, John, *The planters plea: Or the grounds of plantations examined* (1630; STC 25399).

Williams, Roger, *A key into the language of America* (1643; Wing W2766).

Wilson, Thomas [clergyman], *A commentarie upon the most divine Epistle of S. Paul to the Romanes* (1614; STC 25791).

Wilson, Thomas [privy councillor], *The arte of rhetorique* (1553; STC 25799).

A discourse uppon usurye by waye of dialogue and oracions (1572; STC 25807).

Wither, George, *Wither's motto* (1621; STC 25928.7).

Wright, Thomas, *The passions of the minde in generall* (1604; STC 26040).

Wyatt, George, 'A letter of advice to the Governor of Virginia, 1624', ed. J. Frederick Fausz and Jon Kukla, *The William and Mary Quarterly*, 34 (1977), 104–29.

The yonger brother his apology by it selfe (St Omer, 1618; STC 715).

Secondary Sources

Anderson, Susan Campbell, 'A Matter of Authority: James I and the Tobacco War', *Comitatus*, 29 (1998), 136–63.

Andrews, K. R., 'Beyond the Equinoctial: England and South America in the Sixteenth Century', *The Journal of Imperial and Commonwealth History*, 10 (1981), 4–24.

Arens, William, *The Man-Eating Myth: Anthropology and Anthropophagy* (New York: Oxford University Press, 1979).

Arlidge, Anthony, *Shakespeare and the Prince of Love: The Feast of Misrule in the Middle Temple* (London: Giles de la Mare, 2000).

Armitage, David, 'The Elizabethan Idea of Empire', *Transactions of the Royal Historical Society*, 14 (2004), 269–77.

'Greater Britain: A Useful Category of Historical Analysis?', *The American Historical Review*, 104 (1999), 427–45.

The Ideological Origins of the British Empire (Cambridge: Cambridge University Press, 2000).

Aston, Margaret, *The King's Bedpost: Reformation and Iconography in a Tudor Group Portrait* (Cambridge: Cambridge University Press, 1993).

At Home with the Empire: Metropolitan Culture and the Imperial World, ed. Catherine Hall and Sonya O. Rose (Cambridge: Cambridge University Press, 2007).

The Atlantic in Global History, 1500–2000, ed. Jorge Cañizares-Esguerra and Erik R. Seeman (Upper Saddle River, NJ: Pearson Prentice Hall, 2007).

The Atlantic World and Virginia, 1550–1624, ed. Peter C. Mancall (Chapel Hill: University of North Carolina Press, 2007).

Avramescu, Cătălin, *An Intellectual History of Cannibalism*, tr. Alistair Ian Blyth (Princeton, NJ: Princeton University Press, 2009).

Bailyn, Bernard, *The Barbarous Years: The Peopling of British North America: The Conflict of Civilizations, 1600–1675* (New York: Knopf, 2012).

Bellany, Alastair and Thomas Cogswell, *The Murder of King James* (New Haven, CT: Yale University Press, 2015).

Bernhard, Virginia, 'Bermuda and Virginia in the Seventeenth Century: A Comparative View', *Journal of Social History*, 19 (1985), 57–70.

'Beyond the Chesapeake: The Contrasting Status of Blacks in Bermuda, 1616–1663', *The Journal of Southern History*, 54 (1988), 554–64.

Berry, Christopher, *The Idea of Luxury: A Conceptual and Historical Investigation* (New York: Cambridge University Press, 1994).

Billings, Warren M., 'Sir William Berkeley and the Diversification of the Virginia Economy', *The Virginia Magazine of History and Biography*, 104 (1996), 433–54.

Black Africans in Renaissance Europe, ed. Thomas Foster Earle and Kate J. P. Lowe (Cambridge: Cambridge University Press, 2005).

Bobbio, Noberto, *Thomas Hobbes and the Natural Law Tradition* (Chicago, IL: University of Chicago Press, 1993).

Boddie, John Bennett, 'Edward Bennett of London and Virginia', *The William and Mary Quarterly*, 13 (1933), 117–30.

Books between Europe and the Americas: Connections and Communities, 1620–1860, ed. Leslie Howsam and James Raven (Basingstoke: Palgrave, 2011).

Bourke, Richard, 'Pocock and the Presuppositions of the New British History', *The Historical Journal*, 53 (2010), 747–70.

Braddick, Michael, 'Introduction: The Politics of Gesture', *Past & Present*, 203 (2009), 9–35.

   State Formation in Early Modern England, 1550–1700 (Cambridge: Cambridge University Press, 2000).

Breen, T. H., *Tobacco Culture: The Mentality of the Great Tidewater Planters on the Eve of the Revolution* (Princeton, NJ: Princeton University Press, 1985).

Brenner, Robert, *Merchants and Revolution: Commercial Change, Political Conflict, and London's Overseas Traders, 1550–1653* (London: Verso, 2003).

Bringing the World to Early Modern Europe: Travel Accounts and Their Audiences, ed. Peter C. Mancall (Leiden: Brill, 2007).

The British Atlantic World, 1500–1800, ed. David Armitage and Michael Braddick (Basingstoke: Palgrave, 2002).

The British Atlantic World, 1500–1800, 2nd ed., ed. David Armitage and Michael J. Braddick (Basingstoke: Palgrave, 2009).

British Interventions in Early Modern Ireland, ed. Ciaran Brady and Jane Ohlmeyer (Cambridge: Cambridge University Press, 2005).

Brooks, Christopher W., *Law, Politics and Society in Early Modern England* (Cambridge: Cambridge University Press, 2009).

   Pettyfoggers and Vipers of the Commonwealth: The Lower Branch of the Legal Profession in Early Modern England (Cambridge: Cambridge University Press, 1986).

Bryson, Anna, *From Courtesy to Civility: Changing Codes of Conduct in Early Modern England* (Cambridge: Cambridge University Press, 1998).

Burns, Eric, *The Smoke of the Gods: A Social History of Tobacco* (Philadelphia, PA: Temple University Press, 2007).

Bushnell, Rebecca, *Green Desire: Imagining Early Modern English Gardens* (Ithaca, NY: Cornell University Press, 2003).

The Cambridge History of the Native Peoples of the Americas, Vol. 3: South America, ed. Frank Salomon and Stuart B. Schwartz (Cambridge: Cambridge University Press, 1999).

Cañizares-Esguerra, Jorge, *Puritan Conquistadors: Iberianizing the Atlantic, 1550–1700* (Stanford, CA: Stanford University Press, 2006).

Cannibalism and the Colonial World, ed. Francis Barker, Peter Hulme, and Margaret Iversen (Cambridge: Cambridge University Press, 1998).

Canny, Nicholas, *The Elizabethan Conquest of Ireland: A Pattern Established, 1565–1576* (Hassocks: Harvester Press, 1976).

'The Ideology of English Colonization: From Ireland to America', *The William and Mary Quarterly*, 30 (1973), 575–98.

Kingdom and Colony: Ireland in the Atlantic World, 1560–1800 (Baltimore, MD: Johns Hopkins University Press, 1988).

Making Ireland British, 1580–1650 (Oxford: Oxford University Press, 2001).

'Writing Early Modern History: Ireland, Britain, and the Wider World', *The Historical Journal*, 46 (2003), 723–47.

Carson, Cary, 'Banqueting Houses and the "Need of Society" among Slave-Owning Planters in the Chesapeake Colonies', *The William and Mary Quarterly*, 70 (2013), 725–80.

Catholics and the 'Protestant Nation': Religious Politics and Identity in Early Modern England, ed. Ethan Shagan (Manchester: Manchester University Press, 2005).

Cell, Gillian T., 'The Newfoundland Company: A Study of Subscribers to a Colonizing Venture', *The William and Mary Quarterly*, 22 (1965), 611–25.

Civil Histories, ed. Peter Burke, Brian Harrison, and Paul Slack (Oxford: Oxford University Press, 2000).

Cogswell, Thomas, 'The Human Comedy in Westminster: The House of Commons, 1604–1629', *Journal of British Studies*, 52 (2013), 370–89.

'"In the Power of the State": Mr Anys's Project and the Tobacco Colonies, 1626–1628', *English Historical Review* (2008), 35–64.

Collecting across Cultures: Material Exchanges in the Early Atlantic World, ed. Daniel Bleichmar and Peter C. Mancall (Philadelphia: University of Pennsylvania Press, 2011).

Conklin, Beth A., *Consuming Grief: Compassionate Cannibalism in an Amazonian Society* (Austin: University of Texas Press, 2001).

Conquest and Union: Fashioning a British State, 1485–1725, ed. Steven G. Ellis and Sarah Barber (London: Longman, 1995).

The Consumption of Culture, 1600–1800: Image, Object, Text, ed. Ann Bermingham and John Brewer (New York: Routledge, 1995).

Coombs, John C., 'The Phases of Conversion: A New Chronology for the Rise of Slavery in Early Virginia', *The William and Mary Quarterly*, 68 (2011), 332–60.

Cooper, John M., 'Aristotle on the Forms of Friendship', *The Review of Metaphysics*, 30 (1977), 619–48.

Cormack, Lesley B., *Charting an Empire: Geography at the English Universities, 1580–1620* (Chicago, IL: University of Chicago Press, 1997).

Cramsie, John, 'Commercial Projects and the Fiscal Policy of James VI and I', *The Historical Journal*, 43 (2000), 345–64.

  Kingship and Crown Finance under James VI and I, 1603–1625 (Woodbridge: Boydell, 2002).

Craven, Wesley Frank, *Dissolution of the Virginia Company: The Failure of a Colonial Experiment* (New York: Oxford University Press, 1932).

Croft, Pauline, *King James* (New York: Palgrave, 2003).

Crouch, Patricia, 'Patronage and Competing Visions of Virginia in George Chapman's "The Memorable Masque" (1613)', *English Literary Renaissance*, 53 (1986), 673–707.

Culture and Cultivation in Early Modern England: Writing and the Land, ed. Michael Leslie and Timothy Raylor (Leicester: Leicester University Press, 1992).

Cultures of Violence: Interpersonal Violence in Historical Perspective, ed. Stuart Carroll (New York: Palgrave, 2007).

Cust, Richard, 'Honour and Politics in Early Stuart England: The Case of Beaumont v. Hastings', *Past & Present*, 149 (1995), 57–94.

Custalow, Linwood 'Little Bear' and Angel Daniel 'Silver Star', *The True Story of Pocahontas: The Other Side of History* (Golden, CO: Fulcrum, 2007).

Das, Nandini, 'Sir Thomas Roe: Eyewitness to a Changing World (Hakluyt Society Annual Lecture)', *The Hakluyt Society* (2018), 1–20.

Davis, Natalie Zemon, *Society and Culture in Early Modern France: Eight Essays* (Stanford, CA: Stanford University Press, 1975).

DeLucia, Christine M., *Memory Lands: King Philip's War and the Place of Violence in the Northeast* (New Haven, CT: Yale University Press, 2018).

The Development of Harvard University since the Inauguration of President Eliot, 1869–1929, ed. Samuel Eliot Morison (Cambridge, MA: Harvard University Press, 1930).

Doan, James E., '"An Island in the Virginian Sea": Native Americans and the Irish in English Discourse, 1585–1640', *New Hibernia Review*, 1 (1997), 79–99.

Dunne, Derek, *Shakespeare, Revenge Tragedy and Early Modern Law: Vindictive Justice* (Basingstoke: Palgrave, 2016).

Eacott, Jonathan, *Selling Empire: India in the Making of Britain and America, 1600–1830* (Chapel Hill: University of North Carolina Press, 2016).

Early Modern Visual Culture: Representation, Race, and Empire in Renaissance England, ed. Peter Erickson and Clark Hulse (Philadelphia: University of Pennsylvania Press, 2000).

Elias, Norbert, *The Civilizing Process*, tr. Edmund Jephcott (Oxford: Blackwell, 1978).

Elliott, J. H., *Spain, Europe, and the Wider World, 1500–1800* (New Haven, CT: Yale University Press, 2009).

Ellis, Steven G., *Ireland in the Age of the Tudors, 1447–1603: English Expansion and the End of Gaelic Rule* (London: Longman, 1998).

Estate Landscapes: Design, Improvement, and Power in the Post-medieval Landscape, ed. Jonathan Field and Katherine Giles (Woodbridge: Boydell, 2007).

European Visions: American Voices, ed. Kim Sloan (London: British Museum, 2009).

The Experience of Authority in Early Modern England, ed. Paul Griffiths, Adam Fox, and Steve Hindle (New York: Macmillan, 1996).

Exploring Cultural History: Essays in Honour of Peter Burke, ed. Melissa Calaresu, Filippo de Vivo, and Joan-Pau Rubiés (Farnham: Ashgate, 2010).

Fausto, Carlos, *Warfare and Shamanism in Amazonia* (Cambridge: Cambridge University Press, 2012).

Fausz, Frederick J., 'An "Abundance of Blood Shed on Both Sides": England's First Indian War, 1609–1614', *The Virginia Magazine of History and Biography*, 98 (1990), 3–56.

　'The Invasion of Virginia: Indians, Colonialism, and the Conquest of Cant: A Review Essay on Anglo–Indian Relations in the Chesapeake', *The Virginia Magazine of History and Biography*, 95 (1987), 133–56.

　'Middlemen in Peace and War: Virginia's Earliest Indian Interpreters', *The Virginia Magazine of History and Biography*, 95 (1987), 41–64.

Festa, Thomas, 'The Metaphysics of Labour in John Donne's Sermon to the Virginia Company', *Studies in Philology*, 106 (2009), 76–99.

Fitzmaurice, Andrew, *Humanism and America: An Intellectual History of English Colonization, 1500–1625* (Cambridge: Cambridge University Press, 2003).

Forsyth, Donald W., 'Beginnings of Brazilian Anthropology: Jesuits and Tupinambá Indians', *Journal of Anthropological Research*, 39 (1983), 147–78.

Foucault, Michel, *Discipline and Punish: The Birth of the Prison*, tr. Alan Sheridan (New York: Vintage Books, 1979).

Froide, Amy M., *Silent Partners: Women as Public Investors during Britain's Financial Revolution, 1690–1750* (Oxford: Oxford University Press, 2017).

Gallivan, Martin, *James River Chiefdoms: The Rise of Social Inequality in the Chesapeake* (Lincoln: University of Nebraska Press, 2003).

Games, Alison, *The Web of Empire: English Cosmopolitans in the Age of Expansion, 1560–1660* (Oxford: Oxford University Press, 2008).

The Gift of Birds: Featherwork of Native South American Peoples, ed. Ruben E. Reina and Kenneth M. Kensinger (Philadelphia, PA: University Museum, 1991).

Goodman, Jordan, *Tobacco in History: The Cultures of Dependence* (London: Routledge, 1993).

　Tobacco in History and Culture: An Encyclopaedia (Farmington Hills, MI: Thompson Gale, 2005).

Green, Adrian, *Building for England: John Cosin's Architecture in Renaissance Durham and Cambridge* (Durham: Institute of Medieval and Early Modern Studies, 2016).

Greenblatt, Stephen, *Marvellous Possessions: The Wonder of the New World* (Chicago, IL: University of Chicago Press, 1991).

   Renaissance Self-Fashioning: From More to Shakespeare (Chicago, IL: University of Chicago Press, 1980).

Greene, Jack P., *Evaluating Empire and Confronting Colonialism in Eighteenth-Century Britain* (Cambridge: Cambridge University Press, 2013).

Guasco, Michael, *Slaves and Englishmen: Human Bondage in the Early Modern Atlantic World* (Philadelphia: University of Pennsylvania Press, 2011).

Habib, Imtiaz, *Black Lives in the English Archives, 1500–1677: Imprints of the Invisible* (London: Routledge, 2008).

Halasz, Alexandra, *The Marketplace of Print: Pamphlets and the Public Sphere in Early Modern England* (Cambridge: Cambridge University Press, 1997).

Hall, Kim F., *Things of Darkness: Economies of Race and Gender in Early Modern England* (Ithaca, NY: Cornell University Press, 1995).

Harkness, Deborah and Jean E. Howard, 'Introduction: The Great World of Early Modern London', *Huntington Library Quarterly*, 71 (2008), 1–9.

Haskell, Alexander B., *For God, King, and People: Forging Commonwealth Bonds in Renaissance Virginia* (Chapel Hill: University of North Carolina Press, 2017).

Healy, Margaret, *Fictions of Disease in Early Modern England: Bodies, Plagues and Politics* (Basingstoke: Palgrave, 2001).

Hechter, Michael, *Internal Colonialism: The Celtic Fringe in British National Development*, 2nd ed. (London: Transaction Publishers, 1999).

Hemming, John, *Red Gold: The Conquest of the Brazilian Indians* (Cambridge, MA: Harvard University Press, 1978).

Herrmann, Rachel B., 'The "tragicall historie": Cannibalism and Abundance in Colonial Jamestown', *The William and Mary Quarterly*, 68 (2011), 47–74.

Himmelman, P. Kenneth, 'The Medicinal Body: An Analysis of Medicinal Cannibalism in Europe, 1300–1700', *Dialectical Anthropology*, 22 (1997), 183–203.

Hindle, Steve, *The State and Social Change in Early Modern England, 1550–1640* (Basingstoke: Palgrave, 2000).

Hirschman, Albert O., *The Passions and the Interest: Political Arguments for Capitalism before Its Triumph* (Princeton, NJ: Princeton University Press, 1977).

Hodder, Ian, *Entangled: An Archaeology of the Relationships between Humans and Things* (Malden, MA: Wiley-Blackwell, 2012).

Hodgen, Margaret T., *Early Anthropology in the Sixteenth and Seventeenth Centuries* (Philadelphia: University of Pennsylvania Press, 1964).

Hollis, Daniel W., 'The Crown Lands and the Financial Dilemma in Stuart England', *Albion*, 26 (1994), 419–42.

Hollis, Gavin, *The Absence of America: The London Stage, 1576–1642* (Oxford: Oxford University Press, 2015).

Horn, James, *Adapting to a New World: English Society in the Seventeenth-Century Chesapeake* (Chapel Hill: University of North Carolina Press, 1994).

    A Land as God Made It: Jamestown and the Birth of America (New York: Basic Books, 2005).

Horn, James, William Kelso, Douglas Owsley, and Beverly Straube, *Jane: Starvation, Cannibalism, and Endurance at Jamestown* (Williamsburg, VA: Colonial Williamsburg Foundation, 2013).

Horning, Audrey, *Ireland in the Virginian Sea: Colonialism in the British Atlantic* (Chapel Hill: University of North Carolina Press, 2013).

Howarth, David, *Lord Arundel and His Circle* (New Haven, CT: Yale University Press, 1985).

Hulme, Peter, *Colonial Encounters: Europe and the Native Caribbean, 1492–1797* (London: Methuen, 1986).

Hume, Ivor Noël, *The Archaeology of Martin's Hundred* (Philadelphia: University of Pennsylvania Press, 2001).

Hunt, Arnold, 'The Lord's Supper in Early Modern England', *Past & Present*, 161 (1998), 39–83.

Hutson, Lorna, 'Rethinking the "Spectacle of the Scaffold": Juridical Epistemologies and English Revenge Tragedy', *Representations*, 89 (2005), 30–58.

    The Usurer's Daughter: Male Friendships and Fictions of Women in Sixteenth-Century England (London: Routledge, 1994).

Inns of Court, ed. Alan H. Nelson and John R. Elliott (Cambridge: D. S. Brewer, 2010).

The Intellectual and Cultural World of the Early Modern Inns of Court, ed. Jayne Elisabeth Archer, Elizabeth Goldring, and Sarah Knight (Manchester: Manchester University Press, 2011).

Irwin, Lee, *Coming Down from Above: Prophesy, Resistance, and Renewal in Native American Religion* (Norman: University of Oklahoma Press, 2008).

James VI and I: Ideas, Authority, and Government, ed. Ralph Houlbrooke (Aldershot: Ashgate, 2006).

James, Mervyn, *Family, Lineage and Civil Society: A Study of Society, Politics and Mentality in the Durham Region, 1500–1640* (Oxford: Clarendon, 1974).

'Jamestown, 1607–2007' special issue, *Post-medieval Archaeology*, 40 (2006).

Jarvis, Michael, *In the Eye of All Trade: Bermuda, Bermudians, and the Maritime Atlantic World, 1680–1783* (Chapel Hill: University of North Carolina Press, 2010).

Johnson, Matthew, *English Houses, 1300–1800: Vernacular Architecture, Social Life* (New York: Routledge, 2010).

Jowitt, Claire, *Voyage Drama and Gender Politics, 1589–1642: Real and Imagined Worlds* (Manchester: Manchester University Press, 2003).

Kerrigan, John, *Archipelagic English: Literature, History, and Politics, 1603–1707* (Oxford: Oxford University Press, 2008).

Kidd, Colin, *British Identities before Nationalism: Ethnicity and Nationhood in the Atlantic World, 1600–1800* (Cambridge: Cambridge University Press, 1999).

King, Richard C., 'The (Mis)uses of Cannibalism in Contemporary Cultural Critique', *Diacritics*, 30 (2000), 106–23.

King, Thomas, *The Inconvenient Indian: A Curious Account of Native People in North America* (Toronto: Anchor, 2013).

Kishlanksy, Mark, *A Monarchy Transformed: Britain 1603–1714* (London: Penguin, 1996).

Klein, Bernhard, *Maps and the Writing of Space in Early Modern England and Ireland* (Basingstoke: Palgrave, 2001).

Knafla, Louis A., *Law and Politics in Jacobean England: The Tracts of Lord Chancellor Ellesmere* (Cambridge: Cambridge University Press, 1977).

Knapp, Jeffrey, 'Elizabethan Tobacco', *Representations*, 21 (1988), 26–66.

An Empire Nowhere: England, America, and Literature from Utopia to the Tempest (Berkeley: University of California Press, 1992).

Kupperman, Karen Ordahl, 'The Founding Years of Virginia – and the United States', *The Virginia Magazine of History and Biography*, 104 (1996), 103–12.

Indians and English: Facing Off in Early America (Ithaca, NY: Cornell University Press, 2000).

The Jamestown Project (Cambridge, MA: Harvard University Press, 2007).

'Presentment of Civility: English Reading of American Self-Presentation in the Early Years of Colonization', *The William and Mary Quarterly*, 54 (1997), 193–228.

Kyle, Chris R., *Theatre of State: Parliament and Political Culture in Early Stuart England* (Stanford, CA: Stanford University Press, 2012).

Lake, Peter and Steve Pincus, 'Rethinking the Public Sphere in Early Modern England', *Journal of British Studies*, 45 (2006), 270–92.

Lake, Peter with Michael Questier, 'Agency, Appropriation and Rhetoric under the Gallows: Puritans, Romanists and the State in Early Modern England', *Past & Present*, 153 (1996), 64–107.

The Antichrist's Lewd Hat: Protestants, Papists, and Players in Post-Reformation England (New Haven, CT: Yale University Press, 2002).

Land, Robert Hunt, 'Henrico and Its College', *The William and Mary Quarterly*, 18 (1938), 453–98.

Lee, Maurice, *Great Britain's Solomon: James VI and I in His Three Kingdoms* (Urbana: University of Illinois Press, 1990).

Lemire, Beverly, *Global Trade and the Transformation of Consumer Cultures: The Material World Remade, 1500–1820* (Cambridge: Cambridge University Press, 2018).

Lemmings, David, *Gentlemen and Barristers: The Inns of Court and the English Bar, 1680–1730* (Oxford: Clarendon, 1990).

Lestringant, Frank, *Cannibals: The Discovery and Representation of the Cannibal from Columbus to Jules Verne*, tr. Rosemary Morris (Cambridge: Polity, 1997).

Levine, David and Keith Wrightson, *The Making of an Industrial Society: Whickham, 1560–1765* (Oxford: Clarendon, 1991).

Liebaert, Alexis and Alain Maya, *The Illustrated History of the Pipe* (Suffolk: Harold Starke Publishers, 1994).

Lindebaum, Shirley, 'Thinking about Cannibalism', *Annual Review of Anthropology*, 33 (2004), 475–98.

Lipman, Andrew, "'A Meanes to Knitt Them Together'": The Exchange of Body Parts in the Pequot War', *The William and Mary Quarterly*, 65 (2008), 3–28.

Lockyer, Roger, *Buckingham: The Life and Political Career of George Villiers, First Duke of Buckingham, 1592–1628* (London: Longman, 1981).

James VI and I (London: Longman, 1998).

London, 1500–1700: The Making of the Metropolis, ed. A. L. Beier and Roger Finlay (London: Longman, 1986).

Lorimer, Joyce, 'The Failure of the English Guiana Ventures 1595–1667 and James I's Foreign Policy', *The Journal of Imperial and Commonwealth History*, 21 (1993), 1–30.

Lubbock, Jules, *The Tyranny of Taste: The Politics of Architecture and Design in Britain, 1550–1960* (New Haven, CT: Yale University Press, 1995).

Lyttleton, James, *The Jacobean Plantations of Seventeenth-Century Offaly: An Archaeology of a Changing World* (Dublin: Four Courts Press, 2013).

MacFaul, Thomas, *Male Friendship in Shakespeare and His Contemporaries* (Cambridge: Cambridge University Press, 2009).

Macmillan, Ken, *The Atlantic Imperial Constitution: Centre and Periphery in the English Atlantic World* (New York: Palgrave, 2011).

Mancall, Peter C., *Hakluyt's Promise: An Elizabethan's Obsession for an English America* (New Haven, CT: Yale University Press, 2006).

'Tales Tobacco Told in Sixteenth-Century Europe', *Environmental History*, 9 (2004), 648–78.

Marenbon, John, *Pagans and Philosophers: The Problem of Paganism from Augustine to Leibniz* (Princeton, NJ: Princeton University Press, 2015).

Marotti, Arthur F., *Religious Ideology and Cultural Fantasy: Catholic and Anti-Catholic Discourses in Early Modern England* (Notre Dame, IN: University of Notre Dame Press, 2005).

Mason, Roger A., 'Scotland, Elizabethan England and the Idea of Britain', *Transactions of the Royal Historical Society*, 14 (2004), 279–93.

Material London, ca. 1600, ed. Lena Cowen Orlin (Philadelphia: University of Pennsylvania Press, 2000).

Maxwell, Susan, 'Thomas Cavendish's Visit to Puná Island in 1587', *The Mariner's Mirror* (103), 136–49.

McGowan, Andrew, 'Eating People: Accusations of Cannibalism against Christians in the Second Century', *Second-Century Journal of Early Christian Studies*, 2 (1994), 413–42.

McRae, Andrew, 'Reading Libels: An Introduction', *Huntington Library Quarterly*, 69 (2006), 1–13.

'To Know One's Own: Estate Surveying and the Representation of the Land in Early Modern England', *Huntington Library Quarterly*, 56 (1993), 333–57.

Menard, Russell, *Sweet Negotiations: Sugar, Slavery, and Plantation Agriculture in Early Barbados* (Charlottesville: University of Virginia Press, 2006).

Mennell, Stephen, *Norbert Elias: An Introduction* (Oxford: Blackwell, 1992).

Mercantilism Reimagined: Political Economy in Early Modern Britain and Its Empire, ed. Philip Stern and Carl Wennerlind (Oxford: Oxford University Press, 2014).

Merritt, J. F., *The Social World of Early Modern Westminster: Abbey, Court, and Community, 1525–1640* (Manchester: Manchester University Press, 2005).

Millstone, Noah, *Manuscript Circulation and the Invention of Politics in Early Stuart England* (Cambridge: Cambridge University Press, 2016).

'Seeing Like a Statesman in Early Stuart England', *Past & Present*, 223 (2014), 77–127.

Montrose, Louis, 'The Work of Gender in the Discourse of Discovery', *Representations*, 33 (1991), 1–41.

Morgan, Edmund S., *American Slavery, American Freedom: The Ordeal of Colonial Virginia* (New York: W. W. Norton, 1975).

Muldrew, Craig, *The Economy of Obligation: The Culture of Credit and Social Relations in Early Modern England* (Basingstoke: Palgrave, 1998).

The Mysterious and the Foreign in Early Modern England, ed. Helen Ostovich, Mary V. Silcox, and Graham Roebuck (Newark: University of Delaware Press, 2008).

Negotiating Power in Early Modern Society: Order, Hierarchy, and Subordination in Britain and Ireland, ed. Michael J. Braddick and John Walter (Cambridge: Cambridge University Press, 2001).

Netzloff, Mark, *England's Internal Colonies: Internal Colonialism in Early Modern England* (Basingstoke: Palgrave, 2003).

Nicholls, Mark and Penry Williams, *Sir Walter Raleigh: In Life and Legend* (London: Continuum, 2011).

Noble, Louise, '"And Make Two Pasties of Your Shameful Heads": Medicinal Cannibalism and Healing the Body Politic in "Titus Andronicus"', *English Literary History*, 70 (2003), 677–708.

Medicinal Cannibalism in Early Modern English Literature and Culture (New York: Palgrave Macmillan, 2011).

Norton, Marcy, *Sacred Gifts, Profane Pleasures: A History of Tobacco and Chocolate in the Atlantic World* (Ithaca, NY: Cornell University Press, 2008).

O'Callaghan, Michelle, *The English Wits: Literature and Sociability in Early Modern England* (Cambridge: Cambridge University Press, 2007).

The 'Shepheards Nation': Jacobean Spenserians and Early Stuart Political Culture, 1612–1625 (Oxford: Clarendon, 2000).

Ogborn, Miles, *Global Lives: Britain and the World, 1550–1800* (Cambridge: Cambridge University Press, 2008).

Indian Ink: Script and Print in the Making of the East India Company (Chicago, IL: University of Chicago Press, 2007).

Ohlmeyer, Jane, *Making Ireland English: The Irish Aristocracy in the Seventeenth Century* (New Haven, CT: Yale University Press, 2012).

'Seventeenth-Century Ireland and the New British and Atlantic Histories', *The American Historical Review*, 104 (1999), 446–62.

Orser, Charles E., *An Archaeology of the English Atlantic World, 1600–1700* (Cambridge: Cambridge University Press, 2018).

The Oxford History of the British Empire: Vol. 1, ed. Nicholas Canny (Oxford: Oxford University Press, 1998).

Pagden, Anthony, *European Encounters with the New World: From Renaissance to Romanticism* (New Haven, CT: Yale University Press, 1993).

Lords of all the World: Ideologies of Empire in Spain, Britain, and France, 1500–1800 (New Haven, CT: Yale University Press, 1995).

Pawlisch, Hans, *Sir John Davies and the Conquest of Ireland: A Study in Legal Imperialism* (Cambridge: Cambridge University Press, 1985).

Peacey, Jason, *Print and Public Politics in the English Revolution* (Cambridge: Cambridge University Press, 2013).

Peck, Linda Levy, *Consuming Splendour: Society and Culture in Seventeenth-Century England* (Cambridge: Cambridge University Press, 2005).

'"For a King not to be bountiful were a fault": Perspectives on Court Patronage in Early Stuart England', *Journal of British Studies*, 25 (1986), 31–61.

Peltonen, Markku, *The Duel in Early Modern England: Civility, Politeness and Honour* (Cambridge: Cambridge University Press, 2003).

'Francis Bacon, the Earl of Northampton, and the Jacobean Anti-duelling Campaign', *The Historical Journal*, 44 (2001), 1–28.

Perry, Graham, *The Trophies of Time: English Antiquarians of the Seventeenth Century* (Oxford: Oxford University Press, 1995).

Pestana, Carla Gardina, *Protestant Empire: Religion and the Making of the Atlantic World* (Philadelphia: University of Pennsylvania Press, 2009).

Pettigrew, William A., *Freedom's Debt: The Royal African Company and the Politics of the Atlantic Slave Trade, 1672–1752* (Chapel Hill: University of North Carolina Press, 2013).

A Pleasing Sinne: Drink and Conviviality in Seventeenth-Century England, ed. Adam Smyth (Woodbridge: Boydell, 2004).

Pluymers, Keith, 'Taming the Wilderness in Sixteenth and Seventeenth-Century Ireland and Virginia', *Environmental History*, 16 (2011), 610–32.

Pocock, J. G. A., *The Machiavellian Moment: Florentine Political Thought and the Atlantic Republican Tradition* (Princeton, NJ: Princeton University Press, 1975).

'The New British History in Atlantic Perspective: An Antipodean Commentary', *The American Historical Review*, 104 (1999), 490–500.

Political Innovation and Conceptual Change, ed. Terence Ball, James Farr, and Russell L. Hanson (Cambridge: Cambridge University Press, 1989).

Political Spaces in Pre-industrial Europe, ed. Beat Kümin (Surrey: Ashgate, 2009).

The Politics of the Public Sphere in Early Modern England, ed. Peter Lake and Steve Pincus (Manchester: Manchester University Press, 2007).

Pollan, Michael, *The Botany of Desire: A Plant's Eye View of the World* (New York: Random House, 2001).

Pollnitz, Aysha, *Princely Education in Early Modern Britain* (Cambridge: Cambridge University Press, 2015).

Popper, Nicholas, 'An Information State for Elizabethan England', *The Journal of Modern History*, 90 (2018), 503–35.

Walter Ralegh's History of the World and the Historical Culture of the Late Renaissance (Chicago, IL: University of Chicago Press, 2012).

Prest, Wilfred R., *The Inns of Court under Elizabeth I and the Early Stuarts, 1590–1640* (London: Longman, 1972).

Puritanism and Emotion in the Early Modern World, ed. Alex Ryrie and Tom Schwanda (Basingstoke: Palgrave, 2016).

Quinn, David B., 'Advice for Investors in Virginia, Bermuda, and Newfoundland, 1611', *The William and Mary Quarterly*, 23 (1966), 135–45.

'Notes by a Pious Colonial Investor, 1608–1610', *The William and Mary Quarterly*, 16 (1959), 551–5.

'Renaissance Influences in English Colonization: The Prothero Lecture', *Transactions of the Royal Historical Society*, 26 (1976), 73–93.

Quitt, Martin H., 'Trade and Acculturation at Jamestown, 1607–1609: The Limits of Understanding', *The William and Mary Quarterly*, 52 (1995), 227–58.

Rabb, Theodore K., *Enterprise and Empire: Merchant and Gentry Investment in the Expansion of England, 1575–1630* (Cambridge, MA: Harvard University Press, 1967).

Jacobean Gentleman: Sir Edwin Sandys, 1561–1629 (Princeton, NJ: Princeton University Press, 1998).

Race in Early Modern England: A Documentary Companion, ed. Jonathan Burton and Ania Loomba (Basingstoke: Palgrave, 2007).

Raffield, Paul, *Images and Cultures of Law in Early Modern England: Justice and Political Power, 1558–1660* (Cambridge: Cambridge University Press, 2004).

Raymond, Joad, *Pamphlets and Pamphleteering in Early Modern Britain* (Cambridge: Cambridge University Press, 2003).

Rebhorn, Wayne A., *The Emperor of Men's Minds* (Ithaca, NY: Cornell University Press, 1997).

Remaking English Society: Social Relations and Social Change in Early Modern England, ed. Steve Hindle, Alexandra Shepard, and John Walter (Woodbridge: Boydell, 2013).

Renaissance Transformations: The Making of English Writing, 1500–1650, ed. Margaret Healy and Tom Healy (Edinburgh: Edinburgh University Press, 2009).

Riggs, David, *The World of Christopher Marlowe* (London: Faber and Faber, 2004).

Roper, L. H., *Advancing Empire: English Interests and Overseas Expansion, 1613–1688* (Cambridge: Cambridge University Press, 2017).

Rose, E. M., 'Notes and Documents: The "Bewitching Lotteries for Virginia", 1616–1621: A List of Sites and Charitable Donations', *Huntington Library Quarterly*, 81 (2018), 107–19.

Rountree, Helen C., *The Powhatan Indians of Virginia* (Norman: University of Oklahoma Press, 1989).

Rouse, Irving, *The Tainos: Rise and Decline of the People Who Greeted Columbus* (New Haven, CT: Yale University Press, 1992).

Royal Subjects: Essays on the Writings of James VI and I, ed. Daniel Fischlin and Mark Fortier (Detroit, MI: Wayne State University Press, 2002).

Rublack, Ulinka, 'Renaissance Dress, Cultures of Making, and the Period Eye', *West 86th: A Journal of Decorative Arts, Design History, and Material Culture*, 23 (2016), 6–34.

Ryrie, Alex, *Being Protestant in Reformation Britain* (Oxford: Oxford University Press, 2013).

Sanday, Peggy Reeves, *Divine Hunger: Cannibalism as a Cultural System* (Cambridge: Cambridge University Press, 1986).

Scots and Britons: Scottish Political Thought and the Union of 1603, ed. Roger A. Mason (Cambridge: Cambridge University Press, 1994).

Sekora, John, *Luxury: The Concept in Western Thought, Eden to Smollet* (Baltimore, MD: Johns Hopkins University Press, 1977).

Selwood, Jacob, *Diversity and Difference in Early Modern London* (Farnham: Ashgate, 2010).

Shagan, Ethan, *The Rule of Moderation: Violence, Religion, and the Politics of Restraint in Early Modern England* (Cambridge: Cambridge University Press, 2011).

Shammas, Carole, *The Pre-industrial Consumer in England and America* (Oxford: Clarendon, 1990).

Sharpe, Kevin, 'Virtues, Passions and Politics in Early Modern England', *History of Political Thought*, 32 (2011), 773–98.

Shepard, Alexandra, *Meanings of Manhood in Early Modern England* (Oxford: Oxford University Press, 2003).

Shrank, Cathy, *Writing the Nation in Reformation England, 1530–1580* (Oxford: Oxford University Press, 2004).

Slack, Paul, *The Invention of Improvement: Information and Material Progress in Seventeenth-Century England* (Oxford: Oxford University Press, 2014).

Sloan, Kim, *A New World: England's First View of America* (London: British Museum Press, 2007).

Smith, David L., *A History of the Modern British Isles, 1603–1707: The Double Crown* (Oxford: Blackwell, 1998).

Smith, Edmond, 'De-personifying Collaert's *Four Continents*: European Descriptions of Continental Diversity, 1585–1625', *European Review of History*, 21 (2014), 817–35.

'The Global Interests of London's Commercial Community, 1599–1625: Investment in the East India Company', *Economic History Review*, 71 (2018), 1118–46.

Smuts, Malcolm, *Court Culture and the Origins of a Royalist Tradition in Early Stuart England* (Philadelphia: University of Pennsylvania Press, 1987).

Culture and Power in England, 1585–1685 (Basingstoke: Macmillan, 1999).

The Social Life of Things: Commodities in Cultural Perspective, ed. Arjun Appadurai (Cambridge: Cambridge University Press, 1992).

Steffen, Lisa, *Defining a British State: Treason and National Identity, 1608–1820* (Basingstoke: Palgrave, 2001).

Stern, Philip J., *The Company-State: Corporate Sovereignty and the Early Modern Foundations of the British Empire in India* (Oxford: Oxford University Press, 2011).

Stewart, Alan, *The Cradle King: A Life of James VI & I* (London: Chatto and Windus, 2003).

Stout, Felicity Jane, *Exploring Russia in the Elizabethan Commonwealth: The Muscovy Company and Giles Fletcher, the Elder (1546–1611)* (Manchester: Manchester University Press, 2015).

Strong, Roy, *Henry, Prince of Wales and England's Lost Renaissance* (London: Thames, 1986).

The Stuart Kingdoms in the Seventeenth Century: Awkward Neighbours, ed. Allan I. Macinnes and Jane Ohlmeyer (Portland, OR: Four Courts Press, 2002).

Sugg, Richard, '"Good Physic but Bad Food": Early Modern Attitudes to Medicinal Cannibalism and Its Suppliers', *Social History of Medicine*, 19 (2006), 225–40.

Survivance: Narratives of Native Presence, ed. Gerald Vizenor (Lincoln: University of Nebraska Press, 2008).

The Taking and Displaying of Human Body Parts as Trophies by Amerindians, ed. Richard J. Chacon and David H. Dye (New York: Springer, 2007).

Thirsk, Joan, *Economic Policy and Projects: The Development of a Consumer Society in Early Modern England* (Oxford: Clarendon, 1978).

Thomas, Keith, *Man and the Natural World: Changing Attitudes in England, 1500–1800* (London: Allen Lane, 1983).

In Pursuit of Civility: Manners and Civilization in Early Modern England (Waltham, MA: Brandeis University Press, 2018).

Thompson, Peter, 'William Bullock's "Strange Adventure": A Plan to Transform Seventeenth-Century Virginia', *The William and Mary Quarterly*, 61 (2004), 107–28.

Thrush, Coll, *Indigenous London: Native Travelers at the Heart of Empire* (New Haven, CT: Yale University Press, 2016).

Tobacco Use by Native North Americans: Sacred Smoke and Silent Killer, ed. Joseph C. Winter (Norman: University of Oklahoma Press, 2000).

Tosh, Will, *Male Friendship and Testimonies of Love in Shakespeare's England* (Basingstoke: Palgrave, 2016).

Travel and Travail: Early Modern Women, English Drama, and the Wider World, ed. Patricia Akhimie and Bernadette Andrea (Lincoln: University of Nebraska Press, 2019).

Trentmann, Frank, *Empire of Things: How We Became a World of Consumers, from the Fifteenth Century to the Twenty-First* (London: Penguin, 2016).

Vaughan, Alden T., *Transatlantic Encounters: American Indians in Britain, 1500–1776* (Cambridge: Cambridge University Press, 2006).

Virginia 1619: Slavery and Freedom in the Making of English America, ed. Paul Musselwhite, Peter C. Mancall, and James Horn (Chapel Hill: University of North Carolina Press, 2019).

de Vries, Jan, *The Industrious Revolution: Consumer Behaviour and the Household Economy, 1650 to the Present* (Cambridge: Cambridge University Press, 2008).

Wallis, Helen M., 'Further Light on the Molyneux Globes', *The Geographical Journal*, 121 (1955), 304–11.

Walsh, Lorena S., *Motives of Honor, Pleasure, & Profit: Plantation Management in the Colonial Chesapeake, 1607–1783* (Chapel Hill: University of North Carolina Press, 2010).

Walsham, Alexandra, '"Domme Preachers"? Post-Reformation English Catholicism and the Culture of Print', *Past & Present*, 168 (2000), 72–123.

    Providence in Early Modern England (Oxford: Oxford University Press, 2001).

    The Reformation of the Landscape: Religion, Identity, and Memory in Early Modern Britain and Ireland (Oxford: Oxford University Press, 2011).

Walter, John, '"Abolishing Superstition with Sedition"? The Politics of Popular Iconoclasm in England, 1640–1642', *Past & Present*, 183 (2004), 79–123.

Walvin, James, *Slavery in Small Things: Slavery and Modern Cultural Habits* (Chichester: John Wiley & Sons, 2017).

Warren, Ian, 'The English Landed Elite and the Social Environment of London, 1580–1700: The Cradle of an Aristocratic Culture?', *English Historical Review*, 126 (2011), 44–74.

Warsh, Molly, *American Baroque: Pearls and the Nature of Empire, 1492–1700* (Chapel Hill: University of North Carolina Press, 2018).

Watson, Kelly, *Insatiable Appetites: Imperial Encounters with Cannibals in the North Atlantic World* (New York: New York University Press, 2015).

Weber: Political Writings, ed. Peter Lassman and Ronald Speirs (Cambridge: Cambridge University Press, 1994).

Welch, Stephen, *The Theory of Political Culture* (Oxford: Oxford University Press, 2013).

The Western Antiquary, Vol. 4, ed. W. H. K. Wright (Plymouth: W. H. Luke, 1885).

Whatley, Janet, 'Food and the Limits of Civility: The Testimony of Jean de Léry', *The Sixteenth Century Journal*, 15 (1984), 387–400.

    'Savage Hierarchies: French Catholic Observers of the New World', *The Sixteenth Century Journal*, 17 (1986), 319–30.

Whitehead, Neil L., 'Hans Staden and the Cultural Politics of Cannibalism', *The Hispanic American Historical Review*, 80 (2000), 721–51.

Whyman, Susan E., *Sociability and Power in Late Stuart England: The Cultural World of the Verneys, 1660–1720* (Oxford: Oxford University Press, 2002).

Williamson, Margaret Holmes, *Powhatan Lords of Life and Death: Command and Consent in Seventeenth-Century Virginia* (Lincoln: University of Nebraska Press, 2003).

Winston, Jessica, *Lawyers at Play: Literature, Law, and Politics at the Early Modern Inns of Court* (Oxford: Oxford University Press, 2016).

Withington, Phil, 'Company and Sociability in Early Modern England', *Social History*, 32 (2007), 291–307.

'Intoxicants and Society in Early Modern England', *The Historical Journal*, 54 (2011), 631–57.

'Introduction: Cultures of Intoxication', *Past & Present: Supplement 9* (2014), 9–33.

The Politics of Commonwealth: Citizens and Freemen in Early Modern England (Cambridge: Cambridge University Press, 2005).

Society in Early Modern England: The Vernacular Origins of Some Powerful Ideas (Cambridge: Polity, 2010).

Wood, Andy, *The Memory of the People: Custom and Popular Senses of the Past in Early Modern England* (Cambridge: Cambridge University Press, 2013).

Riot, Rebellion, and Popular Politics in Early Modern England (Basingstoke: Palgrave, 2002).

Wood, Neal, *Cicero's Social and Political Thought* (Berkeley: University of California Press, 1991).

Working, Lauren, 'Locating Colonization at the Jacobean Inns of Court', *The Historical Journal*, 61 (2018), 29–51.

Wormald, Jenny, 'A Very British Problem: The Stuart Crown and the Plantation of Ulster', *History Ireland*, 17 (2009), 20–3.

Wrightson, Keith, *English Society, 1580–1680* (London: Routledge, 1993).

'Mutualities and Obligations: Changing Social Relationships in Early Modern England', *Proceedings of the British Academy*, 139 (2006), 157–94.

Yates, Candida, *The Play of Political Culture, Emotion and Identity* (Basingstoke: Palgrave, 2015).

Ziser, Michael, 'Sovereign Remedies: Natural Authority and the "Counterblaste to Tobacco"', *The William and Mary Quarterly*, 62 (2005), 719–44.

Index